The Shapley value

The Shapley value

Essays in honor of Lloyd S. Shapley

Edited by
Alvin E. Roth

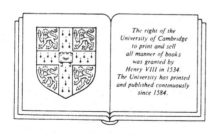

The right of the
University of Cambridge
to print and sell
all manner of books
was granted by
Henry VIII in 1534.
The University has printed
and published continuously
since 1584.

CAMBRIDGE UNIVERSITY PRESS
Cambridge
New York   New Rochelle   Melbourne   Sydney

CAMBRIDGE UNIVERSITY PRESS
Cambridge, New York, Melbourne, Madrid, Cape Town, Singapore, São Paulo

Cambridge University Press
The Edinburgh Building, Cambridge CB2 2RU, UK

Published in the United States of America by Cambridge University Press, New York

www.cambridge.org
Information on this title: www.cambridge.org/9780521361774

First published 1988
This digitally printed first paperback version 2005

A catalogue record for this publication is available from the British Library

Library of Congress Cataloguing in Publication data
The Shapley value : essays in honor of Lloyd S. Shapley / edited by
Alvin E. Roth.
p. cm.
Bibliography: p.
ISBN 0-521-36177-X
1. Economics, Mathematical. 2. Game theory. 3. Shapley, Lloyd
S., 1923– . I. Shapley, Lloyd S., 1923– . II. Roth, Alvin E.,
1951– .
HB144.S533   1988
330′.01′5193 – dc19131   88-2983

ISBN-13 978-0-521-36177-4 hardback
ISBN-10 0-521-36177-X hardback

ISBN-13 978-0-521-02133-3 paperback
ISBN-10 0-521-02133-2 paperback

Contents

Preface   *page* vii

1   Introduction to the Shapley value   1
    Alvin E. Roth

I   Ancestral papers

2   A value for *n*-person games   31
    Lloyd S. Shapley

3   A method for evaluating the distribution of power
    in a committee system   41
    Lloyd S. Shapley and Martin Shubik

II   Reformulations and generalizations

4   The expected utility of playing a game   51
    Alvin E. Roth

5   The Shapley-Shubik and Banzhaf power indices as
    probabilities   71
    Philip D. Straffin, Jr.

6   Weighted Shapley values   83
    Ehud Kalai and Dov Samet

7   Probabilistic values for games   101
    Robert James Weber

8   Combinatorial representations of the Shapley
    value based on average relative payoffs   121
    Uriel G. Rothblum

9   The potential of the Shapley value   127
    Sergiu Hart and Andreu Mas-Colell

10   Multilinear extensions of games   139
     Guillermo Owen

III Coalitions

11   Coalitional value   155
     Mordecai Kurz

12   Endogenous formation of links between players
     and of coalitions: an application of the Shapley value   175
     Robert J. Aumann and Roger B. Myerson

IV Large games

13   Values of large finite games   195
     Myrna Holtz Wooders and William R. Zame

14   Payoffs in nonatomic economies: an axiomatic
     approach   207
     Pradeep Dubey and Abraham Neyman

15   Values of smooth nonatomic games: the method
     of multilinear approximation   217
     Dov Monderer and Abraham Neyman

16   Nondifferentiable TU markets: the value   235
     Jean-François Mertens

V Cost allocation and fair division

17   Individual contribution and just compensation   267
     H. P. Young

18   The Aumann-Shapley prices: a survey   279
     Yair Tauman

VI NTU games

19   Utility comparison and the theory of games   307
     Lloyd S. Shapley

20   Paths leading to the Nash set   321
     Michael Maschler, Guillermo Owen, and Bezalel Peleg

Preface

This volume is in honor of the 1000001st (binary) birthday of Lloyd Shapley.

Each of its twenty chapters concerns some aspect of the Shapley value. The aim of the volume is to make accessible the large body of work that has grown out of Shapley's seminal 1953 paper. Three of the chapters are reprints of "ancestral" papers: Chapter 2 is Shapley's original 1953 paper defining the value, Chapter 3 is the 1954 paper by Shapley and Shubik applying the value to voting models, and Chapter 19 is Shapley's 1969 paper defining a value for games without transferable utility. The other seventeen chapters were contributed especially for this volume. Each is written so as to be largely self-contained, and there is a little diversity of terminology and notation among them, which reflects the diversity in the literature at large. However, the first chapter introduces the subject and each paper in the volume in a unified way. It also contains a very brief account of a few of Shapley's other major contributions to game theory.

CHAPTER 1

Introduction to the Shapley value

Alvin E. Roth

Among the obligations facing a community of scholars is to make accessible to a wider community the ideas it finds useful and important. A related obligation is to recognize lasting contributions to ideas and to honor their progenitors. In this volume we undertake to fill part of both obligations.

The papers in this volume review and continue research that has grown out of a remarkable 1953 paper by Lloyd Shapley. There he proposed that it might be possible to evaluate, in a numerical way, the "value" of playing a game. The particular function he derived for this purpose, which has come to be called the Shapley value, has been the focus of sustained interest among students of cooperative game theory ever since. In the intervening years, the Shapley value has been interpreted and reinterpreted. Its domain has been extended and made more specialized. The same value function has been (re)derived from apparently quite different assumptions. And whole families of related value functions have been found to arise from relaxing various of the assumptions.

The reason the Shapley value has been the focus of so much interest is that it represents a distinct approach to the problems of complex strategic interaction that game theory seeks to illuminate. To explain this, we need to recount some history of game theory. (Even when we are not speaking of the Shapley value, the history of game theory is inextricably connected with other aspects of Shapley's work. To avoid too many diversions, we defer discussion of Shapley's other work until the concluding section of this introduction.)

Although game-theoretic ideas can be traced earlier, much of the modern theory of games traces its origins to the monumental 1944 book by John von Neumann and Oskar Morgenstern, *Theory of games and economic behavior*. In seeking a way to analyze potentially very complex patterns of strategic behavior, their approach was to, in their phrase, "divide the difficulties," by finding simple models of the strategic environment itself.

Their first step was to find a way to summarize each alternative facing an individual decision maker by a single number. Their solution to this problem – expected utility theory – has left its own indelible mark on economic theory, quite independently of the impact the theory of games has had. Briefly, their contribution was to specify conditions on an individual's preferences over possibly risky alternatives sufficient so that his choice behavior could be modeled as if, faced with a choice over any set of alternatives, he chose the one that maximized the expected value of some real-valued function, called his utility function. In this way, a complex probability distribution over a diverse set of alternatives could be summarized by a single number, equal to the expected utility of the lottery in question.

Having reduced the alternatives facing each individual to a numerical description, von Neumann and Morgenstern proceeded to consider (among other things) a class of games in which the opportunities available to each coalition of players could also be described by a single number. They considered cooperative games in *characteristic function form* (now sometimes also called "coalitional form") defined by a finite set $N = \{1, \ldots, n\}$ of players, and a real-valued "characteristic function" v, defined on all subsets of N (with $v(\phi) = 0$). The interpretation of v is that for any subset S of N the number $v(S)$ is the worth of the coalition, in terms of how much "utility" the members of S can divide among themselves in any way that sums to no more than $v(S)$ if they all agree. The only restriction on v that von Neumann and Morgenstern proposed was that it be superadditive; that is, if S and T are two disjoint subsets of N, then $v(S \cup T) \geq v(S) + v(T)$. This means that the worth of the coalition $S \cup T$ is equal to at least the worth of its parts acting separately.

The characteristic function model assumes the following things about the game being modeled. First, utility can be embodied in some medium of exchange – "utility money" – that is fully transferable among players, and such that an additional unit of transferable utility always adds a unit to any player's utility function. (For example, if all players are risk neutral in money – that is, if their utility functions are all linear in money – then ordinary money can be the necessary medium of exchange in a game in which all outcomes can be evaluated in monetary terms and in which money is freely transferable.) Second, the possibilities available to a coalition of players can be assessed without reference to the players not included in the coalition. Third, a coalition can costlessly make binding agreements to distribute its worth in any way agreed to by all the members, so it is not necessary to model explicitly the actions that players must take to carry out these agreements. In recognition of the importance of the assumption that utility is transferable, these games are sometimes called transferable utility (TU) games.

Although these simplifying assumptions are obviously substantial, the characteristic function model has proved to be surprisingly useful as a simple model of strategic interaction. Consider, for example, the interaction between a potential seller and two potential buyers of some object that the seller (the current owner) values at ten dollars, the first buyer values at twenty dollars, and the second buyer values at thirty dollars. If the players can freely transfer money among themselves, and if they are risk neutral (although for many purposes this latter assumption is not really necessary), this situation can be modeled as the game $\Gamma_1 = (N,v)$ with players $N = \{1,2,3\}$ and v given by $v(1) = 10$, $v(2) = v(3) = v(23) = 0$, $v(12) = 20$, $v(13) = v(123) = 30$. This reflects the fact that only coalitions containing the seller, player 1, and at least one buyer can engage in any transactions that change their collective wealth. A coalition that contains player 1 is worth the maximum that the object in question is worth to any member of the coalition.

The tools of cooperative game theory applied to this model reflect some of the important features of such an interaction. For example, the core of the game [which for TU games is equal to the set of payoff distributions with the property that the sum of the payoffs to the members of each coalition S is at least $v(S)$] corresponds to the set of outcomes at which the seller sells to the buyer with the higher reservation price, at some price between twenty and thirty dollars, and no other transfers are made. This corresponds to what we would expect if the buyers compete with each other in an auction, for example. Von Neumann and Morgenstern proposed a more comprehensive kind of "solution" for such a game, which today is called a *stable set* or a *von Neumann–Morgenstern solution*. There are infinitely many von Neumann–Morgenstern solutions to this game, each of which consists of the core plus a continuous curve corresponding to a rule for sharing between the two buyers the wealth at each price less than twenty dollars (should they be able to agree to avoid bidding against one another, for example).

Von Neumann and Morgenstern's interpretation of this multiplicity of solutions was that each represented a particular "standard of behavior" that might be exhibited by rational players of the game. Which standard of behavior we might expect to observe in a particular game would generally depend on features of the environment – for example, institutional, social, or historical features – not modeled by the characteristic function. Thus their view was that much of the complexity of strategic interactions that was omitted from the characteristic function model reemerged through the complexity of the set of solutions. This very complexity nevertheless made it difficult to make a simple evaluation of a game in terms of its von Neumann – Morgenstern solutions. Partly for this reason, much of the subsequent analysis of such games has focused instead on the core. Although the core is much simpler than the von Neumann – Morgenstern solutions, it may be empty in some games and a large set of outcomes in others. And various "noncompetitive" modes of behavior (such as the formation of a bidders' cartel in our earlier example) might lead to outcomes outside the core, so a great deal of complexity remains.

This complexity is to a large extent a reflection of the underlying complexity of strategic interaction. Indeed, much current work in game theory is in the direction of putting more institutional and other detail into game-theoretic models in order to be able to more fully describe and better understand these complexities. (To a certain extent the same can be said of individual choice theory, in which there has been in recent years some exploration of more complex models than utility maximization.) However the underlying complexity of the phenomena only increases the need for a simple way to make a preliminary evaluation of games.

1   The Shapley value

Shapley's 1953 paper (reprinted as Chapter 2 of this volume) proposed to fill this need, essentially by carrying the reductionist program of von Neumann and Morgenstern a step further. Because it had proved so useful to represent each alternative facing a player by a single number expressing its expected utility, and to summarize the opportunities facing a coalition in a game by a single number expressing its worth in units of transferable utility, Shapley proposed to summarize the complex possibilities facing each player in a game in characteristic function form by a single number representing the "value" of playing the game. Thus the value of a game with a set $N = \{1, \ldots, n\}$ of players would be a vector of n numbers representing the value of playing the game in each of its n positions. The connection to what I have called the reductionist program of von Neumann and Morgenstern is made clearly in the first paragraph of Shapley's paper, which begins "At the foundation of the theory of games is the assumption that the players of a game can evaluate, in their utility scales, every 'prospect' that might arise as a result of a play. . . . [O]ne would normally expect to be permitted to include, in the class of 'prospects,' the prospect of having to play a game."

Shapley's approach was to consider the space of all games that might be played by some potentially very large set of players (denoted by the letter U, to signify the universe of all possible players). In a particular game v, the players actually involved are contained in any *carrier*, which is a subset N of U such that $v(S) = v(S \cap N)$ for any subset of players $S \subset U$. If a carrier N for a game v does not contain some player i, then i is a *null* player, because i does not influence the worth $v(S)$ of any coalition S. So any set containing a carrier is itself a carrier of a game, and any player not contained in every carrier is a null player.

Shapley defined a *value* for games to be a function that assigns to each game v a number $\phi_i(v)$ for each i in U. He proposed that such a function obey three axioms. The *symmetry* axiom requires that the names of the players play no role in determining the value, which should be sensitive only to how the characteristic function responds to the presence of a player in a coalition. In particular, the symmetry axiom requires that players who are treated identically by the characteristic function be treated identically by the value.

The second axiom, usually called the *carrier* axiom, requires that the sum of $\phi_i(v)$ over all players i in any carrier N equal $v(N)$. Because this must hold for *any* carrier, it implies that $\phi_i(v) = 0$ if i is a null player in v. Sometimes this axiom is thought of as consisting of two parts: the *efficiency* axiom ($\Sigma_{i \in N} \phi_i(v) = v(N)$ for some carrier N), and the *null player* (or sometimes "dummy player"[1]) axiom.

The third axiom, now called the *additivity* axiom, requires that, for any games v and w, $\phi(v) + \phi(w) = \phi(v + w)$ (i.e., $\phi_i(v) + \phi_i(w) = \phi_i(v + w)$ for all i in U, where the game $[v + w]$ is defined by $[v + w](S) = v(S) + w(S)$ for any coalition S). This axiom, which specifies how the values of different games must be related to one another, is the driving force behind Shapley's demonstration that there is a unique function ϕ defined on the space of all games that satisfies these three axioms.

The easiest way to understand why this function exists and is unique is to think of a characteristic function v as a vector with $2^U - 1$ components, one for each nonempty subset of U. (For simplicity, take the universe U of players to be finite.) Then the set G of all (not necessarily superadditive) characteristic function games coincides with euclidean space of dimension $2^U - 1$. The additivity axiom says that if we know a value function on some set of games that constitute an additive basis for G, then we can determine the value for any game.

A set of games that will permit us to accomplish this is the set consisting of the games v_R, defined for each subset R of U by

$$v_R(S) = 1 \quad \text{if } R \subset S,$$
$$= 0 \quad \text{otherwise.}$$

Any player not in R is a null player in this game, which is sometimes called the *pure bargaining* or *unanimity* game among the players in R, because they must all agree among themselves how to split the available wealth. Because the players in R are all symmetric, the symmetry axiom requires that $\phi_i(v_R) = \phi_j(v_R)$ for all i and j in R. Because the null player axiom requires that $\phi_k(v_R) = 0$ for all k not in R, the efficiency axiom allows us to conclude that $\phi_i(v_R) = 1/r$ for all i in R, where r is the number of players in R. (For any finite coalition S, we will denote by s the number of players in S.) Thus the value is uniquely defined on all games of the form v_R or, for that matter, on games of the form cv_R for any number c (where $cv_R(S) = c$ if $R \subset S$ and 0 otherwise). (Note that cv_R is superadditive when c is non-negative.)

But the games v_R form a basis for the set of all games, because there are $2^U - 1$ of them, one for each nonempty subset R of U, and because they are linearly independent. Therefore any game v can be written as the sum of games of the form cv_R. (For example, the game Γ_1 discussed earlier with one seller and two buyers is given by $\Gamma_1 = 10v_{(1)} + 10v_{(12)} + 20v_{(13)} - 10v_{(123)}$.) And so the additivity axiom implies that there is a unique value obeying Shapley's axioms defined on the space of all games.

Shapley showed that this unique value ϕ is

$$\phi_i(v) = \sum_{S \subset N} \frac{(s-1)!(n-s)!}{n!} [v(S) - v(S-i)],$$

where N is any finite carrier of v, with $|N| = n$. This formula expresses the Shapley value for player i in game v as a weighted sum of terms of the form $[v(S) - v(S - i)]$, which are player i's marginal contribution to coalitions S. (In Chapter 17 Peyton Young shows how the Shapley value may be axiomatized in terms of the marginal contributions.) In fact, $\phi_i(v)$ can be interpreted as the *expected* marginal contribution of player i, where the distribution of coalitions arises in a particular way.

Specifically, suppose the players enter a room in some order and that all $n!$ orderings of the players in N are equally likely. Then $\phi_i(v)$ is the expected marginal contribution made by player i as she enters the room. To see this, consider any coalition S containing i and observe that the probability that player i enters the room to find precisely the players in $S - i$ already there is $(s - 1)!(n - s)!/n!$. (Out of $n!$ permutations of N there are $(s - 1)!$ different orders in which the first $s - 1$ players can precede i, and $(n - s)!$ different orders in which the remaining $n - s$ players can follow, for a total of $(s - 1)!(n - s)!$ permutations in which precisely the players $S - i$ precede i.)

Although this is not meant to be a literal model of coalition formation (a topic that will be addressed by two of the papers in this volume), thinking of the value in this way is often a useful computational device. In our example of one seller and two buyers, the three players can enter in six possible orders. If they enter in order 1,2,3, their marginal contributions are $(0,20,10)$, and their Shapley values are the average of these marginal contributions over all six orders: $\phi(v) = (18.33, 3.33, 8.33)$.

For a more challenging example, consider a game loosely modeled on the United Nations Security Council, which consists of fifteen members. Five of these are permanent members and have a veto, and ten are rotating members. The voting rule is that a motion is passed if it receives nine votes and no vetoes. We model this here by taking $v(S) = 1$ if S contains all five permanent members and four or more other members, and $v(S) = 0$ otherwise.

Because 15! is a number on the order of 10^{12}, we obviously cannot proceed to calculate the Shapley value by enumerating all possible orderings of the players. But we can use the random-order property, together with symmetry and efficiency, to calculate the value. To do this, note that by symmetry all rotating members have the same value $\phi_r(v)$, all permanent members have the same value $\phi_p(v)$, and efficiency requires that $10\phi_r(v) + 5\phi_p(v) = 1$. In order for a rotating member to make a positive marginal contribution in a random order, all five permanent members and exactly three of the other nine rotating members must precede him or her. There are $9!/3!6!$ such coalitions, corresponding to the different ways to choose three out of the nine other rotating members. As we said, each such coalition S (of size $s = 9$) occurs with probability $(s - 1)!(n - s)!/n!$, and the marginal contribution of the last rotating member is $[v(S) - v(S - i)] = 1$. So the Shapley value of a rotating member is $\phi_r(v) = (9!/3!6!)(8!6!/15!) = .00186$, and the Shapley value of a permanent member is $\phi_p(v) = (1 - 10\phi_r(v))/5 = .196$, which is over 100 times greater.

1.1   The Shapley–Shubik Index

The results of a similar calculation, using the then existing rules of the Security Council, are described in the 1954 paper of Shapley and Martin Shubik, which is reprinted as Chapter 3. That paper was the first to propose applying the Shapley value to the class of simple games, which are natural models of voting rules.

A *simple* game is a game represented by a characteristic function v that takes on only the values 0 and 1. A coalition S is called *winning* if $v(S) = 1$, and *losing* if $v(S) = 0$, and the usual assumption is that every coalition containing a winning coalition is itself winning or, equivalently, that every subset of a losing coalition is itself a losing coalition. (A simple game is called *proper* if the complement of a winning coalition is always losing.) If v is a simple game among some set N of players, then an equivalent representation is simply the list of winning coalitions of N, or even the list of minimal winning coalitions (i.e., winning coalitions none of whose subsets are winning). For some classes of games, even terser representations may be natural: For example, a "weighted majority game" with n voters, such as might arise among the stockholders of a corporation, can be represented by the vector $[q; w_1, \ldots , w_n]$, where w_i denotes the number of votes cast by player i, and q denotes the number of votes needed by a winning coalition. The winning coalitions are then precisely those coalitions S with enough votes; that is, S is winning if and only if $\Sigma_{i \in S} w_i \geq q$.

Because simple games are essentially no more than lists of winning coalitions, they are often natural models of situations in which the full weight of the usual assumptions about characteristic function games may not be justified. Thus, for example, we may want to model a bicameral legislature by noting that the winning coalitions are those containing a majority of members in each house, and without assuming that the log-rolling opportunities available to members are sufficient so that a winning coalition can divide up the spoils in a transferable utility way. When we are interpreting a simple game as something other than a transferable utility characteristic function game, we may want to interpret the Shapley value of each player differently than we otherwise would. In recognition of this, the Shapley value applied to simple games is often called the *Shapley–Shubik index*. The marginal values $[v(S) - v(S - i)]$ in a simple game are always equal to 0 or 1, so a player's Shapley–Shubik index equals the proportion of random orders in which he or she is a "pivotal" player, the proportion of orders in which the set of players $S - i$ who precede him or her form a losing coalition that is transformed into a winning coalition S by the arrival of player i. (In each ordering of the players, only one player is pivotal.)

Analyzing voting rules that are modeled as simple games abstracts away from the particular personalities and political interests present in particular voting environments, but this abstraction is what makes the analysis focus on the rules themselves rather than on other aspects of the political environment. This kind of analysis seems to be just what is needed to analyze the voting rules in a new constitution, for example, long before the specific issues to be voted on arise or the specific factions and personalities that will be involved can be identified.

The task of assessing how much influence a voting system gives to each voter has assumed legal importance in evaluating legislative reapportionment schemes, following court rulings that valid schemes must give voters equal representation (i.e., must be systems that give "one man, one vote"). This has proved a difficult concept to define when voters are represented by legislators elected by district, particularly in systems in which districts of different sizes may be represented by different numbers of legislators or by legislators with different numbers of votes. A measure of voter influence related to the Shapley–Shubik index, called the Banzhaf index after the lawyer who formulated it in this context (Banzhaf 1965, 1968; Coleman 1971; Shapley 1977), has gained a measure of legal authority, particularly in New York State, in court decisions concerning these issues (Lucas 1983). Instead of looking at random orders of players, the Banzhaf index simply counts the number of coalitions in which a player is a "swing" voter. That is, the Banzhaf index of a voter i is proportional to the number of coalitions S such that S is winning but $S - i$ is losing. (A comprehensive treatment of the mathematical properties of the Banzhaf index is given by Dubey and Shapley 1979). Although the Banzhaf and Shapley–Shubik indices have certain obvious similarities, in any particular game they may not only give different numerical evaluations of a player's position but they may rank players differently, so the voter with more influence according to the Shapley–Shubik index may have less influence according to the Banzhaf index.

2   The other papers in this volume

Chapters 2 and 3, by Shapley and by Shapley and Shubik, are the "ancestral" papers from which the rest of the papers in this volume follow. Chapters 4 through 10 are concerned with reformulating these ideas in order to better understand them. As often as not, these reformulations also lead to generalizations, so by coming to understand the Shapley value or Shapley–Shubik index in new ways, we are also led to different ways to assess the value of playing a game or of measuring the influence of a voter.

2.1   *Reformulations and generalizations*

Chapter 4, "The expected utility of playing a game," investigates the implications of taking seriously the idea that the Shapley value can be interpreted as a utility function. It turns out that there is a strong and precise analogy between the Shapley value as a utility for positions in games and the expected value as a utility for monetary gambles, because both are risk-neutral utility functions. However, two kinds of risk neutrality are involved in interpreting the Shapley value as a utility: The first involves gambles ("ordinary risk") among games, and the second involves games that need not involve any probabilistic uncertainty but only the *strategic* risk associated with the unknown outcome of the interactions among the players. Neutrality to ordinary risk turns out to be equivalent to additivity of the utility function, and neutrality to strategic risk turns out to be closely associated with the efficiency axiom. The class of utility functions that represent preferences that are not neutral to strategic risk (and that are therefore "inefficient" value functions) is also characterized, provided that the preferences remain neutral to ordinary risk over games. (The characterization of utilities for preferences that are not neutral to ordinary risk remains an open problem.) The chapter concludes by considering the implications of this for understanding the comparisons among positions in games that are implicit in the Shapley value.

Philip Straffin's chapter, "The Shapley–Shubik and Banzhaf power indices as probabilities," is concerned with simple games, and shows that both the Shapley–Shubik and Banzhaf indices can be interpreted as the answer to the question: "What is the probability that a given voter's vote will affect the outcome of the vote on a bill?" To pose this question, one needs to specify a model of voter probabilities. Straffin observes that the Shapley–Shubik index answers this question if we assume voters' opinions are homogeneous in a certain sense, and the Banzhaf index gives the answer if we assume voters' opinions are independent in a particular way. His analysis not only casts new light on the similarities and differences between these two indices, but also suggests how this method of modeling voters might be adapted to particular situations to create new indices when other assumptions about voters are appropriate.

Ehud Kalai and Dov Samet, in "Weighted Shapley values," consider the class of value functions that need not be symmetric but obey Shapley's other axioms. In other words, they report on possible generalizations of the Shapley theory that apply to nonanonymous players. This line of work was begun by Shapley in his dissertation (Shapley 1953b), who introduced the nonanonymity by assigning different positive weights to the players. In a pure bargaining game v_R the players in R receive payoffs proportional to their weights. Owen (1968) provided an interpretation of the weighted Shapley values by considering random arrival times. A high weight corresponds to a high probability of arriving later. Kalai and Samet consider more general lexicographic weight systems. Using a novel consistency axiom in place of symmetry, they show that all such values must be of this generalized weighted type. Their "partnership consistency" axiom concerns players who are only valuable to a coalition when they are in it together. They also discuss a family of dual weighted values that have natural interpretations in cost allocation problems (Shapley 1983). These values are in turn characterized by an axiom system that contains a dual to the partnership consistency axiom, and it is shown that when the two axioms are imposed together they yield the (symmetric) Shapley value. As a consequence of these characterizations, for consistent values, lack of symmetries between players may be viewed as being due to asymmetries in size. That is, different players may be viewed as representing "blocks" of different sizes. (A recent result by Monderer, Samet, and Shapley shows that the set of weighted Shapley values of a given game always contains the core of the game. Coincidence of the two sets occurs if and only if the game is convex.)

In "Probabilistic values for games," Robert Weber returns to the consideration of symmetric values that need not be efficient, as well as efficient values that need not be symmetric. He pays careful attention to the effect of applying the axioms to different classes of games, including superadditive and simple games, and observes that on sufficiently rich classes of games the values obtained by discarding the efficiency axiom can all be characterized as expected marginal contributions. He draws a different connection than that developed in Chapter 4 between values that do not assume efficiency and a kind of strategic risk aversion of the player evaluating the game.

In Chapter 8, Uriel Rothblum considers three formulas for the Shapley value that differ from its representation as the expected marginal contribution when all orders are equally likely. It is important to recognize that the random-order representation, although familiar and useful, has no special status. In particular, the significance of the Shapley value does not rest on the stylized model of "coalition formation" embodied in the standard formula. Rothblum presents three other, equivalent, formulas for the Shapley value, each of which permits us to compute it as a kind of average taken over coalitions of the same size. Just as the random-order representation has proved useful in facilitating certain kinds of computations (as in the computation involving the Security Council example), each of these other representations can be of similar use for games whose special structure makes one of these other averages easy to compute.

In "The potential of the Shapley value," Sergiu Hart and Andreu Mas-Colell carry a step further the reductionist program begun by von Neumann and Morgenstern and continued by Shapley. Instead of summarizing the opportunities available to each player in a game by a single number, and thus summarizing the game by a vector, Hart and Mas-Colell propose to summarize each game by a single number, $P(N,v)$, to be called its *potential*. (I have spoken of a reductionist program in terms of models: utility, characteristic functions, values, and now potentials. Hart and Mas-Colell speak of a parallel program in terms of solution concepts: stable sets, core, value, and potential.) The marginal contribution of a player in terms of the potential is the difference $P(N,v) - P(N - i,v)$, that is, the difference between the potential of the game with its full set N of players and the game without player i. Strictly speaking, Hart and Mas-Colell define a function on games to be a potential only if the sum of these marginal contributions over all the players equals $v(N)$, and they show that there is a unique such potential with respect to which each player's marginal contribution equals his or her Shapley value. (And thus the use of the term *potential* conforms to standard mathematical usage, because the potential of a vector-valued function ϕ is a real-valued function P whose gradient is ϕ.) Representing the value by the potential proves to be a useful technical tool (at least one with great potential), as is shown by the results concerning the consistency of the value. As the authors remark, this treatment provides a natural approach for viewing the Shapley value as a tool for cost allocation (a subject to which we will return), although their caution about avoiding inappropriate interpretations is well taken.

The final chapter in this section, "Multilinear extensions of games" by Guillermo Owen, could well have been grouped with the chapters on large games, because it concerns an extension of the characteristic function model that permits a large-game interpretation, among others. For a game played by n players, consider an n-dimensional unit cube. Its vertices, which are vectors of 0's and 1's, can be interpreted as coalitions of players, with player i being in the coalition associated with a given vertex if the ith component of the associated vector is a 1. Owen defines the multilinear extension of a given characteristic function v as a function defined on the whole cube, which agrees with v on the vertices and interpolates in a linear way on other parts of the cube. Owen shows that this extension provides a powerful computational and conceptual tool. Points in the cube other than vertices can be interpreted in various ways. The large-game interpretation arises, for example, if we view each of the n players of the game as representing a continuum of players of a certain type. Then a point in the cube can be interpreted as corresponding to a coalition of players, with the ith coordinate indicating the percentage of players of type i in the coalition. It turns out that the Shapley value is determined by the value of the multilinear extension only on the "main diagonal" of the cube (i.e., on the points of the cube in which all n components are equal). This "diagonal property," which plays a significant role in the study of the values of large games (see, e.g., Neyman 1977), has a natural intuitive interpretation in that context related to the random-order property of the Shapley value. In a game with finitely many types of players, consider a coalition of some size arising from the random entry of players (think of the number of players of each type as very large but finite, in order to avoid for the moment the difficulties with defining a random order of an infinite game). Then by the law of large numbers, most of the coalitions of this size will have the same proportion of each type of player as is found in the game as a whole. The diagonal property says that only such coalitions need be considered in computing the Shapley value.

2.2   *Coalitions*

The next two chapters deal with attempts to use the Shapley value and related concepts to begin to develop the elements of a theory of how players in a game might choose to organize themselves, which remains one of the most difficult and important problems in game theory. The traditional approach to this problem has been to consider coalition structures, which are partitions of players into disjoint coalitions. In order to consider how players might organize themselves into coalitions, one first must be able to assess how any given structure of coalitions will influence each player's payoff. "Coalitional value," by Mordecai Kurz considers some ways in which the Shapley value may be adapted to this task, and goes on to consider some ways in which the answers to this question can inform the discussion of which coalitions might be expected to form.

The chapter by Robert Aumann and Roger Myerson uses an extension of the Shapley value proposed earlier by Myerson, to suggest a novel approach to the question of how cooperation among players might be organized. Rather than looking only at disjoint coalitions, they examine cooperation structures, which consist of bilateral links between players. They then consider a linking game in which players may choose whether and with whom to establish such links, using the extension of the Shapley value to cooperation structures to evaluate the payoffs to the players from each resulting set of links. They call a cooperation structure "natural" if it can arise as the subgame perfect equilibrium of such a game. The chapter contains examples that give insight into the problems involved in this area of game theory. The chapter itself is a good example of how, even in the absence of a fully worked out theory, much insight can often be obtained by creatively applying game-theoretic tools.

2.3   *Large games*

Chapters 13 through 16 concern very large games, such as arise in economic models of perfect competition, in which agents are negligibly small relative to the size of the market. In the literature concerning the core (Edgeworth 1881; Shubik 1959; Debreu and Scarf 1963), it has been observed that, as the number of agents in an exchange economy increases, the core shrinks in the limit to include just the competitive allocations. Aumann (1964) modeled a perfectly competitive economy as consisting of a nonatomic continuum of agents, and he showed that the core and the competitive allocations coincide in such a model. The literature concerning the Shapley value of large games began with a set of papers entitled "The value of large games, I–VII" by Shapley and various coauthors (Shapley and Shapiro 1960; Milnor and Shapley 1961; Shapley 1961a; Mann and Shapley 1960; Shapley 1961b; Mann and Shapley 1962; Shapley 1964a,b). (See also Shapley 1962a–c; Mann and Shapley 1964; Shapley and Shubik 1969.) It continued with the seminal book by Aumann and Shapley, *Values of non-atomic games*, which may have directly inspired more Ph.D. dissertations than any other book in game theory, except von Neumann and Morgenstern's. They showed that in economies with a nonatomic continuum of agents, value allocations coincide with core allocations (and hence with competitive allocations), even though value and core allocations may be quite unrelated in finite markets.

The opening chapter of this section, by Myrna Wooders and William Zame, reports on their recent work concerning large finite games. In these games, not necessarily markets, players are drawn from some metric space of attributes. This makes it possible to speak of two players as being close to one another in attributes, and of games that treat similar players similarly. A game can then be thought of as large if there are sufficiently many near substitutes for every player in the game. The main result of the paper is that, under fairly weak conditions, the Shapley value for a large game is not far from the core – that is, is in the ϵ-core – of the game.

The chapter "Payoffs in nonatomic economies: an axiomatic approach," by Pradeep Dubey and Abraham Neyman follows the presentation of their 1984 *Econometrica* paper of the same name and considers what properties the value shares with other solution concepts that all coincide on nonatomic economies. (The only widely studied solution concept that does *not* coincide with the competitive allocations in standard continuum economies is the von Neumann – Morgenstern solution; see Hart 1974.) One of their key axioms is a weakening of additivity. Their results can be thought of as an axiomatization of the value on a class of nonatomic economies.

In their chapter, "Values of smooth nonatomic games: the method of multilinear approximation," Dov Monderer and Abraham Neyman provide new, short proofs of some of the classical results about the value of nonatomic measure games. They do this by establishing that a general class of nonatomic games can be approximated by nonatomic measure games that are multilinear functions of a finite number of measures. Thus, among other things, this chapter establishes an even closer connection between infinite games and the multilinear extensions of games discussed by Owen in Chapter 10. They also prove a result related to the results presented by Young in Chapter 17.

Since the publication of Aumann and Shapley's book, a great deal has been learned about how to relax some of their assumptions and expand the class of infinite games on which values can be defined and characterized. Among the hardest kinds of games to deal with, and the source of difficult and perplexing counterexamples, have been infinite games whose characteristic function need not be smooth. In the most technically demanding chapter in this volume, Jean-Francois Mertens characterizes the value on a class of market games without the usual differentiability assumptions.

2.4   *Cost allocation and fair division*

The next two chapters concern the application of the Shapley value to problems of allocating costs. This subject has been of interest both to game theorists and accountants (Moriarty 1983). One of the first papers to suggest this particular use was Shubik (1962). Two conceptual approaches have developed around this application. One is to view cost allocation problems as games and to interpret the allocation of costs implied by the Shapley value in the same way that one interprets the Shapley value generally. In this spirit, Billera, Heath, and Raanan (1978) looked at allocation of costs for telephone calls at different times of day as an application of Aumann and Shapley's work on nonatomic games (in which instants of telephone time occupied the role of players in the game), and Roth and Verrecchia (1979) proposed that Shapley cost allocations by a central administration could be viewed (in the manner of Chapter 4) as those which would give risk-neutral managers the same utility as allowing them to negotiate with one another about how to share costs. The second approach, which has focused on the case of a continuum of goods, has been to axiomatize cost allocation rules directly, without necessarily considering the problem as a game. This approach thus yields axioms that directly concern how commodities enter a production function, for example.

Peyton Young's chapter, "Individual contribution and just compensation," deals with both of these approaches. It is motivated by ideas of distributive justice and by economic ideas about cost allocation as well. The first part of his chapter concerns finite games in characteristic function form, interpreted as production functions that give the joint output for any coalition of agents. He shows that the Shapley value is the unique symmetric value function that fully distributes all gains and in which each agent's share depends only on his or her own marginal contributions. (Formally, this characterization of the Shapley value is in terms of the requirement that if player i has the same vector of marginal contributions in two games, then his or her values for those two games must be equal.) The second part of the chapter concerns a firm whose production is a function of a vector of inputs that can vary continuously, and considers how to impute profits to each factor of production. He shows that a requirement of monotonicity (if factor i has a higher marginal contribution at every level of input under one production function than under another, then it is imputed a higher share of the profit under the first production function), together with an appropriate version of symmetry and of full distribution of profits among the factors of production is sufficient to characterize the Aumann–Shapley pricing rule in this context.

The next chapter, by Yair Tauman, gives a comprehensive survey of the direct axiomatic approach to cost allocation that has grown out of the work of Aumann and Shapley on nonatomic games, which grew out of the direct axiomatizations given by Billera and Heath (1982) and by Mirman and Tauman (1982). The chapter reviews the principal results that have been obtained to date, and indicates the connections to related work in the game-theoretic literature on the value. Consequently, this chapter is related to numerous other chapters in this volume.

2.5 *NTU games*

We have so far been concentrating on games with transferable utility. Although the chapters in this book make abundantly clear why it is frequently productive to model situations as if utility were transferable, it is nevertheless also clear why it is often desirable to avoid such a strong assumption. Indeed, there are situations in which the assumption that utility is transferable would obscure some of the most important features of the economic environment. For this reason, much of the game-theoretic literature has been concerned with NTU (nontransferable utility) games, in which utility is not assumed to be transferable. In such a game, the opportunities available to a coalition S may be represented by a *set* $V(S)$ of utility vectors rather than by a single number $v(S)$. (A TU game given by the characteristic function v can be thought of as the special case of an NTU game in which, for each coalition S, $V(S) = \{(x_1, \ldots, x_n) | \Sigma_{i \in S} x_i \leq v(S)\}$.) For example, in an exchange economy, the set function V would be determined by the trades each coalition of traders S can accomplish among themselves, together with their utilities for the resulting commodity bundles. Modeling a market in this way rather than as a TU game allows factors such as the indivisibility of certain kinds of commodities to play a role and, even when money is present in the economy, avoids the necessity of assuming that all commodities enter the traders' utility functions as money.

John Nash (1950, 1953) considered the class of *pure bargaining* NTU games. (A pure bargaining game among a set of r players is one in which any agreement requires the unanimous consent of all the players.) Nash represented such an NTU game by a pair (S,d), where S is a set of r-dimensional utility vectors corresponding to the feasible agreements that can be reached if all the players agree, and d is the vector of utility payoffs that the players will get if bargaining ends in disagreement (i.e., in the absence of a unanimous agreement on some other alternative). The TU pure bargaining game v_R is simply the game whose feasible set S corresponds to all the ways the players can split a fixed sum – that is, it is bounded by the hyperplane $\Sigma_{i \in R} x_i = 1$ – and in which disagreement gives each player a utility of 0. Nash proposed that a *solution* of a pure bargaining NTU game should be a function that (like the Shapley value) selects a unique feasible outcome for any pure bargaining game.

Nash characterized a particular solution, using an axiomatic framework that has a close conceptual (but not mathematical) relationship to the axiomatic characterization of the Shapley value. Nash's axioms, like Shapley's, include symmetry and efficiency, which therefore fix the outcome for the TU game v_R to be the one that gives each player $1/r$. Where Shapley used additivity to generalize this result to arbitrary TU games, Nash used two "independence" axioms to generalize this to arbitrary NTU pure bargaining games. (The first axiom specifies that the agreement corresponding to the utility payoff selected by the solution should not depend on how the utilities of the bargainers are scaled. This is meant to capture the idea that the payoffs are stated in terms of players' von Neumann–Morgenstern utility functions, which have arbitrary origins and units and do not permit interpersonal comparisons. The second axiom, called "independence of irrelevant alternatives," specifies that if two games have the same disagreement point and the feasible outcomes of one are contained in those of the other, then the solution of the larger game is also the solution of the smaller game whenever it is feasible.) As is the case with the Shapley value, relaxing the assumptions of efficiency and symmetry leads to a class of solutions that preserve the essential character of the original solution (see, e.g., Roth 1979 for a review of this literature and Roth 1987 for a discussion of experimental evidence concerning the strengths and weaknesses of these solutions as descriptive tools).

Shapley's 1969 paper, reprinted as Chapter 19, establishes a way to generalize the Shapley value from the class of TU games to NTU games. (In fact, the paper proposes a method that can potentially be used for generalizing any value function for TU games to NTU games, but most subsequent work has looked at the generalization of the Shapley value.) This generalization coincides with Nash's solution on the set of pure bargaining games, so it can also be viewed as a generalization of Nash's solution from the class of bargaining games to the class of all NTU games. Another generalization of Nash's solution had been proposed by Harsanyi (1963), and Shapley writes that "The value definition developed here was first contrived in an attempt to approximate Harsanyi's 1963 bargaining value by something that might prove analytically more tractable in dealing with economic models having large numbers of participants."

Shapley's paper begins with a consideration of two-person pure bargaining NTU games and the demonstration that no nontrivial single-point solution exists that depends only on the independently scaled ordinal utilities of the players. (This conclusion does not hold for the n-person pure bargaining problem with $n > 2$; see Shapley and Shubik 1974; Shubik 1982, chap. 5.) It then goes on to consider cardinal solutions and to interpret Nash's solution for pure bargaining games as making an implicit comparison of the bargainers' utilities. This kind of comparison is the basis of the proposed generalization to a value for general NTU games. The basic idea is to use the TU value to find the NTU value. Note that if we transform an NTU game into a TU game by allowing the unrestricted transfer of utility among the players, then we are enlarging the set of outcomes. The TU value of this game might not, therefore, be a feasible outcome of the original NTU game. However, Shapley proves, via a fixed-point argument, that one can always find a vector λ of weights, one for each player, such that when each player's utility is multiplied by his or her weight, the resulting game will have the property that the TU value ϕ is feasible in the NTU game. Shapley called the resulting vector ϕ the "λ-transfer value" for the original NTU game, noting that "As a companion to each value vector, ϕ, obtained under this definition, there will be a vector, λ, of intrinsic utility-comparison weights." (In the subsequent literature, the λ-transfer value is sometimes called the NTU value.) The connection with Nash's axiom of independence of irrelevant alternatives is clear, because the λ-transfer value takes the solution of the NTU game to be the solution of the associated TU game (with a larger feasible set) when this is feasible (Aumann 1975).

There has been some controversy about the interpretation of the λ-transfer value (and also of Harsanyi's 1963 value). Researchers have questioned whether the value for NTU games can support, on the class of NTU games for which it is defined, the various interpretations given to the TU value and, if not, what other interpretations or what restricted class of games might be called for. Particular targets of concern have been the interpretation of the utility comparisons, the implications of "independence of irrelevant alternatives" in games in which more than one coalition may be important, and the extent to which the λ-transfer value can respond to features of NTU games that differ from TU games. These concerns have made their way into the literature via the analysis of particular games, typically games with few players (Owen 1972; Roth 1980, 1986; Shafer 1980; Harsanyi 1980; Scafuri and Yannelis 1984). However, no consensus has yet emerged on the significance of these concerns, which have been addressed directly (Aumann 1985a, 1986, 1987) and indirectly in numerous explorations of the λ-transfer value as a tool for analyzing games and markets, particularly large markets (see, e.g., the references in Aumann 1985a). The λ-transfer value remains by far the most easily computable of proposed alternative NTU values, and considerable progress in understanding its mathematical properties has been made in the axiomatization presented by Aumann (1985b), which is strikingly similar to Shapley's axiomatization of the TU value. A closely related axiomatization of Harsanyi's NTU value has been presented by Hart (1985a); see also Hart (1985b).

The final chapter of this volume, by Michael Maschler, Guillermo Owen, and Bezalel Peleg, returns to the case of pure bargaining NTU games. Games whose feasible sets need not be convex are considered, on which the NTU value – Nash solution may not select a unique outcome. Rather than characterizing the outcomes axiomatically, this paper explores a dynamic process of adjustment that leads to the indicated outcomes. The paper can thus be viewed as providing a different way of understanding the NTU value – Nash solution on the class of pure bargaining games.

In closing, I should hasten to add that research on the Shapley value has proceeded in so many directions that it has not proved possible to cover them all in this volume. One recent area of investigation is the study of the Shapley value using the tools of noncooperative game theory. For example, Harsanyi (1981) proposes to study cooperative games by means of noncooperative bargaining models, using the notions of risk dominance he has developed in conjunction with Reinhard Selten to select a unique equilibrium. He identifies an equilibrium that corresponds with the Shapley value on one class of games, although not on all of the games that can be modeled in this way. A similarly motivated paper by Gul (1986) analyzes the equilibria of certain market games modeled as sequential bargaining games, and shows that the Shapley value corresponds to a subgame perfect equilibrium. A somewhat different strategic question is asked by Thomson (in press), who considers the strategic game that results if the Shapley value is employed as a rule to allocate resources among players, based on parameters of the game announced by the players (each of whom is the only one to know his or her own utility function). Thomson considers the strategic problem facing each player about what utility function to state, and characterizes the ways in which this kind of resource allocation mechanism can be manipulated.

3   Some remarks on the work of Lloyd Shapley

As the papers in this volume attest, Lloyd Shapley's contribution to game theory would have been significant even if he had done no more than introduce the value and some of its principal extensions and uses. But, especially because the particular occasion for this volume is to mark the sixty-fifth birthday of a major scholar, it seems proper to at least briefly mention the nature and scope of Shapley's other contributions to game theory.

The first formal definitions of the core of a game as an independent solution concept are generally attributed to Shapley (1953c) and Gillies (1953a,b). Shapley's subsequent work on when the core of a game is nonempty led to the notion of "balancedness," which in TU games is related to the theory of linear programming (Shapley 1967a; Bondareva 1963). The same notion can be generalized to the case of NTU games (see Scarf 1967; and Shapley 1973) with much the same effect, and this work has had important applications, such as the computational work initiated by Scarf (1973). Shapley and Shubik (1969a) showed that the TU games that can be formulated as exchange economies (with continuous and concave utility functions) are precisely those that are "totally balanced," that is, those for which the subgame for each subset of players is a balanced game. Another important class of games with nonempty core, the class of convex games, was introduced in Shapley (1971). Still another family of games with nonempty cores was introduced by Gale and Shapley (1962), who studied an NTU model (the "marriage" game), and by Shapley and Shubik (1972), who studied a TU model (the "assignment" game). This family of games has in recent years attracted a good deal of interest among economists interested in labor markets and other kinds of two-sided matching processes (see, e.g., Roth 1984; Roth and Sotomayor in press).

Although the core has become one of the most important game-theoretic ideas, particularly for the study of markets, the initial interest in the core grew out of the research agenda established by von Neumann and Morgenstern (1944), because the core is contained in every stable set of outcomes of the kind that they proposed as solutions for games. Although the theory of stable sets does not occupy the central place in contemporary game theory that von Neumann and Morgenstern anticipated, a good deal of what we know about both the strengths and weaknesses of stable sets as a tool for analyzing games is due to Shapley. On the one hand, Shapley explored the stable sets of various classes of games and showed how understanding them could lead to a better understanding of the strategic possibilities facing coalitions of players. His 1959 paper on symmetric market games falls into this category, as does his paper on solutions of "quota" games (Shapley 1953d). In a series of papers on simple games, motivated explicitly by models of political and committee decision making, he showed the power of this kind of theory for a class of games with empty cores (Shapley 1962a, 1963, 1964a, 1967b). Quite apart from the study of solutions of simple games, much of the way we think of simple games derives from Shapley's (1962b) taxonomy. At the same time, Shapley's work played an equally important role in clarifying the limitations of stable sets as an analytical tool, not only because of the computational intractability of stable sets but also because many games have solutions that cannot support any interpretation in terms of the features of the game. A good example of this part of his work is found in Shapley (1959b). Shapley's work set the stage for the demonstration by Lucas (1968, 1969) of a characteristic function game for which no solution exists, which resolved in the negative a famous conjecture of von Neumann and Morgenstern.

In noncooperative game theory, quite a large literature has grown out of Shapley's paper on stochastic games (Shapley 1953e), which introduced a model in which the actions of the players jointly determine not only their payoffs but also the transition probabilities to a subsequent stage of the game. This was a natural extension of the study of (single-agent) Markovian decision processes in the operations research literature, and was also among the first important examples of a multistage game. Shapley showed the existence of a value and of stationary optimal strategies in the discounted game. Some subsequent milestones in the work that followed were by Gillette (1957), who extended the results to the undiscounted game under an ergodicity assumption, and by Blackwell and Ferguson (1968), who solved a game proposed by Gillette. Further generalizations were obtained by Kohlberg (1974) and Bewley and Kohlberg (1976), in which an algebraic approach was used to prove the existence of an asymptotic value for any stochastic game with finite sets of states and moves. Mertens and Neyman (1981) proved the existence of a value for a general class of infinitely repeated stochastic games. Algorithms for solving stochastic games have also received a good deal of attention; see, for example, Raghavan (undated). In addition, stochastic games are closely related to repeated games of incomplete information (cf. Kohlberg and Zamir 1974).

This brief account of Shapley's work is by no means complete. However, even a more adequately detailed account, if it concentrated only on Shapley's published work, or even on his voluminous unpublished and sometimes unwritten work that forms much of the folklore of game theory, would fail to convey the critical role he played in game theory's development. Indeed, in the years following the work of von Neumann and Morgenstern, Shapley became the very personification of game theory, such was the role he played in shaping the agenda of game-theoretic research.

I cannot speak from personal experience of the early years, but when I received my Ph.D. in 1974 I made the customary pilgrimage to Santa Monica to discuss my work with Shapley. I was moved by his passion for and generosity with ideas and overwhelmed by his encyclopedic knowledge. I have since found that this experience was shared by many game theorists of my generation.

All game theorists owe Shapley a considerable intellectual debt, part of which we seek to acknowledge with this volume.

NOTES

1 A dummy player in a game v is a player i such that for all coalitions S containing i, $v(S) - v(S - i) = v(i)$. When $v(i) = 0$, a dummy player is a null player.

REFERENCES

Aumann, Robert J. [1964], "Markets with a Continuum of Traders," *Econometrica*, 32, 39–50.

[1975], "Values of Markets with a Continuum of Traders," *Econometrica*, 43, 611–46.

[1985a], "On the Non-transferable Utility Value: A Comment on the Roth–Shafer Examples," *Econometrica*, 53, 667–77.

[1985b], "An Axiomatization of the Non-Transferable Utility Value," *Econometrica*, 53, 599–612.

[1986], "Rejoinder," *Econometrica*, 54, 985–9.

[1987], "Value, Symmetry and Equal Treatment: A Comment on Scafuri and Yannelis," *Econometrica*, 55, 1461–4.

Aumann, Robert J. and Lloyd S. Shapley [1974], *Values of Non-Atomic Games*, Princeton, Princeton University Press.

Banzhaf, John F. III [1965], "Weighted Voting Doesn't Work: A Mathematical Analysis," *Rutgers Law Review*, 19, 317–43.

[1968], "One Man, 3,312 Votes: A Mathematical Analysis of the Electoral College," *Villanova Law Review*, 13, 303–46.

Bewley, Truman and Elon Kohlberg [1976], "The Asymptotic Theory of Stochastic Games," *Mathematics of Operations Research*, 1, 197–208.

Billera, L. J., D. C. Heath, and J. Raanan [1978], "Internal Telephone Billing Rates: A Novel Application of Non-atomic Game Theory," *Operations Research*, 26, 956–65.

Billera, L. J. and D. C. Heath [1982], "Allocation of Shared Costs: A Set of Axioms Yielding a Unique Procedure," *Mathematics of Operations Research*, 7, 32–39.

Blackwell, D. and T. S. Ferguson [1968], "The Big Match," *Annals of Mathematical Statistics*, 39, 159–63.

Bondareva, O. N. [1963], "Some Applications of Linear Programming Methods to the Theory of Cooperative Games," *Problemy Kibernetiki,* 10, 119–39. (in Russian)

Coleman, James S. [1971], "Control of Collectivities and the Power of a Collectivity to Act," in *Social Choice,* B. Lieberman, editor, Gordon and Breach, New York, pp. 269–300.

Debreu, Gerard and Herbert Scarf [1963], "A Limit Theorem on the Core of an Economy," *International Economic Review,* 4, 235–46.

Dubey, Pradeep and Lloyd S. Shapley [1979], "Mathematical Properties of the Banzhaf Power Index," *Mathematics of Operations Research,* 4, 99–131.

Edgeworth, F. Y. [1881], *Mathematical Psychics,* London, C. Kegan Paul.

Gale, David and Lloyd Shapley [1962], "College Admissions and the Stability of Marriage," *American Mathematical Monthly,* 69, 9–15.

Gillette, D. [1957], "Stochastic Games with Zero Stop Probabilities," in *Contribution to the Theory of Games,* M. Dresher, A. W. Tucker, and P. Wolfe, editors, vol. III, Ann. Math. Studies, 39, Princeton University Press, Princeton, New Jersey.

Gillies, D. B. [1953a], "Locations of Solutions," in *Report of an Informal Conference on the Theory of N-Person Games,* H. W. Kuhn, editor, Princeton University, mimeo.

[1953b], *Some Theorems on N-Person Games,* Ph.D. dissertation, Department of Mathematics, Princeton University.

Gul, Faruk [1986], "Bargaining Foundations of the Shapley Value," Princeton University, Department of Economics, mimeo.

Harsanyi, John C. [1963], "A Simplified Bargaining Model for the *n*-Person Cooperative Game," *International Economic Review,* 4, 194–220.

[1977], *Rational Behavior and Bargaining Equilibrium in Games and Social Situations,* Cambridge University Press, Cambridge.

[1980], "Comments on Roth's Paper: "Values for Games without Side Payments", *Econometrica,* 48, 477.

[1981], "The Shapley Value and the Risk-Dominance Solutions of Two Bargaining Models for Characteristic-Function Games," in *Essays in Game Theory and Mathematical Economics in Honor of Oskar Morgenstern,* V. Bohn, editor, B. I. Wissenschaftsverlag, Mannheim, pp. 43–68.

Hart, Sergiu [1974], "Formation of Cartels in Large Markets," *Journal of Economic Theory,* 7, 453–66.

[1985a], "An Axiomatization of Harsanyi's Nontransferable Utility Solution," *Econometrica,* 53, 1295–1313.

[1985b], "Nontransferable Utility Games and Markets: Some Examples and the Harsanyi Solution," *Econometrica,* 53, 1445–50.

Kohlberg, E. [1974], "Repeated Games with Absorbing States," *Annals of Statistics,* 2, 724–38.

Kohlberg, Elon and Shmuel Zamir [1974], "Repeated Games of Incomplete Information: The Symmetric Case," *Annals of Statistics,* 2, 1040–41.

Lucas, William F. [1968], "A Game with No Solution," *Bulletin of the American Mathematical Society,* 74, 237–9.

[1969], "The Proof That a Game May Not Have a Solution," *Transactions of the American Mathematical Society,* 137, 219–29.

[1983], "Measuring Power in Weighted Voting Systems," in *Political and Related Models*, S. Brams, W. Lucas, and P. Straffin, editors, Springer, Berlin, pp. 183–238.

Mann, I. and Lloyd S. Shapley [1960], *Values of Large Games, IV: Evaluating the Electoral College by Montecarlo Techniques*, RM-2651, The Rand Corporation, Santa Monica.

[1962], *Values of Large Games, VI: Evaluating the Electoral College Exactly*, RM-3158, The Rand Corporation, Santa Monica.

[1964], "The *a priori* Voting Strength of the Electoral College," in *Game Theory and Related Approaches to Social Behavior*, M. Shubik, editor, Wiley, New York, pp. 151–64.

Mertens, Jean-Francois and Abraham Neyman [1981], "Stochastic Games," *International Journal of Game Theory*, 10, 53–66.

Milnor, John W. and Lloyd S. Shapley [1961], *Values of Large Games, II: Oceanic Games*, RM-2649, The Rand Corporation, Santa Monica. (Also *Mathematics of Operations Research*, 3, 1978, 290–307.)

Mirman, Leonard J. and Yair Tauman [1982], "Demand Compatible Equitable Cost Sharing Prices," *Mathematics of Operations Research*, 7, 40–56.

Moriarity, Shane (editor) [1983], *Joint Cost Allocation*, University of Oklahoma Press, Tulsa.

Nash, John F. [1950], "The Bargaining Problem," *Econometrica*, 28, 155–62.

[1953], "Two-Person Cooperative Games," *Econometrica*, 21, 129–40.

Neyman, Abraham [1977], "Continuous Values Are Diagonal," *Mathematics of Operations Research*, 2, 338–42.

Owen, Guillermo [1968], "A Note on Shapley Values," *Management Science*, 14, 731–32.

[1972], "Values of Games without Sidepayments," *International Journal of Game Theory*, 1, 95–108.

Raghavan, T. E. S. [undated], "Algorithms for Stochastic Games: A Survey," Department of Mathematics, University of Illinois at Chicago, mimeo.

Roth, Alvin E. [1979], *Axiomatic Models of Bargaining*, Springer, Berlin.

[1980], "Values for Games without Sidepayments: Some Difficulties with Current Concepts," *Econometrica*, 48, 457–65.

[1984], "The Evolution of the Labor Market for Medical Interns and Residents: A Case Study in Game Theory," *Journal of Political Economy*, 92, 991–1016.

[1986], "On the Non-Transferable Utility Value: A Reply to Aumann," *Econometrica*, 54, 981–4.

[1987], "Bargaining Phenomena and Bargaining Theory," in *Laboratory Experimentation in Economics: Six Points of View*, A. E. Roth, editor, Cambridge University Press, Cambridge, pp. 14–41.

Roth, Alvin E. and Marilda Sotomayor [In press], *Two-Sided Matching: A Study in Game-Theoretic Modelling and Analysis*. Econometric Society Monograph, Cambridge University Press, Cambridge.

Roth, Alvin E. and Robert E. Verrecchia [1979], "The Shapley Value as Applied to Cost Allocation: A Reinterpretation," *Journal of Accounting Research*, 17, 295–303.

Scafuri, Allen J. and Nicholas C. Yannelis [1984], "Non-Symmetric Cardinal Value Allocations," *Econometrica*, 52, 1365–8.

Scarf, Herbert [1967], "The Core of an *N*-Person Game," *Econometrica*, 37, 50–69.

[1973], *The Computation of Economic Equilibria*, with the collaboration of Terje Hansen, Yale University Press, New Haven.

Shafer, Wayne J. [1980], "On the Existence and Interpretation of Value Allocations," *Econometrica*, 48, 467–76.

Shapley, Lloyd S. [1953a], "A Value for *n*-Person Games," in *Contributions to the Theory of Games*, vol. II, H. W. Kuhn and A. W. Tucker, editors, Ann. Math. Studies 28, Princeton University Press, Princeton, New Jersey, pp. 307–17 [reprinted in this volume].

[1953b], *Additive and Non-Additive Set Functions*, Ph.D. thesis, Department of Mathematics, Princeton University.

[1953c], "Open Questions," in *Report of an Informal Conference on the Theory of N-Person Games*, H. W. Kuhn, editor, Princeton University, mimeo.

[1953d] "Quota Solutions of *n*-Person Games," in *Contributions to the Theory of Games*, vol. II, H. W. Kuhn and A. W. Tucker, editors, Ann. Math. Studies 28, Princeton University Press, Princeton, New Jersey, pp. 343–59.

[1953e] "Stochastic Games," *Proceedings of the National Academy of Sciences*, 39, 1095–1100.

[1959a], "The Solutions of a Symmetric Market Game," *Annals of Mathematics Studies*, 40, 145–62.

[1959b], "A Solution Containing an Arbitrary Closed Component," *Annals of Mathematics Studies*, 40, 87–93.

[1961a], *Values of Large Games, III: A Corporation with Two Large Stockholders*, RM-2650, The Rand Corporation, Santa Monica.

[1961b], *Values of Large Games, V: An 18-person Market Game*, RM-2860, The Rand Corporation, Santa Monica.

[1962a], "Compound Simple Games. I: Solutions of Sums and Products," RM-3192-PR, The Rand Corporation, Santa Monica.

[1962b], "Simple Games: An Outline of the Descriptive Theory," *Behavioral Science*, 7, 59–66.

[1962c], "Values of Games with Infinitely Many Players," in *Recent Advances in Game Theory*, M. Maschler, editor (proceedings of a Princeton University Conference, October 4–6, 1961), Ivy Curtis Press, Philadelphia, Pennsylvania, pp. 113–18. (Also Rand RM-2912.)

[1963], "Compound Simple Games. II: Some General Composition Theorems," RM-3643-PR, The Rand Corporation, Santa Monica.

[1964a], "Solutions of Compound Simple Games," *Annals of Mathematics Studies*, 52, 267–305.

[1964b], *Values of Large Games, VII: A General Exchange Economy with Money*, RM-4248, The Rand Corporation, Santa Monica.

[1967a], "On Balanced Sets and Cores," *Naval Research Logistics Quarterly*, 14, 453–60.

[1967b], "On Committees," in *New Methods of Thought and Procedure*, F. Zwicky and A. G. Wilson, editors, Springer, New York, pp. 246–70.

[1969], "Utility Comparison and the Theory of Games," in *La Decision: Aggregation et Dynamique des Ordres de Preference,* Editions du Centre National de la Recherche Scientifique, Paris, pp. 251–63 [reprinted in this volume].

[1971], "Cores of Convex Games," *International Journal of Game Theory,* 1, 11–26.

[1973], "On Balanced Games without Side Payments," in *Mathematical Programming,* T. C. Hu and S. M. Robinson, editors, Academic Press, New York, pp. 261–90.

[1977], "A Comparison of Power Indices and a Nonsymmetric Generalization," Paper P-5872, The Rand Corporation, Santa Monica.

[1983], "Discussant's Comment," in *Joint Cost Allocation,* S. Moriarity, editor, University of Oklahoma Press, Tulsa.

Shapley, Lloyd S. and N. Z. Shapiro [1960], *Values of Large Games, I: A Limit Theorem,* RM-2648, The Rand Corporation, Santa Monica. (Appearing as "Values of Large Games, A Limit Theorem," *Mathematics of Operations Research,* 3, 1978, 1–9.)

Shapley, Lloyd S. and Martin Shubik [1954], "A Method for Evaluating the Distribution of Power in a Committee System," *American Political Science Review,* 48, 787–92 [reprinted in this volume].

[1969a], "On Market Games," *Journal of Economic Theory,* 1, 9–25.

[1969b], "Pure Competition, Coalitional Power, and Fair Division," *International Economic Review* 10, 337–62.

[1972], "The Assignment Game. I: The Core," *International Journal of Game Theory,* 1, 111–30.

[1974], "Game Theory in Economics–Chapter 4: Preferences and Utility," R-904/4 NSF, The Rand Corporation, Santa Monica.

Shubik, Martin [1959], "Edgeworth Market Games," in *Contributions to the Theory of Games,* vol. IV, Princeton University Press, Princeton, New Jersey, pp. 267–78.

[1962], "Incentives, Decentralized Control, the Assignment of Joint Costs and Internal Pricing," *Management Science,* 325–43.

[1982], *Game Theory in the Social Sciences,* MIT Press, Cambridge.

Thomson, William [in press], "The Manipulability of the Shapley Value," *International Journal of Game Theory.*

von Neumann, John and Oskar Morgenstern [1944], *Theory of Games and Economic Behavior,* Princeton University Press, Princeton, New Jersey.

PART I

Ancestral papers

CHAPTER 2

A value for *n*-person games

Lloyd S. Shapley

1   Introduction

At the foundation of the theory of games is the assumption that the players of a game can evaluate, in their utility scales, every "prospect" that might arise as a result of a play. In attempting to apply the theory to any field, one would normally expect to be permitted to include, in the class of "prospects," the prospect of having to play a game. The possibility of evaluating games is therefore of critical importance. So long as the theory is unable to assign values to the games typically found in application, only relatively simple situations – where games do not depend on other games – will be susceptible to analysis and solution.

In the finite theory of von Neumann and Morgenstern[1] difficulty in evaluation persists for the "essential" games, and for only those. In this note we deduce a value for the "essential" case and examine a number of its elementary properties. We proceed from a set of three axioms, having simple intuitive interpretations, which suffice to determine the value uniquely.

Our present work, though mathematically self-contained, is founded conceptually on the von Neumann – Morgenstern theory up to their introduction of characteristic functions. We thereby inherit certain important underlying assumptions: (a) that utility is objective and transferable; (b) that games are cooperative affairs; (c) that games, granting (a) and (b), are adequately represented by their characteristic functions. However, we are not committed to the assumptions regarding rational behavior embodied in the von Neumann – Morgenstern notion of "solution."

We shall think of a "game" as a set of rules with specified players in the

Reprinted from *Contributions to the Theory of Games,* vol. 2, eds. H. Kuhn and A. W. Tucker (Princeton: Princeton University Press, 1953), pp. 307–17. The preparation of this paper was sponsored in part by the RAND Corporation.

playing positions. The rules alone describe what we shall call an "abstract game." Abstract games are played by *roles* – such as "dealer," or "visiting team" – rather than by *players* external to the game. The theory of games deals mainly with abstract games.[2] The distinction will be useful in enabling us to state in a precise way that the value of a "game" depends only on its abstract properties. (Axiom 1 below.)

2   Definitions

Let U denote the universe of players, and define a *game* to be any super-additive set-function v from the subsets of U to the real numbers, thus:

$$v(O) = 0, \tag{1}$$

$$v(S) \geq v(S \cap T) + v(S - T) \qquad (\text{all } S, T \subseteq U). \tag{2}$$

A *carrier* of v is any set $N \subseteq U$ with

$$v(S) = v(N \cap S) \qquad (\text{all } S \subseteq U). \tag{3}$$

Any superset of a carrier of v is again a carrier of v. The use of carriers obviates the usual classification of games according to the number of players. The players outside any carrier have no direct influence on the play since they contribute nothing to any coalition. We shall restrict our attention to games which possess finite carriers.

The *sum* ("superposition") of two games is again a game. Intuitively it is the game obtained when two games, with independent rules but possibly overlapping sets of players, are regarded as one. If the games happen to possess disjoint carriers, then their sum is their "composition."[3]

Let $\Pi(U)$ denote the set of permutations of U – that is, the one to one mappings of U onto itself. If $\pi \in \Pi(U)$, then, writing πS for the image of S under π, we may define the function πv by

$$\pi v(\pi S) = v(S) \qquad (\text{all } S \subseteq U). \tag{4}$$

If v is a game, then the class of games πv, $\pi \in \Pi(U)$, may be regarded as the "abstract game" corresponding to v. Unlike composition, the operation of addition of games cannot be extended to abstract games.

By the *value* $\phi[v]$ of the game v we shall mean a function which associates with each i in U a real number $\phi_i[v]$, and which satisfies the conditions of the following axioms. The value will thus provide an additive set-function (an *inessential game*) $\bar{v}$:

$$\bar{v}(S) = \sum_S \phi_i[v] \qquad (\text{all } S \subseteq U), \tag{5}$$

to take the place of the superadditive function v.

Axiom 1. For each π in $\Pi(U)$,

$$\phi_{\pi i}[\pi v] = \phi_i[v].$$

Axiom 2. For each carrier N of v,

$$\sum_N \phi_i[v] = v(N).$$

Axiom 3. For any two games v and w,

$$\phi[v + w] = \phi[v] + \phi[w].$$

Comments: The first axiom ("symmetry") states that the value is essentially a property of the abstract game. The second axiom ("efficiency") states that the value represents a distribution of the full yield of the game. This excludes, for example, the evaluation $\phi_i[v] = v((i))$, in which each player pessimistically assumes that the rest will all cooperate against him. The third axiom ("law of aggregation") states that when two independent games are combined, their values must be added player by player. This is a prime requisite for any evaluation scheme designed to be applied eventually to systems of *inter*dependent games.

It is remarkable that no further conditions are required to determine the value uniquely.[4]

3 Determination of the value function

Lemma 1. If N is a finite carrier of v, then, for $i \not\in N$,

$$\phi_i[v] = 0.$$

Proof: Take $i \not\in N$. Both N and $N \cup (i)$ are carriers of v; and $v(N) = v(N \cup (i))$. Hence $\phi_i[v] = 0$ by Axiom 2, as was to be shown.

We first consider certain symmetric games. For any $R \subseteq U$, $R \neq 0$ define v_R:

$$v_R(S) = \begin{cases} 1 & \text{if } S \supseteq R, \\ 0 & \text{if } S \not\supseteq R. \end{cases} \tag{6}$$

The function cv_R is a game, for any non-negative c, and R is a carrier.

In what follows, we shall use $r, s, n, \ldots$ for the numbers of elements in $R, S, N, \ldots$ respectively.

Lemma 2. For $c \geq 0$, $0 < r < \infty$, we have

$$\phi_i[cv_R] = \begin{cases} c/r & \text{if } i \in R, \\ 0 & \text{if } i \notin R. \end{cases}$$

Proof: Take i and j in R, and choose $\pi \in \Pi(U)$ so that $\pi R = R$ and $\pi i = j$. Then we have $\pi v_R = v_R$, and hence, by Axiom 1,

$$\phi_j[cv_R] = \phi_i[cv_R].$$

By Axiom 2,

$$c = cv_R(R) = \sum_{j \in R} \phi_j[cv_R] = r\phi_i[cv_R],$$

for any $i \in R$. This, with Lemma 1, completes the proof.

Lemma 3.[5] Any game with finite carrier is a linear combination of symmetric games v_R:

$$v = \sum_{\substack{R \subseteq N \\ R \neq 0}} c_R(v)v_R, \tag{7}$$

N being any finite carrier of v. The coefficients are independent of N, and are given by

$$c_R(v) = \sum_{T \subseteq R} (-1)^{r-t} v(T) \qquad (0 < r < \infty). \tag{8}$$

Proof: We must verify that

$$v(S) = \sum_{\substack{R \subseteq N \\ R \neq 0}} c_R(v)v_R(S) \tag{9}$$

holds for all $S \subseteq U$, and for any finite carrier N of v. If $S \subseteq N$, then (9) reduces, by (6) and (8), to

$$v(S) = \sum_{R \subseteq S} \sum_{T \subseteq R} (-1)^{r-t} v(T)$$

$$= \sum_{T \subseteq S} \left[\sum_{r=t}^{s} (-1)^{r-t} \binom{s-t}{r-t} \right] v(T).$$

The expression in brackets vanishes except for $s = t$, so we are left with the identity $v(S) = v(S)$. In general we have, by (3),

$$v(S) = v(N \cap S) = \sum_{R \subseteq N} c_R(v) v_R(N \cap S) = \sum_{R \subseteq N} c_R(v) v_R(S).$$

This completes the proof.

Remark: It is easily shown that $c_R(v) = 0$ if R is not contained in every carrier of v.

An immediate corollary to Axiom 3 is that $\phi[v - w] = \phi[v] - \phi[w]$ if v, w, and $v - w$ are all games. We can therefore apply Lemma 2 to the representation of Lemma 3 and obtain the formula:

$$\phi_i[v] = \sum_{\substack{R \subseteq N \\ R \ni i}} c_r(v)/r \qquad \text{(all } i \in N). \tag{10}$$

Inserting (8) and simplifying the result gives us

$$\phi_i[v] = \sum_{\substack{S \subseteq N \\ S \ni i}} \frac{(s-1)!(n-s)!}{n!} v(S)$$

$$- \sum_{\substack{S \subseteq N \\ S \not\ni i}} \frac{s!(n-s-1)!}{n!} v(S) \qquad \text{(all } i \in N). \tag{11}$$

Introducing the quantities

$$\gamma_n(s) = (s-1)!(n-s)!/n!, \tag{12}$$

we now assert:

Theorem. A unique value function ϕ exists satisfying Axioms 1–3, for games with finite carriers; it is given by the formula

$$\phi_i[v] = \sum_{S \subseteq N} \gamma_n(s)[v(S) - v(S - (i))] \qquad \text{(all } i \in U), \tag{13}$$

where N is any finite carrier of v.

Proof: (13) follows from (11), (12), and Lemma 1. We note that (13), like (10), does not depend on the particular finite carrier N; the ϕ of the theorem is therefore well defined. By its derivation it is clearly the only value function which could satisfy the axioms. That it does in fact satisfy the axioms is easily verified with the aid of Lemma 3.

4   Elementary properties of the value

Corollary 1. We have

$$\phi_i[v] \geq v((i)) \qquad \text{(all } i \in U), \tag{14}$$

with equality if and only if i is a *dummy*–i.e., if and only if

$$v(S) = v(S - (i)) + v((i)) \qquad \text{(all } S \ni i). \tag{15}$$

Proof: For any $i \in U$ we may take $N \ni i$ and obtain, by (2),

$$\phi_i[v] \geq \sum_{\substack{S \subseteq N \\ S \ni i}} \gamma_n(s) v((i)),$$

with equality if and only if (15), since none of the $\gamma_n(s)$ vanishes. The proof is completed by noting that

$$\sum_{\substack{S \subseteq N \\ S \ni i}} \gamma_n(s) = \sum_{s=1}^{n} \binom{n-1}{s-1} \gamma_n(s) = \sum_{s=1}^{n} \frac{1}{n} = 1. \tag{16}$$

Only in this corollary have our results depended on the super-additive nature of the functions v.

Corollary 2. If v is *decomposable*–i.e., if games $w^{(1)}, w^{(2)}, \ldots, w^{(p)}$ having pairwise disjunct carriers $N^{(1)}, N^{(2)}, \ldots, N^{(p)}$ exist such that

$$v = \sum_{k=1}^{p} w^{(k)},$$

–then, for each $k = 1, 2, \ldots, p$,

$$\phi_i[v] = \phi_i[w^{(k)}] \qquad \text{(all } i \in N^{(k)}).$$

Proof: By Axiom 3.

Corollary 3. If v and w are *strategically equivalent*–i.e., if

$$w = cv + \bar{a}, \tag{17}$$

where c is a positive constant and $\bar{a}$ an additive set-function on U with finite carrier[6]–then

$$\phi_i[w] = c\phi_i[v] + \bar{a}((i)) \qquad \text{(all } i \in U).$$

Proof: By Axiom 3, Corollary 1 applied to the inessential game $\bar{a}$, and the fact that (13) is linear and homogeneous in v.

Corollary 4. If v is *constant-sum* – i.e., if

$$v(S) + v(U - S) = v(U) \qquad \text{(all } S \subseteq U\text{),} \tag{18}$$

– then its value is given by the formula:

$$\phi_i[v] = 2 \left[\sum_{\substack{S \subseteq N \\ S \ni i}} \gamma_n(s)v(S) \right] - v(N) \qquad \text{(all } i \in N\text{).} \tag{19}$$

where N is any finite carrier of v.

Proof: We have, for $i \in N$,

$$\phi_i[v] = \sum_{\substack{S \subseteq N \\ S \ni i}} \gamma_n(s)v(S) - \sum_{\substack{T \subseteq N \\ T \not\ni i}} \gamma_n(t + 1)v(T)$$

$$= \sum_{\substack{S \subseteq N \\ S \ni i}} \gamma_n(s)v(S) - \sum_{\substack{S \subseteq N \\ S \ni i}} \gamma_n(n - s + 1)[v(N) - v(S)].$$

But $\gamma_n(n - s + 1) = \gamma_n(s)$; hence (18) follows with the aid of (16).

5   Examples

If N is a finite carrier of v, let A denote the set of *n*-vectors (α_i) satisfying

$$\sum_N \alpha_i = v(N), \quad \alpha_i \geq v((i)) \qquad \text{(all } i \in N\text{).}$$

If v is inessential A is a single point; otherwise A is a regular simplex of dimension $n - 1$. The value of v may be regarded as a point ϕ in A, by Axiom 2 and Corollary 1. Denote the centroid of A by θ:

$$\theta_i = v((i)) + \frac{1}{n}\left[v(N) - \sum_{j \in N} v((j)) \right].$$

Example 1. For *two-person* games, *three-person constant-sum* games, and *inessential* games, we have

$$\phi = \theta. \tag{20}$$

The same holds for arbitrary symmetric games – i.e., games which are invariant under a transitive group of permutations of N – and, most generally, games strategically equivalent to them. These results are demanded by symmetry, and do not depend on Axiom 3.

Example 2. For general *three-person* games the positions taken by ϕ in A cover a regular hexagon, touching the boundary at the midpoint of each 1-dimensional face (see figure). The latter cases are of course the decomposable games, with one player a dummy.

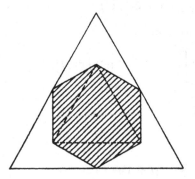

Example 3. The *quota games*[7] are characterized by the existence of constants ω_i satisfying

$$\omega_i + \omega_j = v((i,j)) \qquad (\text{all } i,j \in N, i \neq j)$$

$$\sum_N \omega_i = v(N).$$

For $n = 3$, we have

$$\phi - \theta = \frac{\omega - \theta}{2}. \tag{21}$$

Since ω can assume any position in A, the range of ϕ is a triangle, inscribed in the hexagon of the preceding example (see the figure).

Example 4. All *four-person constant-sum* games are quota games. For them we have

$$\phi - \theta = \frac{\omega - \theta}{3}. \tag{22}$$

The quota ω ranges over a certain cube,[8] containing A. The value ϕ meanwhile ranges over a parallel, inscribed cube, touching the boundary of A at the midpoint of each 2-dimensional face. In higher quota games the points ϕ and ω are not so directly related.

Example 5. The *weighted majority games*[9] are characterized by the existence of "weights" w_i such that never $\Sigma_S w_i = \Sigma_{N-S} w_i$, and such that

$$v(S) = n - s \quad \text{if } \sum_S w_i > \sum_{N-S} w_i,$$

$$v(S) = -s \quad \text{if } \sum_S w_i < \sum_{N-S} w_i.$$

The game is then denoted by the symbol $[w_1, w_2, \ldots, w_n]$. It is easily shown that

$$\phi_i < \phi_j \quad \text{implies} \quad w_i < w_j \quad \text{(all } i, j \in N) \tag{23}$$

in any weighted majority game $[w_i, w_2, \ldots, w_n]$. Hence "weight" and "value" rank the players in the same order.

The exact values can be computed without difficulty for particular cases. We have

$$\phi = \frac{n-3}{n-1}(-1, -1, \ldots, -1, n-1)$$

for the game $[1, 1, \ldots, 1, n-2]$,[10] and

$$\phi = \tfrac{2}{5}(1, 1, 1, -1, -1, -1)$$

for the game $[2, 2, 2, 1, 1, 1]$,[11] etc.

6   Derivation of the value from a bargaining model

The deductive approach of the earlier sections has failed to suggest a bargaining procedure which would produce the value of the game as the (expected) outcome. We conclude this paper with a description of such a procedure. The form of our model, with its chance move, lends support to the view that the value is best regarded as an *a priori* assessment of the situation, based on either ignorance or disregard of the social organization of the players.

The players constituting a finite carrier N agree to play the game v in a grand coalition, formed in the following way: (1) Starting with a single member, the coalition adds one player at a time until everyone has been admitted. (2) The order in which the players are to join is determined by chance, with all arrangements equally probable. (3) Each player, on his admission, demands and is promised the amount which his adherence contributes to the value of the coalition (as determined by the function v).

The grand coalition then plays the game "efficiently" so as to obtain the amount $v(N)$: exactly enough to meet all the promises.

The expectations under this scheme are easily worked out. Let $T^{(i)}$ be the set of players preceding i. For any $S \ni i$, the payment to i if $S - (i) = T^{(i)}$ is $v(S) - v(S - (i))$, and the probability of that contingency is $\gamma_n(s)$. The total expectation of i is therefore just his value, (13), as was to be shown.

NOTES

1   Reference [3] at the end of this paper. Examples of infinite games without values may be found in [2], pp. 58–9, and in [1], p. 110. See also Karlin [2], pp. 152–3.
2   An exception is found in the matter of symmetrization (see for example [2], pp. 81–83), in which the players must be distinguished from their roles.
3   See [3], Sections 26.7.2 and 41.3.
4   Three further properties of the value which might suggest themselves as suitable axioms will be proved as Lemma 1 and Corollaries 1 and 3.
5   The use of this lemma was suggested by H. Rogers.
6   This is McKinsey's "S-equivalence" (see [2], p. 120), wider than the "strategic equivalence" of von Neumann and Morgenstern ([3], Section 27.1).
7   Discussed in [4].
8   Illustrated in [4], Figure 1 (page 353).
9   See [3], Section 50.1.
10   Discussed at length in [3], Section 55.
11   Discussed in [3], Section 53.2.2.

REFERENCES

[1] Borel, E. and Ville, J., "Applications aux jeux de hasard," *Traité du Calcul des Probabilités et de ses Applications,* vol. 4, part 2 (Paris, Gauthier-Villars, 1938).
[2] Kuhn, H. W. and Tucker, A. W., eds., *Contributions to the Theory of Games* (Annals of Mathematics Study No. 24), Princeton, 1950.
[3] von Neumann, J. and Morgenstern, O., *Theory of Games and Economic Behavior,* Princeton 1944, 2nd ed. 1947.
[4] Shapley, L. S., "Quota solutions of n-person games," in H. W. Kuhn and A. W. Tucker, eds., *Contributions to the Theory of Games,* vol. II (Annals of Mathematics Study No. 28), Princeton, 1950, pp. 343–59.

CHAPTER 3

A method for evaluating the distribution of power in a committee system

Lloyd S. Shapley and Martin Shubik

In the following paper we offer a method for the *a priori* evaluation of the division of power among the various bodies and members of a legislature or committee system. The method is based on a technique of the mathematical theory of games, applied to what are known there as "simple games" and "weighted majority games." [1] We apply it here to a number of illustrative cases, including the United States Congress, and discuss some of its formal properties.

The designing of the size and type of a legislative body is a process that may continue for many years, with frequent revisions and modifications aimed at reflecting changes in the social structure of the country; we may cite the role of the House of Lords in England as an example. The effect of a revision usually cannot be gauged in advance except in the roughest terms; it can easily happen that the mathematical structure of a voting system conceals a bias in power distribution unsuspected and unintended by the authors of the revision. How, for example, is one to predict the degree of protection which a proposed system affords to minority interests? Can a consistent criterion for "fair representation" be found? [2] It is difficult even to *describe* the net effect of a double representation system such as is found in the U.S. Congress (i.e., by states and by population), without attempting to deduce it *a priori*. The method of measuring "power" which we present in this paper is intended as a first step in the attack on these problems.

Our definition of the power of an individual member depends on the chance he has of being critical to the success of a winning coalition. It is easy to see, for example, that the chairman of a board consisting of an even number of members (including himself) has no power if he is allowed to

Reprinted from *The American Political Science Review* 48 (1954), pp. 787–92.

vote only to break ties. Of course he may have prestige and moral influence and will even probably get to vote when someone is not present. However, in the narrow and abstract model of the board he is without power. If the board consists of an odd number of members, then he has exactly as much power as any ordinary member because his vote is "pivotal"–i.e., turns a possible defeat into a success–as often as the vote of any other member. Admittedly he may not cast his vote as often as the others, but much of the voting done by them is not necessary to ensure victory (though perhaps useful for publicity or other purposes). If a coalition has a majority, then extra votes do not change the outcome. For any vote, only a minimal winning coalition is necessary.

Put in crude economic terms, the above implies that if votes of senators were for sale, it might be worthwhile buying forty-nine of them, but the market value of the fiftieth (to the same customer) would be zero. It is possible to buy votes in most corporations by purchasing common stock. If their policies are entirely controlled by simple majority votes, then there is no more power to be gained after one share more than 50% has been acquired.[3]

Let us consider the following scheme: There is a group of individuals all willing to vote for some bill. They vote in order. As soon as a majority[4] has voted for it, it is declared passed, and the member who voted last is given credit for having passed it. Let us choose the voting order of the members randomly. Then we may compute the frequency with which an individual belongs to the group whose votes are used and, of more importance, we may compute how often he is *pivotal*. This latter number serves to give us our index. It measures the number of times that the action of the individual actually changes the state of affairs. A simple consequence of this formal scheme is that where all voters have the same number of votes, they will each be credited with $1/n$th of the power, there being n participants. If they have different numbers of votes (as in the case of stockholders of a corporation), the result is more complicated; more votes mean more power, as measured by our index, but not in direct proportion (see below).

Of course, the actual balloting procedure used will in all probability be quite different from the above. The "voting" of the formal scheme might better be thought of as declarations of support for the bill, and the randomly chosen order of voting as an indication of the relative degrees of support by the different members, with the most enthusiastic members "voting" first, etc. The *pivot* is then the last member whose support is needed in order for passage of the bill to be assured.

Analyzing a committee chairman's tie-breaking function in this light, we see that in an *odd* committee he is pivotal as often as an ordinary member, but in an *even* committee he is never pivotal. However, when the number of members is large, it may sometimes be better to modify the strict interpretation of the formal system, and say that the number of members in attendance is about as likely to be even as odd. The chairman's index would then be just half that of an ordinary member. Thus, in the U.S. Senate the power index of the presiding officer is – strictly – equal to 1/97. Under the modified scheme it is 1/193. (But it is zero under either interpretation when we are considering decisions requiring a two-thirds majority, since ties cannot occur on such votes.) Recent history shows that the "strict" model may sometimes be the more realistic: in the present Senate (1953–54) the tie-breaking power of the Vice President, stemming from the fact that 96 is an even number, has been a very significant factor. However, in the passage of ordinary legislation, where perfect attendance is unlikely even for important issues, the modified scheme is probably more appropriate.

For Congress as a whole we have to consider three separate bodies which influence the fate of legislation. It takes majorities of Senate and House, with the President, or two-thirds majorities of Senate and House without the President, to enact a bill. We take all the members of the three bodies and consider them voting[5] for the bill in every possible order. In each order we observe the relative positions of the straight-majority pivotal men in the House and Senate, the President, and also the 2/3-majority pivotal men in House and Senate. One of these five individuals will be the pivot for the whole vote, depending on the order in which they appear. For example, if the President comes after the two straight-majority pivots, but before one or both of the 2/3-majority pivots, then he gets the credit for the passage of the bill. The frequency of this case, if we consider all possible orders (of the 533 individuals involved), turns out to be very nearly 1/6. This is the President's power index. (The calculation of this value and the following is quite complicated, and we shall not give it here.) The values for the House as a whole and for the Senate as a whole are both equal to 5/12, approximately. The individual members of each chamber share these amounts equally, with the exception of the presiding officers. Under our "modified" scheme they each get about 30% of the power of an ordinary member; under the "strict" scheme, about 60%. In brief, then, the power indices for the three bodies are in the proportion 5:5:2. The indices for a *single* congressman, a *single* senator, and the President are in the proportion 2:9:350.

In a multicameral system such as we have just investigated, it is obviously easier to defeat a measure than to pass it.[6] A coalition of senators, sufficiently numerous, can block passage of any bill. But they cannot push through a bill of their own without help from the other chamber. This suggests that our analysis so far has been incomplete – that we need an index of "blocking power" to supplement the index already defined. To this end, we could set up a formal scheme similar to the previous one, namely: arrange the individuals in all possible orders and imagine them casting *negative* votes. In each arrangement, determine the person whose vote finally defeats the measure and give him credit for the block. Then the "blocking power" index for each person would be the relative number of times that he was the "blocker."

Now it is a remarkable fact that the new index is exactly equal to the index of our original definition. We can even make a stronger assertion: *any scheme for imputing power among the members of a committee system either yields the power index defined above or leads to a logical inconsistency.* A proof, or even a precise formulation, of this assertion would involve us too deeply in mathematical symbolism for the purposes of the present paper.[7] But we can conclude that the scheme we have been using (arranging the individuals in all possible orders, etc.) is just a convenient conceptual device; the indices which emerge are not peculiar to that device but represent a basic element of the committee system itself.

We now summarize some of the general properties of the power index. In pure *bi*cameral systems using simple majority votes, each chamber gets 50% of the power (as it turns out), regardless of the relative sizes. With more than two chambers, power varies inversely with size: the smallest body is most powerful, etc. But no chamber is completely powerless, and no chamber holds more than 50% of the power. To illustrate, take Congress without the provision for overriding the President's veto by means of two-thirds majorities. This is now a pure tricameral system with chamber sizes of 1, 97, and 435. The values come out to be slightly under 50% for the President, and approximately 25% each for the Senate and House, with the House slightly less than the Senate. The exact calculation of this case is quite difficult because of the large numbers involved. An easier example is obtained by taking the chamber sizes as 1, 3, and 5. Then the division of power is in the proportions $32:27:25$. The calculation is reproduced at the end of this paper.

The power division in a multicameral system also depends on the type of majority required to pass a bill. Raising the majority in *one* chamber (say from one-half to two-thirds) increases the relative power of that chamber.[8] Raising the required majority in all chambers simultaneously weakens the smaller house or houses at the expense of the larger. In the extreme case, where unanimity is required in every house, each individual in the whole legislature has what amounts to a veto, and is just as powerful as any other individual. The power index of each chamber is therefore directly proportional to its size.

We may examine this effect further by considering a system consisting of a governor and a council. Both the governor and some specified fraction of the council have to approve a bill before it can pass. Suppose first that council approval has to be unanimous. Then (as we saw above) the governor has no more power than the typical councilman. The bicameral power division is in the ratio $1:N$, if we take N to be the number of councilmen. If a simple majority rule is adopted, then the ratio becomes $1:1$ between governor and council. That is, the governor has N times the power of a councilman. Now suppose that the approval of only one member of the council is required. This means that an individual councilman has very little chance of being pivotal. In fact the power division turns out to be $N:1$ in favor of the governor.[9] If votes were for sale, we might now expect the governor's price to be N^2 times as high as the average councilman's.

Several other examples of power distribution may be given. The indices reveal the decisive nature of the veto power in the United Nations Security Council. The Council consists of eleven members, five of whom have vetoes. For a substantive resolution to pass, there must be seven affirmative votes and no vetoes. Our power evaluation gives 76/77 or 98.7% to the "Big Five" and 1/77 or 1.3% to the remaining six members. Individually, the members of the "Big Five" enjoy a better than 90 to 1 advantage over the others.

It is well known that usually only a small fraction of the stock is required to keep control of a corporation. The group in power is usually able to muster enough proxies to maintain its position. Even if this were not so, the power of stockholders is not directly proportional to their holding, but is usually biased in favor of a large interest. Consider one man holding 40% of a stock while the remaining 60% is scattered among 600 small shareholders, with 0.1% each. The power index of the large holder is 66.6%, whereas for the small holders it is less than 0.06% apiece. The 400:1 ratio in holdings produces a power advantage of better than 1000:1.[10]

The preceding was an example of a "weighted majority game." Another example is provided by a board with five members, one of whom casts two extra votes. If a simple majority (four out of seven votes) carries the day, then power is distributed 60% to the multivote member, 10% to each of the others. To see this, observe that there are five possible positions for the strong man, if we arrange the members in order at random. In three of these positions he is pivotal. Hence his index is equal to 3/5. (Similarly, in the preceding example, we may compute that the strong man is pivotal 400 times out of 601.)

The values in the examples given above do not take into account any of the sociological or political superstructure that almost invariably exists in a legislature or policy board. They were not intended to be a representation of present day "reality." It would be foolish to expect to be able to catch all the subtle shades and nuances of custom and procedure that are to be found in most real decision-making bodies. Nevertheless, the power index computations may be useful in the setting up of norms or standards, the departure from which will serve as a measure of, for example, political solidarity, or regional or sociological factionalism, in an assembly. To do this we need an empirical power index, to compare with the theoretical. One possibility is as follows: The voting record of an individual is taken. He is given no credit for being on the losing side of a vote. If he is on the winning side, when n others voted with him, then he is awarded the probability of his having been the pivot (or blocker, in the case of a defeated motion), which is $1/(n + 1)$. His probabilities are then averaged over all votes. It can be shown that this measure gives more weight than the norm does to uncommitted members who hold the "balance of power" between extreme factions. For example, in a nine-man committee which contains two four-man factions which always oppose each other, the lone uncommitted member will always be on the winning side, and will have an observed index of 1/5, compared to the theoretical value of 1/9.

A difficulty in the application of the above measure is the problem of finding the correct weights to attach to the different issues. Obviously it would not be proper to take a uniform average over all votes, since there is bound to be a wide disparity in the importance of issues brought to a vote. Again, in a multicameral legislature (or in any more complicated system), many important issues may be decided without every member having had an opportunity to go on record with his stand. There are many other practical difficulties in the way of direct applications of the type mentioned. Yet the power index appears to offer useful information concerning the basic design of legislative assemblies and policy-making boards.

Appendix

The evaluation of the power distribution for a tricameral legislature with houses of 1, 3, and 5 members is given below:

There are 504 arrangements of five X's, three O's, and one ϕ, all equally likely if the nine items are ordered at random. In the following tabulation, the numbers indicate the number of permutations of predecessors ( ) and successors [ ] of the final pivot, marked with an asterisk. The dots indicate the pivots of the three separate houses.

```
O Ȯ O X X φ̇ Ẋ X X ⎫                 O Ȯ O X X Ẋ X X φ̇ ⎫
   (60)      *  [1] ⎪ 150 pivots        (56)          *  ⎪
O Ȯ X X φ̇ Ẋ O X X  ⎬ for X          O Ȯ O X X Ẋ X X φ̇ X ⎪
   (30)    *  [3]   ⎭                   (35)        *  [1] ⎪
                                    O Ȯ O X X Ẋ φ̇ X X    ⎪
                                       (20)        *  [1] ⎬ 192 pivots
O X X Ẋ X X φ̇ Ȯ O  ⎫                 O Ȯ X X Ẋ X X φ̇ O   ⎪  for φ
   (42)      *  [1] ⎪                   (21)        *  [1] ⎪
O X X Ẋ X φ̇ Ȯ O X  ⎬ 162 pivots     O Ȯ X X Ẋ X X φ̇ O X ⎪
   (30)    *  [2]   ⎪ for O              (15)      *  [2]  ⎪
O X X Ẋ φ̇ Ȯ O X X  ⎪                 O Ȯ X X Ẋ φ̇ O X X   ⎪
   (20)    *  [3]   ⎭                   (12)  *     [3]    ⎭
```

Power indices for the houses are 192/504, 162/504, and 150/504, and hence are in the proportion 32 : 27 : 25, with the smallest house the strongest. Powers of the individual members are as 32 : 9 : 9 : 9 : 5 : 5 : 5 : 5 : 5.

NOTES

1   See J. von Neumann and O. Morgenstern, *Theory of Games and Economic Behavior* (Princeton, 1944, 1947, 1953), pp. 420 ff.

2   See K. J. Arrow, *Social Choice and Individual Values* (New York, 1951), p. 7.

3   For a brief discussion of some of the factors in stock voting see H. G. Gothman and H. E. Dougall, *Corporate Financial Policy* (New York, 1948), pp. 56–61.

4   More generally, a minimal winning coalition.

5   In the formal sense described above.

6   This statement can be put into numerical form without difficulty, to give a quantitative description of the "efficiency" of a legislature.

7   The mathematical formulation and proof are given in L. S. Shapley, "A Value for N-Person Games," *Annals of Mathematics Study No. 28* (Princeton, 1953), pp. 307–17. Briefly stated, any alternative imputation scheme

would conflict with either *symmetry* (equal power indices for members in equal positions under the rules) or *additivity* (power distribution in a committee system composed of two strictly independent parts the same as the power distributions obtained by evaluating the parts separately).

8 As a general rule, if one component of a committee system (in which approval of all components is required) is made less "efficient"–i.e., more susceptible to blocking maneuvers–then its share of the total power will increase.

9 In the general case the proportion is $N - M + 1 : M$, where M stands for the number of councilmen required for passage.

10 If there are two or more large interests, the power distribution depends in a fairly complicated way on the sizes of the large interests. Generally speaking, however, the small holders are better off than in the previous case. If there are two big interests, equal in size, then the small holders actually have an advantage over the large holders, on a power per share basis. This suggests that such a situation is highly unstable.

PART II

Reformulations and generalizations

CHAPTER 4

The expected utility of playing a game

Alvin E. Roth

1 Introduction

This chapter is concerned with how the Shapley value can be interpreted as an expected utility function, the consequences of interpreting it in this way, and with what other value functions arise as utility functions representing different preferences.

These questions brought themselves rather forcefully to my attention when I first taught a graduate course in game theory. After introducing utility theory as a way of numerically representing sufficiently regular individual preferences, and explaining which comparisons involving utility functions are meaningful and which are not, I found myself at a loss to explain precisely what comparisons could meaningfully be made using the Shapley value, if it was to be interpreted as a utility as suggested in the first paragraph of Shapley's 1953 paper. In order to state the problem clearly, it will be useful to remark briefly on some of the familiar properties of utility functions.

First, utility functions represent preferences, so individuals with different preferences will have different utility functions. When preferences are measured over risky as well as riskless prospects, individuals who have the same preferences over riskless prospects may nevertheless have different preferences over lotteries, and so may have different expected utility functions.

Second, there are some arbitrary choices involved in specifying a utility function, so the information contained in an individual's utility function is really represented by an equivalence class of functions. When preferences are defined over riskless prospects without any information about relative intensities of preference, then the class of utility functions equivalent to a given utility function *u* consists of all monotone transformations of *u*. When preferences are defined over risky prospects as well, then the class of expected utility functions equivalent to a given expected utility function u consists of all positive linear transformations of u. That is, the (only) arbitrary elements in an expected utility function are the choice of the zero point and unit.

A *meaningful* statement about preferences, in terms of a utility function, must be true for every equivalent utility function. (In just this sense it is not a meaningful statement about temperature to say that water boils at between six and seven times the temperature at which it freezes: This is a statement about the Fahrenheit temperature scale that does not hold in the equivalent Celsius scale.) Similarly, because different individuals' expected utility functions have arbitrary origins and units, they are not comparable. For example, they cannot meaningfully be added. That is, no information about preferences is conveyed by saying that a particular outcome maximizes the sum of the utilities of the players in a game, because this is not independent of the scale of each utility function: If an individual's utility is multiplied by 100 (which yields an equivalent representation of the individual's preferences), the outcome that maximizes the sum of the utilities would not stay the same in general.[1]

The original derivation of the Shapley value does not resemble the derivation of utility functions, in that all conditions are stated directly on the value function, so there is no clear connection to underlying preferences. Hence, the following questions present themselves.

1. *If the Shapley value is to be interpreted as a utility, why is it unique?* Won't different individuals with different preferences and risk postures have different utility functions? If so, what can be said about those preferences for which the Shapley value is a utility function? What will other utility functions for games look like?

2. *What are the meaningful statements about preferences that can be conveyed by the Shapley value?* What are the arbitrary elements in the Shapley value as a utility – what normalization has been chosen? Under what circumstances can the Shapley value of a game be compared to the utility of other kinds of alternatives?

3. *What does the additivity axiom mean?* What statement about preferences is made by a utility function that relates the sum of the utilities of games v and w to the utility of another game, $v + w$?

4. *How can the efficiency axiom be interpreted in the context of a utility function?* It specifies that the values for each position in a game v must sum to $v(N)$: Is there some assumption hidden here that interpersonal comparisons can be made, and that sums of utilities are meaningful? If not, what is the significance of specifying the sum?[2]

To answer these questions, we need to consider preferences over games. The viewpoint I take is that the preferences in question are those of a single individual, faced with choices over positions in a game, and in different games. The resulting utility function can be thought of, like the Shapley value, as a function defined on games that assigns a real number to each position in a game. It turns out that whether such a utility function conforms to the efficiency axiom depends on the attitude of the individual in question to a certain kind of risk, and whether it conforms to the additivity axiom depends on the individual's attitude toward another kind of risk. When the individual is what I call "risk neutral" to both kinds of risk, then his or her expected utility for playing a game is equal to the Shapley value. Other attitudes toward risk yield other utility functions.

This chapter attempts to integrate the material originally presented in Roth (1977a,b,c). Section 2 briefly reviews how an expected utility for an abstract set of alternatives is derived. Sections 3 and 4 then consider how to apply and extend this treatment to include positions in games as alternatives. Section 5 considers the special case of simple games, and may be skipped by those interested only in the main ideas. Section 6 concludes by considering the answers to the questions posed earlier.

2   Utility theory

We summarize here an elegant axiomatization of expected utility developed by Herstein and Milnor (1953). A set M of alternatives is a *mixture set* if for any elements $a, b \in M$ and for any probability $p \in [0,1]$ we can associate another element of M, denoted by $[pa;(1-p)b]$ and called a *lottery* between a and b. (Henceforth the letters p and q will be reserved for elements of [0,1].) We assume that lotteries have the following properties for all $a, b \in M$:

$$[1a;0b] = a,$$
$$[pa;(1-p)b] = [(1-p)b;pa],$$
$$[q[pa;(1-p)b];(1-q)b] = [pqa;(1-pq)b].$$

A *preference relation* on M is defined to be a binary relation $\geq*$ such that for any $a, b \in M$ either $a \geq* b$ or $b \geq* a$ must hold, and if $a \geq* b$ and $b \geq* c$ then $a \geq* c$. We write $a >* b$ if $a \geq* b$ and $b \not\geq* a$, and $a \sim b$ if $a \geq* b$ and $b \geq* a$. (So $a >* b$ means that the individual whose preferences we are considering prefers a to b; $a \geq* b$ means he likes a at least as well as b; and $a \sim b$ means he is indifferent between the two alternatives.) A real-valued function u defined on a mixture set M is an *expected utility* *function* for the preference $\geq*$ if it is order preserving (i.e., if for all a and b in M, $u(a) > u(b)$ if and only if $a >* b$), and if it evaluates the utility of lotteries by their expected utility; that is, if for any lottery $[pa;(1-p)b]$,

$$u([pa;(1-p)b]) = pu(a) + (1-p)u(b).$$

If $\geq*$ is a preference ordering on a mixture set M, then the following conditions ensure that an expected utility function exists:

Continuity: For any a, b, $c \in M$, the sets $\{p | [pa;(1-p)b] \geq* c\}$ and $\{p | c \geq* [pa;(1-p)b]\}$ are closed.

Substitutability: If a, $a' \in M$ and $a \sim a'$, then for any $b \in M$, $[\frac{1}{2}a;\frac{1}{2}b] \sim [\frac{1}{2}a';\frac{1}{2}b]$.

The utility function is unique up to an affine transformation; that is, if u is an expected utility function representing the preferences $\geq*$, then so is v if and only if $v = c_1 u + c_2$, where c_1 and c_2 are real numbers and $c_1 > 0$. Another way to say this is that in specifying a utility function u representing the preferences $\geq*$, we are free to choose arbitrarily any alternatives a_1 and a_0 in M, such that $a_1 >* a_0$, and set $u(a_1) = 1$ and $u(a_0) = 0$. When these arbitrary elements are specified, the value of $u(a)$ for any other alternative a is then completely determined by the preferences.[3] For example, if the alternative a is such that $a_1 \geq* a \geq* a_0$, then $u(a) = p$, where p is the probability such that $a \sim [pa_1;(1-p)a_0]$. (This follows since the utility of the lottery is p, its expected utility.)

3   Comparing positions in games

In what follows, we will consider for simplicity the class G of superadditive characteristic function games[4] v defined on a universe of positions N, where N is taken to be finite. To make comparison between positions in a game and in different games, we shall consider a preference relation defined on the set $N \times G$ of positions in a game. So $(i,v) >* (j,w)$ means "it is preferable to play position i in game v than to play position j in game w." As before, $\sim$ will denote indifference, and $\geq*$ will denote weak preference.

We consider preference relations that are also defined on the mixture set M generated by $N \times G$ (i.e., the smallest mixture set containing $N \times G$). That is, preferences are also defined over lotteries whose outcomes are positions in a game. Denote by $[q(i,v);(1-q)(j,w)]$ the lottery that, with probability q, has a player take position i in game v and, with probability $1 - q$, take position j in game w. We henceforth consider only preference relations that have the standard properties of continuity and substitutability on M and that ensure the existence of an expected utility function unique up to the choice of origin and unit. Denote this function by θ, and write $\theta_i(v) \equiv \theta((i,v))$ and $\theta(v) \equiv (\theta_1(v), \ldots, \theta_n(v))$. Because θ is an expected utility function, $\theta_i(v) > \theta_j(w)$ if and only if the individual whose preferences are being modeled prefers to play position i in game v rather than position j in game w, and the utility of a lottery is its expected utility: that is,

$$\theta([p(i,v);(1-p)(j,w)]) = p\theta_i(v) + (1-p)\theta_j(w).$$

Recall that the games v we are considering are themselves defined in terms of some transferable commodity that reflects the expected utility of the players for some underlying outcomes (e.g., as in note 2). Some additional regularity conditions on preferences for positions in games will be needed in order that the preferences, and the resulting utility function for positions in games, be consistent with the underlying utility function in terms of which the games are defined.

It will be convenient to define, for each position i, the game v_i by

$$\begin{aligned} v_i(S) &= 1 \quad &&\text{if } i \in S, \\ &= 0 \quad &&\text{otherwise.} \end{aligned}$$

All positions other than i are null players in games of the form cv_i, so the player in position i may be sure of getting a utility of c. (This observation will provide the appropriate normalization for the utility θ.) Denote by v_0 the game in which all players are null players (i.e., the game $v_0(S) = 0$ for all S), and let G_{-i} be the class of games in which position i is null.

The first regularity condition we impose on the preferences is

R1.   If $v \in G_{-i}$, then $(i,v) \sim (i,v_0)$. Also, $(i,v_i) >* (i,v_0)$.

This condition says that being a null player in a game is not preferable to being a null player in any other game (in particular in the game v_0), and that the position (i,v_i) is preferable to playing a null position.

The second regularity condition is

R2.   For all $i \in N$, $v \in G$, and for any permutation π, $(i,v) \sim (\pi i, \pi v)$.

This condition says simply that the names of the positions do not affect their desirability. An immediate consequence is that the utility function for games will obey the symmetry axiom.

Lemma 1. $\theta_{\pi i}(\pi v) = \theta_i(v)$.

By R1 we can choose (i,v_i) and (i,v_0) to be the unit and origin of the utility scale, so $\theta_i(v_i) = 1$ and $\theta_i(v_0) = 0$. These are the natural normalizations, reflecting the fact that a player in position i of game v_0 is assured of receiving a payoff of 0 (in terms of her underlying utility function for the outcomes of the games), and a player in position i of v_i is assured of receiving 1.

The last regularity condition reflects that the games v are defined in terms of an *expected* utility function.

R3.   For any number $c > 1$ and for every (i,v) in $N \times G$,

$$(i,v) \sim [(1/c)(i,cv);(1 - 1/c)(i,v_0)].$$

Condition R3 reflects the fact that games v and cv are identical except for the scale of the rewards. These rewards are expressed in terms of a player's expected utility for the underlying consequences, so a player is indifferent between receiving a utility of 1 or of having the lottery that gives him or her a utility of c with probability $1/c$, and 0 with probability $1 - 1/c$. Condition R3 says that, whatever a player's expectation from playing position i in game v, it is related by the same sort of lottery to his or her expectation for playing position i in game cv.

Lemma 2. For any $c \geq 0$ and any $(i,v) \in N \times G$, $\theta_i(cv) = c\theta_i(v)$.

Proof: Without loss of generality we can take $c \geq 1$ (because if $c = 0$, the result follows from condition R1 and the normalization that $\theta_i(v_0) = 0$, and if $0 < c < 1$ we can simply consider $c' = 1/c$). By R3

$$(i,v) \sim [(1/c)(i,cv); (1 - 1/c)(i,v_0)],$$

so

$$\begin{aligned}
\theta_i(v) &= \theta([(1/c)(i,cv); (1 - 1/c)(i,v_0)]) \\
&= (1/c)\theta_i(cv) + (1 - 1/c)\theta_i(v_0) \\
&= (1/c)\theta_i(cv).
\end{aligned}$$

These regularity conditions, together with the normalization that $\theta_i(v_i) = 1$ and $\theta_i(v_0) = 0$, place some constraints on the utility function θ that allow us to interpret it as an extension of the underlying utility function defining the games. (We can regard the alternative (i,cv_i) as "embedding" in the mixture space M of positions in games the underlying payoffs of the games themselves, because the opportunity to play position

i in the game cv_i is essentially the same as being given a prize with utility c, and $\theta_i(cv_i) = c$.) We will call a utility function on M normalized in this way and satisfying R1–R3 an *extended* utility function, because it extends to the space of positions in games the utility function used to define the games. However, infinitely many extended utility functions still could arise, because the preferences that an agent could have over games still have many degrees of freedom. In particular, we turn now to consider an individual's attitude toward different kinds of risk.

4   Risk posture

We distinguish between two kinds of risk. *Ordinary risk* involves the uncertainty that arises from lotteries, whereas *strategic risk* involves the uncertainty that arises from the strategic interaction of the players in a game.

4.1   *Ordinary risk*

Recall that when we consider preferences defined over money, we say that an individual is "risk neutral" if his utility for any lottery is equal to its expected monetary value. Analogously, we say that an individual is "risk neutral to ordinary risk over games" if her preferences obey the following condition.

Neutrality to ordinary risk over games:

$$(i, (qw + (1 - q)v)) \sim [q(i,w);(1 - q)(i,v)].$$

The condition says that the individual is indifferent between the alternative on the right, which is a lottery that will result in playing position i in either game w or game v, and the alternative on the left, which is to play position i in the game whose characteristic function is equal to the expected value of the characteristic function of the lottery. That is, consider some coalition $S \subset N$. Its expected worth in the lottery on the right is $qw(S) + (1 - q)v(S)$, which is precisely its worth in the game on the left. So a player is risk neutral with respect to ordinary risk over games if he or she is indifferent between playing position i in the "expected game" $qw + (1 - q)v$ or to having the appropriate lottery between the games w and v.

Note that $v = (1/c)cv + (1 - (1/c)v_0)$, so neutrality to ordinary risk over games implies regularity condition R3. In fact, it is a much stronger condition, and in Section 6 we briefly consider why an individual might not be neutral to ordinary risk over games, even if he or she was risk neutral in terms of the transferable commodity used to define them. However, the next result shows that this kind of risk neutrality is just what is involved in assuming that the utility function θ is additive.

Theorem 1 (Additivity). $\theta(v + w) = \theta(v) + \theta(w)$ for all $v,\ w \in G$ if and only if preferences are neutral to ordinary risk over games.

Proof: For each $i \in N$,

$$\theta_i(v + w) = \theta_i(2(\tfrac{1}{2}v + \tfrac{1}{2}w)) = 2\theta_i(\tfrac{1}{2}v + \tfrac{1}{2}w)$$

by Lemma 2. But by ordinary risk neutrality over games,

$$\theta_i(\tfrac{1}{2}v + \tfrac{1}{2}w) = \theta_i([\tfrac{1}{2}(i,v);\tfrac{1}{2}(i,w)]) = \tfrac{1}{2}\theta_i(v) + \tfrac{1}{2}\theta_i(w),$$

because θ is an expected utility function. So $\theta_i(v + w) = \theta_i(v) + \theta_i(w)$. The other direction is equally straightforward, after the initial task of proving that additivity of an extended utility function (together with continuity) implies the conclusions of Lemma 2.

There is uncertainty in playing a game even if no lotteries are involved. In Roth (1977a,b) this was called *strategic* risk. Given that an individual is neutral to ordinary risk over games, we will now show that the individual's posture toward strategic risk uniquely determines his or her utility for a position in a game.

4.2   *Strategic risk*

Any game with more than one strategic (i.e., nondummy) position involves some potential uncertainty as to the outcome, arising from the interaction of the strategic players. To describe a given player's preferences for situations involving strategic risk, it will be convenient for us to consider it on the games v_R defined for each subset R of N by

$$\begin{aligned} v_R(S) &= 1 \qquad \text{if } R \subset S, \\ &= 0 \qquad \text{otherwise.} \end{aligned}$$

A "pure bargaining game" of the form v_R is essentially the simplest game that can be played among r strategic players. (The cardinality of sets R, S, $T, \ldots$ is denoted by $r, s, t, \ldots$.)

Define the *certain equivalent* of a strategic position in a game v_R to be the number $f(r)$ such that the prospect of receiving $f(r)$ for certain is exactly as desirable as the prospect of playing the strategic position.[5] That is, $f(r)$ is the number such that, for $i \in R$, $(i,v_R) \sim (i,f(r)v_i)$. Note that $f(1) = 1$, and that $f(r)$ is a measure of a player's opinion of his or her own bargaining ability in pure bargaining games of size r.

Using the terminology of Roth (1977a), we say that the preference is *neutral to strategic risk* if $f(r) = 1/r$ for $r = 1, \ldots, n$. The preference is *strategic risk averse* if $f(r) \le 1/r$, and *strategic risk preferring* if $f(r) \ge 1/r$. (Note that preferences may be none of these; e.g., if $f(2) > 1/2$ but $f(3) < 1/3$.) The utility of playing a position in a game v_R is given by the following lemma.

Lemma 3.

$$\begin{aligned}\theta_i(v_R) &= f(r) &&\text{if } i \in R,\\ &= 0 &&\text{otherwise.}\end{aligned}$$

Proof: If $i \notin R$, then $v_R \in G_{-i}$ and $\theta_i(v_R) = \theta_i(v_0) = 0$, by R1. If $i \in R$, then $\theta_i(v_R) = \theta_i(f(r)v_i) = f(r)\theta_i(v_i) = f(r)$, by Lemma 2.

If preferences are neutral to ordinary risk over games, then Theorem 1 implies that the utility function is completely determined by the numbers $f(r)$, because the games v_R are an additive basis. We have the following result.

Shapley value theorem. The Shapley value is the utility function of an individual who is both neutral to ordinary risk over games and neutral to strategic risk. That is, when preferences are neutral to both kinds of risk,

$$\theta_i(v) = \phi_i(v) = \sum_{S \subset N} \frac{(s-1)!(n-s)!}{n!}\,[v(S) - v(S - i)].$$

Proof: Neutrality to ordinary risk over games implies that θ is additive, and strategic risk neutrality implies that θ agrees with the Shapley value ϕ on all games of the form v_R. Because the games v_R constitute a basis of the space of games, it follows that θ agrees with ϕ on all games.

As the Shapley value theorem and its proof make clear, neutrality to ordinary risk together with different strategic risk preferences (as expressed by the numbers $f(r)$, $r = 2, \ldots, n$) will determine utility functions that differ from the Shapley value. These other utility functions for games are given by the next result.

Representation theorem. When preferences are neutral to ordinary risk over games, the utility function θ has the form

$$\theta_i(v) = \sum_{T \subseteq N} k(t)[v(T) - v(T - i)], \tag{1}$$

where

$$k(t) = \sum_{r=t}^{n} (-1)^{r-t} \binom{n-t}{r-t} f(r).$$

Proof: Every game v is a sum of games of the form v_R. In fact (see Shapley 1953 and Chapter 2 of this volume), $v = \sum_{R \subseteq N} c_R v_R$, where $c_R = \sum_{T \subseteq R} (-1)^{r-t} v(T)$. By Lemma 2 and Theorem 1,

$$\theta_i(v) = \sum_{\substack{R \subseteq N}} c_R \theta_i(v_R) = \sum_{\substack{R \subseteq N \\ i \in R}} c_R f(r) = \sum_{\substack{R \subseteq N \\ i \in R}} \sum_{T \subseteq R} (-1)^{r-t} v(T) f(r).$$

Reversing the order of summation, we obtain

$$\theta_i(v) = \sum_{T \subseteq N} \left\{ \sum_{\substack{R \subseteq N \\ R \supseteq (T \cup i)}} (-1)^{r-t} f(r) \right\} v(T).$$

If we denote the term in braces by $g_i(T)$, then we note that $g_i(T) = -g_i(T - i)$ when $i \in T$. So

$$\theta_i(v) = \sum_{\substack{T \subseteq N \\ i \in T}} g_i(T)[v(T) - v(T - i)].$$

But there are $\binom{n-t}{r-t}$ coalitions of size r that contain T, so

$$g_i(T) = \sum_{r=t}^{n} (-1)^{r-t} \binom{n-t}{r-t} f(r) = k(t).$$

Because $[v(T) - v(T - i)] = 0$ unless $i \in T$, we are done.

   An immediate consequence of this representation theorem is that when preferences are neutral to ordinary risk (i.e., when the utility function is additive), then the utility of playing a null position is 0, because the utility is the weighted sum of marginal contributions. The effect of strategic risk neutrality, and the special feature of the Shapley value, is that the sum over positions equals $v(N)$. In a purely axiomatic framework (Roth 1977d), the theorem can be restated to say that any symmetric and additive value θ that gives null players 0 (or, equivalently, with the property that $\Sigma_{i\in T}\theta_i(v) = \Sigma_{i\in S}\theta_i(v)$ for any carriers T, S of a game v) is a weighted sum of marginal contributions as given in the theorem. Such values, which need not sum to $v(N)$, have subsequently been called *semivalues* (Dubey, Neyman, and Weber 1981; Einy 1987; Weber Chapter 7 this volume).

The semivalue that has received perhaps the most attention in the literature (cf. Banzhaf 1965; Coleman 1971; Owen 1975; Dubey 1975a; Roth 1977b,c; Dubey and Shapley 1979; Straffin Chapter 5 this volume) is the Banzhaf index $\beta' = (\beta'_1, \ldots ,\beta'_n)$ given by

$$\beta'_i(v) = \sum_{S \subseteq N} \frac{1}{2^{n-1}} [v(S) - v(S - i)].$$

Banzhaf (1965) originally proposed a version of this index in the context of simple games (see Chapters 1 and 5), but the extension to general games is straightforward, the major difference being that the marginal contributions $v(S) - v(S - i)$ may take on values other than 0 and 1. The factor $1/2^{n-1}$ is a convenient normalization, but others could be chosen. The important point for the following result is that the normalization does not depend on the game v. (In some treatments of the Banzhaf index for simple games, the index is normalized so that $\beta_i = \beta'_i/\Sigma_{i\in N}\beta'_i$ for β' as defined here, so $\Sigma\beta_i = 1$. But this involves a different divisor for each game, so the resulting index is not additive – i.e., not neutral to ordinary risk.)

The Banzhaf index β' as normalized here is an extended utility function reflecting preferences averse to strategic risk and neutral to ordinary risk. We state without proof the following corollary of the representation theorem, from Roth (1977d).

Corollary. If $f(r) = 1/2^{r-1}$, then the extended utility function equals the Banzhaf index; that is, $\theta(v) = \beta'(v)$.

Thus the Banzhaf index is a utility function in which a player's utility for a strategic position in a game v_R is inversely proportional to the number of ways the $r - 1$ other strategic players can form coalitions.

5   Simple games

As discussed in Chapter 1, the Banzhaf index, like the Shapley–Shubik (1954) index, was proposed in connection with voting processes modeled by simple games. However, the characterization of the Shapley value and Banzhaf index for general games given here, like Shapley's axiomatic characterization of the Shapley value, makes crucial use of nonsimple games. If the universe of games we are interested in consists only of simple games, then symmetry, efficiency, and additivity do not uniquely characterize the Shapley value. In particular, the Banzhaf index β, normalized so as to sum to 1, also obeys these three axioms when they are applied only to simple games. The reason is that additivity (equivalently, neutrality to ordinary risk) loses all its force when applied only to simple games, because the class of simple games is not closed under addition. So if v and w are nontrivial simple games, $v(N) = w(N) = 1$ and the game $v + w$ is not simple, because $v(N) + w(N) = 2$. In this section we follow Roth (1977c) in considering how the Shapley–Shubik index can be (uniquely) characterized as a risk-neutral utility function defined on the class of simple games.

Dubey (1975a,b) axiomatically characterized the Shapley–Shubik index on the class of simple games by replacing additivity with the following axiom (which Weber, in Chapter 5, has called the *transfer axiom*).

Transfer axiom. For any simple games v, w,

$$\phi(v \vee w) + \phi(v \wedge w) = \phi(v) + \phi(w),$$

where the games $v \vee w$ and $v \wedge w$ are defined by

$$(v \vee w)(S) = 1 \quad \text{if } v(S) = 1 \text{ or } w(S) = 1,$$
$$= 0 \quad \text{otherwise,}$$

and

$$(v \wedge w)(S) = 1 \quad \text{if } v(S) = 1 \text{ and } w(S) = 1,$$
$$= 0 \quad \text{otherwise.}$$

Perhaps the easiest way to understand the transfer axiom is to recast it in terms of preferences over games and lotteries over games, as a form of neutrality to ordinary risk over simple games. Viewed in that way, it takes the following form.

Ordinary risk neutrality for simple games: For all simple games v, w

$$[\tfrac{1}{2}(v,i);\tfrac{1}{2}(w,i)] \sim [\tfrac{1}{2}((v \vee w),i);\tfrac{1}{2}((v \wedge w),i)].$$

This condition specifies indifference between two lotteries. One lottery results in either the game v or the game w, and the other results in either the game $v \vee w$ or the game $v \wedge w$. What makes this a condition of risk neutrality is that any given coalition S has the same probability of being a winning coalition in either lottery. It follows immediately from the fact that θ is an expected utility function that if it is neutral to ordinary risk it obeys the transfer axiom.

In order to state all conditions on preferences in terms of simple games only, we also need to rewrite neutrality to strategic risk, because the game $f(r)v_i$ is not a simple game. The following condition involves only simple games.

Strategic risk neutrality for simple games: For all $R \subset N$ and $i \in R$,

$$(v_R,i) \sim [\tfrac{1}{r}(v_i,i);(1 - \tfrac{1}{r})(v_0,i)].$$

It is easy to see that, when the utility function is normalized as in the previous sections so that $\theta_i(v_i) = 1$ and $\theta_i(v_0) = 0$, strategic risk neutrality for simple games continues to imply that θ coincides with ϕ on the class of pure bargaining games.

Dubey proved the following result.

Proposition. The Shapley–Shubik index is the unique function ϕ defined on simple games that obeys Shapley's symmetry and carrier axioms as well as the transfer axiom.

In terms of utilities, we can now recast this result as follows.

Shapley–Shubik index theorem. The Shapley–Shubik index is the unique utility θ, normalized so that $\theta_i(v_i) = 1$ and $\theta_i(v_0) = 0$, corresponding to preferences that obey conditions R1 and R2 and that are neutral to both strategic and ordinary risk defined over simple games.

Proof: We have already observed that θ is symmetric (Lemma 1) and obeys the transfer axiom, and that for every $R \subset N$, $\theta(v_R) = \phi(v_R)$; that is, θ coincides with the Shapley–Shubik index on the pure bargaining games

v_R. To complete the proof of the theorem, we show that θ coincides with ϕ on every simple game v.

Let $R_1, R_2, \ldots, R_k \subset N$ be all the distinct minimal winning coalitions[6] of v. Then we say the game v is in class k, and note that $v = v_{R1} \vee v_{R2} \vee \cdots \vee v_{Rk}$. If v is in class $k = 0$, then $v = v_0$ and $\theta(v) = \phi(v) = 0$. If v is in class $k = 1$, then $v = v_{R1}$ is a pure bargaining game, and $\theta(v) = \phi(v)$.

Suppose that for games v in classes $k = 1, 2, \ldots, m$ it has been shown that θ is well defined and coincides with the Shapley–Shubik index. Consider a game v in class $m + 1$. Then

$$v = v_{R1} \vee v_{R2} \vee \cdots \vee v_{Rm} \vee v_R = w \vee v_R,$$

where w is a game in class m. Hence, by neutrality to ordinary risk over simple games (which implies that the utility θ obeys the transfer axiom),

$$\theta_i(v) = \theta_i(w \vee v_R) = \theta_i(w) + \theta_i(v_R) - \theta_i(w \wedge v_R).$$

But we show that the game $w \wedge v_R$ cannot be in a class higher than w, so by the inductive hypothesis the terms on the right side of the preceding expression are uniquely determined and equal to the Shapley–Shubik index. Consequently, we will have shown that $\theta(v) = \phi(v)$ for all simple games v.

To see that the game $w' = (w \wedge v_R)$ cannot be in a class higher than the game w, consider a minimal winning coalition S' of the game w'. By the definition of w' we know that $S' \supset R$ and $w(S') = 1$. If $S' = R$, then $w' = v_R$ and we are done (because except for the game v_0, every game has at least one minimal winning coalition). Otherwise, $S' = S \cup R$, where S is a minimal winning coalition in the game w. (Of course, S and R need not be disjoint.)

Consider now a coalition T' that is minimal winning in w'. Then $T' = T \cup R$, where T is minimal winning in w. If $T' \neq S'$, then $T \neq S$. Consequently, every minimal winning coalition in w' can be identified with a distinct minimal winning coalition in w, so w' cannot be in a class higher than w. This completes the proof.

6   Discussion

To see what has been accomplished by considering the Shapley value as a utility function, let us consider what kind of answers have been obtained to the questions raised in the introduction to this chapter.

    1. The "uniqueness" of the Shapley value as a utility function for

games is associated with its risk neutrality. Perhaps a good way to think of this is by analogy with utility functions for money: The risk-neutral utility function is the one that evaluates lotteries at their expected value. Although few of us consider only the expected value when choosing among risky investments, for example, the expected value is nevertheless enormously important to know and can give us at least a rough indication of what our preferences are likely to be upon closer investigation. In the same way, the Shapley value gives an indication of what our preferences over positions in games are likely to be, even if we are not neutral to both strategic and ordinary risk over games. And for preferences that are neutral to ordinary risk over games, we have been able to characterize the utility functions that reflect different attitudes toward strategic risk. However, the systematic behavior of utility functions that reflect different attitudes toward ordinary risk over games remains an open question.

2. We have seen that the Shapley value "inherits" the normalization of the utility function used to define the games being considered. That is, underlying any game is a concrete set of outcomes that are represented by utility payoffs in terms of utility functions with arbitrary origin and unit. An individual's Shapley value is an extension of this utility function, with the same normalization. Thus the meaningful utility comparisons that can be made with the Shapley value are precisely those that can be made with expected utility functions. For example, in Chapter 1 the Shapley value was calculated for a simple model of the U.N. Security Council, yielding a Shapley value of .00186 for a rotating member and a Shapley value of .196 for a permanent member. Viewing the Shapley value as an expected utility function, we can now determine which statements about these numbers are meaningful comparisons reflecting the underlying preferences, and which are not. For example, an individual who is neutral to both ordinary and strategic risk would be indifferent between playing the game in the position of a permanent member or to having a lottery that gave a .196 probability of being a dictator in the game, and otherwise made him a null player (or for that matter having a lottery that gave a .196 probability of receiving any prospect with a utility of 1, and otherwise receiving a utility of 0). Similarly, such an individual would be indifferent between playing the position of a rotating member or having a lottery that gave her a probability of $p = .00186/.196 = .0095$ of playing the position of a permanent member and otherwise being a null player. To put it another way, this individual would prefer a 1 in 100 chance of being a permanent member (and a 99 in 100 chance of being a null player) to the prospect of being a rotating member. But it would not be a meaningful

comparison to say that the prospect of playing a position in a game is over 100 times as desirable as another prospect (which could be either a position in a game or a lottery over prizes), because this depends on the (arbitrary) normalization chosen for the underlying utility function.

3. We have seen that the additivity axiom on the value function is equivalent to assuming that the preferences that the value represents as a utility function are neutral with respect to ordinary risk over games. Perhaps the best way to understand what this entails at this point is to consider why an individual might *not* be neutral to this kind of risk. For example, let v be the three-person majority game given by $v(1) = v(2) = v(3) = 0$ and $v(12) = v(13) = v(23) = v(123) = 1$, and let $w = v_{(12)}$ be the two-person pure bargaining game (with player 3 a null player). Then the game $z = v + w$ is given by $z(1) = z(2) = z(3) = 0$, $z(13) = z(23) = 1$, $z(12) = z(123) = 2$. Although v and w are both symmetric among the nonnull players, z is not. In particular, the symmetry of v makes it not unreasonable to suppose that each of the two-person coalitions is as likely to form as any other, and that if the three-person coalition forms it will divide equally. So the fact that $\phi(v) = (\frac{1}{3},\frac{1}{3},\frac{1}{3})$ seems reasonable, as does the fact that $\phi(w) = (\frac{1}{2},\frac{1}{2},0)$. So our evaluation of the two games separately is that each two-person coalition is equally likely to form in v, but in w the coalition $\{12\}$ will form.

Therefore the coalition $\{12\}$ should be especially easy to form in the game z because players 1 and 2 are essential for the game to be worth 2, and player 3 can make no further marginal contribution. (This is clearly reflected in the core of z, which is the single payoff vector $(1,1,0)$.) But the Shapley value is $\phi(z) = (\frac{5}{6},\frac{5}{6},\frac{1}{3})$. That is, an individual whose utility is the Shapley value is indifferent between playing position 3 in the game z or in the game v. Although this preference may be consistent with plausible models of how the game might be played (because game z gives 3 a less advantageous position but has higher stakes than game v), I think that for most purposes I would personally prefer to play position 3 of game v rather than of game z. So, although neutrality to ordinary risk is an easy to understand and plausible condition on preferences that gives rise to tractable (i.e., additive) utility functions, it is by no means an inescapable requirement for plausible preferences, either for all individuals or for a given individual over all games.

4. Finally, we have seen that, when preferences are neutral to ordinary risk so that the utility function is additive, the vector θ of utility for each position in a game is "efficient" if and only if the preferences are neutral to strategic risk. The quotation marks reflect the fact that under the interpretation presented here the vector θ is not a distribution of utility among

different players but simply a vector of utilities for the different positions. Indeed, whether the vector $(\theta_1(v), \ldots, \theta_n(v))$ is even a *feasible* outcome of the game, let alone an efficient one, appears to arise in this context essentially by accident.[7] The risk-neutral utility – the Shapley value – always happens to coincide with an outcome of the game, but utility vectors that do not reflect neutrality to strategic risk do not share this property.[8] In any event no interpersonal comparisons are implied, because all comparisons are those of a single agent evaluating alternative positions.

As to whether we should expect individuals to be neutral to strategic risk, just as many individuals do not judge monetary lotteries only by their expected value, I imagine that many are not indifferent between bargaining among r individuals or receiving $1/r$ of the proceeds for sure. Certainly some aversion to strategic risk would appear to be justified by the experimental evidence, which reveals a nonnegligible frequency of disagreement (see Roth 1987), and by the growing theoretical understanding about how differences in information, ability to make commitments, or long-term concerns may lead to disagreements (see, e.g., the papers in Roth 1985 or Binmore and Dasgupta 1987). So, like additivity, efficiency arises from assumptions about preferences that are plausible but by no means inescapable.

In conclusion, the analogy between the Shapley value, which is the risk-neutral utility for playing a game, and the expected value, which is the risk-neutral utility for monetary gambles, seems to be a strong one. (Note that this is *not* because of the interpretation of the Shapley value as an expected marginal contribution. The Banzhaf index and other non-risk-neutral utilities can also be interpreted as expected marginal contributions; see, e.g., Weber Chapter 7 this volume.) When we consider a specific individual or a specific choice among games, we may be able to find a more precise indicator. But when we are considering a first approximation, both the expected value of monetary gambles and the Shapley value of transferable utility games seem to work in similar ways. And even if we conclude that most individuals are not risk neutral, the assumptions of risk neutrality implicit in the Shapley value, like the expected value, may be a more natural proxy for the utility of some unspecified individual than would any assumption of a particular risk posture.

NOTES

1   In the same way, the arithmetic mean of players' utilities is not meaningful. But the geometric mean of expected utilities is: This forms the basis for Nash's celebrated model of bargaining (see Nash 1950; Roth 1979).

2   Of course, a similar question arises concerning transferable utility games, in which the "transferable utility" payoffs to the players are assumed to sum to (at most) $v(N)$. No assumption that utilities are interpersonally comparable needs to be made to consider such a game. For example, if the payoffs are all in money and the players are all risk neutral, then the characteristic function form representation of the game simply involves a common (but still arbitrary) normalization of the players' utility functions. To see that no fundamental comparisons are involved, observe that we could construct a characteristic function form game among players, all of whom receive quite different commodities and among whom no actual physical transfers can take place. Consider three players, one of whom will ultimately be paid in French francs, one in baskets of fruit, and one in wine. For each player, a utility function is constructed for possible payoffs. The arbitrary elements in each utility representation are chosen without reference to the others. A given characteristic function game v defined on $N = \{1,2,3\}$ can now be created by allowing the members of each coalition $S \subset N$ (who can communicate by telephone and sign contracts as needed) to divide an amount $v(S)$ of a fictitious commodity – "utility money" – in any way they choose. At the conclusion of the game, each player may exchange whatever utility money he has earned for the amount of the commodity in which he is to be paid that gives him that amount of utility, according to the arbitrarily scaled utility function established for him before the game.

3   In general, for any element $x \in M$, the utility of x is

$$u(x) = (p_{ab}(x) - p_{ab}(a_0))/(p_{ab}(a_1) - p_{ab}(a_0))$$

where a, b, a_1, and a_0 are elements of M such that $a \geq^* x \geq^* b$ and $a \geq^* a_1 \geq^* a_0 \geq^* b$, and for any $y \in M$ such that $a \geq^* y \geq^* b$, $p_{ab}(y)$ is defined by $y \sim [p_{ab}(y)a;(1 - p_{ab}(y))b]$.

It can be shown that the numbers $p_{ab}(\cdot)$ are well defined, and the function $u(\cdot)$ is independent of the choice of a and b. Note that $u(a_1) = 1$ and $u(a_0) = 0$.

4   The class of superadditive games is sufficiently large, but we could consider a larger class of games without changing the results presented here.

5   We take the point of view that a player does not know who will occupy the other positions in a game. Consequently, her certain equivalent for a game v_R depends only on r.

6   A coalition $R \subset N$ is minimal winning in v if $v(R) = 1$ and if $S \subset R$, $S \neq R$, implies $v(S) = 0$.

7   Note that, by analogy, expected values of money gambles aren't necessarily feasible outcomes: for example, the 50-50 gamble for plus or minus one dollar has an expected value of 0, although that isn't a feasible outcome. For transferable utility games feasibility comes along with risk neutrality, but this does not appear to be the case for NTU games. It seems to me that this may be part of the trouble in interpreting the value for NTU games along the lines of the Shapley value for TU games (see the references in this connection in Chapter 1).

8   This is so for utilities that are strategic risk averse as well as strategic risk

preferring. It is clear that a vector of utilities that are strategically risk preferring will not always coincide with a feasible outcome: Because $f(r) > 1/r$, such a utility vector isn't a feasible outcome in a pure bargaining game v_R, because $rf(r) > v_R(N) = 1$. For a risk-averse utility, consider the Banzhaf index β', with $f(r) = 1/2^{r-1}$. For the three-person majority game, $\beta'(\dot{v}) = (\frac{1}{2},\frac{1}{2},\frac{1}{2})$, so $\Sigma\beta_i' > v(N) = 1$. To see what is going on here, note that $v = v_{(12)} + v_{(13)} + v_{(23)} - 2v_{(123)}$, and so $\beta_i'(v) = \beta_i'(v_{(12)}) + \beta_i'(v_{(13)}) + \beta_i'(v_{(23)}) - 2\beta_i'(v_{(123)})$. But when $r = 2$, $1/2^{-1} = \frac{1}{2}$, so the Banzhaf index agrees with the Shapley value on the two-person pure bargaining games. But when $r = 3$, the strategic risk aversion of the Banzhaf agent comes into play, with $\beta_i'(v_{(123)}) = \frac{1}{4}$ for each $i = 1, 2, 3$ (in contrast to the Shapley value $\phi_i'(v_{(123)}) = \frac{1}{3}$). Because $v_{(123)}$ enters the expression for the three-person majority game v with a negative coefficient, this means that the relatively greater strategic risk aversion of the Banzhaf agent, which causes him to evaluate the three-person pure bargaining game less favorably than does the Shapley agent, nevertheless causes him to evaluate the three-person majority game more favorably. Thus, in the presence of neutrality to ordinary risk (i.e., additivity) differences in strategic risk aversion can have effects that are difficult to anticipate.

There are (at least) two ways to think about these effects of strategic risk aversion. On the one hand, they appear to parallel similar effects of ordinary risk aversion found in game-theoretic models of bargaining (Roth and Rothblum 1982; Harrington 1987). On the other hand, they are also intimately related to the assumption of neutrality to ordinary risk and the resulting additivity of the utility function, and so these effects may also provide some further cause to be cautious about the assumption of additivity.

REFERENCES

Banzhaf, John F. III [1965], "Weighted Voting Doesn't Work: A Mathematical Analysis," *Rutgers Law Review,* 19, 317–43.

Binmore, Ken and Partha Dasgupta (editors) [1987], *The Economics of Bargaining,* Oxford, Basil Blackwell.

Coleman, James S. [1971], "Control of Collectivities and the Power of a Collectivity to Act," in *Social Choice,* B. Lieberman, editor, Gordon and Breach, New York, pp. 269–300.

Dubey, Pradeep [1975a], "Some Results on Values of Finite and Infinite Games," Ph.D. thesis, Cornell University.

[1975b], "On the Uniqueness of the Shapley Value," *International Journal of Game Theory,* 4, 131–9.

Dubey, Pradeep, Abraham Neyman, and Robert Weber [1981], "Value Theory without Efficiency," *Mathematics of Operations Research,* 6, 122–8.

Dubey, Pradeep and Lloyd S. Shapley [1979], "Mathematical Properties of the Banzhaf Power Index," *Mathematics of Operations Research,* 4, 99–131.

Einy, Ezra [1987], "Semivalues of Simple Games," *Mathematics of Operations Research,* 12, 185–92.

Harrington, Joseph E., Jr. [1987], "The Role of Risk Preferences in Bargaining for the Class of Symmetric Voting Rules," Department of Political Economy, Johns Hopkins, mimeo.

Herstein, I. N. and J. Milnor [1953], "An Axiomatic Approach to Measurable Utility," *Econometrica,* 21, 291 – 7.

Nash, John F. [1950], "The Bargaining Problem," *Econometrica,* 54, 155 – 62.

Owen, Guillermo [1975], "Multilinear Extensions and the Banzhaf Value," *Naval Research Logistics Quarterly,* 22, 741 – 750.

Roth, Alvin E. [1977a], "The Shapley Value as a von Neumann – Morgenstern Utility," *Econometrica,* 45, 657 – 64.

[1977b], "Bargaining Ability, the Utility of Playing a Game, and Models of Coalition Formation," *Journal of Mathematical Psychology,* 16, 153 – 60.

[1977c], "Utility Functions for Simple Games," *Journal of Economic Theory,* 16, 481 – 9.

[1977d], "A Note on Values and Multilinear Extensions," *Naval Research Logistics Quarterly,* 24, 517 – 20.

[1979], *Axiomatic Models of Bargaining,* Lecture Notes in Economics and Mathematical Systems, No. 170, Springer-Verlag, New York.

editor, [1985], *Game-Theoretic Models of Bargaining,* Cambridge University Press, Cambridge.

[1987], "Bargaining Phenomena and Bargaining Theory," *Laboratory Experimentation in Economics: Six Points of View,* A. E. Roth, editor, Cambridge University Press, Cambridge, pp. 14 – 41.

Roth, Alvin E. and Uriel Rothblum [1982], "Risk Aversion and Nash's Solution for Bargaining Games With Risky Outcomes, *Econometrica,* 50, 639 – 47.

Shapley, Lloyd S. [1953], "A Value for *n*-Person Games," *Contributions to the Theory of Games,* vol. II, H. W. Kuhn and A. W. Tucker, editors, Ann. of Math. Studies 28, Princeton University Press, Princeton, New Jersey, pp. 307 – 17.

Shapley, Lloyd S. and Martin Shubik [1954], "A Method for Evaluating the Distribution of Power in a Committee System," *American Political Science Review,* 48, 787 – 92.

CHAPTER 5

The Shapley–Shubik and Banzhaf power indices as probabilities

Philip D. Straffin, Jr.

1 The Shapley–Shubik and Banzhaf indices

In 1954 Lloyd Shapley and Martin Shubik published a short paper [12] in the *American Political Science Review,* proposing that the specialization of the Shapley value to simple games could serve as an index of voting power. That paper has been one of the most frequently cited articles in social science literature of the past thirty years, and its "Shapley–Shubik power index" has become widely known. Shapley and Shubik explained the index as follows:

> There is a group of individuals all willing to vote for some bill. They vote in order. As soon as a majority has voted for it, it is declared passed, and the member who voted last is given credit for having passed it. Let us choose the voting order of the members randomly. Then we may compute the frequency with which an individual . . . is *pivotal.* This latter number serves to give us our index. It measures the number of times that the action of the individual actually changes the state of affairs. . . .
>
> Of course, the actual balloting procedure used will in all probability be quite different from the above. The "voting" of the formal scheme might better be thought of as declarations of support for the bill and the randomly chosen order of voting as an indication of the relative degrees of support by the different members, with the most enthusiastic members "voting" first, etc. The *pivot* is then the last member whose support is needed in order for passage of the bill to be assured.

Thus to calculate the Shapley–Shubik indices in the weighted voting game

$$[3;2,1,1],$$
$$ABC \qquad\qquad (1)$$

we write down the 3! orders in which A, B, C might declare their support for a bill, and in each order we circle the pivot voter:

$$A \,\textcircled{B}\, C \quad A \,\textcircled{C}\, B \quad B \,\textcircled{A}\, C \quad B C \,\textcircled{A} \quad C \,\textcircled{A}\, B \quad C B \,\textcircled{A}.$$

The Shapley–Shubik power indices are $\phi_A = \frac{2}{3}$, $\phi_B = \frac{1}{6}$, and $\phi_C = \frac{1}{6}$.

In 1965 John Banzhaf[1] explicitly rejected the Shapley–Shubik index and proposed a new index of voting power for use in court cases involving issues of equal representation. The Banzhaf index was endorsed by the New York Court of Appeals in two 1966 cases and has been used in cases since then [5]. Banzhaf argued that the order in which voters join a coalition in favor of a bill should not be the crucial factor: "It seems unreasonable to credit a legislator with different amounts of voting power depending on when and for what reasons he joins a particular voting coalition. His joining is a use of his voting power – not a measure of it." Instead [1],

> Since the determination of legislative outcomes is the only legitimate use and purpose of legislative power and since usually an individual legisla-tor can only determine outcomes when the others are closely divided, the appropriate measure of a legislator's power is simply the number of different situations in which he is able to determine the outcome. More explicitly, in a case where there are N legislators, each acting indepen-dently and each capable of influencing the outcome only by means of his votes, the ratio of the power of legislator X to the power of legislator Y is the same as the ratio of the number of possible voting combinations of the entire legislature in which X can alter the outcome by changing his vote to the number of combinations in which Y can alter the outcome by changing his vote.

Thus to calculate Banzhaf indices in the weighted voting game (1), we would write down the winning coalitions and in each one circle the *swing* voters, those who by changing their vote could change the coalition from winning to losing:

$$\textcircled{A}\,\textcircled{B} \quad \textcircled{A}\,\textcircled{C} \quad \textcircled{A}\, B \, C.$$

The Banzhaf indices for A, B, C are in the ratio $3 : 1 : 1$. One might norma-lize the Banzhaf index by dividing by the total number of swings, getting $\beta_A = \frac{3}{5}, \beta_B = \frac{1}{5}$, and $\beta_C = \frac{1}{5}$. On the other hand, Banzhaf saw clearly that it is the ratio of power that is most meaningful, and for our purposes it is more natural to divide by the maximal number of swings that any voter could possibly have – 2^{n-1} when there are n voters. If we do this, we get a *nonnormalized* Banzhaf index $\beta'_A = \frac{3}{4}$, $\beta'_B = \frac{1}{4}$, and $\beta'_C = \frac{1}{4}$.

For a general simple game with n players, the definitions of the Shapley–Shubik and Banzhaf power indices for voter i are

$$\phi_i = \frac{1}{n!} \sum_{i \text{ swings in } S} (s-1)!(n-s)! \qquad (s = |S|),$$

$$\beta'_i = \frac{1}{2^{n-1}} \sum_{i \text{ swings in } S} 1.$$

The phrase "i swings in S" means that the sum is taken over all coalitions S such that i is in S, S is winning, but $S - \{i\}$ is losing. The Banzhaf index simply counts these coalitions. The Shapley–Shubik index weights each such coalition by the number of orders in which i could exercise his or her swing: $(s-1)!$ is the number of orders in which the other members of S could vote, followed by i as pivot, followed by the voters not in S in $(n-s)!$ possible orders. For more details and examples, see [6] and [16].

2 Comparison of the indices

In the three-person game (1) the Shapley–Shubik and Banzhaf indices give fairly similar results. This is not always true, even for games of moderate size. For example, in their 1954 paper Shapley and Shubik considered a legislative system consisting of a president P, three senators SSS, and five house members HHHHH. Legislation must be approved by the president and a majority of both the Senate and the House. The Shapley–Shubik power indices are $\phi_P = .381$, $\phi_S = .107$, and $\phi_H = .059$. The ratios of power of P, S, and H are $6.4 : 1.8 : 1$. In contrast, the Banzhaf indices for this system are $\beta'_P = .250$, $\beta'_S = .125$, and $\beta'_H = .094$, with ratios $2.7 : 1.3 : 1$. In the eight-person game

$$[2;1,1,1,1] \otimes [3;2,1,1,1],$$
$$AAAA BCCC$$

where the $\otimes$ notation from [10] means that a bill must be approved in *both* of the two weighted voting bodies, the Shapley–Shubik and Banzhaf indices even rank the power of the voters differently:

$$\phi_A = .093 \qquad \phi_B = .314 \qquad \phi_C = .105$$

$$\beta'_A = .188 \qquad \beta'_B = .516 \qquad \beta'_C = .172$$

The Shapley–Shubik index says a C is more powerful than an A, and the Banzhaf index says the reverse.

In large games the differences between the power indices can be extreme. For example, in the United States legislative scheme with president P, 101 senators S (including the vice-president), and 435 House members H, the Shapley–Shubik power ratios of P to S to H are $870:4.3:1$, whereas the Banzhaf ratios are $27:2.1:1$. In the other direction, consider a corporation with one stockholder who holds 10 percent of the stock and a large "ocean" of small stockholders who hold the remaining 90 percent. The Shapley–Shubik index gives 11 percent of the power to the large stockholder [9]; the Banzhaf index gives close to 100 percent of the power to the large stockholder [4].

If the power indices can give such different results, it is important in applications to have criteria to decide which index is more applicable to a given situation. Most early discussions of the difference between the indices concentrated on the fact that Shapley and Shubik's "story" for their index involved the idea of winning coalitions forming in some order, whereas Banzhaf's justification focused only on the final winning coalition. Banzhaf himself characterized the difference as one of permutations versus combinations ([1], p. 331). Hence it seemed that the Shapley–Shubik index might be more applicable to legislative situations in which there is considerable communication among voters and coalition building is actively pursued. The Banzhaf index might be more applicable if coalition building was absent and only final votes were observable.

I argued in [13], and plan to argue here, that the permutation–combination distinction between the indices is illusory, because both indices can be derived from a simple probability model of voting in which order plays no part. The probability model will suggest that the important distinction between the indices has to do with the degree of statistical independence among the voters.

3   A probability model for the power indices

When an individual in a voting body considers his or her voting power, the most natural question to ask is, "What difference will my vote make?" Notice from the quotations in Section 1 that this question is the basis for both the Shapley–Shubik and Banzhaf power indices. Hence we will begin by defining voter i's power in a voting system to be the answer to his or her

Question of individual effect: What is the probability that my vote will affect the outcome of the vote on a bill? In other words, what is the probability that a bill will pass if I vote for it, but fail if I vote against it?

To answer this question, we need to specify a probability model for bills. Because we are concerned with how voters vote, we will characterize a bill by its *acceptability vector* $(p_1, \ldots, p_n)$, where n is the number of voters and $0 \leq p_k \leq 1$ is the probability that voter k will vote for a bill. Our problem is then to define a joint probability distribution for the p_k's. There are many ways in which this could be done, but at the level of abstraction suitable for power indices two possible assumptions have a claim to naturalness.

Independence assumption: Each p_k is chosen independently from the uniform distribution on $[0,1]$.

Homogeneity assumption: A number p is chosen from the uniform distribution on $[0,1]$, and $p_k = p$ for all k.

The Independence Assumption just says that voters behave independently of each other. In contrast, the Homogeneity Assumption says that voter decisions are correlated in a specific way. We could think of voters as judging bills by some uniform standard, and the number p as the bill's *acceptability level* by that standard. If there seemed to be reason to do so, the uniform distribution could be replaced by some other distribution in these definitions (see [14]). However, with the uniform distribution, we have

Theorem 1. The answer to voter i's Question of Individual Effect under the Homogeneity Assumption is given by voter i's Shapley–Shubik power index ϕ_i.

Theorem 2. The answer to voter i's Question of Individual Effect under the Independence Assumption is given by voter i's nonnormalized Banzhaf power index β_i'.

In other words, the Shapley–Shubik and Banzhaf power indices appear as answers to a natural probabilistic question about voter influence, under two different assumptions about the correlation of voters' votes for bills. In particular, the Shapley–Shubik power index is defined in a natural context in which there is no mention of the order in which voters declare support for a bill.

Proof of the theorems. Voter i's vote will affect the outcome on a bill exactly when i is a swing voter in some coalition S, all the other members of S vote for the bill, and all voters not in S vote against the bill. The probability that this will happen is

$$g_i(p_1, \ldots, p_n) = \sum_{i \text{ swings in } S} \prod_{j \in S-\{i\}} p_j \prod_{k \in N-S} 1 - p_k,$$

where N is the set of all voters. Notice that this polynomial in $p_1, \ldots, p_n$ does not involve p_i. The probability that voter i's vote will affect the outcome is independent of what that vote is.

Under the Independence Assumption, voter i's power is

$$\int_0^1 \int_0^1 \cdots \int_0^1 g_i(p_1, \ldots, p_n) \, dp_1 \cdots dp_n$$

$$= \sum_{i \text{ swings in } S} \prod_{j \in S-\{i\}} \int_0^1 p_j \, dp_j \prod_{k \in N-S} \int_0^1 1 - p_k \, dp_k$$

$$= \sum_{i \text{ swings in } S} \left(\frac{1}{2}\right)^{n-1} = \beta_i'.$$

Under the Homogeneity Assumption, voter i's power is

$$\int_0^1 g_i(p, \ldots, p) \, dp = \sum_{i \text{ swings in } S} \int_0^1 p^{s-1}(1-p)^{n-s} \, dp$$

$$= \sum_{i \text{ swings in } S} \frac{(s-1)!(n-s)!}{n!} = \phi_i.$$

The crucial equality in this second derivation is the beta function identity

$$\int_0^1 x^a (1-x)^b \, dx = \frac{a!b!}{(a+b+1)!}. \qquad \text{Q.E.D.}$$

For calculation purposes, it is convenient to define $f_i(p) = g_i(p, \ldots, p)$. I have called $f_i(p)$ voter i's *power polynomial* [13,15,16]. Then notice that

$$\phi_i = \int_0^1 f_i(p) \, dp \qquad \text{and} \qquad \beta_i' = f_i(\tfrac{1}{2})$$

(cf. Owen Chapter 10 this volume).

4   Examples and calculations

In the weighted voting game

$$[3;2,1,1]$$
$$A \, B \, C$$

the power polynomials are simple to compute. For example, B's vote will matter only if A votes yes (otherwise the bill would fail regardless of how B votes) and C votes no (otherwise, given A's yes vote, the bill would pass regardless of how B votes). Hence

$$f_B(p) = p(1-p) = p - p^2.$$
$$A \text{ yes}; C \text{ no}$$

Of course, C's power polynomial is the same as B's. A's vote will matter unless both B and C vote no, so

$$f_A(p) = 1 - (1-p)^2 = 2p - p^2$$

Integrating between 0 and 1 gives $\phi_A = \frac{2}{3}$, $\phi_B = \phi_C = \frac{1}{6}$. Evaluating at $p = \frac{1}{2}$ gives $\beta'_A = \frac{3}{4}$, $\beta'_B = \beta'_C = \frac{1}{4}$.

As voting games get larger, the power polynomials become more difficult to compute, but they remain reasonable to do by hand for medium-size games. For example, for Shapley and Shubik's nine-person legislative government the power polynomials are

$$f_P(p) = [3p^2(1-p) + p^3][10p^3(1-p)^2 + 5p^4(1-p) + p^5],$$
$$2 \text{ or } 3 \text{ S's yes}; \qquad 3, 4, \text{ or } 5 \text{ H's yes}$$

$$f_S(p) = p[2p(1-p)][10p^3(1-p)^2 + 5p^4(1-p) + p^5],$$
$$P \text{ yes; other S's split}; \quad 3, 4, \text{ or } 5 \text{ H's yes}$$

$$f_H(p) = p[3p^2(1-p) + p^3][6p^2(1-p)^2].$$
$$P \text{ yes; } 2 \text{ or } 3 \text{ S's yes}; \quad \text{other H's split}$$

You can check that integrating from 0 to 1 gives the Shapley–Shubik indices, and evaluating at $\frac{1}{2}$ gives the Banzhaf indices.

5 Implications for using the power indices

Many early applications of power indices were to questions of fairness at the constitutional level. Does a certain voting rule give each representative close to the amount of power to which that representative is entitled by some independent criterion? For example, power indices were used to analyze the fairness of voting methods in New York county boards [5], the U.S. electoral college (see [6]), and a proposed Canadian constitutional amendment scheme [7,13].

At this constitutional level, data about voting correlations may not be available, and it is arguable that it should not be used even if it is available. The fairness of the structure we design should not depend on the particular voters who will fill positions in that structure. As John Rawls might put it, formal justice should be designed behind a veil of ignorance. Neverthe-less, even at the constitutional level there may be philosophical indica-tions as to whether society is conceived of as a collection of individuals acting independently or as a group judging social welfare by common standards. To the extent there are such indications, the Banzhaf or Shapley–Shubik indices, respectively, would be more appropriate.

If we use power indices to analyze an existing voting body, we will have historical information available about patterns of voting in the body. Because members and preferences change over time, it would be inappro-priate to extrapolate historical information at too fine a level, but it may be possible to draw conclusions at the level of generality of the Independ-ence versus Homogencity Assumptions. For example, I argued in [13] that the Homogeneity Assumption, and hence the Shapley–Shubik index, is more appropriate for the United States legislative scheme and for voting in most corporations. On the other hand, the Independence As-sumption seems better to measure the spirit of voting among Canadian provinces. My point is that the level of generality of the Independence and Homogeneity Assumptions may match rather well the qualitative nature of political analyses of existing voting bodies.

There is another interesting possibility. At this level of generality, we might conclude that some groups of voters behave homogeneously among themselves but independently of other groups. This observation could be modeled in the framework of our probabilistic model by an appropriate *partial homogeneity* assumption, thus leading to a specifi-cally tailored power index combining features of both the Shapley–Shubik and Banzhaf indices.

6   Partial homogeneity assumptions: a political example

Suppose in Shapley and Shubik's PSSSHHHHH legislative system that there are two parties, Republican (R) and Democratic (D). As an approx-imation, let us suppose that the members of each party are homogeneous among themselves (in the sense of the Homogeneity Assumption) but vote independently of members of the other party. We can then calculate the power of voters in this system by answering the Question of Individual Effect with this partial homogeneity assumption. I will consider two cases.

In the first case, we suppose that the president is a Republican, but there are Democratic majorities in both legislative houses: Republicans PSHH; Democrats SSHHH. How much power does each type of voter have? The calculations involve double integrals of polynomials in p (the

Table 1. *(Nonnormalized) power indices for the Shapley–Shubik legislative example under different partial homogeneity assumptions.*

Type of voter	Rep. pres. Dem. major.	Rep. pres. Rep. major.	Homogeneous (ϕ)	Independent (β')
P	.350	.350	.381	.250
Republican S	.100	.162	.107	.125
Democratic S	.132	.100		
Republican H	.067	.108	.059	.094
Democratic H	.078	.073		

probability that a Republican will vote yes) and q (the probability that a Democrat will vote yes). For example, the power of a House Republican is

$$\int_0^1 \int_0^1 p[2pq(1 - q) + (1 - p)q^2 + pq^2](3pq(1 - q)^2$$
$$+ 3(1 - p)q^2(1 - q)]\ dp\ dq,$$

$$\text{P yes;} \qquad \text{2 or 3 S's yes;} \qquad \text{2 H's yes, 2H's no}$$

which works out to be 48/720 or .067. The complete results are given in the second column of Table 1.

In the second case, we suppose the president is still a Republican, but now the Republicans have a majority in both houses: Republicans PSSHHH; Democrats SHH. The partial homogeneity calculations are similar, and the results are given in column 3 of Table 1. For comparison, columns 4 and 5 give the Shapley–Shubik and nonnormalized Banzhaf indices. All figures in Table 1 can be interpreted directly as the probability that a voter of the given type will affect the outcome of voting on a bill, given the appropriate homogeneity–independence assumption.

One interesting observation from Table 1 is that, in accordance with intuition, congressmen in the majority party have more voting power than those in the minority party. This is true regardless of which party holds the presidency, but the gap is about twice as large if the president is a member of the majority party in congress. A congressman definitely gains power if his party captures the presidency.

On the other hand, notice that the president's voting power is not affected by which party has a majority in Congress. A president does *not* gain power if his party captures Congress. If this seems contrary to political intuition, it is nevertheless a direct consequence of our definition of power. The chance that the president's vote will matter is exactly the chance that a bill will pass both houses of Congress, and if we make only party-free assumptions about the distribution of bills to be voted on, this chance will be independent of which party has a majority.

One way to recover the element of ideological satisfaction – of liking the outcome of voting – is to ask, instead of the Question of Individual Effect, the

Question of group – individual agreement: What is the probability that the group decision on a bill will agree with my individual vote? In other words, what is the probability that I vote for a bill that passes, or vote against a bill that fails?

Answers to this question give indices that have been called *satisfaction indices.* They are related to power indices in interesting ways [2,14,17].

The next logical step in this kind of ideologizing of the classical power indices might be to introduce ideological opposition as well as, or in addition to, independence. In other words, have the Republicans be homogeneous among themselves and the Democrats homogeneous among themselves, but when Republicans vote for a bill with probability p, Democrats vote for it with probability $1 - p$. This kind of approach is analyzed in [17]. Alternative approaches are proposed in [8] and [11].

7   Other approaches to comparing the power indices

The Shapley–Shubik power index is a specialization to simple games of the Shapley value, which is characterized by Shapley's axioms. These axioms are attractive for general games in characteristic function form, and Shapley and Shubik [12] claimed that "any scheme for imputing power among the members of a committee system either yields the power index defined above [the Shapley–Shubik power index] or leads to a logical inconsistency." However, the key axiom for the Shapley value is the linearity axiom, and the sum of simple games is not always simple. Hence this axiomatic approach goes outside the class of simple games to justify an index that could well be considered only on that class, and the justification is correspondingly weakened.

In the 1970s Dubey clarified the situation by giving comparable axioms for the Shapley–Shubik and Banzhaf indices, entirely within the context of simple games [3,4,16]. Dubey's axiomatic approach is very elegant, but I believe that it is less effective than the probability approach in giving clear heuristic advice about which power index is applicable to which voting situations.

REFERENCES

1. Banzhaf, J. F., "Weighted voting doesn't work: a mathematical analysis," *Rutgers Law Review* 19 (1965), 317–43.
2. Brams, S. J. and M. Lake, "Power and satisfaction in a representative democracy," pp. 529–62 in P. Ordeshook, ed., *Game Theory and Political Science,* NYU Press, 1978.
3. Dubey, P., "On the uniqueness of the Shapley value," *International Journal of Game Theory* 4 (1975), 131–40.
4. Dubey, P. and L. S. Shapley, "Mathematical properties of the Banzhaf power index," *Mathematics of Operations Research* 4 (1979), 99–131.
5. Imrie, R. W., "The impact of the weighted vote on representation in municipal governing bodies in New York state," *Annals of the New York Academy of Sciences* 219 (1973), 192–9.
6. Lucas, W. F., "Measuring power in weighted voting systems," pp. 183–238 in Brams, S., Lucas, W., and Straffin, P., eds., *Political and Related Models,* Springer-Verlag, 1983.
7. Miller, D. R., "A Shapley value analysis of the proposed Canadian constitutional amendment scheme," *Canadian Journal of Political Science* 6 (1973), 140–43.
8. Owen, G., "Political Games," *Naval Research Logistics Quarterly* 18 (1971), 345–55.
9. Shapiro, N. Z. and L. S. Shapley, "Values of large games. I: a limit theorem," *Mathematics of Operations Research* 3 (1978), 1–9.
10. Shapley, L. S., "Simple games: an outline of the descriptive theory," *Behavioral Science* 7 (1962), 59–66.
11. "A comparison of power indices and a non-symmetric generalization," RAND Corporation, Santa Monica, Paper P-5872, 1977.
12. Shapley, L. S. and M. Shubik, "A method for evaluating the distribution of power in a committee system," *American Political Science Review* 48 (1954), 787–92.
13. Straffin, P. D., "Homogeneity, independence, and power indices," *Public Choice* 30 (1977), 107–18.
14. "Probability models for power indices," pp. 477–510 in P. Ordeshook, ed., *Game Theory and Political Science,* NYU Press, 1978.
15. "Using integrals to evaluate voting power," *Two-Year College Mathematics Journal* 10 (1979), 179–81.
16. "Power indices in politics," pp. 256–321 in Brams, Lucas, and Straffin, eds., *Political and Related Models,* Springer-Verlag, 1983.
17. Straffin, P. D., M. Davis, and S. Brams, "Power and satisfaction in an ideologically divided voting body," pp. 239–55 in M. Holler, ed., *Power, Voting, and Voting Power,* Physica-Verlag, 1981.

CHAPTER 6

Weighted Shapley values

Ehud Kalai and Dov Samet

1 Background and summary

One of the main axioms that characterizes the Shapley value is the axiom of symmetry. However, in many applications the assumption that, except for the parameters of the games the players are completely symmetric, seems unrealistic. Thus, the use of nonsymmetric generalizations of the Shapley value was proposed in such cases.

Weighted Shapley values were discussed in the original Shapley (1953a) Ph.D. dissertation. Owen (1968, 1972) studied weighted Shapley values through probabilistic approaches. Axiomatizations of nonsymmetric values were done by Weber (Chapter 7 this volume), Shapley (1981), Kalai and Samet (1987), and Hart and Mas-Colell (1987).

Consider, for example, a situation involving two players. If the two players cooperate in a joint project, they can generate a unit profit that is to be divided between them. On their own they can generate no profit. The Shapley value views this situation as being symmetric and would allocate the profit from cooperation equally between the two players. However, in some applications lack of symmetry may be present. It may be, for example, that for the project to succeed, a greater effort is needed on the part of player 1 than on the part of player 2. Another example arises in situations where player 1 represents a large constituency with many individuals and player 2's constituency is small (see, for example, Kalai 1977 and Thomson 1986). Other examples where lack of symmetry is present can easily be constructed for problems of cost allocations (see, for example, Shapley 1981). Also, lack of symmetry may arise when players have different bargaining abilities (see, for example, Roth 1977).

The family of weighted Shapley values was introduced by Shapley (1953a). Each weighted Shapley value associates a positive weight with each player. These weights are the proportions in which the players share in unanimity games. The symmetric Shapley value is the special case where all the weights are the same. The notion of "weights" was extended to "weight systems" by Kalai and Samet (1987), enabling a weight of zero for some players. In Section 2 the notion of the weighted Shapley value with a given weight system is defined and related to a procedure of dividend allocation that was proposed by Harsanyi (1959) (see also Owen 1982) for games without sidepayments. In Section 3 we give an equivalent definition of the weighted Shapley value by random orders, which generalizes the random-order approach to the symmetric Shapley value. In Section 4, following Kalai and Samet (1987), we give an axiomatic characterization of the family of weighted Shapley values – that is, we provide a list of properties of a solution that is satisfied only by weighted Shapley values.

Shapley (1981) also proposed a family of weighted cost allocation schemes and axiomatically characterized, for exogenously given weights, the schemes associated with these weights. This family of solutions is related to the weighted Shapley values by duality. In Section 5, following Kalai and Samet (1987), we illustrate the relationship between these two families, provide an axiomatization of the latter family (which does not use the weights explicitly in the axioms as Shapley's axioms do), and get as a result an axiomatization of the symmetric Shapley value that does not use the symmetry axiom.

Owen (1968, 1972, and Chapter 10 this volume) showed that weighted Shapley values can be computed by a "diagonal formula," providing another interpretation of the weights associated with the players. In Section 6 we present an extension due to Kalai and Samet (1987) of the diagonal formula for weight systems and cost allocation schemes.

Finally, we note that if one accepts the axioms in Section 4, one is obliged to use a weighted Shapley value, but no recommendation of the weights is implied by the axioms. The weights should be determined by considering such factors as bargaining ability, patience rates, or past experience. In Section 7, following Kalai and Samet (1987), we illustrate cases in which the "sizes" of the players (where the players themselves are groups of individuals) are appropriate weights for the players. It follows that any nonsymmetric solution (one satisfying the axioms in this chapter and leaving out the symmetry axiom) can always be mathematically viewed as being due to nonsymmetries in the size of the constituencies the players represent.

2   Weighted Shapley values

Let N be a finite set of n *players*. Subsets of N are called *coalitions*, and N is called the *grand coalition*. For each coalition S we denote by E^S the $|S|$-dimensional Euclidian space indexed by the players of S. A *game* v is a function that assigns to each coalition a real number and, in particular, $v(\varnothing) = 0$. The set of all games on N is denoted by Γ. Addition of two games v and w in Γ is defined by $(v + w)(S) = v(S) + w(S)$ for each S; multiplication of the game v by a scalar α is defined by $(\alpha v)(S) = \alpha v(S)$ for each coalition S. Thus Γ is a vector space. For each coalition S the *unanimity game of the coalition S, u_S,* is defined by $u_S(T) = 1$ if $T \supseteq S$ and $u_S(T) = 0$ otherwise. It is well known that the family of games $\{u_S\}_{S \subseteq N}$ is a basis for Γ.

The Shapley value ϕ is the linear function $\phi \colon \Gamma \to E^N$, which for each unanimity game u_S is defined by $\phi_i(u_S) = 1/|S|$ if $i \in S$ and $\phi_i(u_S) = 0$ otherwise. Intuitively, in the game u_S any coalition that contains S can split one unit between its members, and therefore players outside S do not contribute anything to the coalition they join. Hence, $\phi_i(u_S) = 0$ for $i \notin S$. The members of S, on the other hand, split equally the one unit between themselves. Since $\{u_S\}_{S \subseteq N}$ is a basis for Γ and ϕ is linear, ϕ is defined for all games. A weighted Shapley value generalizes the Shapley value by allowing different ways to split one unit between the members of S in u_S. We prescribe a vector of positive weights $\lambda = (\lambda_i)_{i \in N}$, and in each u_S players split proportionally to their weights. We want to allow some players to have weight zero. This means that if they split one unit with players who have positive weights, they get zero. But then we have to specify how these zero-weight players split a unit when no positive-weight players are present. This brings us to the following lexicographic definition of a weight system.

A *weight system* ω is a pair (λ, Σ), where $\lambda \in E^N_{++}$ (the strictly positive quadrant of E^N) and $\Sigma = (S_1, \ldots, S_m)$ is an ordered partition of N. A weight system $\omega = (\lambda, \Sigma)$ is called *simple* if $\Sigma = (N)$. The *weighted Shapley value with weight system ω* is the linear map $\phi_\omega \colon \Gamma \to E^N$, which is defined for each unanimity game u_S as follows.

Let $k = \max\{j | S_j \cap S \neq \varnothing\}$ and denote $\bar{S} = S \cap S_k$. Then

$$(\phi_\omega)_i(u_S) = \lambda_i \bigg/ \sum_{j \in \bar{S}} \lambda_j \qquad \text{for } i \in \bar{S},$$
$$= 0 \qquad\qquad\qquad \text{otherwise.}$$

In other words, the weights of players in S_i are 0 with respect to players in S_j with $j > i$. The positive weights of players in S_i are used only for games u_S such that no player from S_j with $j > i$ is in S. Observe that ϕ_ω is the (symmetric) Shapley value if and only if $\omega = (\lambda, (N))$ and λ is proportional to the vector $(1, 1, \ldots, 1)$.

Another computation procedure of $\phi_\omega(v)$ is along the lines proposed by Harsanyi (1959). In this procedure each coalition S allocates dividends to its members after all the proper subcoalitions of S have done it. The dividend allocation proceeds as follows. We first allocate to each player i his or her worth $v(\{i\})$. Suppose that all the coalitions of size k or less have already allocated dividends, and let S be a coalition of size $k + 1$. Denote by $z(S)$ the sum of the dividends that members of S were paid by proper subcoalitions of S. Then $v(S) - z(S)$ (which is possibly zero or negative) is the amount that S will allocate to its members. To determine how the amount is divided, we define the coalition $\bar{S}$ (which is a subset of S) as before. The members of $\bar{S}$ will divide $v(S) - z(S)$ in proportion to their weights, and the rest of the players in S get nothing. The total amount that each player accumulated at the end of the procedure (i.e., after N allocated its dividends) is exactly $(\phi_\omega)_i(v)$. To see this, one can easily prove by induction that if $v = \Sigma_{S \subseteq N} \alpha_S u_S$ then for each coalition S, $v(S) - z(S) = \alpha_S$, and the dividend allocation is therefore the allocation of the coefficients α_S in accordance with the definition of ϕ_ω.

A generalization of this procedure for the computation of the Shapley value was proposed by Maschler (1982). The same generalization applies also for ϕ_ω. We start by choosing any coalition S with $v(S) \neq 0$ and allocating $v(S)$ according to ω. In later steps of the computation, we choose for dividend allocation any S for which $v(S) - z(S) \neq 0$, where $z(S)$ is the sum of the dividends paid for the players in S by subcoalitions of S that already allocated dividends (notice that a coalition may be chosen several times in this procedure). The procedure ends when $v(S) - z(S) = 0$ for all the coalitions. The proof that such a procedure always terminates and gives ϕ_ω is the same as in Maschler (1982).

Harsanyi (1959) also defined a procedure of weighted dividend allocation for games without sidepayments. A family of solutions, called egalitarian, obtained by these procedures was axiomatized by Kalai and Samet (1985). It is shown there that the restriction of each egalitarian solution to games with sidepayments is a weighted Shapley value.

In the next section we provide a probabilistic approach to the weighted Shapley values, one that generalizes the probabilistic formula of the (symmetric) Shapley value.

3 Probabilistic definition of weighted Shapley values

Let $\mathbf{R}(S)$ denote the set of all orders R of players in the coalition S. For an order R in $\mathbf{R}(N)$ we denote by $B^{R,i}$ the set of players preceding i in R. For an ordered partition $\Sigma = (S_1, \ldots, S_m)$ of N, $\mathbf{R}_\Sigma$ is the set of orders of N in which all the players of S_i precede those of S_{i+1} for $i = 1, \ldots, m - 1$. Each R in $\mathbf{R}_\Sigma$ can be described as $R = (R_1, \ldots, R_m)$, where $R_i \in \mathbf{R}(S_i)$, $i = 1, \ldots, m$.

Let $|S| = s$ and let $\lambda \in E^S_{++}$. We associate with λ a probability distribution P_λ over $\mathbf{R}(S)$. For $R = (i_1, \ldots, i_s)$ in $\mathbf{R}(S)$, we define

$$P_\lambda(R) = \prod_{j=1}^{s} \lambda_{i_j} \bigg/ \sum_{k=1}^{j} \lambda_{i_k}.$$

One way to obtain this probability distribution is by arranging the players of S in an order, starting from the *end*, such that the probability of adding a player to the beginning of a partially created line is the ratio between the player's weight and the total weight of the players of S that are not yet in the line.

With each weight system $\omega = (\lambda, \Sigma)$, where $\Sigma = (S_1, \ldots, S_m)$, we associate a probability distribution P_ω over $\mathbf{R}(N)$ as follows. The distribution P_ω vanishes outside $\mathbf{R}_\Sigma$, and for $R = (R_1, \ldots, R_m)$ in $\mathbf{R}_\Sigma$, $P_\omega(R) = \Pi_{i=1}^{m} P_{\lambda_{S_i}}(R_i)$, where λ_{S_i} is the projection of λ on E^{S_i}.

For a given game v and order R in $\mathbf{R}(N)$ the *contribution* of player i is $C_i(v,R) = v(B^{R,i} \cup \{i\}) - v(B^{R,i})$. We now prove

Theorem 1. For each player $i \in N$, weight system ω, and game v,

$$(\phi_\omega)_i(v) = E_{P_\omega}(C_i(v, \cdot)),$$

where the right side is the expected contribution of player i with respect to the probability distribution P_ω.

Proof: We say that i is *last for S* in the order R if $i \in S$ and $S \subseteq B^{R,i} \cup \{i\}$. For a given order R and player i the coalition $N \setminus (B^{R,i} \cup \{i\})$ is called *the tail of i in R*. A coalition T is said to be a *tail for R* if for some i, T is a tail of i in R.

Let $\omega = (\lambda, (S_1, \ldots, S_m))$ be a weight system, and let S be a coalition. Now let $k = \max\{j | S \cap S_j \neq \varnothing\}$ and $\bar{S} = S \cap S_k$. We show that for each

$i \in S \backslash \bar{S}$, $P_\omega(i$ is last for $S) = 0$; for each $i \in \bar{S}$, $P_\omega(i$ is last for $S) > 0$; and for each $j, i \in \bar{S}$

$$\frac{P_\omega(i \text{ is last for } S)}{P_\omega(j \text{ is last for } S)} = \frac{\lambda_i}{\lambda_j}. \tag{*}$$

Indeed, if $i \in S \backslash \bar{S}$, then in order to be last for S, i must be preceded by players from S_k, which occurs with probability 0. Now suppose $i, j \in \bar{S}$. Let $A = (\cup_{t \geq k} S_t) \backslash S$. Then

$$\begin{aligned}
P_\omega(i \text{ is last for } S) &= \sum_{T \subseteq A} P_\omega(T \text{ is a tail of } i) \\
&= \sum_{T \subseteq A} P_\omega(T \text{ is a tail of } i | T \text{ is a tail}) P_\omega(T \text{ is a tail}) \\
&= \sum_{T \subseteq A} \lambda_i \left(1 \bigg/ \sum_{r \in S_k \backslash T} \lambda_r \right) P_\omega(T \text{ is a tail}) \\
&= \lambda_i h, \qquad \text{where } h \text{ is positive.}
\end{aligned}$$

Similarly, $P_\omega(j$ is last for $S) = \lambda_j h$, and (*) follows.

Now consider the game u_S. The contribution of $i \notin S$ is 0 in each order, and thus $E_{P_\omega}(C_i(u_S, \cdot)) = 0 = (\phi_\omega)(u_S)$. The contribution of $i \in S$ in the order R is 1 if i is last for S in R, and is 0 otherwise. If $i \in S \backslash \bar{S}$, then

$$E_{P_\omega}(C_i(u_S, \cdot)) = P_\omega(i \text{ is last for } S) = 0 = (\phi_\omega)_i(u_S).$$

If $i, j \in \bar{S}$, then

$$\frac{E_{P_\omega}(C_i(u_S, \cdot))}{E_{P_\omega}(C_j(u_S, \cdot))} = \frac{P_\omega(i \text{ is last for } S)}{P_\omega(j \text{ is last for } S)} = \frac{\lambda_i}{\lambda_j}.$$

But

$$\sum_{i \in N} E_{P_\omega}(C_i(u_S, \cdot)) = E_{P_\omega}\left(\sum_{i \in N} C_i(u_S, \cdot) \right) = E_{P_\omega}(1) = 1.$$

On the other hand, as we have shown,

$$\sum_{i \in N} E_{P_\omega}(C_i(u_S, \cdot)) = \sum_{i \in S} E_{P_\omega}(C_i(u_S, \cdot)),$$

and therefore for each $i \in \bar{S}$,

$$E_{P_\omega}(C_i(u_S, \cdot)) = \lambda_i \bigg/ \sum_{j \in \bar{S}} \lambda_j = (\phi_\omega)_i(u_S).$$

Clearly $E_{P_\omega}(C_i(v, \cdot))$ is a linear map from Γ to E and so is $(\phi_\omega)_i(v)$; therefore, because they coincide on the basis consisting of the unanimity games, they coincide on Γ.   Q.E.D.

4 An axiomatic characterization of the family of weighted Shapley values

A solution for Γ is a function ϕ from Γ to E^N. For a coalition S we denote by $\phi(v)(S)$ the sum $\Sigma_{i \in S}\phi_i(v)$. A coalition S is said to be a *partnership* in the game v if for each $T \subsetneq S$ and each $R \subseteq N\backslash S$, $v(R \cup T) = v(R)$.

Consider now the following axioms imposed on ϕ. For all games $v, w \in \Gamma$:

1. **Efficiency.** $\qquad\qquad\qquad\phi(v)(N) = v(N)$.

2. **Additivity.** $\qquad\qquad\qquad\phi(v + w) = \phi(v) + \phi(w)$.

3. **Positivity.** $\qquad\qquad\qquad$ If v is monotonic (i.e., $v(T) \geq v(S)$ for each T and S such that $T \supseteq S$), then $\phi(v) \geq 0$.

4. **Dummy Player.** $\qquad\qquad$ If i is a dummy player in the game v (i.e., for each S, $v(S \cup \{i\}) = v(S)$), then $\phi_i(v) = 0$.

5. **Partnership Consistency.** If S is a partnership in v, then $\phi_i(v) = \phi_i(\phi(v)(S)u_S)$, for each $i \in S$.

Axioms 1–4 are standard in various axiomatizations of the Shapley value. Axiom 5 expresses a consistency of ϕ in the following sense. Let S be a partnership in v. If we use ϕ to allocation $v(N)$, then the members of S receive together $\phi(v)(S)$. Suppose we want to reallocate $\phi(v)(S)$ among the members of S. Remembering that each proper subcoalition of S is powerless, we find it natural to allocate $\phi(v)(S)$ by applying ϕ to the game $\phi(v)(S)u_S$. Axiom 5 says that each player in S receives after the reallocation exactly what he or she received before. More recently, Hart and Mas-Colell (1987) strengthened Axiom 5 by requiring consistency of ϕ with respect to any coalition that is not necessarily a partnership. In their axiom, $\phi(v)(S)$ is reallocated by applying ϕ to a reduced game defined by v and S. We note that for a partnership this reduced game is just the unanimity game $\phi(v)(S)u_S$ used here in Axiom 5.

Theorem 2. A solution ϕ satisfies Axioms 1–5 if and only if there exists a weight system ω such that ϕ is the weighted Shapley value ϕ_ω.

Proof: We first show that for $\omega = (\lambda, (S_1, \ldots, S_m))$, ϕ_ω satisfies Axioms 1–5. To prove efficiency, we observe that for each v and R, $\Sigma_{i \in N} C_i(v, R) = v(N)$, and therefore

$$\phi_\omega(v)(N) = \sum_{i \in N} (\phi_\omega)_i (v) = \sum_{i \in N} E_{P_\omega}(C_i(v, \cdot)) = E_{P_\omega}\left(\sum_{i \in N} C_i(v, \cdot)\right)$$
$$= v(N).$$

The additivity of ϕ_ω follows from the additivity of E_{P_ω} and C_i. The positivity and the dummy player axioms also follow immediately. To check the partnership consistency axiom, assume that S is a partnership in a game v. Observe first that because S is a partnership, a player i in S makes a nonzero contribution in an order R only if i is last for S in R. Now let $k = \max\{j | S_j \cap S \neq \varnothing\}$, and let $\bar{S} = S \cap S_k$. For $i \in S \backslash \bar{S}$ the orders in which i is last for S have probability 0, so $(\phi_\omega)_i(v) = 0$. For $i \in \bar{S}$,

$$(\phi_\omega)_i(v) = E_{P_\omega}(C_i(v, \cdot))$$
$$= \sum_{T \subseteq N \backslash S} E_{P_\omega}(C_i(v, \cdot) | T \text{ is a tail of } i) P_\omega(T \text{ is a tail of } i).$$

But $E_{P_\omega}(C_i(v_j, \cdot) | T$ is a tail of $i)$ is the same for every $i \in \bar{S}$ because S is a partnership. Moreover, as shown in the proof of Theorem 1, $P_\omega(T$ is a tail of $i)$ is of the form $\lambda_i h(T)$, where $h(T)$ is the same for each $i \in S$.

Thus, there exists a constant K such that for every $i \in S$, $(\phi_\omega)_i(v) = \lambda_i K$, which shows that ϕ_ω satisfies the partnership consistency property.

Now let ϕ be a solution that satisfies Axioms 1–5, and we will show that for some weight system ω, $\phi = \phi_\omega$. We first define a weight system $\bar{\omega} = (\lambda, (\bar{S}_1, \ldots, \bar{S}_m))$ as follows. The coalition $\bar{S}_1$ contains all players i for which $\phi_i(u_N) \neq 0$ ($\bar{S}_1 \neq \varnothing$ because of the efficiency axiom). We define $\lambda_1 = \phi_i(u_N)$ for each $i \in \bar{S}_1$. Assuming that the coalitions $\bar{S}_1, \ldots, \bar{S}_k$ are already defined, then denote $T = N \backslash (\bar{S}_1 \cup \cdots \cup \bar{S}_k)$, let $\bar{S}_{k+1}$ contain all the players i for which $\phi_i(u_T) \neq 0$, and define $\lambda_i = \phi_i(u_T)$ for all $i \in \bar{S}_{k+1}$. ($\bar{S}_{k+1}$ is not empty because of the efficiency and dummy player axioms.) By the positivity axiom, $\lambda > 0$. Now for $i = 1, \ldots, m$ we define $S_i = \bar{S}_{m-i+1}$ and $\omega = (\lambda, (S_1, S_2, \ldots, S_m))$.

Next we show that ϕ is homogeneous; that is, $\phi(tv) = t\phi(v)$ for each game v and scalar t. Because every game is the difference of two monotonic games, it is enough, by the additivity axiom, to consider only monotonic games. Again by additivity, homogeneity follows for rational scalars. Let v be a monotonic game. Choose sequences of rationals $\{r_k\}$ and $\{s_k\}$ that converge to t from above and below, correspondingly. By the additivity and positivity axioms, $\phi(r_k v) - \phi(tv) = \phi((r_k - t)v) \geq 0$, and similarly $\phi(tv) - \phi(s_k v) \geq 0$. But $\phi(r_k v) - \phi(s_k v) = (r_k - s_k)\phi(v) \to 0$ as $k \to \infty$, and therefore $\phi(r_k v) \to \phi(tv)$ and $\phi(r_k v) = r_k\phi(v) \to t\phi(v)$, which proves the homogeneity of ϕ. Because both ϕ and ϕ_ω are linear maps on Γ, it suffices to show, as we do next, that ϕ and ϕ_ω coincide on each unanimity game.

For a unanimity game u_S define $k = \max\{j | S \cap S_j \neq \varnothing\}$, and let $\bar{S} = S \cap S_k$. Let $T = \cup_{j=1}^k S_j$. The coalition S is a partnership in u_T (as each subset of T is), and by the partnership axiom for each $i \in S$

$$\phi_i(u_T) = \phi_i(\phi(u_T)(S)u_S) = \phi(u_T)(S)\phi_i(u_S).$$

By the definition of T the only members of T who have nonzero payoffs in u_T are those of S_k; thus $\phi(u_T)(S) = \Sigma_{j \in \bar{S}}\lambda_j > 0$ and

$$\phi_i(u_S) = \phi_i(u_T) \Big/ \sum_{j \in \bar{S}} \lambda_j.$$

It follows that for $i \in \bar{S}$,

$$\phi_i(u_S) = \lambda_i \Big/ \sum_{j \in \bar{S}} \lambda_j,$$

and for $i \notin \bar{S}$, $\phi_i(u_S) = 0$; that is, $\phi(u_S) = (\phi_\omega)(u_S)$.   Q.E.D.

The family of all weighted Shapley values ϕ_ω for simple weight systems ω can also be characterized by slightly changing the positivity axiom. We now replace Axiom 3 by the following one.

3′. Positivity. If v is monotonic and has no dummy players, then $\phi(v) > 0$.

Theorem 3. A solution ϕ satisfies Axioms 1, 2, 3′, 4, and 5 if and only if there exists a simple weight system $\omega = (\lambda, (N))$ such that $\phi = \phi_\omega$.

Proof: If ω is a simple weight system, then for each order R in $\mathbf{R}(N)$, $P_\omega(R) > 0$. If v satisfies the condition of Axiom 3′, then for each player i, $C_i(v, \cdot) \geq 0$ and for some R, $C_i(v, R) > 0$, which shows that $\phi_\omega(v) > 0$.

The proof of the other direction is similar to the proof of Theorem 2. The only difference is that, because of Axiom 3′, $\phi(u_N) > 0$, so the partition built in the proof of Theorem 2 contains only N.   Q.E.D.

In the next theorem we show that weighted Shapley values can be approximated by simple weighted Shapley values.

Theorem 4. For each weight system $\omega = (\lambda,(S_1, \ldots ,S_m))$ there exists a sequence of simple weight systems $\omega^t = (\lambda^t,(N))$ such that for each game v, $\phi_{\omega^t}(v) \to \phi_\omega(v)$ as $t \to \infty$.

Proof: Let $0 < \epsilon < 1$ and define for each t, $1 \le l \le m$, and $i \in S_l$, $\lambda_i^t = \epsilon^{t(m-l+1)}\lambda_i$ and $\omega^t = (\lambda^t,(N))$. It is easy to see that for each S, $\phi_{\omega^t}(u_S) \to \phi(u_S)$, and, because ϕ_ω and ϕ_{ω^t} are linear, $\phi_{\omega^t}(v) \to \phi_\omega(v)$ for each v.

5   Duality

The dual of a game v, denoted by v^*, is defined by

$$v^*(S) = v(N) - v(N \backslash S) \qquad \text{for each } S \subseteq N.$$

The transformation $v \to v^*$ is a one-to-one linear map from Γ onto itself. In particular, the set $\{u_S^*\}_{S \subseteq N}$ is a basis for Γ. Observe that $u_S^*(T) = 0$ for each T with $T \cap S = \varnothing$, and $u_S^*(T) = 1$ if $T \cap S \neq \varnothing$. We call the game u_S^* the *representation game for the coalition S*. The game $-u_S^*$ has a natural interpretation as a cost game, where $u_S^*(T)$ is the cost incurred by T. The presence of any number of members of S in T incurs a unit cost (compare Shapley 1981). For a weight system $\omega = (\lambda,(S_1, \ldots ,S_m))$ we define a linear map $\phi_\omega^*: \Gamma \to R^N$ by defining ϕ_ω^* on the basis $\{u_S^*\}_{S \subseteq N}$ as follows. For a given S let $k = \max\{j|S_j \cap S \neq \varnothing\}$ and let $\bar{S} = S \cap S_k$. Then

$$(\phi_\omega^*)_i(u_S^*) = \lambda_i \bigg/ \sum_{j \in \bar{S}} \lambda_j \qquad \text{for } i \in \bar{S},$$
$$= 0 \qquad \text{if } i \notin \bar{S}.$$

An equivalent random-order approach is defined for ϕ_ω^*. For an order R we denote by R^* the reverse order. For a given probability distribution P over $\mathbf{R}(N)$ we define P^* by $P^*(R) = P(R^*)$. We now have the following equivalence.

Theorem 1*. For each player i, weight system ω, and game v,

$$(\phi_\omega^*)_i(v) = E_{P_\omega^*}(C_i(v, \cdot)).$$

The proof is analogous to the proof of Theorem 1, where the notion "i is last for S in R" is replaced by "i is first for S in R," which means $S \cap B^{R,i} = \varnothing$. The solutions ϕ_ω and ϕ_ω^* can be related in a simple way.

Theorem 5. For each game v and weight system ω,

$$\phi_\omega^*(v) = \phi_\omega(v^*).$$

Proof: Consider the game $v = u_S^*$. Then $v^* = (u_S^*)^* = u_S$, and by the definition of ϕ_ω and ϕ_ω^*, $\phi_\omega^*(v) = \phi_\omega(v^*)$. Now let $v = \Sigma_{S \subseteq N} \alpha_S u_S^*$. Then

$$\phi_\omega^*(v) = \sum_{S \subseteq N} \alpha_S \phi_\omega^*(u_S^*) = \sum_{S \subseteq N} \alpha_S \phi_\omega(u_S)$$

$$= \phi_\omega \left(\sum_{S \subseteq N} \alpha_S u_S \right) = \phi_\omega(v^*). \qquad \text{Q.E.D.}$$

An axiomatic characterization of the set $\{\phi_\omega^*\}$ is obtained by changing Axiom 5. We say that a coalition S is a *family* in the game v if for each $R \supset S$ and $T \subsetneq S$, $v(R \backslash T) = v(R)$. Here again, as in the case of a partnership, a family can be considered as one individual represented by several agents. But in the "family" case any nonempty subcoalition of agents has the same effect as the coalition of all agents, whereas in the "partnership" case all the proper subcoalitions of agents are powerless. Common to both families and partnerships is the fact that the inner coalitional structure of such coalitions is trivial. Axiom 5* is analogous to Axiom 5; it requires that if S is a family in the game v, then the profit shared by each member is the same as the member's profit would be when the family reallocates its total payoff, $\phi^*(v)(S)$, among itself. Clearly by the nature of the family this bargaining is represented by the game $\phi^*(v)(S)u_S^*$.

Axiom 5* (Family consistency). If S is a family in v, then $\phi_i(v) = \phi_i(\phi(v)(S)u_S^*)$ for each $i \in S$.

Theorem 2*. A solution ϕ satisfies Axioms 1 – 4 and 5* if and only if there exists a weight system ω such that $\phi = \phi_\omega^*$.

Theorem 3*. A solution ϕ satisfies Axioms 1, 2, 3', 4, and 5* if and only if there exists a simple weight system $\omega = (\lambda,(N))$ such that $\phi = \phi_\omega^*$.

The proofs are analogous to those of Theorems 2 and 3.

One might expect that ϕ_ω^* can be obtained from ϕ_ω by an appropriate transformation of the weight system. To see that this is not the case, we first examine simple weight systems.

Theorem 6. Let $|N| \geq 3$. If $\omega = (\mu,(N))$ and $\omega' = (\lambda,(N))$ are two simple weight systems and $\phi_\omega^*(v) = \phi_{\omega'}(v)$ for each game v, then both λ and μ are multiples of the vector $(1,1, \ldots ,1)$, so ϕ_ω^* and $\phi_{\omega'}$ are the Shapley values.

Proof: Assume $\phi_{\omega'} = \phi_\omega^*$. Then for any coalition $\{i,j\} \subseteq N$, $(\phi_{\omega'})_i(u_{(i,j)}) = (\phi_\omega^*)_i(u_{(i,j)})$. But

$$(\phi_{\omega'})_i(u_{(i,j)}) = \frac{\lambda_i}{\lambda_i + \lambda_j}$$

and

$$(\phi_\omega^*)_i(u_{(i,j)}) = (\phi_\omega)_i(u_{(i,j)}^*) = (\phi_\omega)_i(u_{(i)} + u_{(j)} - u_{(i,j)}) = \frac{\mu_j}{\mu_i + \mu_j}.$$

Therefore, for each i and j in N,

$$\frac{\lambda_i}{\lambda_i + \lambda_j} = \frac{\mu_j}{\mu_i + \mu_j},$$

from which we conclude that $\lambda_i\mu_i = \lambda_j\mu_j$ for each $i, j \in N$. It follows that there exists a positive number C for which $\lambda_i = C/\mu_i$ for each $i \in N$. Consider now a coalition $\{i,j,k\}$. We find that

$$(\phi_{\omega'})_i(u_{(i,j,k)}) = \frac{\lambda_i}{\lambda_i + \lambda_j + \lambda_k} = \frac{C/\mu_i}{C/\mu_i + C/\mu_j + C/\mu_k}$$

$$= \frac{\mu_j\mu_k}{\mu_j\mu_k + \mu_i\mu_j + \mu_i\mu_k}. \tag{1}$$

Using the probabilistic definition of ϕ_ω^*, we can compute

$$(\phi_\omega^*)_i(u_{(i,j,k)}) = \frac{\mu_k}{\mu_i + \mu_j + \mu_k}\frac{\mu_j}{\mu_i + \mu_j} + \frac{\mu_j}{\mu_i + \mu_j + \mu_k}\frac{\mu_k}{\mu_i + \mu_k}. \tag{2}$$

Equating expressions (1) and (2), dividing by $\mu_j\mu_k$, and multiplying by $\mu_i + \mu_j + \mu_k$, we find that

$$\frac{1}{\mu_i + \mu_j} + \frac{1}{\mu_i + \mu_k} = \frac{\mu_i + \mu_j + \mu_k}{\mu_j\mu_k + \mu_i\mu_j + \mu_i\mu_k}. \tag{3}$$

We can obtain an equation similar to (3) for $(\phi_{\omega'})_j$ and $(\phi_\omega^*)_j$ applied to the game $u_{(i,j,k)}$. By symmetry the right side of this equation will be the same as in (3), so by equating the left sides we get

$$\frac{1}{\mu_i + \mu_j} + \frac{1}{\mu_i + \mu_k} = \frac{1}{\mu_j + \mu_i} + \frac{1}{\mu_j + \mu_k}.$$

From that we conclude $\mu_i = \mu_j$ and therefore $\lambda_i = \lambda_j$. Because this is true for any $i, j \in N$, the proof is completed. Q.E.D.

In different words, Theorem 6 states that for $|N| \ge 3$, $\{\phi_\omega | \omega$ is simple$\} \cap \{\phi_\omega^* | \omega$ is simple$\} = \{$the Shapley value$\}$. From this theorem we can derive

Corollary 1. For $|N| \ge 3$, the only distribution common to the family of distributions $\{P_\omega\}$ and the family $\{P_\omega^*\}$, where ω ranges over all simple weight systems, is P_{ω_0}, where $\omega_0 = ((1, \ldots, 1), (N))$.

By Theorems 3, 3*, and 6, we characterize the (symmetric) Shapley value without using the symmetry axiom.

Theorem 7. For $|N| \ge 3$ a solution ϕ satisfies Axioms 1, 2, 3′, 4, 5, and 5* if and only if it is the Shapley value.

For $|N| = 2$ we have $\{\phi_\omega | \omega$ is simple$\} = \{\phi_\omega^* | \omega$ is simple$\}$; moreover, there exists a transformation $\omega \to \omega^*$ of simple weight systems such that $\phi_\omega^* = \phi_{\omega^*}$. Indeed, it is easy to see that if for $\omega = (\lambda, (N))$ we set $\omega^* = (\lambda^*, (N))$, where $\lambda^* = (\lambda_2, \lambda_1)$, then $\phi_\omega^* = \phi_{\omega^*}$. We now state the extension of Theorem 6 to general weight systems and omit the proof.

Theorem 8. If $\omega = (\mu, (S_1, \ldots, S_m))$ and $\omega' = (\lambda, (T_1, \ldots, T_k))$ are weight systems for which $\phi_\omega^* = \phi_{\omega'}$, then

(1) $m = k$.
(2) $S_i = T_{m+1-i}$ for $i = 1, \ldots, m$.
(3) If $|S_i| > 3$, then μ_{S_i} and $\lambda_{T_{m+1-i}}$ are proportional to $(1, 1, \ldots, 1)$.
(4) If $|S_i| = 2$, then μ_{S_i} is proportional to $\lambda_{T_{m+1-i}}^*$.

6   Other formulas for ϕ_ω and ϕ_ω^*

Owen (1972 and Chapter 10 this volume) has shown that $\phi_\omega(v)$ for $\omega = (\lambda, (N))$ can be computed as an integral of the gradient of the multilinear extension over some path. We now present a generalization of this result (Kalai and Samet 1987) for general weight systems and develop an integration formula for $\phi_\omega^*(v)$. The multilinear extension for a game v is the function F_v defined on the unit cube $[0, 1]^n$ as follows:

$$F_v(x_1, \ldots, x_n) = \sum_{S \subseteq N} \prod_{i \in S} x_i \prod_{j \notin S} (1 - x_j) v(S).$$

The coordinate x_i can be interpreted as the probability that player i will join the game to form a coalition, and $F_v(x_1, \ldots, x_n)$ is the expected payoff made. For a given $\omega = (\lambda, (S_1, \ldots, S_m))$ define for $i \in S_k$,

$$
\begin{aligned}
\xi_i(t) &= 0 && \text{if } t \le \frac{k-1}{m}, \\
&= \left[m \left(t - \frac{k-1}{m} \right) \right]^{\lambda_i} && \text{if } \frac{k-1}{m} \le t \le \frac{k}{m}, \\
&= 1 && \text{if } \frac{k}{m} \le t.
\end{aligned}
$$

Intuitively, $\xi_i(t)$ is the probability that player i will join the game until time t. One can prove that

$$
(\phi_\omega)_i(v) = \int_0^1 \left. \frac{\partial F_v}{\partial x_i} \right|_{\xi(t)} \frac{d\xi_i(t)}{dt} \, dt
$$

just by checking the equality for $v = u_S$, because the right side is linear in v (observe that $F_{u_S}(x) = \Pi_{i \in S} x_i$). It is easy to see that if the players' arrival time is distributed according to the ξ_i's, then the probability that they arrive in a certain order R is $P_\omega(R)$.

Now define F_v^* by

$$
F_v^*(x_1, \ldots, x_n) = v(N) - F_v(1 - x_1, \ldots, 1 - x_n).
$$

It is easy to check that $F_{v^*}(x) = F_v^*(x)$. Therefore

$$
(\phi_\omega^*)_i(v) = (\phi_\omega)_i(v^*) = \int_0^1 \left. \frac{\partial F_v^*}{\partial x_i} \right|_{\xi(t)} \frac{d\xi_i(t)}{dt} \, dt.
$$

Set $\eta_i(t) = 1 - \xi_i(t)$ and observe that

$$
\left. \frac{\partial F_v^*}{\partial x_i} \right|_{\xi(t)} = \left. \frac{\partial F_v}{\partial x_i} \right|_{\eta(t)} \quad \text{and} \quad \frac{d\xi_i}{dt} = -\frac{d\eta_i}{dt}.
$$

It follows that

$$
(\phi_\omega^*)_i(v) = \int_1^0 \left. \frac{\partial F_v}{\partial x_i} \right|_{\eta(t)} \frac{d\eta_i(t)}{dt} \, dt.
$$

$\eta_i(t)$ can be interpreted as the probability that player i arrives after time t.

7   Reduction of partnerships and families

Part of the reasoning of the partnership consistency axiom is that a coalition of partners can be treated in a certain sense as one individual. In this section, following Kalai and Samet (1987), we show how a partnership can be practically defined as one player, thereby reducing the size of the game. Let us fix a coalition S_0 with more than one player. Consider the set $\bar{N}$ that consists of all the players of N except that all the players in S_0 are replaced by a single player denoted by s; that is, $\bar{N} = (N \backslash S_0) \cup \{s\}$. For any game v on N we define a game $\bar{v}$ on $\bar{N}$ by $\bar{v}(S) = v(S)$ if $s \notin S$ and $\bar{v}(S) = v((S \backslash \{s\}) \cup S_0)$ if $s \in S$. Let $\omega = (\lambda, (S_1, \ldots, S_m))$ be a weight system for N, and let k be the highest index for which $S_k \cap S_0 \neq \varnothing$. The weight system $\bar{\omega} = (\bar{\lambda}, (\bar{S}_1, \ldots, \bar{S}_m))$ for $\bar{N}$ is defined as follows. For each $i \neq s$, $\bar{\lambda}_i = \lambda_i$ and $\bar{\lambda}_s = \Sigma_{i \in S_0} \lambda_i$. For each $j \neq k$, $\bar{S}_j = S_j \backslash S_0$ and $\bar{S}_k = (S_k \backslash S_0) \cup \{s\}$. We can now state

Theorem 9. If S_0 is a partnership in v, then for each $i \neq s$,

$$(\phi_{\bar{\omega}})_i(\bar{v}) = (\phi_\omega)_i(v) \quad \text{and} \quad (\phi_{\bar{\omega}})_s(\bar{v}) = \sum_{i \in S_0} (\phi_\omega)_i(v).$$

Similarly, if S_0 is a family, then for each $i \neq s$,

$$(\phi_{\bar{\omega}}^*)_i(\bar{v}) = (\phi_\omega^*)_i(v) \quad \text{and} \quad (\phi_{\bar{\omega}}^*)_s(\bar{v}) = \sum_{i \in S_0} (\phi_\omega^*)_i(v).$$

To prove this theorem we use the following lemmas.

Lemma 1. If i is a dummy player in v and $v = \Sigma_{S \subseteq N} \alpha_S u_S$, then $\alpha_S = 0$ for each S that contains i.

Proof: By induction on the size of S. For $S = \{i\}$, $0 = v(\{i\}) = \alpha_{\{i\}}$. Suppose we proved the lemma for all coalitions of size k that contain i, and let S be a coalition of size $k + 1$ such that $i \in S$. Then

$$0 = v(S) - v(S \backslash \{i\}) = \sum_{T \subseteq S} \alpha_T - \sum_{T \subseteq S \backslash i} \alpha_T = \sum_{i \in T \subseteq S} \alpha_T.$$

But for $i \in T \subsetneq S$, $\alpha_T = 0$, so $\alpha_S = 0$. Q.E.D.

Lemma 2. Let S_0 be a partnership in v, and let $v = \Sigma_{S \subseteq N} \alpha_S u_S$. Then $\alpha_S = 0$ for each S that satisfies $S \cap S_0 \neq \varnothing$ and $S \cap S_0 \neq S_0$.

Proof: For a coalition T and a game v denote by v^T the restriction of the game v to the coalition T. Because $v \to v^T$ is a linear map from the space of games on N to the space of games on T and because $u_S(T) = 0$ if $S \nsubseteq T$, it follows that

$$v^T = \sum_{S \subseteq N} \alpha_S u_S(T) = \sum_{S \subseteq T} \alpha_S u_S(T). \tag{*}$$

Now if T satisfies $T \cap S_0 \neq \emptyset$ and $T \cap S_0 \neq S_0$, then all the players of $T \cap S_0$ are dummies in the game v^T. In particular, we conclude by Lemma 1 and (*) that $\alpha_T = 0$.
Q.E.D.

Proof of Theorem 9: It can be easily shown by Lemma 2 that if $v = \Sigma \alpha_S u_S$, then

$$\bar{v} = \sum_{s \in S} \alpha_S \bar{u}_S + \sum_{s \notin S} \alpha_S \bar{u}_S.$$

When S_0 is a partnership, then by Lemma 2

$$v = \sum_{s \notin S} \alpha_S u_S + \sum_{s \in S} \alpha_S u_S.$$

Therefore for $i \neq s$,

$$(\phi_{\bar{\omega}})_i(\bar{v}) = \sum_{s \notin S} \frac{\bar{\lambda}_i}{\sum_{j \in S} \bar{\lambda}_j} \alpha_S + \sum_{s \in S} \frac{\bar{\lambda}_i}{\sum_{j \in S} \bar{\lambda}_j} \alpha_S$$

$$= \sum_{S \subseteq N \setminus S_0} \frac{\lambda_i}{\sum_{j \in S} \lambda_j} \alpha_S + \sum_{S \supseteq S_0} \frac{\lambda_i}{\sum_{j \in S} \lambda_j} \alpha_S = (\phi_\omega)_i(v).$$

For $i = s$,

$$(\phi_{\bar{\omega}})_s(\bar{v}) = \sum_{s \in S} \frac{\bar{\lambda}_s}{\sum_{j \in S} \bar{\lambda}_j} \alpha_S = \sum_{S \supseteq S_0} \frac{\sum_{i \in S_0} \lambda_i}{\sum_{j \in S} \lambda_j} \alpha_S = \sum_{i \in S_0} (\phi_\omega)_i(v).$$

Now if S_0 is a family in v, then S_0 is a partnership in v^*. To prove the second half of the theorem, we only observe that $(\bar{v})^* = \bar{v^*}$ and use the equality of Theorem 5.
Q.E.D.

The next corollary follows from Theorem 9. It is important for applications in which the players themselves are, or are representing, groups of individuals. Such is the case, for example, when the players are parties, cities, or management boards. The use of the symmetric Shapley value seems to be unjustified in certain cases of this type because the players represent constituencies of different sizes. A natural candidate for a solution is the weighted Shapley value, where the players are weighted by the size of the constituencies they stand for. The following corollary shows that such a procedure is justified whenever players represent constituencies as represented in games v_1 or v_2 as follows.

Corollary 2. Let v be a game on $N(|N| = n)$ in which each player i is a set of individuals M_i with m_i members. Consider the set of individuals $\overline{N} = \cup_{i \in N} M_i$ and the games v_1 and v_2 defined on $\overline{N}$ as follows. For each $S \subseteq \overline{N}$,

$$v_1(S) = v(\{i|M_i \subseteq S\}),$$

$$v_2(S) = v(\{i|M_i \cap S \neq \varnothing\}).$$

Let ω be the simple weight system $((m_1, \ldots, m_n), (\overline{N}))$. Then for each i,

$$(\phi_\omega)_i(v) = \phi(v_1)(M_i) \quad \text{and} \quad (\phi_\omega^*)_i(v) = \phi(v_2)(M_i),$$

where ϕ is the symmetric Shapley value.

REFERENCES

Harsanyi, J. C. [1959], "A Bargaining Model for Cooperative n-Person Games," in *Contributions to the Theory of Games* IV (Annals of Mathematics Studies 40), A. W. Tucker and R. D. Luce (eds.), pp. 325–55. Princeton: Princeton University Press.

Hart, S. and A. Mas-Colell [1987], "Potential, Value and Consistency," *Econometrica,* forthcoming.

Kalai, E. [1977], "Non-Symmetric Nash Solutions and Replications of 2-Person Bargaining," *International Journal of Game Theory,* Vol. 6, No. 3, pp. 129–33.

Kalai, E. and D. Samet [1985], "Monotonic Solutions to General Cooperative Games," *Econometrica,* Vol. 14, No. 11, pp. 307–327.

[1987], "On Weighted Shapley Values," *International Journal of Game Theory,* Vol. 16, Issue 3, pp. 205–22.

Maschler, M. [1982], "The Worth of a Cooperative Enterprise to Each Member," in *Games, Economic Dynamics and Time Series Analysis,* IHS-Studies No. 2, M. Deister, E. Furst and G. Schwodiauer (eds), pp. 67–73, Physica-Verlag.

Owen, G. [1968], "A Note on the Shapley Value," *Management Science,* Vol. 14, No. 11, pp. 731–2.

[1972], "Multilinear Extensions of Games, *Management Science,* Vol. 18, No. 5, pp. P64–P79.

[1982], *Game Theory,* 2nd Edition. New York: Academic Press.

Roth, A. E. [1977], "Bargaining Ability, the Utility of Playing a Game, and Models of Coalition Formation," *Journal of Mathematical Psychology,* Vol. 16, No. 2, pp. 153–60.

Shapley, L. S. [1953a], "Additive and Non-Additive Set Functions," Ph.D. Thesis, Department of Mathematics, Princeton University.

[1953b], "A Value for n-Person Games," in *Contributions to the Theory of Games* II (Annals of Mathematics Studies 28), H. W. Kuhn and A. W. Tucker (eds.), pp. 307–17. Princeton: Princeton University Press.

Shapley, L. S. [1981], "Discussant's Comment," in *Joint Cost Allocation,* S. Moriarity (ed.). Tulsa: University of Oklahoma Press.

Thomson, W. [1986], "Replication Invariance of Bargaining Solutions," *The International Journal of Game Theory,* Vol. 15, No. 1, pp. 59–63.

CHAPTER 7

Probabilistic values for games

Robert James Weber

1   Introduction

The study of methods for measuring the "value" of playing a particular role in an *n*-person game is motivated by several considerations. One is to determine an equitable distribution of the wealth available to the players through their participation in the game. Another is to help an individual assess his prospects from participation in the game.

When a method of valuation is used to determine equitable distributions, a natural defining property is "efficiency": The sum of the individual values should equal the total payoff achieved through the cooperation of all the players. However, when the players of a game individually assess their positions in the game, there is no reason to suppose that these assessments (which may depend on subjective or private information) will be jointly efficient.

This chapter presents an axiomatic development of values for games involving a fixed finite set of players. We primarily seek methods for evaluating the prospects of individual players, and our results center around the class of "probabilistic" values (defined in the next section). In the process of obtaining our results, we examine the role played by each of the Shapley axioms in restricting the set of value functions under consideration, and we trace in detail (with occasional excursions) the logical path leading to the Shapley value.

The research reported in this paper was supported by grant NOOO14-77-C-0518 from the Office of Naval Research and by grant SOC77-27401 from the National Science Foundation.
The beneficial influence of conversations (and friendships) with Pradeep Dubey and with Lloyd Shapley is gratefully acknowledged.

101

2   Definitions and notation

For our purposes, we fix a particular set $N = \{1,2, \ldots ,n\}$ of *players*. The collection of *coalitions* (subsets) in N is denoted by 2^N. A *game* on N is a real-valued function $v: 2^N \to R$ that assigns a "worth" to each coalition and satisfies $v(\varnothing) = 0$. Let $\mathscr{G}$ be the collection of all games on N (note that $\mathscr{G}$ is a $(2^n - 1)$-dimensional vector space), and let v be any game in $\mathscr{G}$. The game v is *monotonic* if $v(S) \geqq v(T)$ for all $S \supset T$; v is *superadditive* if $v(S \cup T) \geqq v(S) + v(T)$ whenever $S \cap T = \varnothing$. The class of all monotonic games is denoted by $\mathscr{M}$, and the class of all superadditive games by $\mathscr{S}$. For future reference, note that $\mathscr{M}$ and $\mathscr{S}$ are cones in $\mathscr{G}$; that is, each is closed under addition, and under multiplication by nonnegative real numbers. Also note that neither class contains the other.

(The *zero-normalization* of a game v is the game $v_{(z)}$, defined for all $T \subset N$ by $v_{(z)}(T) = v(T) - \Sigma_{i \in T} v(i)$. The game v is *zero-monotonic* if $v_{(z)}$ is monotonic. The class of all zero-monotonic games is denoted by $\mathscr{Z}$. Every superadditive game is zero-monotonic; however, neither $\mathscr{M}$ nor $\mathscr{Z}$ contains the other. In this chapter we obtain results for the class $\mathscr{S}$ of superadditive games. All of these results can also be obtained for the class $\mathscr{Z}$.)

If the game v takes only the values 0 and 1, then v is *simple*. If $v(S) = 1$, then S is a *winning coalition;* otherwise S is a *losing coalition*. $\mathscr{G}^*, \mathscr{M}^*$, and $\mathscr{S}^*$ denote, respectively, the classes of all simple games on N, those which are monotonic, and those which are superadditive. For simple games, superadditivity implies monotonicity; hence, $\mathscr{M}^* \supset \mathscr{S}^*$. (Some authors prefer to restrict the term *simple game* to elements of $\mathscr{M}^*$; the more general games $\mathscr{G}^*$ are then called *0-1 games*.)

Two special types of games play an important role in our work. For any nonempty coalition T, let v_T be defined by $v_T(S) = 1$ if $S \supset T$, and 0 otherwise. Also, let $\hat{v}_T$ be defined by $\hat{v}_T(S) = 1$ if $S \supsetneqq T$, and 0 otherwise. Let $\mathscr{C} = \{v_T : \varnothing \neq T \subset N\}$ and $\hat{\mathscr{C}} = \{\hat{v}_T : \varnothing \neq T \subset N\}$. Every game in $\mathscr{C}$ or $\hat{\mathscr{C}}$ is monotonic, superadditive, and simple. We shall occasionally refer to the game $\hat{v}_\varnothing$ defined by $\hat{v}_\varnothing(S) = 1$ for all nonempty coalitions S. This game is monotonic and simple but not superadditive.

For any collection $\mathscr{T} \subset \mathscr{G}$ of games and for any player $i \in N$, a *value* for i on $\mathscr{T}$ is a function $\phi_i : \mathscr{T} \to R$. As we have previously indicated, the value $\phi_i(v)$ of a particular game v represents an assessment by i of his or her prospects from playing the game. This definition stands somewhat in contrast to the more traditional definition of a *group value* $\phi = (\phi_1, \phi_2, \ldots, \phi_n)$, which associates an n-vector with each game. The construction of group values from our individual values will be treated later in the chapter.

Fix a player i, and let $\{p_T^i: T \subset N \backslash i\}$ be a probability distribution over the collection of coalitions not containing i. (We shall often omit the braces when writing one-player coalitions such as $\{i\}$.) A value ϕ_i for i on $\mathcal{T}$ is a *probabilistic value* if, for every $v \in \mathcal{T}$,

$$\phi_i(v) = \sum_{T \subset N \backslash i} p_T^i [v(T \cup i) - v(T)].$$

Let i view his participation in a game as consisting merely of joining some coalition S, and then receiving as a reward his marginal contribution $v(S \cup i) - v(S)$ to the coalition. If, for each $T \subset N \backslash i$, p_T^i is the (subjective) probability that he joins coalition T, then $\phi_i(v)$ is simply his expected payoff from the game.

Both the Shapley and Banzhaf values are instances of probabilistic values. The *Banzhaf value* (for an individual player i) arises from the subjective belief that the player is equally likely to join any coalition; that is, $p_T^i = 1/2^{n-1}$ for all $T \subset N \backslash i$. The *Shapley value* arises from the belief that the coalition he joins is equally likely to be of any size t ($0 \leq t \leq n - 1$) and that all coalitions of size t are equally likely; that is,

$$p_T^i = \frac{1}{n} \binom{n-1}{t}^{-1} = \frac{t!(n-t-1)!}{n!} \qquad \text{for all } T \subset N \backslash i,$$

where $t = |T|$.

In the following sections, we investigate several reasonable conditions that a value might be expected to satisfy. We will find that the only values that satisfy these conditions are closely related to probabilistic values.

3   The linearity and dummy axioms

Given a game v and any constant $c > 0$, consider the game cv defined by $(cv)(S) = c \cdot v(S)$ for all $S \subset N$. It seems reasonable to assume that such a rescaling of the original game would simply rescale a player's assessment of his prospects from playing the game. Similarly, let v and w be games and consider the game $v + w$ defined by $(v + w)(S) = v(S) + w(S)$ for all $S \subset N$. A rational player, facing the latter game, might well consider his prospective gain to be the sum of his prospective gains from the two original games.

Consider a cone $\mathcal{T}$ of games in $\mathcal{G}$. A *linear function* on $\mathcal{T}$ is a function $f: \mathcal{T} \to R$ satisfying $f(v + w) = f(v) + f(w)$ and $f(cv) = c \cdot f(v)$ for all $v, w \in \mathcal{T}$ and $c > 0$. Let ϕ_i be a value for i on $\mathcal{T}$. The preceding comments are reflected in the following criterion.

Linearity axiom. ϕ_i is a linear function on $\mathcal{T}$.

Because $\mathcal{G}, \mathcal{M}$, and $\mathcal{S}$ are all cones in $\mathcal{G}$, the following theorem applies to a value on any of these domains.

Theorem 1. Let ϕ_i be a value for i on a cone $\mathcal{T}$ of games. Assume that ϕ_i satisfies the linearity axiom. Then there is a collection of constants $\{a_T: T \subset N\}$ such that for all $v \in \mathcal{T}$,

$$\phi_i(v) = \sum_{T \subset N} a_T v(T).$$

Proof: ϕ_i has a unique linear extension to the linear subspace $\mathcal{L} \subset \mathcal{G}$ spanned by $\mathcal{T}$. We can, in turn, extend this extension to a linear function ϕ_i^{ext} on all of $\mathcal{G}$, by defining ϕ_i^{ext} arbitrarily on a basis of the orthogonal complement of $\mathcal{L}$. For any nonempty $T \subset N$, define the game w_T by $w_T(S) = 1$ if $S = T$, and 0 otherwise. Then $\{w_T: \varnothing \neq T \subset N\}$ is a basis for $\mathcal{G}$, and ϕ_i^{ext} is uniquely determined by its values on this basis. Any $v \in \mathcal{G}$ can be written as $v = \Sigma_{\varnothing \neq T \subset N} v(T) w_T$; because ϕ_i^{ext} is linear,

$$\phi_i^{\text{ext}}(v) = \sum_{\varnothing \neq T \subset N} v(T) \phi_i^{\text{ext}}(w_T).$$

However, ϕ_i is simply the restriction of ϕ_i^{ext} to $\mathcal{T}$. Therefore, upon taking $a_T = \phi_i^{\text{ext}}(w_T)$ for all nonempty $T \subset N$, and defining $a_\varnothing$ arbitrarily, we obtain the desired result. $\square$

A player i is a *dummy* in the game v if $v(S \cup i) = v(S) + v(i)$ for every $S \subset N \backslash i$. This terminology derives from the observation that such a player has no meaningful strategic role in the game; no matter what the situation, he contributes precisely $v(i)$. Therefore, the following criterion seems reasonable. Let ϕ_i be a value for i on a collection $\mathcal{T}$ of games.

Dummy axiom. If i is a dummy in $v \in \mathcal{T}$, then $\phi_i(v) = v(i)$.

This axiom actually has two aspects. While specifying the prospective gain of a dummy in a game v, it implicitly states that ϕ_i and v are measured in common units, under a common normalization. These aspects are exploited separately in the proof of the following result. Recall that $\mathcal{C}$ denotes the collection $\{^v T\}$.

Theorem 2. Let ϕ_i be a value for i on a collection $\mathcal{T}$ of games, defined by $\phi_i(v) = \Sigma_{T \subset N} a_T v(T)$ for every $v \in \mathcal{T}$. Assume that ϕ_i satisfies the dummy axiom and that $\mathcal{T}$ contains $\mathscr{C}$. Then there is a collection of constants $\{p_T: T \subset N\backslash i\}$ satisfying $\Sigma_{T \subset N\backslash i} p_T = 1$ such that for every $v \in \mathcal{T}$,

$$\phi_i(v) = \sum_{T \subset N/i} p_T[v(T \cup i) - v(T)].$$

Proof: First, note that for any nonempty $T \subset N\backslash i$, player i is a dummy in $v_T \in \mathscr{C}$. Therefore, $\phi_i(v_T) = v_T(i) = 0$. It follows that $\phi_i(v_{N\backslash i}) = a_N + a_{N\backslash i} = 0$. For inductive purposes, assume it has been shown that $a_{T \cup i} + a_T = 0$ for every $T \subset N\backslash i$ with $|T| \geq k \geq 2$. (The case $k = n - 1$ has just been established.) Take any fixed $S \subset N\backslash i$ with $|S| = k - 1$. Then

$$\phi_i(v_S) = \sum_{T \supset S} a_T = \sum_{\substack{T \subset N\backslash i \\ T \supsetneq S}} (a_{T \cup i} + a_T) + (a_{S \cup i} + a_S)$$

$$= a_{S \cup i} + a_S = 0;$$

the next-to-last equality follows from the induction hypothesis, and the last follows from the dummy axiom.

Therefore, $a_{T \cup i} + a_T = 0$ for all $T \subset N\backslash i$ with $0 < |T| \leq n - 1$. For every such T, define $p_T = a_{T \cup i} = -a_T$. Also, define $p_\varnothing = a_i$. Then for every $v \in \mathcal{T}$,

$$\phi_i(v) = \sum_{T \subset N} a_T v(T) = \sum_{T \subset N\backslash i} p_T[v(T \cup i) - v(T)].$$

Consider $v_i \in \mathscr{C}$. Player i is a dummy in this game; indeed, every player is a dummy in v_i. Therefore, $\phi_i(v_i) = v_i(i) = 1$. But, since $v_i(T \cup i) - v_i(T) = 1$ for every $T \subset N\backslash i$, the expression in the preceding paragraph yields $\phi_i(v_i) = \Sigma_{T \subset N\backslash i} p_T.$ $\square$

When this theorem is taken in conjunction with the preceding one, we obtain the following result.

Theorem 3. Let ϕ_i be a value for i on $\mathscr{G}$, $\mathscr{M}$, or $\mathscr{S}$. Assume that ϕ_i satisfies the linearity and dummy axioms. Then there is a collection of constants $\{p_T: T \subset N\backslash i\}$ satisfying $\Sigma_{T \subset N\backslash i} p_T = 1$ such that for every game v in the domain of ϕ_i,

$$\phi_i(v) = \sum_{T \subset N\backslash i} p_T[v(T \cup i) - v(T)].$$

4   The monotonicity axiom

Let v be any monotonic game. A player i facing the prospect of playing this game may be uncertain concerning his eventual payoff. However, for every $T \subset N \setminus i$, $v(T \cup i) - v(T) \geqq 0$; therefore player i knows at least that his presence will never "hurt" a coalition. This motivates the following criterion. Let ϕ_i be a value for i on a collection $\mathscr{T}$ of games.

Monotonicity axiom. If $v \in \mathscr{T}$ is monotonic, then $\phi_i(v) \geqq 0$.

The following proposition will be of value.

Proposition. Let ϕ_i be a value for i on a collection $\mathscr{T}$ of games. Assume that there is a collection of constants $\{p_T : T \subset N \setminus i\}$ such that for all $v \in \mathscr{T}$,

$$\phi_i(v) = \sum_{T \subset N \setminus i} p_T[v(T \cup i) - v(T)].$$

Further assume that $\mathscr{T}$ contains the game $\hat{v}_T$ for some $T \subset N \setminus i$ (note that T may be empty), and assume that ϕ_i satisfies the monotonicity axiom. Then $p_T \geqq 0$.

Proof: The game $\hat{v}_T$ is monotonic. Therefore, $\phi_i(\hat{v}_T) = p_T \geqq 0$. $\square$

The collections of games $\mathscr{G}$ and $\mathscr{M}$ contain both $\hat{\mathscr{C}}$ and $\hat{v}_\varnothing$. On the other hand, $\mathscr{S}$ contains $\hat{\mathscr{C}}$ but not $\hat{v}_\varnothing$. Therefore, we have the following theorems.

Theorem 4. Let ϕ_i be a value for i on $\mathscr{G}$ or $\mathscr{M}$. Assume that ϕ_i satisfies the linearity, dummy, and monotonicity axioms. Then ϕ_i is a probabilistic value. Furthermore, every probabilistic value on $\mathscr{G}$ or $\mathscr{M}$ satisfies these three axioms.

Theorem 5. Let ϕ_i be a value for i on $\mathscr{S}$. Assume that ϕ_i satisfies the linearity, dummy, and monotonicity axioms. Then there is a collection of constants $\{p_T : T \subset N \setminus i\}$ satisfying $\sum_{T \subset N \setminus i} p_T = 1$ and $p_T \geqq 0$ for all nonempty $T \subset N \setminus i$, such that for every game $v \in \mathscr{S}$,

$$\phi_i(v) = \sum_{T \subset N \setminus i} p_T[v(T \cup i) - v(T)].$$

Furthermore, every such value on $\mathscr{S}$ satisfies these three axioms.

For values on $\mathscr{G}$ or $\mathscr{M}$ we thus have a natural axiomatic characterization of the probabilistic values. However, for values on $\mathscr{S}$ we are unable to rule out the possibility that $p_\varnothing < 0$. This phenomenon is investigated in the next section.

5 Values for superadditive games

It is natural to seek an explanation of the preceding results. A value for a class of games yields a relative evaluation of one's prospects from playing the various games. If the class of games is sufficiently rich, the only evaluation functions satisfying certain reasonable criteria are the probabilistic values. Why, if one's consideration is restricted solely to superadditive games, does the class of reasonable evaluation functions broaden in the indicated manner? We shall attempt to provide a rationale.

Consider any particular game v. A player i faced with the prospect of playing this game may seek to determine the amount of gain that he is "guaranteed," in the sense that he contributes at least this amount to any coalition that he joins. When v is superadditive, this "floor" to his expectation is precisely $v(i)$, because $v(T \cup i) - v(T) \geq v(i)$ for all $T \subset N \setminus i$ (and because when $T = \varnothing$, his marginal contribution is exactly $v(i)$). Taking this amount as ensured, the player will then strive to achieve as great a reward as he can in the new game $v^{(i)}$ defined by

$$v^{(i)}(S) = \begin{cases} v(S) & \text{if } i \notin S, \\ v(S) - v(i) & \text{otherwise.} \end{cases}$$

(This is the game that he perceives himself to be playing after having mentally "withdrawn" the amount $v(i)$ from the original game.) However, any gain from this new game is uncertain and depends upon factors such as the bargaining ability of the player. Hence, the two amounts under consideration, $v(i)$ and his gain from playing $v^{(i)}$, are measured respectively in "certain" and "uncertain" units.

Assume that the player's attitude toward risk is such that 1 unit of uncertain gain is worth γ units of certain gain to him. (Hence, $\gamma < 1$ corresponds to risk aversion, and $\gamma = 1$ to risk neutrality.) Further assume that he evaluates his prospects from any game v with $v(i) = 0$ in terms of a probabilistic value $\phi_i(v)$. Then his evaluation of any superadditive game v, expressed in units of certain gain, will be

$$\xi_i(v) = \gamma \phi_i(v^{(i)}) + v(i).$$

One would expect an aversion to risk to limit a player's options. That such is the case is the impact of the next theorem. Let P be the set of probabilistic values on $\mathscr{S}$, and for any $\gamma \geq 0$ let $V(\gamma) = \{\xi_i : \xi_i$ is a value on $\mathscr{S}$, and for some $\phi_i \in P$, $\xi_i(v) = \gamma \phi_i(v^{(i)}) + v(i)$ for all $v \in \mathscr{S}\}$. This is the set of all evaluation functions on $\mathscr{S}$ arising from the considerations discussed previously, when γ represents player i's attitude toward uncertain gain.

Theorem 6. A value ξ_i on $\mathscr{S}$ satisfies the linearity, dummy, and monotonicity axioms if and only if $\xi_i \in V = \cup_{\gamma \geqq 0} V(\gamma)$. If $0 \leqq \gamma' < \gamma$, then $V(\gamma') \subsetneqq V(\gamma)$. Furthermore, $V(1) = P$.

Proof: Let ξ_i satisfy the indicated axioms on $\mathscr{S}$. Then ξ_i is associated with a collection $\{p_T^i : T \subset N \backslash i\}$ of constants, as in Theorem 5. Let $\gamma = 1 - p_\varnothing^i \geqq 0$. If $\gamma > 0$, define the probability distribution $\{q_T^i : T \subset N \backslash i\}$ by $q_T^i = p_T^i / \gamma$ if $T \neq \varnothing$, and $q_\varnothing^i = 0$; if $\gamma = 0$, take any probability distribution $\{q_T^i\}$. Then if ϕ_i is the probabilistic value associated with $\{q_T^i\}$, $\xi_i(v) = \gamma \phi_i(v^{(i)}) + v(i)$ for all $v \in \mathscr{S}$. Hence, $\xi_i \in V(\gamma) \subset V$.

Conversely, it is easily verified that any $\xi_i \in V$ satisfies the axioms on $\mathscr{S}$. (It is essential to this verification that, for every monotonic $v \in \mathscr{S}$, $v^{(i)}$ is a monotonic game; hence $\xi_i(v) = \gamma \phi_i(v^{(i)}) + v(i) \geqq v(i) \geqq 0$.)

If $0 \leqq \gamma' < \gamma$, then any $\xi_i \in V(\gamma')$ corresponds to some $\phi_i' \in P$, which is in turn associated with a probability distribution $\{p_T : T \subset N \backslash i\}$. But then let $\phi_i \in P$ be associated with the probability distribution $\{q_T : T \subset N \backslash i\}$, where $q_T = (\gamma'/\gamma)p_T$ for all nonempty $T \subset N \backslash i$ and $q_\varnothing = 1 - \Sigma_{T \neq \varnothing} q_T$. It follows that $\xi_i(v) = \gamma \phi_i(v^{(i)}) + v(i)$ for all $v \in \mathscr{S}$, so $\xi_i \in V(\gamma)$. Hence, $V(\gamma') \subset V(\gamma)$.

Consider any probability distribution $\{p_T : T \subset N \backslash i\}$ such that $p_\varnothing = 0$. Then if ϕ_i is the associated probabilistic value on $\mathscr{S}$, $\xi_i(v) = \gamma \phi_i(v^{(i)}) + v(i)$ defines a value $\xi_i \in V(\gamma)$ that is not in $V(\gamma')$ for any $\gamma' < \gamma$. Hence the indicated containment is strict.

Finally, observe that when $\gamma = 1$, every value ξ_i in $V(\gamma) = V(1)$ is of the form

$$
\begin{aligned}
\xi_i(v) &= \phi_i(v^{(i)}) + v(i) \\
&= \left\{ \sum_{T \subset N \backslash i} p_T[v(T \cup i) - v(i) - v(T)] \right\} + v(i) \\
&= \sum_{T \subset N \backslash i} p_T[v(T \cup i) - v(T)] \\
&= \phi_i(v);
\end{aligned}
$$

so $V(1) = P$. $\square$

This theorem can be viewed in several ways. One might ask whether the addition of some other natural axiom will lead to the conclusion that $p_\varnothing \geqq 0$. For example, it has been suggested by Milnor (1952) that it is unreasonable for any player $i \in N$ to hope to attain more than $b_i(v) = \max_{S \subset N \setminus i}[v(S \cup i) - v(S)]$. If we require that $\phi_i(v) \leqq b_i(v)$ for all $v \in \mathcal{S}$, then

$$\phi_i(\hat{v}_{(i)}) = \sum_{\varnothing \neq T \subset N \setminus i} p_T = 1 - p_\varnothing \leqq b_i(\hat{v}_{(i)}) = 1.$$

Hence, $p_\varnothing \geqq 0$.

Another point of view is that, if a player wishes to evaluate his prospects from superadditive games, he can satisfy our criteria of rationality while still basing his evaluation in part on his posture toward risk. However, these same criteria, when applied to the evaluation of broader classes of games, force the player into a posture of risk neutrality.

6 Values for simple games

Simple games, particularly those which are monotonic, are often used to represent political situations. A value for a player may then indicate the player's perceived political power in any situation. Under this interpretation, the dummy and monotonicity axioms remain reasonable. However, the linearity axiom does not seem to apply; indeed, the sum of simple games is generally not simple.

An alternative axiom has been suggested by Dubey (1975) (see Roth Chapter 4 this volume). For any games v and w, define $v \vee w$ by $(v \vee w)(S) = \max(v(S), w(S))$ and $v \wedge w$ by $(v \wedge w)(S) = \min(v(S), w(S))$ for all $S \subset N$. If v and w are simple, then $v \vee w$ and $v \wedge w$ are also simple. A coalition is winning in $v \vee w$ if it wins in either v or w; it is winning in $v \wedge w$ if it wins in both. Therefore, each coalition wins as often in v and w together as it does in $v \vee w$ and $v \wedge w$ together. Let ϕ_i be a value for i on a collection $\mathcal{T}$ of games.

Transfer axiom. If v, w, $v \vee w$, and $v \wedge w$ are all in $\mathcal{T}$, then $\phi_i(v) + \phi_i(w) = \phi_i(v \vee w) + \phi_i(v \wedge w)$.

The name of this axiom is motivated by the following observation. The game $v \wedge w$ arises from v when all of the coalitions that win only in v are made losing; $v \vee w$ arises from w when these same coalitions are made winning. Hence, $v \wedge w$ and $v \vee w$ arise from v and w when winning coalitions are "transferred" from one game to the other.

We require several definitions. Let v be a simple game. A *minimal winning coalition* in v is a winning coalition with no proper subsets that are also winning; a *hole* in v is a losing coalition with a winning subset. Note that the monotonic simple games are precisely those without holes.

Let $\mathcal{T}$ be a collection of simple games, and let v be any game in $\mathcal{T}$. We define two types of operations that can be performed on v. Let T be a minimal winning coalition in v. Define the game v^{-T} by $v^{-T}(S) = v(S)$ for all $S \neq T$, with $v^{-T}(T) = 0$; v^{-T} arises from v by the *deletion* of a minimal winning coalition. On the other hand, let T be a hole in v, and define the game v^{+T} by $v^{+T}(S) = v(S)$ for all $S \neq T$, with $v^{+T}(T) = 1$; v^{+T} arises from v by the *insertion* of a (new) winning coalition. The collection $\mathcal{T}$ is *closed under deletion and insertion* if these operations, applied to any game in $\mathcal{T}$, give rise only to other games in $\mathcal{T}$. In particular, $\mathcal{G}^*, \mathcal{M}^*$, and $\mathcal{S}^*$ are all closed under deletion and insertion.

The following result is an analogue of Theorem 1.

Theorem 7. Let $\mathcal{T}$ be a collection of simple games that contains $\mathcal{C}$ and is closed under deletion and insertion. Let ϕ_i be a value for i on $\mathcal{T}$, and assume that $\phi_i(\hat{v}_N) = 0$. Finally, assume that ϕ_i satisfies the transfer axiom. Then there is a collection of constants $\{a_T : T \subset N\}$ such that, for all games $v \in \mathcal{T}$,

$$\phi_i(v) = \sum_{T \subset N} a_T v(T).$$

Proof: We claim that ϕ_i is determined on all of $\mathcal{T}$ by its values on $\mathcal{C}$. To verify this claim, first consider the collection $\mathcal{T}_M$ of monotonic games in $\mathcal{T}$. This subcollection of $\mathcal{T}$ is also closed under deletion and insertion and contains $\mathcal{C}$. Because $v_N \in \mathcal{C}$, the claim is trivially true for this game. Assume that the claim has been verified for all games in $\mathcal{T}_M$ that have at most k winning coalitions (the only game in $\mathcal{T}_M$ with just one winning coalition is v_N), and let $v \in \mathcal{T}_M$ be any game with $k+1$ winning coalitions. Let T be any minimal winning coalition in v and consider the games v_T, v^{-T}, and $v_T \wedge v^{-T}$. The first is in $\mathcal{C}$, and the latter two are in $\mathcal{T}_M$ and have no more than k winning coalitions. Because $v_T \vee v^{-T} = v$, we have from the transfer axiom that $\phi_i(v) = \phi_i(v_T) + \phi_i(v^{-T}) - \phi_i(v_T \wedge v^{-T})$. It follows from the induction hypothesis that $\phi_i(v)$ depends only on the values of ϕ_i on $\mathcal{C}$. This verifies the claim throughout $\mathcal{T}_M$. (Note that the game $\hat{v}_N$ requires special treatment; because it has no winning coalitions, it is not covered by the induction.)

Next, assume that the claim holds for all games in $\mathcal{T}$ that have at most k holes (the case $k = 0$ has just been treated), and let $v \in \mathcal{T}$ be a game with $k+1$ holes. Let T be any hole of maximum cardinality and consider the games v_T, $v \wedge v_T = \hat{v}_T$, and $v \vee v_T = v^{+T}$. The first of these is in $\mathscr{C}$, the second is in $\mathscr{T}_M$, and the third is in $\mathscr{T}$ and has only k holes. Because $\phi_i(v) = \phi_i(v \vee v_T) + \phi_i(v \wedge v_T) - \phi_i(v_T)$, it follows (by induction) that $\phi_i(v)$ depends only on the values of ϕ_i on $\mathscr{C}$. This completes the verification of the claim.

We have just seen that ϕ_i is determined by its values on $\mathscr{C}$. Because $\mathscr{C}$ is a basis for $\mathscr{G}$, there is a unique linear function ϕ_i^{lin} on $\mathscr{G}$ that coincides with ϕ_i on $\mathscr{C}$. This linear function must satisfy the transfer axiom because $(v \vee w) + (v \wedge w) = v + w$ for all v and w in $\mathscr{G}$. Therefore, ϕ_i^{lin} and ϕ_i must coincide on $\mathscr{T}$. Because ϕ_i^{lin} can be expressed in terms of its values on the basis $\{w_T : \varnothing \neq T \subset N\}$ of $\mathscr{G}$ (see the proof of Theorem 1), it follows that ϕ_i has the desired form. $\square$

We can now invoke Theorem 2 and the proposition concerning monotonicity to obtain analogues of Theorems 4 and 5.

Theorem 8. Let ϕ_i be a value for i on $\mathscr{G}^*$ or $\mathscr{M}^*$. Assume that ϕ_i satisfies the transfer, dummy, and monotonicity axioms. Then ϕ_i is a probabilistic value. Furthermore, every probabilistic value on $\mathscr{G}^*$ or $\mathscr{M}^*$ satisfies these three axioms.

Theorem 9. Let ϕ_i be a value for i on $\mathscr{S}^*$. Assume that ϕ_i satisfies the transfer, dummy, and monotonicity axioms. Then there is a collection of constants $\{p_T : T \subset N \backslash i\}$ satisfying $\Sigma_{T \subset N \backslash i} p_T = 1$ and $p_T \geqq 0$ for all nonempty $T \subset N \backslash i$, such that for every game $v \in \mathscr{S}^*$.

$$\phi_i(v) = \sum_{T \subset N \backslash i} p_T[v(T \cup i) - v(T)].$$

Furthermore, every such value on $\mathscr{S}^*$ satisfies these three axioms.

The discussion of the previous section, interpreting the class of values on $\mathscr{S}$, applies with equal validity to $\mathscr{S}^*$.

7 Symmetric values

A value assesses the relative desirability of being a particular player in various games. At times, one might also want to compare the desirability of playing various roles within a particular game. Such comparisons can be facilitated by the use of a collection $\phi = (\phi_1, \ldots, \phi_n)$ of values, with $\phi_i(v)$ representing the value of being player i in game v. Such a collection is a *group value*.

Let $\pi = (\pi(1), \ldots, \pi(n))$ be any permutation of N. For any $S \subset N$, define $\pi S = \{\pi(i) : i \in S\}$. The game πv is defined by $(\pi v)(\pi S) = v(S)$ for all $S \subset N$. (πv arises upon the relabeling of players $1, \ldots, n$ with the labels $\pi(1), \ldots, \pi(n)$.) Let $\mathcal{T}$ be a collection of games with the property that, if $v \in \mathcal{T}$, then every $\pi v \in \mathcal{T}$; such a collection is *symmetric*.

Let $\phi = (\phi_1, \ldots, \phi_n)$ be a group value on $\mathcal{T}$. For the comparison of roles in a game to be meaningful, the evaluation of a particular position should depend on the structure of the game but not on the labels of the players.

Symmetry axiom. For every $v \in \mathcal{T}$, every permutation π of N, and every $i \in N$, $\phi_i(v) = \phi_{\pi(i)}(\pi v)$.

Observe that each of the classes $\mathcal{G}, \mathcal{M}, \mathcal{S}, \mathcal{G}^*, \mathcal{M}^*$, and $\mathcal{S}^*$ contains both $\mathcal{C}$ and $\hat{\mathcal{C}}$; furthermore, each class is symmetric. Therefore, Theorem 10 applies to values on any of these classes.

Theorem 10. Let $\mathcal{T}$ be a symmetric collection of games containing $\mathcal{C}$ and $\hat{\mathcal{C}}$. Let $\phi = (\phi_1, \ldots, \phi_n)$ be a group value on $\mathcal{T}$ such that for each $i \in N$ and $v \in \mathcal{T}$,

$$\phi_i(v) = \sum_{T \subset N \backslash i} p_T^i [v(T \cup i) - v(T)].$$

Assume that ϕ satisfies the symmetry axiom. Then there are constants $\{p_t\}_{t=0}^{n-1}$ such that for all $i \in N$ and $T \subset N \backslash i$, $p_T^i = p_{|T|}$.

Proof: For any $i \in N$, let T_1 and T_2 be any two coalitions in $N \backslash i$ satisfying $0 < |T_1| = |T_2| < n - 1$. Consider a permutation π of N that takes T_1 into T_2 while leaving i fixed. Then $p_{T_1}^i = \phi_i(\hat{v}_{T_1}) = \phi_i(\hat{v}_{T_2}) = p_{T_2}^i$, where the central equality is a consequence of the symmetry axiom.

Next, let i and j be distinct players in N, and let T be a nonempty coalition in $N \backslash \{i, j\}$. Consider the permutation π that interchanges i and j while leaving the remaining players fixed. Then $\pi \hat{v}_T = \hat{v}_T$ and $p_T^i = \phi_i(\hat{v}_T) = \phi_j(\hat{v}_T) = p_T^j$, where the central equality is again a consequence of the symmetry axiom. Combining this with the previous result, we find that for every $0 < t < n - 1$ there is a p_t such that $p_T^i = p_t$ for every $i \in N$ and $T \subset N \backslash i$ with $|T| = t$.

Again, for distinct players i and j, let π interchange i and j while leaving the remaining players fixed. Then $p_{N \backslash i}^i = \phi_i(v_N) = \phi_j(v_N) = p_{N \backslash j}^j$. Let p_{n-1} be this common value. Then for all $i \in N$, $p_{N \backslash i}^i = p_{n-1}$.

Finally, for each $i \in N$,

$$p_{\varnothing}^i = \phi_i(v_i) - \sum_{\substack{T \subseteq N \setminus i \\ T \neq \varnothing}} p_T^i = \phi_i(v_i) - \sum_{t=1}^{n-1} \binom{n-1}{t} p_t.$$

By symmetry, $\phi_i(v_i) = \phi_j(v_j)$. Therefore, $p_{\varnothing}^i = p_{\varnothing}^j$ for all $i, j \in N$. Letting p_0 be this common value completes the proof of the theorem. $\square$

8   Efficiency without symmetry: Random-order values

Consider a collection $\phi = (\phi_1, \ldots, \phi_n)$ of values all on the domain $\mathscr{T}$, one for each player in N. Depending on the game v under consideration, the players' assessments, as a group, of their individual prospects may be either optimistic or pessimistic; that is, $\Sigma_{i \in N} \phi_i(v)$ may be either greater than or less than $v(N)$. However, if the group assessment is neither optimistic nor pessimistic, the payoff vector $\phi(v) = (\phi_1(v), \ldots, \phi_n(v))$ may be taken as an equitable distribution of the resources available to the grand coalition N. Therefore, it is of interest to study those collections of values $\phi = (\phi_1, \ldots, \phi_n)$ that meet the following criterion.

Efficiency axiom. For every $v \in \mathscr{T}$, $\Sigma_{i \in N} \phi_i(v) = v(N)$.

A group value satisfying this axiom is said to be *efficient*, and provides a fair distribution scheme for the games in $\mathscr{T}$. The next theorem characterizes all such group values.

Theorem 11. Let $\phi = (\phi_1, \ldots, \phi_n)$ be a group value on $\mathscr{T}$, defined for all $i \in N$ and all $v \in \mathscr{T}$ by

$$\phi_i(v) = \sum_{T \subseteq N \setminus i} p_T^i [v(T \cup i) - v(T)].$$

Assume that $\mathscr{T}$ contains $\mathscr{C}$ and $\hat{\mathscr{C}}$. Then ϕ satisfies the efficiency axiom if and only if $\Sigma_{i \in N} p_{N \setminus i}^i = 1$ and $\Sigma_{i \in T} p_{T \setminus i}^i = \Sigma_{j \notin T} p_T^j$ for every nonempty $T \subseteq N$.

Proof: For any $v \in \mathscr{T}$, let $\phi_N(v) = \Sigma_{i \in N} \phi_i(v)$. Then

$$\phi_N(v) = \sum_{\substack{i \in N \\ T \subseteq N \setminus i}} \sum p_T^i [v(T \cup i) - v(T)]$$

$$= \sum_{T \subseteq N} v(T) \left(\sum_{i \in T} p_{T \setminus i}^i - \sum_{j \notin T} p_T^j \right).$$

It is immediately clear that any ϕ that satisfies the conditions of the theorem is efficient; that is, $\phi_N(v) = v(N)$.

For any nonempty $T \subset N$, consider the games v_T and $\hat{v}_T$. Because $v_T(S) = \hat{v}_T(S)$ for all $S \neq T$, and $v_T(T) = 1$ while $\hat{v}_T(T) = 0$, it follows from the preceding equation that

$$\phi_N(v_T) - \phi_N(\hat{v}_T) = \sum_{i \in T} p^i_{T \setminus i} - \sum_{j \notin T} p^j_T.$$

However, $v_T(N) - \hat{v}_T(N)$ is 1 if $T = N$, and is 0 otherwise. Therefore, if ϕ satisfies the efficiency axiom, then the indicated conditions must also hold. $\square$

It is conceivable that the efficiency of a group value is an artifact, existing in spite of the fact that the players have grossly different views of the world. However, we can define a family of efficient group values, each of which arises from a viewpoint common to all of the players. Let $\{r_\pi : \pi \in \Pi\}$ be a probability distribution over the set Π of $n!$ orderings of N. For any ordering $\pi = (i_1, \ldots, i_n)$, let $\pi^{i_k} = \{i_1, \ldots, i_{k-1}\}$ be the set of predecessors of i_k in π. A *random-order value* $\xi = (\xi_1, \ldots, \xi_n)$ on $\mathcal{T}$ is defined by

$$\xi_i(v) = \sum_{\pi \in \Pi} r_\pi [v(\pi^i \cup i) - v(\pi^i)]$$

for all $i \in N$ and all $v \in \mathcal{T}$.

To interpret this definition, assume that the players have as their goal the eventual formation of the grand coalition N. Further assume that they see coalition formation as a sequential process: Given any ordering π of the players, each player i joins with his predecessors in π, making the marginal contribution $v(\pi^i \cup i) - v(\pi^i)$ in the game v. Then if the players share a common perception $\{r_\pi : \pi \in \Pi\}$ of the likelihood of the various orderings, the expected marginal contribution of a player is precisely his component of the random-order value.

Theorem 12. Let $\xi = (\xi_1, \ldots, \xi_n)$ be a random-order value on $\mathcal{T}$. Then each component of ξ is a probabilistic value on $\mathcal{T}$, and ξ satisfies the efficiency axiom.

Proof: Let $\{r_\pi : \pi \in \Pi\}$ be any probability distribution defining ξ. For any $i \in N$ and $v \in \mathcal{T}$,

$$\xi_i(v) = \sum_{\pi \in \Pi} r_\pi[v(\pi^i \cup i) - v(\pi^i)]$$
$$= \sum_{T \subset N \backslash i} \left(\sum_{(\pi \in \Pi: \pi^i = T)} r_\pi \right) [v(T \cup i) - v(T)].$$

Hence, ξ_i is a probabilistic value.

Furthermore, for any $v \in \mathcal{T}$,

$$\sum_{i \in N} \xi_i(v) = \sum_{i \in N} \sum_{\pi \in \Pi} r_\pi[v(\pi^i \cup i) - v(\pi^i)]$$
$$= \sum_{\pi \in \Pi} r_\pi \sum_{i \in N} [v(\pi^i \cup i) - v(\pi^i)]$$
$$= \sum_{\pi \in \Pi} r_\pi v(N) = v(N). \qquad \square$$

Theorem 13. Let $\phi = (\phi_1, \ldots, \phi_n)$ be a collection of probabilistic values on $\mathcal{T}$. Assume that $\mathcal{T}$ contains $\mathcal{C}$ and $\hat{\mathcal{C}}$ and that ϕ satisfies the efficiency axiom. Then ϕ is a random-order value.

Proof: Let ϕ be defined for all $i \in N$ and all $v \in \mathcal{T}$ by

$$\phi_i(v) = \sum_{T \subset N \backslash i} p_T^i[v(T \cup i) - v(T)].$$

For any $i \in N$ and $T \subset N \backslash i$, define $A^d(T) = \sum_{j \notin T} p_T^j$ and $A(i; T) = p_T^i / A^d(T)$. (If $A^d(T) = 0$ set $A(i;T) = 0$.) Consider any ordering $\pi = (i_1, \ldots, i_n) \in \Pi$, and define

$$r_\pi = p_\varnothing^{i_1} A(i_2; \{i_1\}) A(i_3; \{i_1, i_2\}) \cdots A(i_n; \{i_1, \ldots, i_{n-1}\}).$$

It is easily verified, by repeated summation, that

$$\sum_{\pi \in \Pi} r_\pi = \sum_{i_1} \sum_{i_2 \notin \{i_1\}} \sum_{i_3 \notin \{i_1, i_2\}} \cdots \sum_{i_n \notin \{i_1, \ldots, i_{n-1}\}} r_{(i_1, \ldots, i_n)} = \sum_{i \in N} p_\varnothing^i = 1,$$

where the final equality follows from induction on the relations in the conclusion of Theorem 11. (More generally, for every $0 \le t \le n - 1$ those relations imply that $\sum_{|T|=t} \sum_{i \notin T} p_T^i = 1$; we use here the case $t = 0$.) Hence, $\{r_\pi: \pi \in \Pi\}$ is a probability distribution on Π.

Let ξ be the random-order value associated with $\{r_\pi: \pi \in \Pi\}$. Because

$$\xi_i(v) = \sum_{T \subset N \backslash i} \left(\sum_{(\pi \in \Pi: \pi^i = T)} r_\pi \right) [v(T \cup i) - v(T)],$$

it will suffice to show that for all $i \in N$ and $T \subset N \backslash i$,

$$p_T^i = \sum_{\{\pi: \pi^i = T\}} r_\pi.$$

Observe that

$$
\sum_{\{\pi:\,\pi^i=T\}} r_\pi = \sum_{i_t \in T}\ \sum_{i_{t-1} \in T\setminus\{i_t\}} \cdots \sum_{i_1 \in T\setminus\{i_t,\,\ldots,\,i_2\}}\ \sum_{i_{t+2} \notin T\cup\{i\}}\ \sum_{i_{t+3}\notin T\cup\{i,i_{t+2}\}}
$$

$$
\cdots \sum_{i_n \notin T\cup\{i,i_{t+2},\,\ldots,\,i_{n-1}\}} r_{(i_1,\,\ldots,\,i_n)}
$$

$$
= \frac{p_T^i}{A^d(T)} \sum_{i_t \in T} \frac{p_{T\setminus\{i_t\}}^{i_t}}{A^d(T\setminus\{i_t\})} \sum_{i_{t-1} \in T\setminus\{i_t\}} \frac{p_{T\setminus\{i_t,i_{t-1}\}}^{i_{t-1}}}{A^d(T\setminus\{i_t,i_{t-1}\})}
$$

$$
\cdots \sum_{i_1 \in T\setminus\{i_t,\,\ldots,\,i_2\}} p_\varnothing^{i_1} \sum_{i_{t+2} \notin T\cup\{i\}} A(i_{t+2};\,T\cup\{i\})
$$

$$
\cdots \sum_{i_n \notin T\cup\{i,i_{t+2},\,\ldots,\,i_{n-1}\}} A(i_n;\,T\cup\{i,i_{t+2},\,\ldots,\,i_{n-1}\}).
$$

This summation can be carried out explicitly. From right to left, the first $n - (t + 1)$ sums each, in turn, have value 1. Continuing leftward, we find that each term of the form $\sum_{i_k \in T_k} p_{T_k\setminus i_k}^{i_k}$ is preceded by a factor with denominator $A^d(T_k) = \sum_{j \notin T_k} p_{T_k}^j$. Each two such sums are equal; this follows from the hypotheses of the theorem and from Theorem 11. Therefore, the entire expression simplifies to p_T^i. $\square$

Combining Theorems 12 and 13, we see that a collection of individual probabilistic values is efficient for all games in its domain precisely when the players' probabilistic views of the world are consistent; that is, only when the various $\{p_T^i:\ T \subset N\setminus i\}$ arise from a single distribution $\{r_\pi:\ \pi \in \Pi\}$.

The family of random-order values associates a set of imputations (efficient group allocations) with each game. This set clearly contains the Shapley value of the game; we next show that it also contains the core of the game.

For any game v on the player set N, and any ordering $\pi \in \Pi$, the *marginal worth vector* $a^\pi(v)$ is the imputation satisfying $a_i^\pi(v) = v(\pi^i \cup i) - v(\pi^i)$ for all $i \in N$. Let $W(v)$ be the convex hull of the set $\{a^\pi(v):\ \pi \in \Pi\}$; $W(v)$ is the set of all imputations associated with v by *some* random-order value. The *core* of a game v with player set N is the set

$$
C(v) = \{x \in R^N:\ x(N) = v(N), x(S) \geq v(S) \text{ for all } S \subset N\},
$$

where for any $S \subset N$ we define $x(S) = \sum_{i \in S} x_i$.

Theorem 14. Let v be any game on N. Then $W(v) \supset C(v)$.

Proof: We proceed by induction on n, the number of players in N. The theorem holds trivially for the case $n = 1$. Assume that the theorem is true for all games with fewer than n players.

Because the core of a game is convex, it will suffice to show that all points in the boundary of $C(v)$ are members of $W(v)$. Let x be a boundary point of $C(v)$. Then for some nonempty $S \subsetneq N$, $x(S) = v(S)$. Define the game u on S by $u(T) = v(T)$ for all $T \subset S$; define w on $N \backslash S$ by $w(T) = v(T \cup S) - v(S)$ for $T \subset N \backslash S$. Let x^S be the projection of x onto R^S. Clearly $x^S \in C(u)$. Furthermore, for any $T \subset N \backslash S$,

$$x(T) = x(T \cup S) - x(S) \geqq v(T \cup S) - v(S) = w(T);$$

hence, $x^{N \backslash S} \in C(w)$.

Express $x^S = \Sigma \, \alpha_\sigma a^\sigma(u)$ as a convex combination of marginal worth vectors in $\{a^\sigma(u): \sigma \in \Pi_S\}$, where Π_S is the set of orderings of S. (This is possible by the induction hypothesis.) Similarly express $x^{N \backslash S} = \Sigma \, \beta_\tau a^\tau(w)$ as a convex combination of vectors in $\{a^\tau(w): \tau \in \Pi_{N \backslash S}\}$. For any $\sigma \in \Pi_S$ and $\tau \in \Pi_{N \backslash S}$, let (σ, τ) be the ordering in Π obtained by appending τ to σ. Then $x = \Sigma \, (\alpha_\sigma \beta_\tau) a^{(\sigma, \tau)}(v)$, and hence $x \in W(v)$, as claimed. $\square$

This theorem bears upon several other results. If a game v is convex (that is, if $v(S \cup T) + v(S \cap T) \geqq v(S) + v(T)$ for all $S, T \subset N$), then $W(v) = C(v)$. (This result is due to Shapley [1971]; the converse has been noted by Ichiishi.) Monderer, Samet, and Shapley (1987) have recently strengthened Theorem 14 by showing that the set of weighted values (see Chapter 6 of this volume) of v is a subset of $W(v)$ and a superset of $C(v)$.

9 The Shapley value

The classical characterization of the Shapley value is as the only (group) value that satisfies the linearity, dummy, symmetry, and efficiency axioms (Shapley 1953). From our previous results, we can quickly prove the uniqueness of the Shapley value, and simultaneously obtain a simple derivation of an explicit formula for the Shapley value. Traditional proofs center around a consideration of the games in $\mathscr{C}$. It appears that our consideration, as well, of the games in $\hat{\mathscr{C}}$ simplifies matters.

Theorem 15. Let $\phi = (\phi_1, \ldots, \phi_n)$ be a group value on $\mathscr{G}$, $\mathscr{M}$, or $\mathscr{S}$. Assume that each ϕ_i satisfies the linearity and dummy axioms, and that ϕ

satisfies the symmetry and efficiency axioms. Then for every v in the domain of ϕ and every $i \in N$,

$$\phi_i(v) = \sum_{T \subset N \backslash i} \frac{t!(n-t-1)!}{n!} [v(T \cup i) - v(T)],$$

where t generically denotes the cardinality of T.

Proof: From Theorems 3 and 10, it follows that there is a sequence $\{p_t\}_{t=0}^{n-1}$ such that each $\phi_i(v) = \sum_{T \subset N \backslash i} p_t[v(T \cup i) - v(T)]$. Specializing Theorem 11 to the symmetric case, we must have $\sum_{i \in N} p_{N \backslash i}^i = n p_{n-1} = 1$ and $\sum_{i \in T} p_{T \backslash i}^i = t p_{t-1} = \sum_{j \notin T} p_T^j = (n-t) p_t$ for all nonempty $T \subseteq N$. Consequently,

$$p_{n-1} = \binom{n-1}{n-1} p_{n-1} = \frac{1}{n}$$

and

$$\binom{n-1}{t} p_t = \binom{n-1}{t-1} p_{t-1}$$

for all $1 \leq t \leq n-1$. It follows that, for each t,

$$\binom{n-1}{t} p_t = \frac{1}{n}, \quad \text{so} \quad p_t = \frac{t!(n-t-1)!}{n!}. \quad \square$$

If we replace the linearity axiom with the transfer axiom, we obtain an analogous result characterizing the Shapley value on $\mathcal{G}^*$, $\mathcal{M}^*$, and $\mathcal{S}^*$.

Remarks: Throughout this paper, we have studied values of games on a fixed finite set of players. Along similar lines, Dubey, Neyman, and Weber (1981) study values defined for all finite-player games in an infinite universe of players and values of infinite-player (nonatomic) games.

Other related work is found in Blair (1976), Roth (1977a,b), Weber (1979), Dubey and Shapley (1979), and Roth (Chapter 4 this volume).

REFERENCES

Blair, Douglas [1976], "Essays in Social Choice Theory," Ph.D. thesis, Yale University.

Dubey, Pradeep [1975], "On the Uniqueness of the Shapley Value," *International Journal of Game Theory*, 4, 131–9.

Dubey, Pradeep, Abraham Neyman, and Robert J. Weber [1981], "Value Theory without Efficiency," *Mathematics of Operations Research,* 6, 122–8.

Dubey, Pradeep and Lloyd S. Shapley [1979], "Mathematical Properties of the Banzhaf Power Index," *Mathematics of Operations Research,* 4, 99–131.

Milnor, John [1952], "Reasonable Outcomes for *n*-Person Games," RAND Memorandum RM-916.

Monderer, Dov, Dov Samet, and Lloyd S. Shapley [1987], "Weighted Values and the Core," manuscript.

Owen, Guillermo [1972], "Multilinear Extensions of Games," *Management Science,* 18, Part 2, 64–79.

Roth, Alvin E. [1977a], "Bargaining Ability, the Utility of Playing a Game, and Models of Coalition Formation," *Journal of Mathematical Psychology,* 16, 153–60.

[1977b], "A Note on Values and Multilinear Extensions," *Naval Research Logistics Quarterly,* 24, 517–20.

Shapley, Lloyd S. [1953], "A Value for *n*-Person Games," *Annals of Mathematics Study,* 28, 307–18.

[1971], "Cores of Convex Games," *International Journal of Game Theory.* 1 11–26.

Weber, Robert J. [1979], "Subjectivity in the Valuation of Games," *Game Theory and Related Topics* (ed. O. Moeschlin and D. Pallaschke), North-Holland Publishing Company, 129–36.

CHAPTER 8

Combinatorial representations of the Shapley value based on average relative payoffs

Uriel G. Rothblum

Abstract

Shapley's combinatorial representation of the Shapley value is embodied in a formula that gives each player his expected marginal contribution to the set of players that precede him, where the expectation is taken with respect to the uniform distribution over the set of all orders of the players. We obtain alternative combinatorial representations that are based on allocating to each player the average relative payoff of coalitions that contain him, where one averages first over the sets of fixed cardinality that contain the player and then averages over the different cardinalities. Different base levels in comparison to which relative payoffs are evaluated yield different combinatorial formulas.

1   Introduction

The familiar representation of the Shapley value gives each player his "average marginal contribution to the players that precede him," where averages are taken with respect to all potential orders of the players; see Shapley (1953). This chapter looks at three alternative representations of the Shapley value, each expressing the idea that a player gets the "average relative payoff to coalitions that contain him." The common feature of the three representations we obtain is the way averages are taken, whereas the distinctive feature is the base level in comparison to which relative payoffs are evaluated. Specifically, in each of our three representations we first average over coalitions having a given cardinality and at a second stage average over the different cardinalities. On the other hand, the base

The research leading to this paper was supported by the Fund for the Promotion of Research at the Technion.

payoffs from which excesses are evaluated are different for the three representations. In the first representation it is the payoff to the given coalition when the particular player in question is excluded, so the relative payoffs coincide with marginal payoffs used by Shapley; in the second representation the base payoff is the payoff to the complement of the given coalition as in Harsanyi (1963, p. 203, equation 4.1); and in the third representation the base payoff is the average payoff to coalitions having the same cardinality as the given one but not including the particular player as in Rothblum (1985, equation 3).

Kleinberg and Weiss (1985) obtained a representation for the Shapley value as a weighted sum of quantities they call relative worth that can be viewed as relative payoffs with respect to a base different from those we consider. However, Kleinberg and Weiss do not give an interpretation of their weights and their formula does not express average relative payoff with respect to any intuitive distribution. Thus, one can view their formula as a qualitative, but not quantitative, expression of the idea of average relative payoffs.

Let $N = \{1, \ldots, n\}$ be the grand coalition consisting of all players, and let $v(N)$ be the payoff to N. The base payoff for computing the relative payoff to the grand coalition is zero under each of the three representations we obtain, and we get a term $v(N)/n$ in each of our formulas. This term can be viewed as the "fair division," whereas the remaining terms can be viewed as adjustments of the fair division "to reflect the relative worth of coalitions that he (the player) belongs to. If a player, for example, belongs consistently to coalitions of above average worth, then he will receive a value which exceeds his fair share." (Kleinberg and Weiss 1985)

Our main result is presented in Section 2, and some extensions are discussed in Section 3.

2   The main result

A *game in characteristic function form on* $N = \{1, \ldots, n\}$ is a real-valued function v on the subsets of N, where $v(\varnothing) = 0$. As usual, elements of N are called *players,* subsets of N are called *coalitions* and for each coalition S, $v(S)$ represents the payoff that the members of S can guarantee themselves without cooperation with the other players. Let G^N be the set of games in characteristic function form on $N = \{1, \ldots, n\}$. The *Shapley value* (Shapley 1953) is the function ϕ mapping G^N into R^n having the explicit representation

$$(\phi v)_i = \sum_{\substack{S \subseteq N \\ i \in S}} \frac{(|S|-1)!(n-|S|)!}{n!} \, [v(S) - v(S\setminus\{i\})], \qquad i \in S, \tag{1}$$

where $|S|$ denotes the cardinality of the set S.

For $\varnothing \neq S \subseteq N$ and $i \in S$, let

$$e_1(S,i) \equiv v(S) - v(S\setminus\{i\}), \tag{2}$$

$$e_2(S,i) \equiv v(S) - v(N\setminus S), \tag{3}$$

and

$$e_3(S,i) \equiv v(S) - \binom{n-1}{|S|}^{-1} \sum_{\substack{i \notin R \\ |R|=|S|}} v(R), \tag{4}$$

where the last term in (4) when $S = N$ is defined to be zero. Each of the expressions (2)–(4) can be viewed as a *relative payoff* to coalition S in comparison to base payoff $v(S\setminus\{i\})$, $v(N\setminus S)$, and $\binom{n-1}{|S|}^{-1}[\sum_{i \notin R; |R|=|S|} v(R)]$, respectively. In particular, $\binom{n-1}{|S|}^{-1}[\sum_{i \notin R; |R|=|S|} v(R)]$ is the average payoff to coalitions of size $|S|$ not including i. Also, $e_1(S,i)$ is the marginal contribution of player i to coalition S, and $e_2(S,i)$ is a measure used by Harsanyi (1963).

Theorem 1. For $t = 1, 2, 3$, $v \in G^N$, and $i \in N$,

$$(\phi v)_i = n^{-1} \sum_{k=1}^{n} \binom{n-1}{k-1}^{-1} \sum_{\substack{i \in S \\ |S|=k}} e_t(S,i). \tag{5}$$

Remark: Because the number of coalitions of size k that include i is $\binom{n-1}{k-1}$, the expression $\binom{n-1}{k-1}^{-1}[\sum_{i \in S; |S|=k} e_t(S,i)]$ is the average relative payoff to such coalitions for the corresponding base payoffs, and the three variants of (5) for $t = 1$, $t = 2$, and $t = 3$ take the average of these averages over the index k. So, the right side of (5) gives three representations of the Shapley value of player i with respect to game v as the average relative payoff to coalitions containing the given player where the different bases for evaluating relative payoffs are used.

Proof of Theorem 1: Consider the functions ψ_1, ψ_2, and ψ_3 mapping G^N into R^n, where for each $v \in G^N$ and $i \in N$,

$$(\psi_1 v)_i = n^{-1} \sum_{k=1}^{n} \binom{n-1}{k-1}^{-1} \sum_{\substack{i \in S \\ |S|=k}} [v(S) - v(S\setminus\{i\})]. \tag{6}$$

$$(\psi_2 v)_i = n^{-1} \sum_{k=1}^{n} \binom{n-1}{k-1}^{-1} \sum_{\substack{i \in S \\ |S|=k}} [v(S) - v(N\setminus S)], \tag{7}$$

and

$$(\psi_3 v)_i = n^{-1} \sum_{k=1}^{n} \binom{n-1}{k-1}^{-1} \sum_{\substack{i \in S \\ |S|=k}} [v(S) - \binom{n-1}{k}^{-1} \sum_{\substack{i \notin R \\ |R|=k}} v(R)]. \tag{8}$$

Our task is to show that for $v \in G^N$ and $i \in N$,

$$(\phi v)_i = (\psi_1 v)_i = (\psi_2 v)_i = (\psi_3 v)_i. \tag{9}$$

By ordering the nonempty subsets of N, we have that G^N can be identified with R^{2^n-1}. Under this identification, ϕ, ψ_1, ψ_2, and ψ_3 are clearly linear functions. Thus, it suffices to establish (9) for elements v in any basis of G^N. The basis corresponding to the set of unit vectors in R^{2^n-1} is the set $\{W_T : \emptyset \neq T \subseteq N\}$, where

$$W_T(S) = \begin{cases} 1 & \text{if } S = T, \\ 0 & \text{if } S \neq T, \end{cases}$$

and we will establish (9) for each v in this basis.

Let $\emptyset \neq T \subseteq N$ be given. We distinguish the cases $i \in T$ and $i \notin T$. First assume that $i \in T$. In this case $W_T(S) = 0$ for each subset $S \subseteq N$ containing i that is different from T, $W_T(S\setminus\{i\}) = W_T(N\setminus S) = 0$ for all subsets $S \subseteq N$ containing i. Also, $W_T(R) = 0$ for all subsets $R \subseteq N$ not containing i. It therefore follows from (1), (6), (7), and (8) that

$$(\phi W_T)_i = \frac{(|T|-1)!(n-|T|)!}{n!} W_T(T) = \frac{(|T|-1)!(n-|T|)!}{n!}$$

and

$$(\psi_1 W_T)_i = (\psi_2 W_T)_i = (\psi_3 W_T)_i = n^{-1} \binom{n-1}{|T|-1}^{-1} W_T(T)$$

$$= \frac{(|T|-1)!(n-|T|)!}{n!}.$$

Then (9) follows for $v = W_T$ and $i \in T$.

Next assume that $i \notin T$. For each subset $S \subseteq N$ containing i we have $W_T(S) = 0$, $W_T(S\setminus\{i\}) = 0$ unless $S = T \cup \{i\}$, and $W_T(N\setminus S) = 0$ unless

$S = N \backslash T$. Also, $W_T(R) = 0$ for each subset $R \subseteq N$ not containing i, except for $R = T$. It therefore follows from (1), (6), (7), and (8) that

$$(\phi W_T)_i = -\frac{(|T \cup \{i\}| - 1)!(n - |T \cup \{i\}|)!}{n!} \, W_T[(T \cup \{i\}) \backslash \{i\}]$$

$$= -\frac{|T|!(n - |T| - 1)!}{n!},$$

$$(\psi_1 W_T)_i = -n^{-1} \binom{n-1}{|T \cup \{i\}| - 1}^{-1} W_T[(T \cup \{i\}) \backslash \{i\}]$$

$$= \frac{|T|!(n - |T| - 1)!}{n!},$$

$$(\psi_2 W_T)_i = -n^{-1} \binom{n-1}{|N \backslash T| - 1}^{-1} W_T[N \backslash (N \backslash T)] = -\frac{|T|!(n - |T| - 1)!}{n!},$$

and

$$(\psi_3 W_T)_i = n^{-1} \sum_{k=1}^{n} \binom{n-1}{k-1}^{-1} \sum_{\substack{i \in S \\ |S| = k}} \left[W_T(S) - \binom{n-1}{k}^{-1} \sum_{\substack{i \notin R \\ |R| = k}} W_T(R) \right]$$

$$= n^{-1} \binom{n-1}{|T| - 1}^{-1} \sum_{\substack{i \in S \\ |S| = |T|}} \left[0 - \binom{n-1}{|T|}^{-1} \sum_{\substack{i \notin R \\ |R| = |T|}} W_T(T) \right]$$

$$= -n^{-1} \binom{n-1}{|T| - 1}^{-1} \binom{n-1}{|T| - 1} \binom{n-1}{|T|}^{-1} = -n^{-1} \binom{n-1}{|T|}^{-1}$$

$$= -\frac{|T|!(n - |T| - 1)!}{n!},$$

and (9) follows for $v = W_T$ and $i \notin T$, thereby completing our proof of Theorem 1. $\square$

3   Extensions

Theorem 1 gives three formulas for expressing the Shapley value as the average relative payoff, where averages are first evaluated over subsets of fixed cardinality that contain a given player, and then, at a second stage, averages are taken over the different cardinalities. In particular, the formulas use equal weight on all possible cardinalities. Possible extensions of those formulas result from putting different weights on the different cardinalities. Specifically, for $q \in R^n$, one can consider functions $\psi_t^q, t = 1, 2, 3$, mapping G^N into R^n, defined by

$$(\psi_t^q v)_i = \sum_{k=1}^n q_k \binom{n-1}{k-1}^{-1} \sum_{\substack{i \in S \\ |S|=k}} e_t(S,i), \qquad i \in N, \tag{10}$$

where the functions $e_1(\cdot, \cdot)$, $e_2(\cdot, \cdot)$, and $e_3(\cdot, \cdot)$ are defined by (2)–(4), respectively. Equation (10) defines parametric measures for the power of players participating in a game determined by v. Other parametric measures were considered by Dubey (1976), Dubey and Weber (1977), Roth (1977a,b,c), and Dubey, Neyman, and Weber (1981). Specifically, they use expressions of the form

$$(\xi^p v)_i \equiv \sum_{\substack{S \subseteq N \\ i \in S}} p(i,S)[v(S) - v(S \setminus \{i\})], \qquad i \in N, \tag{11}$$

where p is a real-valued function on pairs (i,S) with $i \in S$ and $S \subseteq N$. Dubey, Neyman, and Weber call the corresponding functions ξ^p *semivalues*.

REFERENCES

Dubey, P. [1976], "Probabilistic generalization of the Shapley value," Cowles Foundation Discussion Paper No. 440, Cowles Foundation for Research in Economics, Yale University, New Haven, Connecticut.

Dubey, P., A. Neyman, and R. J. Weber [1981], "Value theory without efficiency," *Mathematics of Operations Research* 6, pp. 122–8.

Dubey, P. and R. J. Weber [1977], "Probabilistic values for games," Cowles Foundation Discussion Paper No. 471, Cowles Foundation for Research in Economics, Yale University, New Haven, Connecticut.

Harsanyi, J. C. [1963], "A simplified bargaining model for the n-person cooperative game," *International Economic Review* 4, pp. 194–220.

Kleinberg, N. L. and J. H. Weiss [1985], "A new formula for the Shapley value," *Economic Letters* 18, pp. 311–5.

Roth. A. E. [1977a], "The Shapley value as a von Neumann–Morgenstern utility," *Econometrica* 45, pp. 657–64.

    [1977b], "A note on values and multilinear extensions," *Naval Research Logistics Quarterly* 24, pp. 517–20.

    [1977c], "Bargaining ability, the utility of playing a game and models of coalition formation," *Journal of Mathematical Psychology* 16, pp. 153–60.

Rothblum, U. G. [1985], "A representation of the Shapley value and other semivalues," unpublished manuscript.

Shapley, L. S. [1953], "A value for n-person games," *Annals of Mathematical Studies* 28, pp. 307–12.

CHAPTER 9

The potential of the Shapley value

Sergiu Hart and Andreu Mas-Colell

1 Introduction

We study multiperson games in characteristic function form with transferable utility. The problem is to *solve* such a game (i.e., to associate to it payoffs to all the players).

Three main solution concepts are as follows. The first was introduced by von Neumann and Morgenstern: A "stable set" of a given game is a *set* of payoff *vectors;* such a set, if it exists, need *not* be *unique.* Next came the "core," due to Shapley and Gillies, which is a *unique set* of payoff *vectors.* Finally, the Shapley "value" consists of just *one* payoff *vector.* There is thus an apparent historical trend from "complexity" to "simplicity" in the structure of the solution.[1,2]

We propose now an even simpler construction: Associate to each game just *one number!* How would the payoffs to *all* players then be determined? by using the "marginal contribution" principle, an approach with a long tradition (especially in economics). Thus, we assign to each player his or her marginal contribution according to the numbers defined earlier. The surprising fact is that only one requirement, that the resulting payoff vector be "efficient" (i.e., that the payoffs add up to the worth of the grand coalition), determines this procedure uniquely.

Clearly it is not possible in general to assign to each player his or her direct marginal contribution to the grand coalition (according to the given characteristic function of the game). This is true simply because these marginal contributions need not add up to the worth of the grand coalition; namely, they will either be not feasible or, if feasible, not Pareto

Dedicated with great admiration to Lloyd S. Shapley on his 65th birthday. This chapter is based on the paper "Potential, Value and Consistency" (1987) and its previous versions (1985,1986). Financial support by the National Science Foundation and the U.S.-Israel Binational Science Foundation is gratefully acknowledged.

optimal (as usual, we refer to this "adding up" requirement as "efficiency"). The way these two principles – marginal contribution and efficiency – are reconciled is by introducing the function that associates to each game a real number, called the *potential* of the game, and computing marginal contributions according to it. The main result can now be stated.

Theorem A. There exists a unique[3] real function on games, called the *potential function,* with respect to which the marginal contributions of all players are always efficient. Moreover, these marginal contributions are precisely the Shapley (1953) value.

Thus the Shapley value, viewed as a vector-valued function on games, is just the (discrete) gradient of the potential function (this explains our choice of name for it). The Shapley value has therefore been singled out as the unique efficient solution concept that admits a potential. More detailed discussions, together with additional results and interpretations, are the subject of Section 2.

The potential, although by its definition just an analytical tool, has nonetheless turned out to be most suggestive and productive. See Hart and Mas-Colell (1987) for details. In Section 3, we present one result obtained by the potential approach: a new way to characterize the Shapley value by an internal "consistency" property.

2   The potential

In this section we formalize the previous discussion and study various properties of the potential.

A cooperative game with sidepayments (or with transferable utility) – in short, a *game* – consists of a pair (N,v), where N is a finite set of *players* and[4] $v: 2^N \to \mathbf{R}$ is the *characteristic function,* satisfying $v(\varnothing) = 0$. A subset[5] $S \subset N$ is called a *coalition,* and $v(S)$ is the *worth* of the coalition S. Given a game (N,v) and a coalition $S \subset N$, we write (S,v) for the *subgame* obtained by restricting v to (the subsets of) S; that is, the domain of the function v is restricted to 2^S.

Let Γ denote the set of all games. Given a function $P: \Gamma \to \mathbf{R}$ that associates a real number[6] $P(N,v)$ to every game (N,v), the *marginal contribution* of a player i in a game (N,v) is defined to be

$$D^i P(N,v) = P(N,v) - P(N\backslash\{i\},v),$$

where $i \in N$; recall that the game $(N\backslash\{i\},v)$ is just the restriction of (N,v) to $N\backslash\{i\}$.

A function $P: \Gamma \to \mathbf{R}$ with[7] $P(\varnothing, v) = 0$ is called a *potential function* if it satisfies the following condition:

$$\sum_{i \in N} D^i P(N, v) = v(N) \tag{1}$$

for all games (N, v). Thus, a potential function is such that its marginals are always efficient; that is, they add up to the worth of the grand coalition. The main result is the next theorem.

Theorem A. There exists a unique potential function P. For every game (N, v) the resulting payoff vector $(D^i P(N, v))_{i \in N}$ of marginal contributions coincides with the Shapley value of the game. Moreover, the potential of a game (N, v) is uniquely determined by (1) applied only to the game and its subgames (i.e., to (S, v) for all $S \subset N$).

Proof: Rewrite (1) as[8]

$$P(N, v) = \frac{1}{|N|} \left[v(N) + \sum_{i \in N} P(N \backslash \{i\}, v) \right]. \tag{2}$$

Starting with $P(\varnothing, v) = 0$, (2) determines $P(N, v)$ recursively. This proves the existence and uniqueness of the potential function P and that $P(N, v)$ is uniquely determined by (1) (or (2)) applied just to (S, v) for all $S \subset N$.

It remains to show that $D^i P(N, v) = \text{Sh}^i(N, v)$ for all games (N, v) and all players $i \in N$, where P is the (unique) potential function and $\text{Sh}^i(N, v)$ denotes the Shapley value of player i in the game (N, v). We prove that all the axioms that uniquely determine the Shapley value are satisfied by[9] $D^i P$. Efficiency is just (1); the other three axioms – dummy (null) player, symmetry, and additivity – are proved inductively using (2). Indeed, let i be a null player in the game (N, v) (i.e., $v(S) = v(S \backslash \{i\})$ for all S). We claim that this implies $P(N, v) = P(N \backslash \{i\}, v)$; hence $D^i P(N, v) = 0$. Assume the assertion holds for all games with less than $|N|$ players; in particular, $P(N \backslash \{j\}, v) = P(N \backslash \{j, i\}, v)$ for all $j \neq i$. Now subtract (2) for $N \backslash \{i\}$ from (2) for N, to obtain

$$|N|[P(N, v) - P(N \backslash \{i\}, v)] = [v(N) - v(N \backslash \{i\})]$$
$$+ \sum_{j \neq i} [P(N \backslash \{j\}, v) - P(N \backslash \{j, i\}, v)]$$
$$= 0.$$

Next, assume players i and j are substitutes in the game (N, v). This implies that $P(N \backslash \{i\}, v) = P(N \backslash \{j\}, v)$ (use (2), noting that i and j are substitutes in $(N \backslash \{k\}, v)$ for all $k \neq i, j$); thus $D^i P(N, v) = D^j P(N, v)$. Finally, another inductive argument on (2) shows that $P(N, v + w) = P(N, v) + P(N, w)$, implying additivity. ∎

Remark 1: The potential approach may be viewed as a *new axiomatic characterization* for the Shapley value. Its significance is twofold: First, *only one* axiom, (1), is needed (though one may view it as the combination of two postulates: "efficiency" and "marginal contributions"; note, however, that no additivity, symmetry, and so on, are assumed). Second, one needs to consider *the given game only;* the potential and a fortiori the Shapley values are uniquely determined by (1) applied just to the game and its subgames (thus, only one characteristic function is taken into account). This is particularly important in applications, where typically just one specific problem is considered. In contrast, all the standard axiomatizations of the Shapley value require, in order to uniquely determine it for any single game, the application of the various axioms (additivity, symmetry, etc.) to a large domain (e.g., all games or all simple games).[10]

Remark 2: Formula (2) yields a simple and straightforward recursive procedure for the computation of the potential and of the Shapley values of the game as well as all its subgames. This seems to be a most efficient algorithm for computing Shapley values (note that (2) has to be applied just once for each one of the $2^{|M|} - 1$ nonempty coalitions).

We now present another way of viewing the potential. Given a game (N, v), the allocation of marginal contributions (i.e., $v(N) - v(N \backslash \{i\})$ to player i) is, in general, not efficient. One way to resolve this difficulty is to add a new player, say player 0, and extend the game to $N_0 = N \cup \{0\}$ in such a way that the allocation of marginal contributions in the extended game becomes efficient. Formally, let (N_0, v_0) be an extension of (N, v) (i.e., $v_0(S) = v(S)$ for all $S \subset N$). Then the requirement is

$$v_0(N_0) = \sum_{i \in N_0} [v_0(N_0) - v_0(N_0 \backslash \{i\})]$$
$$= [v_0(N_0) - v(N)] + \sum_{i \in N} [v_0(N_0) - v_0(N_0 \backslash \{i\})]. \qquad (3)$$

This reduces to

$$v(N) = \sum_{i \in N} [v_0(N_0) - v_0(N_0 \backslash \{i\})], \qquad (4)$$

which, when compared to (1), yields the following restatement of the result of Theorem A.

Corollary 1. There exists a unique extension v_0 of v whose marginal contributions to the grand coalition are always efficient (more precisely, (3) is satisfied for the game and all its subgames); it is given by $v_0(S \cup \{0\}) = P(S,v)$ for all $S \subset N$, where P is the potential function.

Note that the payoffs to the original players (in N) add up correctly to $v(N)$ (see (4); these are the Shapley values). Player 0, whose payoff is the residual $P(N,v) - v(N)$, may be regarded as a "hidden player," similarly to the "hidden factor" introduced by McKenzie[11] in the study of production functions in order to explain the residual profit (or loss).[12]

In (1) and (2) the potential is only given implicitly. We now present two explicit formulas. The T-unanimity game u_T (where T is a nonempty finite set) is defined by $u_T(S) = 1$ if $S \supset T$, and $u_T(S) = 0$ otherwise. It is well known that these games form a linear basis for Γ: Each game (N,v) has a unique representation (e.g., see Shapley 1953)

$$v = \sum_{T \subset N} \alpha_T u_T,$$

where, for all $T \subset N$,

$$\alpha_T \equiv \alpha_T(N,v) = \sum_{S \subset T} (-1)^{|T|-|S|} v(S). \tag{5}$$

Proposition 1. The potential function P satisfies

$$P(N,v) = \sum_{T \subset N} \frac{1}{|T|} \alpha_T$$

for all games (N,v), where α_T is given by (5).

Proof: Let $Q(N,v)$ denote the right-hand side in the preceding formula. Then $Q(\varnothing,v) = 0$ and $Q(N,v) - Q(N\setminus\{i\},v) = \sum_{T \ni i} \alpha_T/|T|$, which when summed up over i shows that Q satisfies (1). Therefore, by Theorem A, Q coincides with the unique potential function P. ∎

The number $\delta_T = \alpha_T/|T|$ is called the *dividend* of each member of the coalition T and $\text{Sh}^i(N,v) = \sum_{T \ni i} \delta_T$ (cf. Harsanyi 1963).

Proposition 2. The potential function P satisfies

$$P(N,v) = \sum_{S \subset N} \frac{(s-1)!(n-s)!}{n!} v(S),$$

where $n = |N|$ and $s = |S|$.

Proof: The marginal contributions of the function on the right side are easily seen to yield the Shapley value. ∎

To interpret this last formula, consider the following probabilistic model of choosing a random nonempty coalition $S \subset N$: First, choose a size $s = 1, 2, \ldots, n = |N|$ uniformly (i.e., with probability $1/n$ each). Second, choose a subset S of size s, again uniformly (i.e., each of the $\binom{n}{s}$) subsets has the same probability). Equivalently, choose a random order of the n elements of N (with probability $1/n!$ each), choose a cutting point s ($1 \leq s \leq n$), and let S be the first s elements in that order. The probability of choosing of a set S with $|S| = s$ is

$$\pi_S = \frac{s!(n-s)!}{n \cdot n!} = \frac{s}{n} \frac{(s-1)!(n-s)!}{n!}.$$

Therefore the formula of Proposition 2 may be rewritten as

$$P(N,v) = \sum_{S \subset N} \pi_S \frac{n}{s} v(S) = E\left[\frac{|N|}{|S|} v(S) \right], \tag{6}$$

where E denotes expectation over S with respect to the foregoing probability model. The interpretation of (6) is that the potential is the *expected normalized worth*, or, equivalently, the *per capita potential* $P(N,v)/|N|$ equals the *average per capita worth* $v(S)/|S|$. This shows that the potential may be viewed as an appropriate "summary" of the characteristic function into one number (from which marginal contributions are then computed).[13]

To study some further properties of the potential function, we regard it as an operator on games. Fix N and let Γ_N be the set of all games with player set N. Let **P** be the operator from Γ_N into itself that associates to each game v another game **P**v given by $(\mathbf{P}v)(S) = P(S,v)$ for all $S \subset N$.

Proposition 3. The operator **P**: $\Gamma_N \to \Gamma_N$ has the following properties (for all $v, w \in \Gamma_N$ and all scalars α, β):

  (i)   **P** is *linear:* $\mathbf{P}(\alpha v + \beta w) = \alpha \mathbf{P}v + \beta \mathbf{P}w$.
  (ii) **P** is *symmetric:* $\mathbf{P}(\theta v) = \theta(\mathbf{P}v)$ for every one-to-one mapping θ of N into itself (i.e., a permutation of the players; for a game w the "permuted" game θw is defined by $(\theta w)(S) = w(\theta S)$ for all $S \subset N$).
  (iii) **P** is *positive:* $v \geq 0$ implies $\mathbf{P}v \geq 0$ (where $w \geq 0$ means $w(S) \geq 0$ for all $S \subset N$).
  (iv) **P** is *one-to-one* and *onto*.

(v) The *fixed points* of **P** are the inessential games (or additive games – games v such that $v(S) = \Sigma_{i \in S} v(\{i\})$ for all $S \subset N$).

Proof: Preposition 1 implies that if we decompose v as $v = \Sigma \alpha_T u_T$, then $\mathbf{P}v = \Sigma(\alpha_T/|T|)u_T$ (both sums are over $T \subset N$ and α_T is given by (5)). From this (i), (ii), (iv), and (v) follow easily, and (iii) is implied by Proposition 2. ∎

From these basic properties additional ones may be derived. For example:

Corollary 2. If the core of (N,v) is not empty (i.e., (N,v) is balanced), then $P(N,v) \leq v(N)$. If (N,v) is a market game (i.e., totally balanced), then $\mathbf{P}v \leq v$.

Proof: Let $x = (x^i)_{i \in N}$ be a payoff vector in the core of (N,v) and consider the inessential game (N,w) given by $w(S) = \Sigma_{i \in S} x^i$ for all $S \subset N$. Then $v \leq w$, implying $\mathbf{P}v \leq \mathbf{P}w = w$ (apply (i), (iii), and (iv) of Proposition 3); hence $P(N,v) = (\mathbf{P}v)(N) \leq w(N) = v(N)$. In a market game this argument applies to all subgames as well. ∎

3   Consistency

This section presents one of the results obtained by the potential approach. It shows that the Shapley value enjoys an internal consistency property, similarly to most solution concepts (see Hart and Mas-Colell 1987, sec. 4 for references).

The "consistency" requirement may be described informally as follows: Let ϕ be a "solution function" that associates a payoff to every player in every game. For any group of players in a game, one defines a "reduced game" among them by considering the amounts remaining after the rest of the players are given the payoffs prescribed by ϕ. Then ϕ is said to be *consistent* if, when it is applied to any reduced game, it always yields the same payoffs as in the original game.

Formally, a *solution function* ϕ is a function defined on Γ, the set of all games, that associates to every $(N,v) \in \Gamma$ a payoff vector $\phi(N,v) = (\phi^i(N,v))_{i \in N} \in \mathbf{R}^N$. Given a solution function ϕ, a game (N,v), and a coalition $T \subset N$, the *reduced game* (T,v^ϕ_T) is defined by

$$v^\phi_T(S) = v(S \cup T^c) - \sum_{i \in T^c} \phi^i(S \cup T^c, v) \tag{7}$$

for all $S \subset T$, where $T^c = N \backslash T$. The solution function ϕ is *consistent* if

$$\phi^j(T, v_T^\phi) = \phi^j(N, v) \tag{8}$$

for every game (N, v), every coalition $T \subset N$, and all $j \in T$.

These definitions may be interpreted as follows. Fix ϕ, (N, v), and $T \subset N$. The members of T – more precisely, every (sub)coalition $S \subset T$ – need to consider the total payoff remaining after the players in T^c are paid according to ϕ. To compute the worth of S (in this reduced game), one assumes that the complementary coalition $T \backslash S$ is not present. Therefore, the game to be considered is $(S \cup T^c, v)$, in which the payoffs are distributed according to ϕ. The amount that remains for S is then precisely that given by (7). Finally, note that, if ϕ is efficient, then

$$v_T^\phi(S) = \sum_{i \in S} \phi^i(S \cup T^c, v). \tag{9}$$

There are alternative definitions of consistency (used for various solution concepts). They differ only in the definition of the reduced game. The appropriateness of definition (7) here depends on the specific situation being modeled, particularly on the concrete assumptions underlying the determination of the characteristic function.

One example where (7) appears to be the natural definition is the problem of allocating joint costs among various projects (or departments, tasks, etc.); these projects are now the "players." The cost imputations are *not* to be interpreted as some kind of "efficiency prices" that are used to make optimal decisions on which projects to undertake, but as an equitable way to distribute exactly the total costs once the set of projects is fixed.

Such an instance arises in multistate corporations that for tax purposes have to allocate the joint costs (and benefits) among the projects in the various states in which they operate. As an example of such a corporation and, say, its Tennessee division, let T be the set of projects in Tennessee. For every subset $S \subset T$ of Tennessee's projects, the "local accountant" has to determine its cost, assuming that it was the only subset of projects to be undertaken in Tennessee. In addition, there is the set T^C of all the projects outside Tennessee (which are not in the domain of this local "gedanken experiment"). Therefore, the cost of S is the amount imputed to it by the "accounting procedure" (= solution function) under consideration when the set of projects to be implemented is $S \cup T^c$. This is exactly given by formula (9). Consistency requires that for T the imputation obtained by the local accountant be no different than that of the general (national) accountant.

It turns out that this consistency requirement is the one satisfied by the Shapley value. Moreover, together with the appropriate initial conditions for two-person games, consistency uniquely characterizes the Shapley value.

A solution function ϕ is *standard for two-person games* if

$$\phi^i(\{i,j\},v) = v(\{i\}) + \tfrac{1}{2}[v(\{i,j\}) - v(\{i\}) - v(\{j\})]$$

for all v and all $i \neq j$; thus, in a two-person game each player first gets his own guaranteed payoff and then the remaining "surplus" is divided equally. Most solutions satisfy this condition. The main result can now be stated.

Theorem B. Let ϕ be a solution function. Then ϕ is (i) consistent and (ii) standard for two-person games, if and only if ϕ is the Shapley value.

Proof: First, we show that the Shapley value is a consistent solution function. Let (N,v) be a game and $T \subset N$ a nonempty coalition. The reduced game $v_T = v_T^\phi$ (where ϕ is the Shapley value) is given by (see (9) and Theorem A)

$$v_T(S) = \sum_{i \in S} [P(S \cup T^c,v) - P(S \cup T^c\backslash\{i\},v)] \tag{10}$$

for every $S \subset T$. By Theorem A, the potential of the game (T,v_T) is uniquely determined by formula (1) applied to the game and all its subgames. Comparing this with (10) implies that

$$P(S,v_T) = P(S \cup T^c,v) + c$$

for all $S \subset T$, where c is an appropriate constant (so as to make $P(\varnothing,v_T) = 0$). Therefore

$$\begin{aligned}
\text{Sh}^i(T,v_T) &= P(T,v_T) - P(T\backslash\{i\},v_T) \\
&= P(N,v) - P(N\backslash\{i\},v) = \text{Sh}^i(N,v)
\end{aligned}$$

for every $i \in T$, proving that the Shapley values of the players in the reduced game and in the original game coincide.

For the converse, one may show that if ϕ satisfies (i) and (ii), then ϕ must admit a potential function (see the proof of Theorem B in Hart and Mas-Colell 1987).[14] We provide here an alternative direct proof (see Lemma 6.8 in Hart and Mas-Colell 1987).

First, we show that (i) and (ii) imply that ϕ is efficient; that is,

$$\sum_{i \in N} \phi^i(N,v) = v(N)$$

for all games (N,v). This holds for $|N| = 2$, by (ii), and for $|N| = 1$ (add a dummy player and apply (ii) and (i) to the resulting two-person game). Now consider a game (N,v) with $|N| \geq 3$. Let $T \subset N$ be a two-person coalition; by consistency

$$\sum_{j \in N} \phi^j(N,v) = \sum_{j \in T} \phi^j(T,v_T^\phi) + \sum_{i \in T^c} \phi^i(N,v).$$

Because $|T| = 2$, the first sum equals $v_T^\phi(T)$; the definition (7) of the reduced game now implies that the right side is $v(N)$.

Second, assume ϕ and ψ are two solution functions satisfying (i) and (ii), and assume by induction that they coincide for all games with less than n players (this is true for $n = 3$). Let (N,v) be an n-person game, and let $i, j \in N$, $i \neq j$. Consider the two reduced games $(\{i,j\}, v_{(i,j)}^\phi)$ and $(\{i,j\}, v_{(i,j)}^\psi)$, which we denote by v^ϕ and v^ψ, respectively. They coincide for singletons (by induction, because only $n - 1$ players matter); therefore, by (ii), $\phi^i(v^\phi) \gtreqless \phi^i(v^\psi)$ if and only if $\phi^j(v^\phi) \gtreqless \phi^j(v^\psi)$ (if and only if $v^\phi(\{i,j\}) \gtreqless v^\psi(\{i,j\})$). Now $\phi = \psi$ for two-person games, and both ϕ and ψ are consistent; therefore

$$\phi^i(N,v) = \phi^i(v^\phi) \gtreqless \phi^i(v^\psi) = \psi^i(v^\psi) = \psi^i(N,v)$$

if and only if, similarly,

$$\phi^j(N,v) \gtreqless \psi^j(N,v).$$

This applies, however, to any two players i and j; because both ϕ and ψ are efficient, we must therefore have $\phi^i(N,v) = \psi^i(N,v)$ for all i. ∎

See Hart and Mas-Colell (1987) for additional results regarding consistency and the Shapley value (and its extensions, the weighted Shapley values and the nontransferable utility case).

NOTES

1 Other solution concepts (e.g., bargaining set, kernel, nucleolus, etc.) may also fit this description.
2 A simpler solution may be easier to study and apply, which increases its usefulness. However, it is important to look at different solution concepts, based on different postulates, because they illuminate the problem from different angles.
3 Up to an additive constant (which does not change the marginal contributions).
4 $\mathbf{R}$ denotes the set of real numbers, $\varnothing$ is the empty set, and the symbol \ is used for set subtraction.

5   All subset inclusions should be understood in the weak sense (i.e., equality is possible).
6   We write $P(N,v)$ rather than $P((N,v))$.
7   There is only one "empty game" $(\varnothing,v)$, because $v(\varnothing) = 0$ always.
8   $|A|$ denotes the number of elements of the finite set A.
9   For another proof see Hart and Mas-Colell (1987).
10 Note that the explicit formula for the Shapley value (=average marginal contribution) also applies to just one game. However, this seems too complex to be viewed as a "basic postulate" (in particular, one has to justify the specific probabilistic model).
11 McKenzie, L. (1959), "On the Existence of General Equilibrium for a Competitive Market," *Econometrica* 27, 54–71.
12 A similar construction is embodied in this story: A sheik died, leaving a will directing his three sons to divide the property as follows: one-half goes to the oldest son, one-third to the middle son, and one-ninth to the youngest. The property consisted of seventeen camels. The problem was solved by the "wise man" who rode into town on his camel. He added his own camel to the seventeen, and then the three brothers took their shares out of the eighteen camels: nine, six, and two, respectively. One camel was left, on which the wise man rode out of town.
13 Formula (6) should hardly be surprising. The Shapley value is the expected marginal contribution; we obtain it here as the marginal contribution to the appropriate expectation – the potential.
14 Another proof has been independently obtained by Michael Maschler.

REFERENCES

Harsanyi, J. C. [1963], "A Simplified Bargaining Model for the *n*-Person Cooperative Game," *International Economic Review* 4, 194–220.

Hart, S. and A. Mas-Colell [1987], "Potential, Value and Consistency," forthcoming in *Econometrica*.

Shapley, L. S. [1953], "A Value for *n*-Person Games," *Contributions to the Theory of Games*, vol. II (*Annals of Mathematics Studies* 28), H. W. Kuhn and A. W. Tucker (eds.), Princeton University Press, Princeton, pp. 307–17.

CHAPTER 10

Multilinear extensions of games

Guillermo Owen

1   Definition

Let v be a game with player set $N = \{1,2, \ldots ,n\}$; that is, v is a real-valued function with domain 2^N. We define the *multilinear extension* (MLE) of v as the function of n real variables

$$f(q_1, \ldots ,q_n) = \sum_{S \subset N} \prod_{j \in S} q_j \prod_{j \notin S} (1 - q_j) v(S). \tag{1}$$

In general, (1) is defined for all real values of q_j. In practice, however, we consider only values of f on the unit cube

$$Q_n = [0,1]^n = \{(q_1, \ldots ,q_n) | 0 \le q_j \le 1 \text{ for all } j\}.$$

The cube Q_n has 2^n vertices (extreme points), namely points where all components are either 0 or 1. There is a natural correspondence between these vertices and the 2^n subsets of N, namely $\alpha^S \leftrightarrow S$, where

$$\alpha_j^S = \begin{cases} 1 & \text{if } j \in S, \\ 0 & \text{if } j \notin S. \end{cases}$$

We call this correspondence the *natural embedding* of 2^N in Q_n. In this sense, 2^N is a subset of Q_n.

Now, for any $T \subset N$,

$$f(\alpha^T) = \sum_{S \subset N} \prod_{j \in S} \alpha_j^T \prod_{j \notin S} (1 - \alpha_j^T) v(S),$$

and it is not too difficult to see that this reduces to

$$f(\alpha^T) = v(T).$$

In this sense, then, f coincides with v on the domain of v (the vertices of Q_n), and we are justified in saying that f is an extension of v. Because, in addition, f is linear in each of the variables q_j, it is a multilinear function.

139

It can be shown, finally (see Owen 1972), that f is the only multi-linear function on Q_n that coincides with v on the vertices. Thus f is *the multilinear extension* of v.

An alternative, equivalent, expression is

$$f(q_1, \ldots ,q_n) = \sum_{S \subset N} \prod_{j \in S} q_j \Delta(S), \qquad (2)$$

where $\Delta(S)$ is the *dividend* of S in game v, given by

$$\Delta(S) = \sum_{T \subset S} (-1)^{s-t} v(T), \qquad (3)$$

s and t being the cardinalities of S and T, respectively.

2   Interpretation

The importance of the MLE is better seen from its applications. Nevertheless, an interpretation is always desirable. We consider two. The first interpretation of the MLE is as an interpolation formula. In fact, a function f is given (by v) on the corners of the cube Q_n. To obtain a value for f at other points of the cube, we might use an interpolation technique. Linear interpolation (with respect to each of the n variables) will give us (1).

This is easiest to see when $n = 2$. In this case, a function $f(x,y)$ is defined at the four points $(0,0)$, $(0,1)$, $(1,0)$, and $(1,1)$. To approximate f at an arbitrary point (x,y), we first interpolate linearly to obtain $f(0,y)$ and $f(1,y)$:

$$f(0,y) = (1 - y)f(0,0) + yf(0,1), \qquad (4)$$

$$f(1,y) = (1 - y)f(1,0) + yf(1,1). \qquad (5)$$

Having obtained these, we proceed to interpolate for $f(x,y)$:

$$f(x,y) = (1 - x)f(0,y) + xf(1,y). \qquad (6)$$

Substituting (4)–(5) in (6), gives

$$f(x,y) = (1 - x)(1 - y)f(0,0) + x(1 - y)f(1,0)$$
$$+ (1 - x)yf(0,1) + xyf(1,1). \qquad (7)$$

It is easy to check that (7) is the same as (1) with $n = 2$, $x = q_1$, $y = q_2$.

An alternative, and more interesting, interpretation of the MLE is as an expected value. In fact, let ß be a random coalition – that is, a random subset of N. We specify the randomization scheme by assuming that, for each $j \in N$, the event $A_j: j \in \text{ß}$ has probability q_j, and that these events A_j are independent. Under these assumptions, it is easy to see that, for a given $S \subset N$,

$$\text{Prob}\{\text{ß} = S\} = \prod_{j \in S} q_j \prod_{j \notin S} 1 - q_j. \tag{8}$$

It follows that

$$f(q_1, \ldots, q_n) = E[v(\text{ß})],$$

where $E[\,\cdot\,]$ denotes the expected value. For this interpretation, see Ben-Dov and Shilony (1985).

3 Relation to the power index

Let f be the MLE of game v. For any $j \in N$ we have the partial derivative

$$\frac{\partial f}{\partial q_j} = \sum_{\substack{S \subset N \\ j \in S}} \prod_{\substack{i \in S \\ i \neq j}} q_i \prod_{i \notin S} (1 - q_i) v(S) - \sum_{\substack{S \subset N \\ j \notin S}} \prod_{i \in S} q_i \prod_{\substack{i \notin S \\ i \neq j}} (1 - q_i) v(S). \tag{9}$$

This can be rewritten as

$$f_j(q_1, \ldots, q_n) = \sum_{\substack{S \subset N \\ j \notin S}} \prod_{i \in S} q_i \prod_{\substack{i \notin S \\ i \neq j}} (1 - q_i)[v(S \cup \{j\}) - v(S)] \tag{10}$$

(the subscript on f denotes differentiation).

Next suppose that $(q_1, \ldots, q_n)$ lies on the main diagonal of the cube (i.e., all the q_i have a common value r). Then

$$f_j(r, \ldots, r) = \sum_{\substack{S \subset N \\ j \notin S}} r^s (1 - r)^{n-s-1}[v(S \cup \{j\}) - v(S)]. \tag{11}$$

Integrating this with respect to r, we have

$$\int_0^1 f_j(r, \ldots, r) \, dr = \sum_{\substack{S \subset N \\ j \notin S}} \int_0^1 r^s (1 - r)^{n-s-1} \, dr \, [v(S \cup \{j\}) - v(S)].$$

The integral in this last expression is a well-known definite integral (the beta function). Thus

$$\int_0^1 f_j(r, \ldots, r) \, dr = \sum_{\substack{S \subset N \\ j \notin S}} \frac{s!(n - s - 1)!}{n!} [v(S \cup \{j\}) - v(S)],$$

and this is the Shapley value or power index. Thus the value ϕ is given by

$$\phi_j[v] = \int_0^1 f_j(r, \ldots, r) \, dr. \tag{12}$$

In other words, the value can be obtained by integrating the gradient of the MLE along the main diagonal of the cube.

Certain modifications come to mind almost immediately:

(a) Integrate along the main diagonal with respect to some measure other than Lebesgue measure.

(b) Integrate along some other curve from $(0, \ldots, 0)$ to $(1, \ldots, 1)$.

(c) Evaluate the gradient at some fixed point, say $(\frac{1}{2}, \ldots, \frac{1}{2})$.

(d) Integrate inside some higher-dimensional subset of Q_n – perhaps some neighborhood of the main diagonal.

We point out that (c)–evaluation of the gradient at the center of the cube – gives the Banzhaf–Coleman index (see Owen 1975b for this.) Integration inside the entire cube with regard to n-dimensional Lebesgue measure also gives the Banzhaf–Coleman index. For (a) see Dubey, Neyman, and Weber (1981), where *semivalues* are discussed. Idea (b) might be useful when dealing with compound games; see Section 4 and Grofman and Owen (1984).

Example. Let v be the four-person apex game – that is, the simple game in which the winning coalitions are $\{1,2\}$, $\{1,3\}$, $\{1,4\}$, plus all three-person and four-person coalitions. If we set $q = (w,x,y,z)$, the MLE is

$$f(w,x,y,z) = wx(1 - y)(1 - z) + wy(1 - x)(1 - z) + wz(1 - x)(1 - y)$$
$$+ wxy(1 - z) + wxz(1 - y) + wyz(1 - x) + xyz(1 - w)$$
$$+ wxyz.$$

Some algebra reduces this to

$$f(x,y,z,w) = wx + wy + wz - wxy - wxz - wyz + xyz,$$

so the partial f_1 (or f_w) is

$$f_1 = x + y + z - xy - xz - yz.$$

On the diagonal, this gives

$$f_1(r,r,r,r) = 3r - 3r^2,$$

so, by (12),

$$\phi_1 = \int_0^1 (3r - 3r^2) \, dr = \tfrac{1}{2}.$$

Similarly,

$$f_2 = w - wy - wz + yz,$$

or

$$f_2(r,r,r,r) = r - r^2,$$

and

$$\phi_2 = \int_0^1 (r - r^2) \, dr = \tfrac{1}{6}.$$

By the game's symmetry, the Shapley value is then $(\tfrac{1}{2},\tfrac{1}{6},\tfrac{1}{6},\tfrac{1}{6})$, as is well known.

We can also evaluate the Banzhaf–Coleman index by evaluating the partials at the midpoint. In fact, $f_1(\tfrac{1}{2},\tfrac{1}{2},\tfrac{1}{2},\tfrac{1}{2}) = \tfrac{3}{4}$, and $f_2(\tfrac{1}{2},\tfrac{1}{2},\tfrac{1}{2},\tfrac{1}{2}) = \tfrac{1}{4}$, giving us the index $(\tfrac{3}{4},\tfrac{1}{4},\tfrac{1}{4},\tfrac{1}{4})$, also a well-known result.

4   Applications to measure games

A measure on N is an additive, nonnegative set function μ defined on 2^N. Because N is finite, we can define μ in terms of a weight vector $(w_1, w_2, \ldots, w_n)$ with nonnegative components: $w_i = \mu(\{i\})$. We consider here games of the form $v = h \circ \mu$, where μ is a measure and h is a well-behaved (read monotone) function. (More generally, μ could be a vector-valued measure. The number of components of μ should, however, be considerably smaller than the number of players in the game.)

Consider, once again, equation (10). Using the probabilistic interpretation, we may restate it as

$$f_j(q_1, \ldots, q_n) = E[v(\mathcal{B} \cup \{j\}) - v(\mathcal{B})], \qquad (13)$$

where $\mathcal{B}$ is a random subset of $N - \{j\}$, defined, as before, by the probabilities q_i (that player i belongs to $\mathcal{B}$) and the independence of these probabilities.

Now, $v = h \circ \mu$, so this reduces to

$$f_j = E[h(Z_j + w_j) - h(Z_j)], \qquad (14)$$

where Z_j is the random variable $\mu(\mathcal{B})$.

In turn, we note that we can express Z_j in the form

$$Z_j = \sum_{i \neq j} Y_i,$$

where Y_i equals w_i if $i \in \text{ß}$, and 0 otherwise. It is easy to see that

$$E[Y_i] = q_i w_i \quad \text{and} \quad \sigma^2(Y_i) = q_i(1 - q_i)w_i^2,$$

so (by independence of the Y_i)

$$E[Z_j] = \sum_{i \neq j} q_i w_i, \tag{15}$$

$$\sigma^2(Z_j) = \sum_{i \neq j} q_i(1 - q_i)w_i^2. \tag{16}$$

For points on the main diagonal, all $q_i = r$, so (15)–(16) reduce to

$$E[Z_j] = r \sum_{i \neq j} w_i, \tag{17}$$

$$\sigma^2(Z_j) = r(1 - r) \sum_{i \neq j} w_i^2. \tag{18}$$

In general, of course, the actual distribution of the random variable Z_j can be quite complicated. In practice, two cases seem of interest:

(a) If all w_j are equal (and in that case they may be assumed to equal 1) then Z_j is a binomial variable with parameters $n - 1$ and r.

(b) If n is large and none of the w_j is much larger than the others, then the central limit theorem will apply and Z_j may be assumed to be (approximately) normal.

Case (a) may be of interest in certain cases. It is the normal approximation (b) that is most useful. For example, consider the electoral college. Treated as a fifty-one-player game, the electoral college is defined by the weight vector $w = (9,3,7, \ldots ,6,11,3)$ corresponding to the states and District of Columbia (in alphabetical order). The game function v is then $v = h \circ \mu$, where μ is the measure determined by vector w, and

$$h(t) = \begin{cases} 1 & \text{if } t > 269.5, \\ 0 & \text{if } t \leq 269.5. \end{cases}$$

Equation (14) now takes the form

$$f_j = \text{Prob}\{269.5 - w_j < Z_j \leq 269.5\}. \tag{19}$$

It is easily seen that

$$\sum_{i \in N} w_i = 538, \qquad \sum_{i \in N} w_i^2 = 9606.$$

Thus, by (17) and (18), Z_j will have mean $(538 - w_j)r$ and variance $(9606 - w_j^2)r(1 - r)$. If we can assume that Z_j is normal, f_j is merely the probability that a normal variable, with such a mean and variance, lies between $269.5 - w_j$ and 269.5. The mean and the variance both depend on r, and it will now be necessary to integrate (numerically) as r goes from 0 to 1. This integration will give the desired value $\phi_j[v]$.

Owen (1975a) compares these results with the exact values (for the 1970 apportionment); the errors are quite small. More recently, Kemperman (1982) carried out the integration (12), using a more sophisticated error analysis to determine (19). His results are extremely close to the exact values.

5   Composite games

Let v be a game with player set $N = \{1,2, \ldots ,n\}$. For each $j \in N$, let w_j be a game with player set M_j, satisfying

$$0 \le w_j(S) \le w_j(M_j) = 1 \tag{20}$$

for all $S \subset M_j$, and assume the sets M_j are pairwise disjoint, with union

$$M^* = \cup_{j=1}^n M_j.$$

We can now define a game u – the *composite game* – on player set M^*. We write $u = v[w_1, w_2, \ldots ,w_n]$, which is defined by setting, for each $T \subset M^*$,

$$u(T) = \sum_{S \subset N} \prod_{j \in S} w_j(T_j) \prod_{j \notin S} (1 - w_j(T_j))v(S), \tag{21}$$

where $T_j = T \cap M_j$. The similarity of (21) to (1) is obvious. Note, moreover, that if each of the games w_j is simple, with $w_j(S) = 0$ or 1, then (21) reduces to

$$u(T) = v(\{j | w_j(T_j) = 1\}). \tag{22}$$

Thus in this case we obtain the standard composition of simple games, treated in Owen (1964) and Shapley (1964). We call u the composite or *compound* game, v is the *quotient* game, and the w_j are the *subgames*. We will use (i, j) to denote the ith player in subgame j.

Subgame w_j has the MLE g_j, which is a function of the m_j variables x_{ij} (fixed j). We have $g_j: Q_{M_j} \to [0,1]$, and the n-tuple of functions $(g_1, \ldots ,g_n)$ can be thought of as a vector-valued function $\mathbf{g}: \times_j Q_{M_j} \to [0,1]^n$ or, equivalently, $\mathbf{g}: Q_{M^*} \to Q_n$. Now let f be the MLE of v. Clearly, $f: Q_n \to R$, and so the composite function $f \circ \mathbf{g}: Q_{M^*} \to R$.

Because the sets M_j are disjoint, it is not difficult to see that $h = f \circ g$ is also multilinear. Hence h is the MLE of some game with player set M^*. It is then quite straightforward to show that h is the MLE of the composite game u. Thus, *composition of games corresponds to composition of the MLEs.*

We now have

$$h(x_{11}, \ldots, x_{mn}) = f(q_1, q_2, \ldots, q_n), \tag{23}$$

where

$$q_j = g_j(x_{1j}, \ldots, x_{mj}), \tag{24}$$

and so

$$\frac{\partial h}{\partial x_{ij}} = \frac{\partial f}{\partial q_j} \frac{\partial g_j}{\partial x_{ij}}. \tag{25}$$

Using the notation $h_{ij} = \partial h/\partial x_{ij}$, $g_{ij} = \partial g_j/\partial x_{ij}$ and setting all $x_{ij} = r$, we get

$$h_{ij}(r, r, \ldots, r) = f_j(y_1, \ldots, y_n)g_{ij}(r, \ldots, r), \tag{26}$$

where

$$y_k = g_k(r, \ldots, r). \tag{27}$$

Now, (12) becomes

$$\phi_{ij}[u] = \int_0^1 f_j(y_1, \ldots, y_n)g_{ij}(r, \ldots, r) \, dr. \tag{28}$$

In many cases, especially when the games w_j are symmetric, we are interested mainly in the sum of the values for the players in one of the subgames. We then have

$$\sum_{M_j} \phi_{ij}[u] = \int_0^1 f_j(y_1, \ldots, y_n) \left\{ \sum_{M_j} g_{ij}(r, \ldots, r) \right\} dr. \tag{29}$$

Note, however, that by (27),

$$\frac{dy_j}{dr} = \sum_{M_j} g_{ij}(r, r, \ldots, r), \tag{30}$$

and so

$$\sum_{M_j} \phi_{ij}[u] = \int_0^1 f_j(y_1, \ldots, y_n) \frac{dy_j}{dr} \, dr. \tag{31}$$

We see that (31) corresponds to integrating the gradient of the MLE f, not along the main diagonal $q_j = r$ but along the more complicated path

$$q_j = y_j(r) = g_j(r,r, \ldots ,r). \tag{32}$$

However, because $w_j(\varnothing) = 0$ and $w_j(M_j) = 1$, then $y_j(0) = 0$ and $y_j(1) = 1$, so path (32) goes from the origin to the unit point $(1,1, \ldots ,1)$.

With regard to this, see Owen (1982, pp. 209–11) for an evaluation of the game corresponding to the Victoria Amendment Procedure, which was once proposed (but rejected) for the Canadian Constitution.

In an important special case, all the w_j are symmetric majority games in which any coalition with a_j (out of m_j) players wins. In that case,

$$y_j = 1 - B(m_j,a_j - 1,r), \tag{33}$$

where $B(\cdot , \cdot , \cdot)$ represents the cumulative binomial distribution – that is, the probability of not more than $a_j - 1$ successes in m_j trials of a simple experiment with success probability r. For large values of m_j this can be approximated by the normal distribution, so in this case (32) could be replaced by

$$y_j = \Phi \left(\frac{rm_j - a_j + \frac{1}{2}}{\sqrt{r(1 - r)m_j}} \right), \tag{34}$$

where Φ represents the (cumulative) normal distribution function.

Owen (1975a) uses this technique to approximate the value of the presidential election game. It is difficult to estimate the error in this procedure, but it should be of the same order of magnitude as in the electoral college (fifty-one-player) game.

6 Generalizations

As a technique for evaluating the value, the MLE approach is logically analogous to the diagonal technique for nonatomic games (see Aumann and Shapley 1974). Applications are found in Billera, Heath, and Ranaan (1978) and Diaz and Owen (1979).

Attempts to adapt the MLE method to games without sidepayments have not been so successful. See, however, Owen (1972a, 1981).

7 Example: The bilateral oligopoly

Let us consider a game of the form

$$v(S) = \min\{\mu_1(S), \mu_2(S)\}, \tag{35}$$

where μ_k ($k = 1,2$) are two measures on the finite set N. We assume they are determined by the two weight vectors $(x_1, \ldots, x_n)$ and $(y_1, \ldots, y_n)$, respectively.

Heuristically, player i has x_i right shoes and y_i left shoes; each pair of shoes is worth one dollar, but unpaired shoes are worthless. Thus, $v(S)$ is equal to the number of pairs that S can form.

There is no loss of generality in assuming that $N = M \cup L$, $M \cap L = \varnothing$, with $x_i = 0$ for all $i \in L$ and $y_i = 0$ for all $i \in M$. In fact, if any player i had x_i and y_i positive, he could form $\min(x_i,y_i)$ pairs and obtain this utility directly. He would then enter the coalition process with only the remaining shoes, which would then be all of one type. Thus, our assumption is equivalent to a normalization of the characteristic function. Therefore, members of M have only right shoes; members of L have only left shoes.

Let us set

$$a = \sum_M x_i, \tag{36}$$

$$b = \sum_L y_i, \tag{37}$$

$$c = \sum_M x_i^2, \tag{38}$$

$$d = \sum_L y_i^2. \tag{39}$$

The exact analysis of this game can be quite complicated. As an approximation, however, we proceed as follows.

If we assume $a \geq b$ (there are at least as many right shoes as left), then $V(N) = b$, so there is one unit of utility available for each left shoe. The moot question concerns the share of this utility, s_L, that the left shoes (or their owners) will get.

From (35) we note that

$$\frac{\partial v}{\partial \mu_2} = \begin{cases} 1 & \text{if } \mu_2 < \mu_1, \\ 0 & \text{if } \mu_2 > \mu_1. \end{cases}$$

Now the MLE is

$$f(q_1, \ldots, q_n) = E[\max\{\mu_1(\beta), \mu_2(\beta)\}], \tag{40}$$

where β was discussed earlier. It should follow that the left shoes' share of the increase in f should be approximately equal to

$$\frac{1}{b} \sum_L f_j \cong \text{Prob}\{\mu_1(\beta) > \mu_2(\beta)\}$$

or, equivalently,

$$\frac{1}{b} \sum_L f_j = \text{Prob}\{Z_2 - Z_1 < 0\},$$

where $Z_k = \mu_k(\beta)$ $(k = 1,2)$.

Now for a point on the diagonal with all $q_i = r$, we see that

$$E[Z_1] = ra, \qquad E[Z_2] = rb,$$
$$\sigma^2(Z_1) = r(1 - r)c, \qquad \sigma^2(Z_2) = r(1 - r)d,$$

so the difference $Y = Z_2 - Z_1$ has mean and variance

$$E[Y] = r(b - a), \tag{41}$$

$$\sigma^2(Y) = r(1 - r)(c + d). \tag{42}$$

If, indeed, Y is approximately normal, then

$$\text{Prob}(Y < 0) \cong \Phi\left(\frac{a - b}{\sqrt{c + d}} \sqrt{\frac{r}{1 - r}}\right),$$

or

$$\text{Prob}(Y < 0) \cong \Phi\left(\alpha \sqrt{\frac{r}{1 - r}}\right), \tag{43}$$

where

$$\alpha = \frac{a - b}{\sqrt{c + d}} \tag{44}$$

and Φ is the normal distribution function.

Thus, by (12) we obtain

$$s_L = \frac{1}{b} \sum_L \phi_j[v] \cong \int_0^1 \Phi\left(\alpha \sqrt{\frac{r}{1 - r}}\right) dr,$$

or

$$s_L \cong \frac{1}{\sqrt{2\pi}} \int_0^1 \int_{-\infty}^{\alpha \sqrt{r/(1-r)}} e^{-x^2/2} \, dx \, dr. \tag{45}$$

Some rather lengthy analysis shows that, for $\alpha \geq 0$, (45) reduces to

$$s_L \cong \frac{1}{2} + \frac{\alpha \Phi(-\alpha)}{2\Psi(\alpha)}, \tag{46}$$

where Ψ is the normal density function.

For large values of α (corresponding to nearly perfect competition) we can further use the asymptotic expansion

$$\Phi(-\alpha) \sim \Psi(\alpha)\left(\frac{1}{\alpha} - \frac{1}{\alpha^3} - \cdots\right), \tag{47}$$

so (46) further reduces to

$$s_L \cong 1 - \frac{1}{2\alpha^2} \tag{48}$$

or

$$s_L \cong 1 - \frac{c + d}{2(a - b)^2}. \tag{49}$$

Thus, for large α the short side of the market will get the lion's share of the utility. Even for small α, however, the short side has a decided advantage: For $\alpha = .3562$, equation (46) gives $s_L \cong .6717$.

It seems difficult to check on the validity of approximation (46) in general. Suppose, however, that $x_i = 1$ for all M, and $y_i = 1$ for all L. Thus, each player has exactly one shoe. For this special case, Shapley (1967) has given us the exact value

$$s_L = \frac{1}{2} + \frac{a - b}{2b} \sum_{k=1}^{b} \frac{a!b!}{(a + k)!(b - k)!}. \tag{50}$$

For $a = 101$, $b = 96$, (50) gives $s_L = .66346$.

On the other hand, we will then have $c = a = 101$, $d = b = 96$, so $\alpha = 5/\sqrt{197} = .3562$ and (46), as mentioned, gives $s_L \cong .6717$. There is an error of 1 percent, which we feel is quite reasonable. Thus (46) seems to be, in general, a useful result.

REFERENCES

Aumann, R. J., and L. S. Shapley. *Values of Non-Atomic Games.* Princeton University Press, 1974.

Ben-Dov, Y., and Y. Shilony. "Power and Importance in a Theory of Lobbying." *Behav. Sci.* 27, 69–76 (1985).

Billera, L., D. Heath, and J. Ranaan. "Internal Telephone Billing Rates." *Op. Res.* 27, 956–65 (1978).

Diaz, H., and G. Owen. "Fair Subsidies for Urban Transportation Systems." In *Applied Game Theory,* ed. S. Brams, A. Schotter, and G. Schwödiauer, Physika-Verlag, 1979, pp. 325–33.

Dubey, P., A. Neyman, and R. J. Weber. "Value Theory without Efficiency." *Math. Op. Res.* 6, 120–8 (1981).

Grofman, B., and G. Owen. "Coalitions and Power in Political Situations." In *Coalitions and Collective Action,* ed. M. J. Holler, Physika-Verlag, 1984, pp. 137–44.

Kemperman, R. H. "Asymptotic Expansions for the Shapley Index of Power." University of Rochester, Dept. of Statistics, 1982.

Owen, G. "Tensor Composition of Non-Negative Games." In *Ann. Math. Study* 52, ed. M. Dresher, L. S. Shapley, and A. W. Tucker, Princeton, 1964, pp. 307–26.

"Multilinear Extensions of Games." *Man. Sci.* 18, P64–P79 (1972).

"Values of Games without Side Payments." *Int. J. Game Thy.* 1, 93–109 (1972a).

"Evaluation of a Presidential Election Game." *Amer. Poli. Sci. Rev.* 69, 947–53 (1975a).

"Multilinear Extensions and the Banzhaf Value." *Nav. Res. Log. Quart.* 22, 741–52 (1975b).

"Values of Market Games without Side Payments." *Rev. Acad. Col. Cienc. Exa.,* 69, 5–24.

Game Theory, second edition. Academic Press, 1982.

Shapley, L. S. "A Value for *n*-Person Games." In *Ann. Math. Study* 28, ed. H. W. Kuhn and A. W. Tucker, 1953, pp. 307–17.

"Solutions of Compound Simple Games." In *Ann. Math. Study* 52, ed. M. Dresher, L. S. Shapley, and A. W. Tucker, 1964, pp. 327–37.

"The Value of the Game as a Tool in Theoretical Economics." RAND Corp. Report P-2658, 1967.

PART III

Coalitions

CHAPTER 11

Coalitional value

Mordecai Kurz

1 Solutions of games with coalition structures

The study of coalition structures has been seriously explored only recently. Coalition structures are already implicit in the von Neumann–Morgenstern (1944) solutions; because of their internal and external stability the solutions isolate those stable coalition structures that generate the final payoffs. This is to be contrasted with the extensive subsequent literature on the core in which "blocking" is merely a criterion for accepting or rejecting a proposed allocation; no specific coalition structure is implicit in any core allocation. Analysis of games in partition function form (see, for example, Thrall and Lucas 1963) is a more explicit way of studying restrictions on coalition structures. Perhaps the best-studied class of games whose core of a coalition structure was investigated is the "central assignment games" (see, for example, Shapley and Shubik 1972; Kaneko 1982; and Quinzii 1984). This class includes the particular case of the "marriage games" (Gale and Shapley 1962) and is closely related to the various variants of the "job matching games" (see, for example, Crawford and Knoer 1981; Kelso and Crawford 1982; Roth 1984a,b). The nonemptiness of the core of the coalition structure of these games is an important result, to which we return in Section 3.

The study of coalition structures was enhanced by the approach taken in the literature on the various bargaining sets. In this literature an explicit definition of coalition structures was given and solution concepts were developed relative to such structures rather than relative to the grand coalition (see, for example, Aumann and Maschler 1964 or Davis and

This work was supported by National Science Foundation Grant IST-85-21838 at the Institute for Mathematical Studies in the Social Sciences, Stanford University, Stanford, California. It is a pleasure to dedicate this chapter to a volume in honor of Lloyd Shapley's 65th birthday. He has been a source of profound inspiration.
The author thanks John Hillas for his comments on an earlier version of this chapter.

Maschler 1967). These developments established the agenda of subsequent research on coalition structures. To lay out this agenda, let $N = \{1,2, \ldots ,n\}$ be the set of players and let (N,v) be a game in characteristic function form. *A coalition structure* $\mathscr{B} = \{B_1,B_2, \ldots ,B_m\}$ is defined to be a finite partition either of the player set N or of the universe of v.[1] The agenda is thus normally composed of three elements:

(i)   One first defines an extension of (N,v) to a game with coalitional structure $\mathscr{B}$. This requires the specification of the restrictions on payoff vectors and on the set of coalitions that are allowed to form. We loosely use the notation $(N,v,\mathscr{B})$ to identify such games.

(ii)   Having defined the extension of (N,v), one then extends the solution concepts of cooperative game theory to the game $(N,v,\mathscr{B})$.

(iii)   Finally one studies the stability of the coalition structure. To this, one needs to specify *a coalition formation game* Γ_v and then define the stable structures to be the solutions of Γ_v.

The important paper of Aumann and Dréze (1974) carried out items (i) and (ii) of the agenda with respect to the six common solution concepts: the von Neumann–Morgenstern solutions, the core, the bargaining set, the nucleolus, the kernel, and the Shapley value. Following Aumann and Dréze (1974), most of the research on coalition structures concentrated on the study of the core and the Shapley value of games with coalition structures, which we denote by $(N,v,\mathscr{B})$. Most of the subsequent research on the core of a coalition structure concentrated on the application to goods and taxation (see Dréze and Greenberg 1980; Greenberg 1979a,b, 1980, 1983; Greenberg and Weber 1982, 1985, 1986; Guesnerie and Oddou 1979, 1981; Ichiishi 1981; Pauly 1967, 1970; Wooders 1978, 1980). On the other hand, Shenoy (1978, 1979) attempted to advance the Dréze–Aumann agenda one step further by proposing two stability criteria for coalitional structure. More specifically, let θ denote a solution concept for a game $(N,v,\mathscr{B})$ and denote by $x^\theta = x^\theta(N,v,\mathscr{B})$ the vector of payoffs to the players under $\mathscr{B}$ and θ. Now let $(x^\theta,\mathscr{B}^1)$ and $(y^\theta,\mathscr{B}^2)$ be two such pairs. Shenoy (1979) then defines a domination relation by the statement

$(x^\theta,\mathscr{B}^1)$ dominates $(y^\theta,\mathscr{B}^2)$ if there exists a coalition $S \in \mathscr{B}^1$ such that $x_i^\theta > y_i^\theta$, $i \in S$.

Relative to this domination relation Shenoy (1979) defines the core and the "dynamic solution" as two stability criteria of a pair $(x^\theta,\mathscr{B})$ among alternative coalition structures and payoffs. The important aspect of this construction is that the solution concept θ adopted for the game $(N,v,\mathscr{B})$ for fixed $\mathscr{B}$ may be different from the core or the dynamic solution concepts adopted for the game of coalition formation where $\mathscr{B}$ is allowed to vary.

The contributions by Owen (1977) and Hart and Kurz (1983, 1984) represent the main effort at the development of the value of coalition structure (CS value) beyond the Aumann–Dréze (1974) value. The exposition of these two value concepts is the main task of the next section.

2 The value of a coalition structure

In attempting to give a complete exposition of the two value concepts discussed earlier, we first proceed formally. We then follow with a discussion.

Let U be an infinite set, the *universe of players* (we follow Shapley's 1953 approach). A *game v* is a real function defined on all subsets of U and satisfying $v(\varnothing) = 0$. A set $N \subset U$ is a *carrier of v* if, for all $S \subset U$, $v(S) = v(S \cap N)$; we consider only *games with finite carriers*. We call $v(S)$ the *worth of S*. The set of all games on N is denoted by G^N.

A *coalition structure* $\mathscr{B}$ is a finite partition $\mathscr{B} = \{B_1, B_2, \ldots, B_m\}$ of U (i.e., $\cup_{k=1}^m B_k = U$ and $B_k \cap B_j = \varnothing$ for $k \neq j$). For a subset of players N (usually taken to be a carrier of some game), we denote by $\mathscr{B}_N$ the restriction of $\mathscr{B}$ to N; namely, $\mathscr{B}_N = \{B_k \cap N \mid k = 1, 2, \ldots, m\}$, which is a partition of N (empty sets $B_k \cap N$ will be discarded). We sometimes abuse notation and do not distinguish between $\mathscr{B}$ and $\mathscr{B}_N$.

2.1 The Aumann–Dréze value

Given N and $\mathscr{B}$, Aumann and Dréze (1974) define what they call a "$\mathscr{B}$ value" to be a function $\phi_\mathscr{B}$ on the set of all games with a finite carrier N that satisfies the following axioms.

Axiom 1 (Relative efficiency). For all k,

$$(\phi_\mathscr{B}v)(B_k) = v(B_k), \qquad B_k \in \mathscr{B}. \tag{1}$$

Axiom 2 (Symmetry). For all permutations π of N under which $\mathscr{B}$ is invariant,

$$(\phi_\mathscr{B}(\pi v))(S) = (\phi_\mathscr{B}v)(\pi S). \tag{2}$$

Axiom 3 (Additivity).

$$\phi_{\mathscr{B}}(v + w) = \phi_{\mathscr{B}}v + \phi_{\mathscr{B}}w. \tag{3}$$

Axiom 4 (Null player condition). If i is a null player, then

$$(\phi_{\mathscr{B}}v)(i) = 0. \tag{4}$$

It is clear that when $\mathscr{B} = \{N\}$, then $\phi_{\mathscr{B}} = \phi$, where $(\phi v) = \mathrm{Sh}\, v$, which is our designation of the Shapley value as developed by Shapley (1953).

For each $S \subset N$, denote by $v|S$ the game on S defined for all $T \subset S$ by $(v|S)(T) = v(T)$.

Theorem 1. Fix N and $\mathscr{B} = (B_1, \ldots, B_m)$. Then there is a unique Aumann–Dréze value (or $\mathscr{B}$ value), given for all $k = 1, \ldots, m$ and all $i \in B_k$ by

$$(\phi_{\mathscr{B}}v)(i) = (\mathrm{Sh}(v|B_k))(i). \tag{5}$$

Remark: Equation (5) asserts that the restriction to B_k of the value $\phi_{\mathscr{B}}$ for the game (N,v) is the value Sh for the game $(B_k, v|B_k)$. In other words, the value of a game with coalition structure $\mathscr{B}$ has the "restriction property": The restriction of the value is the value of the restriction of the game. An important implication of this property is that $\phi_{\mathscr{B}}$ can be computed by computing $\mathrm{Sh}(v|B_k)$ separately for each k.

Proof: The operator defined by (5) satisfies (1)–(4), so there is at least one $\mathscr{B}$ value. We must prove that there is only one. For each nonempty $T \subset N$, define the T-unanimity game v_T by

$$v_T(S) = \begin{cases} 1 & \text{if } S \supset T, \\ 0 & \text{otherwise.} \end{cases}$$

Using standard procedures, we show that the games v_T form a basis for G^N; therefore every game on N is a linear combination of the games v_T. By the additivity axiom, it then follows that if the $\mathscr{B}$ value is unique on all games of the form αv_T, where α is a constant, then it is unique.

Consider therefore a game of the form αv_T. By (4) $(\phi_{\mathscr{B}}(\alpha v_T))(i) = 0$ whenever $i \notin T$. From (2) it follows that if i and j are in T and in the same member B_k of $\mathscr{B}$ then

$$(\phi_{\mathscr{B}}(\alpha v_T))(i) = (\phi_{\mathscr{B}}(\alpha v_T))(j).$$

Hence from (1) it follows that if $i \in B_k$, then

$$(\phi_{\mathscr{B}}(\alpha v_T))(i) = \begin{cases} \alpha/|T| & \text{if } T \subset B_k, \\ 0 & \text{otherwise.} \end{cases}$$

This determines $\phi_{\mathscr{B}}(\alpha v_T)$, and so completes the proof.

Clearly the Aumann–Dréze value $\phi_{\mathscr{B}}$ is easy to compute. Under this value concept the payoff to any player does not depend upon his contribution to any coalition outside the coalition to which he belongs. That is, for any $i \in B_k$, $(\phi_{\mathscr{B}}v)(i)$ does not depend on $v(S)$, $S \not\subset B_k$, or upon the contribution of i to any S such that $S \not\subset B_k$. It is obvious that the main reason for this conclusion is Axiom 1. This result, which is true for the Aumann–Dréze value but not for the other solution concepts, stands in sharp contrast to the Aumann–Dréze interpretation of how the coalitional bargaining would operate under Axiom 1. On pp. 231–2 they explain that

> Whereas the *implications* of a coalition structure are quite clear, the *idea* of a coalition structure needs some clarification. On the one hand, the players are constrained to "form the coalitions $B_1, \ldots, B_m$ that make up the structure $\mathscr{B}$. On the other hand, considerations of other coalitions, including those that "cut across" the B_k, is by no means excluded. Such coalitions are used to dominate as in the definition of core and VON NEUMANN–MORGENSTERN solution, and to object as in the bargaining set and its relatives; the excesses of these coalitions enter into the definition of nucleolus and kernel. This raises the question: what, precisely, does the "constraint" to the structure $\mathscr{B}$ mean?
>
> The scenario usually associated with the coalition structure idea is as follows: the players consider forming the coalitions $B_1, \ldots, B_m$; one may think of them as going to business lunches in m different groups, each B_k forming a group. At these lunches they negotiate the division of the payoff, on the assumption that the coalitions $B_1, \ldots, B_m$ will be formed. In such negotiations, it is perfectly reasonable for each coalition B_k to base the division of the payoff on the opportunities that its members have outside of B_k. The negotiations at the lunch may of course break down, and at no time is it asserted that they will or even should succeed. What is being asserted is only that *if* the structure $\mathscr{B}$ forms, then the B_k should divide the payoff in whatever way the particular solution concept under consideration dictates.

One is inclined to conclude that the Aumann–Dréze interpretation may not apply universally, and if real coalition bargaining is to be an important element in a value of a coalition structure, then Axiom 1 is not likely to be satisfied in many situations. This is the essential view of the CS value due to Owen (1977) and refined and simplified by Hart and Kurz (1983, 1984). This value is more complex than the Aumann–Dréze (1974) value; we follow here the Hart–Kurz (1983) exposition.

2.2   The CS value

A *coalition structure value* (CS value) is an operator ϕ that assigns to every game v with a finite carrier, every coalition structure $\mathscr{B}$, and every player $i \in U$ a real number $\phi^i(v,\mathscr{B})$. Equivalently, one may think of $\phi(v,\mathscr{B})$ as a (finitely) additive measure on U defined by

$$\phi(v,\mathscr{B})(S) = \sum_{i \in S} \phi^i(v,\mathscr{B}) \qquad \text{for } S \subset U.$$

We will consider the following axioms on ϕ (assumed to hold for all games v and v' and all coalition structures $\mathscr{B}$ and $\mathscr{B}'$).

Axiom 1 (Carrier). Let N be a carrier of v. Then

(i) $\phi(v,\mathscr{B})(N) \equiv \Sigma_{i \in N} \phi^i(v,\mathscr{B}) = v(N)$.

(ii)   If $\mathscr{B}_N = \mathscr{B}'_N$, then $\phi(v,\mathscr{B}) = \phi(v,\mathscr{B}')$.

Axiom 2 (Symmetry). Let π be a permutation of the players. Then

$$\phi(\pi v, \pi \mathscr{B}) = \pi \phi(v,\mathscr{B}).$$

Axiom 3 (Additivity).

$$\phi(v + v', \mathscr{B}) = \phi(v,\mathscr{B}) + \phi(v',\mathscr{B}).$$

Given a game v and a coalition structure $\mathscr{B} = \{B_1, B_2, \ldots, B_m\}$, we say that *the game among coalitions is inessential* if

$$v\left(\bigcup_{k \in K} B_k\right) = \sum_{k \in K} v(B_k)$$

for all subsets K of $\{1, 2, \ldots, m\}$; that is, v restricted to the field generated by $\mathscr{B}$ is additive.

Axiom 4 (Inessential games). Let v and $\mathscr{B} = \{B_1, B_2, \ldots, B_m\}$ be such that the game among coalitions is inessential. Then

$$\phi(v,\mathscr{B})(B_k) = v(B_k) \qquad \text{for all } k = 1, 2, \ldots, m.$$

We discuss now the four axioms. The carrier axiom actually contains three parts. If i is a null player in a game v (i.e., $U \backslash \{i\}$ is a carrier of v or, equivalently, $v(S \cup \{i\}) = v(S)$ for all $S \subset U$), then his value is 0 in all coalition structures. Moreover, if such i "moves" from one B_k to another, it does not affect anyone's values. And last, for all coalition structures the value is efficient.

The efficiency of the CS value is an essential feature. It differs from the Aumann and Dréze (1974) approach, where each coalition $B_k \in \mathcal{B}$ gets only its worth (i.e., $v(B_k)$). The idea is that coalitions form not in order to get their worth, but *to be in a better position when bargaining with the others on how to divide the maximal amount available* [i.e., the worth of the grand coalition, which for superadditive games is no less than $\Sigma_{k=1}^{m} v(B_k)$]. It is assumed that the amount $v(N)$ will be distributed among the players and thus that all collusions and group formations are done with this in mind. A coalition B forms when all its members commit themselves to bargain with the others as one unit.[2]

This further clarifies Axiom 4: When the game between the coalitions is inessential, each coalition gets only its worth and there is no surplus to be bargained over. The other two axioms are straightforward.

Although Theorem 2 indicates that these axioms characterize Owen's value, the significant difference between these axioms and Owen's is to be found in Axiom 4. Owen's corresponding Axiom A3 assumed that for *all* games v and all coalition structures $\mathcal{B}$, the total value of each coalition B_k in $\mathcal{B}$ depends only on the restriction of v to (the field generated by) $\mathcal{B}$. In contrast, Hart and Kurz (1983, 1984) assume this to hold for *inessential games only,* in which case it is easier to justify. The problem of bargaining among coalitions arises when there is a surplus that is available when such coalitions combine. Because there is no such surplus in inessential games (among coalitions), there is nothing to divide; thus each one gets its worth. What is surprising is that this natural condition, in conjunction with Axioms 1-3, implies Owen's Axiom A3.

Theorem 2. The unique CS value ϕ satisfying Axioms 1-4 is Owen's (1977) value.

Let N be a finite set of players, and $\mathcal{B} = \{B_1, B_2, \ldots, B_m\}$ a coalition structure. A complete (linear) *order on N is consistent* with $\mathcal{B}$ if, for all $k = 1, 2, \ldots, m$ and all $i, j \in B_k$, all elements of N between i and j also belong to B_k. A *random order on N consistent with $\mathcal{B}$* (or, given $\mathcal{B}$) is a random variable whose values are the orders on N that are consistent with $\mathcal{B}$, all equally probable (i.e., each with probability $(m!, b_1! b_2! \ldots b_n!)^{-1}$, where b_k is the number of elements in $B_k \cap N$). The interpretation is as follows: The players arrive randomly but such that all members of the same coalition do so successively. This is the same as randomly ordering first the coalitions and then the members within each coalition.

Proposition 3. The unique CS value ϕ satisfying Axioms 1–4 is

$$\phi^i(v,\mathscr{B}) = E[v(\mathscr{P}^i \cup \{i\}) - v(\mathscr{P}^i)], \tag{6}$$

where the expectation E is over all random orders on a carrier N of v that are consistent with $\mathscr{B}$, and $\mathscr{P}^i$ denotes the (random) set of predecessors of i.

Theorem 2 and Proposition 3 will be proved together. Although the main ideas are standard, the use of the weaker Axiom 4 necessitates some additional work.

Proofs of Theorem 2 and Proposition 3: It can easily be checked that the operator given by (6) indeed satisfies Axioms 1–3; as for Axiom 4, let i_k be the first member of B_k in a random order; the fact that all the other players of B_k follow i_k implies that

$$\sum_{j \in B_k} [v(\mathscr{P}^j \cup \{j\}) - v(\mathscr{P}^j)] = v(\mathscr{P}^{i_k} \cup B_k) - v(\mathscr{P}^{i_k}),$$

which, for an inessential game among coalitions, equals $v(B_k)$ (because $\mathscr{P}^{i_k}$ is a union of B's). Thus all four axioms are indeed satisfied.

In order to complete the proof, we have to show uniqueness, namely that Axioms 1–4 determine ϕ. Axiom 3 (additivity) implies that it suffices to check basic games only–that is, games v of the form

$$v(S) = \begin{cases} c & \text{if } S \supset R, \\ 0 & \text{otherwise,} \end{cases}$$

where c is a fixed constant and $R \subset U$ is a fixed finite and nonempty set.

Let $R_k = R \cap B_k$ and assume, without loss of generality, that R_k is not empty for $k = 1, 2, \ldots, l$ (where $1 \leq l \leq m$). Let $\rho = \max_k |R_k|,$[3] and let R'_k, for $k = 1, 2, \ldots, l$, be disjoint sets of players such that $|R'_k| = \rho$ and $R'_k \supset R_k$ (here we use the fact that U is an infinite set). Let $R' = \cup_{k=1}^m R'_k$, $\mathscr{B}' = \{R'_1, R'_2, \ldots, R'_l, U \backslash R'\}$, and

$$v'(S) = \begin{cases} c & \text{if } S \supset R', \\ 0 & \text{otherwise.} \end{cases}$$

Consider $\phi(v', \mathscr{B}')$. All players outside R' get 0, and all players in R' are identical (because R'_k are of the same size ρ for all $1 \leq k \leq l$). Axioms 1 and 2 imply that, for all $i \in R'$,

$$\phi^j(v',\mathscr{B}') = \frac{c}{|R'|} = \frac{c}{\rho l}.$$

Hence, for all $1 \leq k \leq l$,

$$\phi(v',\mathscr{B}')(R'_k) = \frac{c}{l}.$$

Next, consider $\phi(v - v',\mathscr{B}')$. It is an inessential game among coalitions, because $(v - v')(\cup_{k \in K} R'_k)$ is either $c - c = 0$ or $0 - 0 = 0$, according to whether or not $K \supset \{1,2, \ldots ,l\}$. Therefore, by Axiom 4,

$$\phi(v - v',\mathscr{B}')(R'_k) = (v - v')(R'_k) = 0$$

for all $1 \leq k \leq l$. Axiom 3 now implies

$$\phi(v,\mathscr{B}')(R'_k) = \phi(v',\mathscr{B}')(R'_k) + \phi(v - v',\mathscr{B}')(R'_k)$$

$$= \frac{c}{l} + 0 = \frac{c}{l}.$$

But R is a carrier of v, and $\mathscr{B}_R = \mathscr{B}'_R$; therefore (Axiom 1)

$$\phi(v,\mathscr{B})(R_k) = \phi(v,\mathscr{B}')(R_k) = \phi(v,\mathscr{B}')(R'_k) = \frac{c}{l}$$

for all $1 \leq k \leq l$. Finally, symmetry among the members of the same R_k gives

$$\phi^i(v,\mathscr{B}) = \begin{cases} \dfrac{c}{l|R_k|} & \text{if } i \in R \cap B_k \equiv R_k, \\ 0 & \text{otherwise,} \end{cases}$$

which implies the uniqueness of ϕ.   Q.E.D.

Remark: It is clear from the use of Axiom 4 in the proof that it may be replaced by the following, slightly weaker, Axiom 4'.

Axiom 4' (Null game). If $v(\cup_{k \in K} B_k) = 0$ for all $K \subset \{1,2, \ldots ,m\}$, then $\phi(v,\mathscr{B})(B_k) = 0$ for all $k = 1, 2, \ldots , m$.

Axioms 5 and 5' may also be used in place of Axiom 4.

Axiom 5 (Dummy coalition). If B_l is such that

$$v\left(\bigcup_{k \in K} B_k \cup B_l\right) = v\left(\bigcup_{k \in K} B_k\right) + v(B_l)$$

for all $K \subset \{1,2, \ldots ,m\}$, then $\phi(v,\mathscr{B})(B_l) = v(B_l)$.

Axiom 5′ (Null coalition). If B_l is such that

$$v\left(\bigcup_{k \in K} B_k \cup B_l\right) = v\left(\bigcup_{k \in K} B_k\right)$$

for all $K \subset \{1,2, \ldots ,m\}$, then $\phi(v,\mathscr{B})(B_l) = 0$.

It is clear that Axiom 5 (5′) implies Axiom 4 (4′); however, together with Axioms 1–3, they all become equivalent.

For a game (N,v) with finite carrier N, we earlier defined Sh v to be its Shapley value; that is, Sh$^i v$ is the value of player i, and (Sh $v)(S) = \Sigma_{i \in S}$Sh$_v^i$ for $S \subset U$.

Corollary 4. For all $B_k \in \mathscr{B}$,

$$\phi(v,\mathscr{B})(B_k) = (\text{Sh } v_\mathscr{B})(B_k),$$

where $(v_\mathscr{B},\mathscr{B})$ is the game v restricted to the field generated by $\mathscr{B}$ (i.e., each $B_k \in \mathscr{B}$ is a "player").

Proof: The proof is immediate from (6).   Q.E.D.

Thus, the total CS value of each coalition in $\mathscr{B}$ is precisely the Shapley value of the game played by the (representatives of the) coalitions in $\mathscr{B}$. Note that if one wants the CS value to satisfy the null player axiom (i.e., adding null players does not change the value), one is necessarily led to regard each coalition in the coalition structure as one "representative," independent of the number of original players it is composed of! Note that Axiom 1 (ii) implies that only the partition of a carrier N of v needs to be specified.

Another notation will be useful: If for any set $S = \{i_1,i_2, \ldots ,i_S\}$, $\mathscr{B}_S = \{\{i_1\},\{i_2\}, \ldots ,\{i_S\}\}$ [i.e., the partition of S is into singletons (one player sets)], then we will write $\mathscr{B}_S = \langle S \rangle$; in contrast, $\mathscr{B}_S = \{S\}$ means that all members of S are "together" in one coalition.

Corollary 5. Let N be a carrier of v. Then

$$\phi(v,\{N\}) = \phi(v,\langle N \rangle) = \text{Sh } v.$$

Proof: Again, it follows from (6).   Q.E.D.

How is the CS value related to the two bargaining processes among the coalitions (i.e., the elements of $\mathscr{B}$) and within each coalition? By Corollary

4, the former is obtained by replacing each $B_k \in \mathscr{B}$ with a single player and taking the Shapley value of the resulting game, "the game among coalitions."

Consider now one coalition $B_k \in \mathscr{B}$. How should its members divide the total amount $\phi(v,\mathscr{B})(B_k)$ that they receive? Their "relative power" must be taken into account, and one way to measure it is by comparing their "prospects" should B_k break apart. For example, suppose $N = \{1,2,3\}$ and $\mathscr{B}_N = \{\{1,2\},\{3\}\}$. The coalition $\{1,2\}$ gets $\phi(v,\mathscr{B})(\{1,2\})$; if they do not agree on the division of this amount and "split," they will get $\phi(v,\langle N\rangle)(\{i\})$ for $i = 1$ and $i = 2$. This may serve as a "disagreement point" in the two-person bargaining problem where the set of possible "agreements" corresponds to all the various ways of dividing $\phi(v_{\mathscr{B}})(\{1,2\})$. According to the Nash (1950) solution, each $i = 1, 2$ will receive

$$\phi(v,\langle N\rangle)(\{i\}) + \tfrac{1}{2}[\phi(v,\mathscr{B})(\{1,2\}) - \phi(v,\langle N\rangle)(\{1,2\})].$$

It turns out that for $i = 1, 2$ this quantity is precisely $\phi(v,\mathscr{B})(\{i\})$!

What happens if B_k contains more than two players? One may choose the n-person generalization of the Nash solution (see Harsanyi 1977), but this is not completely satisfactory, for two reasons. First, all possible subcoalitions of B_k, not only the singletons, should be taken into account. Second, it would be preferable to use the same solution concept for the bargaining *within* B_k as the one used for the bargaining *among* the coalitions. It is precisely this consistency that one should seek.

To formalize this discussion, let v, $\mathscr{B} = \{B_1,B_2, \ldots ,B_m\}$ and $B_k \in \mathscr{B}$ be given. Define a new game w_k on B_k by

$$w_k(S) = \phi(v,\mathscr{B}|S)(S) \tag{7}$$

for all $S \subset B_k$, where $\mathscr{B}|S$ is the coalition structure obtained from $\mathscr{B}$ by replacing B_k with S and $B_k\backslash S$; that is,

$$\mathscr{B}|S = \{B_1, \ldots ,B_{k-1},S,B_k\backslash S,B_{k+1}, \ldots ,B_m\}. \tag{8}$$

Note that $w_k(\varnothing) = 0$; hence w_k is indeed a game and, moreover, has a finite carrier whenever v does.

Theorem 6 (Consistency). Given a game v and a coalition structure $\mathscr{B} = \{B_1,B_2, \ldots ,B_m\}$, the following equality holds:

$$\phi^i(v,\mathscr{B}) = \phi(w_k,\langle B_k\rangle)(\{i\}),$$

where $i \in B_k \in \mathscr{B}$ and w_k is given by (7) and (8).

This result shows that the CS value enjoys the following consistency property: The bargaining procedure within coalitions may be derived from the one among coalitions. Indeed, because $S \in \mathcal{B}|S$ and $\{i\} \in \langle B_k \rangle$, both $w_k(S)$ and $\phi(w_k, \langle B_k \rangle)(\{i\})$ are CS values to *coalitions* in the corresponding coalition structures; they do not depend in any way on the division of payoffs within coalitions.

In (8) we defined $\mathcal{B}|S$, for $S \subset B_k$, by replacing B_k with S and $B_k \backslash S$. By doing so we assumed that the members of the complement of S "stay together." An alternative possibility is that, when S "leaves," the rest of B_k will break apart into individuals (singletons). In this case, we would define $\mathcal{B}|S$ by

$$\mathcal{B}|S = \{B_1, \ldots, B_{k-1}, S, \{j_1\}, \ldots, \{j_t\}, B_{k+1}, \ldots, B_m\}, \quad (9)$$

where $B_k \backslash S = \{j_1, j_2, \ldots, j_t\}$. This induces by (7) a new game w_k on B_k. However, we have the following result.

Theorem 7 (Consistency). Theorem 6 is true with $\mathcal{B}|S$ given by (9) instead of (8).

This means that the CS value enjoys the consistency property independently of the way w_k is defined; although (8) and (9) define two different games w_k, Theorem 7 states that their values coincide. This additional feature is important particularly in view of the well-known ambiguity of the "complement's behavior": When a coalition acts together, does its complement react as a coalition or as individuals? In the case of the CS value, it does not matter!

Proof of Theorems 6 and 7: The proof amounts to checking that $\phi(v, \mathcal{B})$, given by $\phi^i(v, \mathcal{B}) = \phi(w_k, \langle B_k \rangle)(\{i\})$ for all $B_k \in \mathcal{B}$ and $i \in B_k$, satisfies Axioms 1–4. Such a check is standard.

3   Stability of coalition structures

The question of stability of coalition structures is nearly equivalent to the question of why coalition structures form to begin with. Some of the reasons have already surfaced earlier in the discussion of the Aumann–Dréze value and the CS value. These two, however, provide two sharply different reasons why a coalition structure would form. Aumann and Dréze regard the coalition structure $\mathcal{B}$ to be such that each coalition $B_k \in \mathcal{B}$ actually forms, "operates," and generates its coalitional payoff

$v(B_k)$. In this sense the Aumann–Dréze coalition is a real entity that is formed to realize its potential $v(B_k)$. Given this, members of B_k bargain only *among themselves* to divide $v(B_k)$. The view of Owen, Hart, and Kurz is that the real entity that forms at the end is the coalition of the whole, N, and the coalition structure $\mathscr{B}$ is formed only as a bargaining tool aiming to increase the payoff of individual members. This entails a subtle bargaining *among individual players within each coalition B_k and among all the coalitions $\{B_1, B_2, \ldots, B_m\}$.*

These observations provide a broad hint for the role played by *superadditivity*. Aumann and Dréze (1974, pp. 232–4) suggest that *nonsuperadditivity of (N,v) is the most compelling explanation for the formation of a coalition structure $\mathscr{B}$*. Other groups of "causes" are proposed in the literature for the formation of coalition structures satisfying Axiom 1 of Aumann and Dréze (1974), including such causes as the existence of legal limitations, geographic and spatial limitations, and communication problems. In all such cases a proper formulation of the game quickly reveals that the coalition of the whole does not (or is not allowed to) do as well as some coalition structure $\mathscr{B}$ that can satisfy Aumann and Dréze's (1974) Axiom 1. This formal appearance of nonsuperadditivity is often perplexing in economic contexts. An example will clarify the issue.

In the Guesnerie and Oddou (1979, 1981) public goods game it is postulated, as a *constitutional* limitation, that whenever a coalition is formed as a taxing constituency it cannot discriminate among members and must impose a uniform tax rate on all members. It is then obvious that in a society with heterogeneous demands for public goods (due to heterogeneous preferences, geographic differences, and other causes) the set of utility payoffs attainable from the taxing ability of society as a whole does not contain the set of allocations attainable from the combined taxing abilities of the different constituencies that consist of a coalition structure $\mathscr{B}$ in which each member establishes a different tax rate. Clearly, this is a nonsuperadditive game. However, a drastically opposing argument in favor of superadditivity may be provided. It goes as follows. Given that the constitution is determined by the coalition of the whole, one must conclude that "nondiscriminatory taxation" as an ethical and political principle had significant utility benefits for the players. Hence, when one considers the broader game in which both the constitution, the tax rates, and the composition of output of public goods are determined together, this game *is* superadditive. In fact, the coalition of the whole can be viewed as choosing the coalition structure $\mathscr{B}$ and endowing each member with the "local" power to tax and produce local public goods.

In our opinion the real issue is one of selecting an effective modeling strategy. One cannot take seriously the preceding argument regarding the constitution. It is obvious that society has so many conflicting needs that it is far from clear that a constitution would emerge simultaneously with a solution of *all* our social problems. In addition, this is not a manageable research agenda. There are well-known compelling arguments why a constitution must be based on general principles only and be established so that it will be difficult to change. With a constitution in place the natural way to model the Guesnerie and Oddou problem of taxation and public goods is the way they did–as a nonsuperadditive game.

In all those circumstances in which a good description of reality would lead to the formation of a structure $\{B_1, B_2, \ldots, B_n\}$ satisfying Axiom 1 of Aumann and Dréze, the CS value would not provide a good solution. However, whenever the game is superadditive, the weight of the argument shifts away from an Aumann–Dréze value and in favor of the CS value.

This brings us back to stability. To understand the issue of stability, note that, having defined value concepts such as $\phi_{\mathscr{B}}$ or $\phi(v, \mathscr{B})$, we can introduce a game Γ of coalition formation whose solution would identify the stable coalition structures. Shenoy (1979) studied the core and the dynamic solution of such a game in relation to $\phi_{\mathscr{B}}$, and Hart and Kurz (1983, 1984) studied the core and the strong equilibria of such a game in relation to $\phi(v, \mathscr{B})$. Although this research uncovered interesting stability properties of many classes of games, no universal stability theorem is available. Relative to every stability concept that has been proposed, non-stable counterexamples were found. We shall briefly review some of the available results.

3.1   *Stability relative to $\phi_{\mathscr{B}}$*

As we indicated in Section 1, Shenoy (1979) defined a domination relation among coalition structures, and in relation to the value the reader may identify x^{θ} with $\phi_{\mathscr{B}}$. Now, given this relation, Shenoy introduces the notion of stability.

Definition (Core). $\mathscr{B}$ is said to be core stable if it is undominated by any other coalition structure.

The following is a sample of Shenoy's results.

1.   Every three-person game has a core-stable coalition structure relative to $\phi_{\mathscr{B}}$.

2. Every straight majority game has a core-stable coalition structure relative to $\phi_{\mathscr{B}}$.

On the other hand, Shenoy (1979, p. 150) gives a very simple example of a four-person weighted majority game [3; 2,1,1,1] (the first player has a weight of 2; the weight of each of the others is 1) that has no core-stable structure. The table of $\phi_{\mathscr{B}}$ for all $\mathscr{B}$ is

$\mathscr{B}$	$(\phi_{\mathscr{B}}v)(i)$
{(1234)}	$(\frac{1}{2}, \frac{1}{6}, \frac{1}{6}, \frac{1}{6})$
{(123),4}	$(\frac{2}{3}, \frac{1}{6}, \frac{1}{6}, 0)$
{(124),3}	$(\frac{2}{3}, \frac{1}{6}, 0, \frac{1}{6})$
{(134),2}	$(\frac{2}{3}, 0, \frac{1}{6}, \frac{1}{6})$
{(12),(34)} or {(12),3,4}	$(\frac{1}{2}, \frac{1}{2}, 0, 0)$
{(13),(24)} or {(13),2,4}	$(\frac{1}{2}, 0, \frac{1}{2}, 0)$
{(14),(23)} or {(14),2,3}	$(\frac{1}{2}, 0, 0, \frac{1}{2})$
{1,(234)}	$(0, \frac{1}{3}, \frac{1}{3}, \frac{1}{3})$
All others	$(0, 0, 0, 0)$

The minimal winning coalitions are (12), (13), (14), (234), but all coalition structures containing minimal winning coalitions are dominated.

Almost all researchers who studied the core of the coalition structure implicitly assumed that nonemptiness of that core represents a stability result, so they saw no need to conduct a core-stability analysis in the sense of Shenoy (1979). The justification is rather straightforward. The core of the coalition structure was defined by Aumann and Dréze (1974) to be the core of $(N,v,\mathscr{B})$. This consists of all payoff vectors x^c that are undominated subject to $x^c(B_k) = v(B_k)$, all $B_k \in \mathscr{B}$. But every coalition S that deviates from $\mathscr{B}$ induces a new structure $\mathscr{B}'$, so it is clear that if S can block x^c then $\mathscr{B}'$ will dominate $\mathscr{B}$ via S. Hence the core of the coalition structure – when nonempty – is equivalent to the core in the sense of Shenoy (1979).

3.2   *Stability relative to $\phi(v,\mathscr{B})$*

Hart and Kurz (1983, 1984) attempted to formulate explicit coalition formation games to identify stable coalition structures. To understand this formulation, recall that the CS value $\phi^i(v,\mathscr{B})$ is interpreted as the utility of player i of participating in the game v when the players are organized according to $\mathscr{B}$. Based on this, each player is able to compare the various coalition structures. Stability will thus occur whenever no group of players can reorganize itself in such a way that, in the new coalition structure, they are all better off (according to the CS value). Depending on the reaction of the other players, two notions of stability are obtained. In the γ-model it is assumed that coalitions left by even one member break apart into singletons; in the δ-model the remaining players instead form one smaller coalition.

The games $\Gamma \equiv \Gamma(N,v)$ and $\Delta \equiv \Delta(N,v)$ are given in normal form as follows:

Model γ: The game Γ consists of the following rules:

The set of *players* is N. (10)

For each $i \in N$, the set Σ^i of *strategies* of i consists of all coalitions S that contain i, namely $\Sigma^i = \{S \subset N | i \in S\}$. (11)

For each n-tuple of strategies $\sigma = (S^1, S^2, \ldots, S^n) \in \Sigma^1 \times \Sigma^2 \times \cdots \times \Sigma^n$ and each $i \in N$, the *payoff* to i is $\phi^i(v, \mathcal{B}_\sigma^{(\gamma)})$, where (12)

$$T_\sigma^i = \begin{cases} S^i & \text{if } S^j = S^i \text{ for all } j \in S^i, \\ \{i\} & \text{otherwise,} \end{cases}$$

and $\mathcal{B}_\sigma^{(\gamma)} = \{T_\sigma^i | i \in N\}$.

Model δ: The game Δ consists of (10), (11), and

For each *n*-tuple of strategies $\sigma = (S^1, S^2, \ldots, S^n) \in \Sigma^1 \times \Sigma^2 \times \cdots \times \Sigma^n$ and each $i \in N$, the *payoff* to i is $\phi^i(v, \mathcal{B}_\sigma^{(\delta)})$, where $\mathcal{B}_\sigma^{(\delta)} = \{T \subset N | i, j \in T \text{ if and only if } S^i = S^j\}$.

For a coalition structure $\mathcal{B}$ and a player $i \in N$, let $S_\mathcal{B}^i$ be that element of $\mathcal{B}$ to which i belongs: $i \in S_\mathcal{B}^i \in \mathcal{B}$ (this defines $S_\mathcal{B}^i$ uniquely); put $\sigma_\mathcal{B} = (S_\mathcal{B}^i)_{i \in N}$. If the players choose $\sigma_\mathcal{B}$, then in both Γ and Δ the coalition structure that results is clearly $\mathcal{B}$.

Definition (Stability). The coalition structure $\mathcal{B}$ is γ-stable (resp., δ-stable) in the game (N,v) if $\sigma_\mathcal{B}$ is a strong equilibrium in $\Gamma(N,v)$ [resp., $\Delta(N,v)$], that is, if there exists no nonempty $T \subset N$ and no $\hat{\sigma}^i \in \Sigma^i$ for all $i \in T$ such that $\phi^i(v, \hat{\mathcal{B}}) > \phi^i(v, \mathcal{B})$ for all $i \in T$, where $\hat{\mathcal{B}}$ corresponds to $((\hat{\sigma}_\mathcal{B}^i)_{i \in T}, (\sigma_\mathcal{B}^j)_{j \in N \setminus T})$ by (12) (resp., (13)).

Hart and Kurz (1984) provide an analysis of the stability properties of a few classes of games. A sample of their results can be summarized as follows:

1. Every three-person game has coalition structures that are both γ- and δ-stable.
2. Every symmetric four-person game has coalition structures that are both γ- and δ-stable.
3. Every Apex game[4] with n $\geq$ 5 has a unique γ-stable coalition structure but no δ-stable coalition structure.

However, Hart and Kurz (1984) also provide an example of a monotone and superadditive game with no stable coalition structure in any of the senses defined. The example found is of a ten-person symmetric majority game in which it takes eight votes to "win." Thus the example is complex and will not be reproduced here (see Hart and Kurz 1984, p. 257).

The merit of studying the stability properties of coalition structures is that when a game has such a structure, the theory provides an important prediction of the ultimate social organization that is likely to prevail. Games without a stable coalition structure may describe intrinsically unstable situations and thus do not permit us such a prediction. This represents an open problem.

NOTES

1 This is a minor distinction. If the universe of players is U and $N \subset U$, then, for all $S \subset U$, $v(S) = v(S \cap N)$ and one can define $B_k \subset U$ with $\mathcal{B}_N = \{B_k \cap N | k = 1, 2, \ldots, m\}$ as the induced coalition structure on N.
2 The question of when this commitment is credible will be answered in the next section; for a stable coalition, it is self-enforcing.
3 The number of elements of a finite set A is denoted by $|A|$.
4 Apex games are simple games with one major player and $n - 1$ minor players. All minimal winning coalitions consist of the major player together with one minor player or all the minor players together.

REFERENCES

Aumann, R. and J. Dréze [1974], "Cooperative Games with Coalition Structures," *International Journal of Game Theory*, 3 (4), 217–37.

Aumann, R. and M. Maschler [1964], "The Bargaining Set for Cooperative Games," in *Advances in Game Theory*, Annals of Math Studies No. 52, Princeton, pp. 443–76.

Crawford, V. P. and E. M. Knoer [1981], "Job Matching with Heterogenous Firms and Workers," *Econometrica* 49, 437–50.

Davis, M. and M. Maschler [1967], "Existence of Stable Payoff Configurations for Cooperative Games," *Essays in Mathematical Economics in Honor of Oskar Morgenstern*, M. Shubik (ed.), Princeton, pp. 39–52.

Dréze, J. and J. Greenberg [1980], "Hedonic Coalitions: Optimality and Stability," *Econometrica* 48, 987–1003.

Gale, D. and L. S. Shapley [1962], "College Admissions and the Stability of Marriage," *American Mathematical Monthly* 69, 9–15.

Greenberg, J. [1979a], "Stability When Mobility Is Restricted by the Existing Coalition Structure," *Journal of Economic Theory* 21, 213–21.

[1979b], "Existence and Optimality of Equilibrium in Labour Managed Economies," *Review of Economic Studies* 144, 419–433.

[1980], "Beneficial Altruism," *Journal of Economic Theory* 22, 12–22.

[1983], "Local Public Goods with Mobility: Existence and Optimality of a General Equilibrium," *Journal of Economic Theory* 30, 17–33.

Greenberg, J. and S. Weber [1982], "Equivalence of Superadditivity and Balancedness of Tax Proportional Games," *Economics Letters* 9, 113–17.

[1985], "Multiparty Equilibria under Proportional Representation," *American Political Science Review* 79, 693–703.

[1986], "Strong Tiebout Equilibrium under Restricted Preferences Domain," *Journal of Economic Theory* 38, 101–17.

Guesnerie, R. and C. Oddou [1979], "On Economic Games Which Are Not Necessarily Superadditive," *Economics Letters* 3, 301–06.

[1981], "Second Best Taxation as a Game," *Journal of Economic Theory* 25, 67–91.

Harsanyi, J. C. [1977], *Rational Behavior and Bargaining Equilibrium in Games and Social Situations,* Cambridge: Cambridge University Press.

Hart, S. and M. Kurz [1983], "Endogenous Formation of Coalitions," *Econometrica* 51, 1047–64.

[1984], "Stable Coalition Structures," in *Coalitions and Collective Action,* M. T. Holler (ed.), Physica-Verlag, Vienna, pp. 236–58.

Ichiishi, T. [1981], "A Social Coalitional Equilibrium Existence Theorem," *Econometrica* 49, 369–77.

Kaneko, M. [1982], "The Central Assignment Game," *Journal of Mathematical Economics* 10, 205–32.

Kelso, A. S., Jr. and V. Crawford [1982], "Job Matching Coalition Formation and Gross Substitutes," *Econometrica* 50, 1483–1504.

Nash, J. F. [1950], "The Bargaining Problem," *Econometrica* 18, 155–62.

Owen, G. [1977], "Values of Games with a priori Unions," *Essays in Mathematical Economics and Game Theory,* R. Henn and O. Moschlin (eds.), Springer-Verlag, New York, pp. 76–88.

Pauly, Mark [1967], "Clubs, Commonality, and the Core: An Integration of Game Theory and the Theory of Public Goods," *Economica* 34, 314–24.

[1970], "Cores and Clubs," *Public Choice* 9, 53–65.

Quinzii, M. [1984], "Core and Competitive Equilibria with Indivisibilities," *International Journal of Game Theory* 13, 41–60.

Roth, A. [1984a], "Stability and Polarization of Interests in Job Matching," *Econometrica* 52, 47–59.

[1984b] "The Evolution of the Labor Market for Medical Interns and Residents: A Case Study in Game Theory," *Journal of Political Economy* 92, 991–1016.

Shapley, L. S. [1953], "A Value for *n*-Person Games," in *Contributions to the Theory of Games,* Vol. II, H. W. Kuhn and A. W. Tucker (eds.), Princeton: Princeton University Press, pp. 307–17.

Shapley, L. S. and M. Shubik [1972], "The Assignment Game. I: The Core," *International Journal of Game Theory* 1, 111–30.

Shenoy, P. P. [1978], "On coalition Formation in Simple Games: A Mathematical Analysis of Caplow's and Gamson's Theories," *Journal of Mathematical Psychology* 18, 177–94.

   [1979], "On Coalition Formation: A Game-Theoretic Approach," *International Journal of Game Theory* 8, 133–64.

Thrall, R. M. and W. F. Lucas [1963], "*N*-person Games in Partition Function Form," *Naval Research Logistics Quarterly* 10, 281–98.

von Neumann, J. and O. Morgenstern [1944], *Theory of Games and Economic Behavior,* Princeton; 3rd ed. 1953.

Wooders, M. [1978], "Equilibria, the Core, and Jurisdiction Structures in Economies with a Local Public Good," *Journal of Economic Theory* 18, 328–48.

   [1980], "The Tiebout Hypothesis: Near Optimality in Local Public Good Economies," *Econometrica* 48, 1467–85.

CHAPTER 12

Endogenous formation of links between players and of coalitions: an application of the Shapley value

Robert J. Aumann and Roger B. Myerson

1   Introduction

Consider the coalitional game v on the player set $\{1,2,3\}$ defined by

$$v(S) = \begin{cases} 0 & \text{if } |S| = 1, \\ 60 & \text{if } |S| = 2, \\ 72 & \text{if } |S| = 3, \end{cases} \tag{1}$$

where $|S|$ denotes the number of players in S. Most cooperative solution concepts "predict" (or assume) that the all-player coalition $\{1,2,3\}$ will form and divide the payoff 72 in some appropriate way. Now suppose that P_1 (player 1) and P_2 happen to meet each other in the absence of P_3. There is little doubt that they would quickly seize the opportunity to form the coalition $\{1,2\}$ and collect a payoff of 30 each. This would happen in spite of its inefficiency. The reason is that if P_1 and P_2 were to invite P_3 to join the negotiations, then the three players would find themselves in effectively symmetric roles, and the expected outcome would be (24,24,24). P_1 and P_2 would not want to risk offering, say, 4 to P_3 (and dividing the remaining 68 among themselves), because they would realize that once P_3 is invited to participate in the negotiations, the situation turns "wide open"–anything can happen.

All this holds if P_1 and P_2 "happen" to meet. But even if they do not meet by chance, it seems fairly clear that the players in this game would seek to form pairs for the purpose of negotiation, and not negotiate in the all-player framework.

Research by Robert J. Aumann supported by the National Science Foundation at the Institute for Mathematical Studies in the Social Sciences (Economics), Stanford University, under Grant Number IST 85-21838.
Research by Roger B. Myerson supported by the National Science Foundation under grant number SES 86-05619.

The preceding example is due to Michael Maschler (see Aumann and Dreze 1974, p. 235, from which much of this discussion is cited). Maschler's example is particularly transparent because of its symmetry. Even in unsymmetric cases, though, it is clear that the framework of negotiations plays an important role in the outcome, so individual players and groups of players will seek frameworks that are advantageous to them. The phenomenon of seeking an advantageous framework for negotiating is also well known in the real world at many levels – from decision making within an organization, such as a corporation or university, to international negotiations. It is not for nothing that governments think hard – and often long – about "recognizing" or not recognizing other governments; that the question of whether, when, and under what conditions to negotiate with terrorists is one of the utmost substantive importance; and that at this writing the government of Israel is tottering over the question not of *whether* to negotiate with its neighbors, but of the *framework* for such negotiations (broad-base international conference or direct negotiations).

Maschler's example has a natural economic interpretation in terms of S-shaped production functions. The first player alone can do nothing because of setup costs. Two players can produce 60 units of finished product. With the third player, decreasing returns set in, and all three together can produce only 72. The foregoing analysis indicates that the form of industrial organization in this kind of situation may be expected to be inefficient.

The simplest model for the concept "framework of negotiations" is that of a *coalition structure,* defined as a partition of the player set into disjoint coalitions. Once the coalition structure has been determined, negotiations take place only within each of the coalitions that constitute the structure; each such coalition B divides among its members the total amount $v(B)$ that it can obtain for itself. Exogenously given coalition structures were perhaps first studied in the context of the bargaining set (Aumann and Maschler 1964), and subsequently in many contexts; a general treatment may be found in Aumann and Dreze (1974). Endogenous coalition formation is implicit already in the von Neumann–Morgenstern (1944) theory of stable sets; much of the interpretive discussion in their book and in subsequent treatments of stable sets centers around which coalitions will "form." However, coalition structures do not have a formal, explicit role in the von Neumann–Morgenstern theory. Recent treatments that consider endogenous coalition structures explicitly within the context of a formal theory include Hart and Kurz (1983), Kurz (Chapter 11 this volume), and others.

Coalition structures, however, are not rich enough adequately to capture the subtleties of negotiation frameworks. For example, diplomatic relations between countries or governments need not be transitive and, therefore, cannot be adequately represented by a partition; thus both Syria and Israel have diplomatic relations with the United States but not with each other. For another example, in salary negotiations within an academic department, the chairman plays a special role; members of the department cannot usually negotiate directly with each other, though certainly their salaries are not unrelated.

To model this richer kind of framework, Myerson (1977) introduced the notion of a *cooperation structure* (or *cooperation graph*) in a coalitional game. This graph is simply defined as one whose vertices are the players. Various interpretations are possible; the one we use here is that a link between two players (an edge of the graph) exists if it is possible for these two players to carry on meaningful direct negotiations with each other. In particular, ordinary coalition structures $(B_1, B_2, \ldots, B_k)$ (with disjoint B_j) may be modeled within this framework by defining two players to be linked if and only if they belong to the same B_j. (For generalizations of this cooperation structure concept, see Myerson 1980.)

Shapley's 1953 definition of the value of a coalitional game v may be interpreted as evaluating the players' prospects when there is full and free communication among all of them – when the cooperation structure is "full," when any two players are linked. When this is not so, the prospects of the players may change dramatically. For an extreme example, a player i who is totally isolated – is linked to no other player – can expect to get nothing beyond his own worth $v(\{i\})$; in general, the more links a player has with other players, the better one may expect his prospects to be. To capture this intuition, Myerson (1977) defined an extension of the Shapley value of a coalitional game v to the case of an arbitrary cooperation structure g. In particular, if g is the complete graph on the all-player set N (any two players are directly linked), then Myerson's value coincides with Shapley's. Moreover, if the cooperation graph g corresponds to the coalition structure $(B_1, B_2, \ldots, B_k)$ in the sense indicated here, then the Myerson value of a member i of B_j is the Shapley value of i as a player of the game $v|B_j$ (v restricted to B_j).

This chapter suggests a model for the endogenous formation of cooperation structures. Given a coalitional game v, what links may be expected to form between the players? Our approach differs from that of previous writers on endogenous coalition formation in two respects: First, we work with cooperation graphs rather than coalition structures, using the Myerson value to evaluate the pros and cons of a given cooperation structure for any particular player. Second, we do not use the usual myopic, here-and-now kind of equilibrium condition. When a player considers forming a link with another one, he does not simply ask himself whether he may expect to be better off with this link than without it, given the previously existing structure. Rather, he looks ahead and asks himself, "Suppose we form this new link, will other players be motivated to form further new links that were not worthwhile for them before? Where will it all lead? Is the *end result* good or bad for me?"

In Section 2 we review the Myerson value and illustrate the "look-ahead" reasoning by returning to the three-person game that opened the chapter. The formal definitions are set forth in Section 3, and the following sections are devoted to examples and counterexamples. The final section contains a general discussion of various aspects of this model, particularly of its range of application.

No new theorems are proved. Our purpose is to study the conceptual implications of the Shapley value and Myerson's extension of it to cooperation structures in examples that are chosen to reflect various applied contexts.

2   Looking ahead with the Myerson value

We start by reviewing the Myerson value. Let v be a coalitional game with N as player set, and g a graph whose vertices are the players. For each player i the *value* $\phi_i^g = \phi_i^g(v)$ is determined by the following axioms.

Axiom 1. If a graph g is obtained from another graph h by adding a single link, namely the one between players i and j, then i and j gain (or lose) equally by the change; that is,

$$\phi_i^g - \phi_i^h = \phi_j^g - \phi_j^h.$$

Axiom 2. If S is a connected component of g, then the sum of the values of the players in S is the worth of S; that is,

$$\sum_{i \in S} \phi_i^g(v) = v(S)$$

(Recall that a *connected component* of a graph is a maximal set of vertices of which any two may be joined by a chain of linked vertices.)

That this axiom system indeed determines a unique value was demonstrated by Myerson (1977). Moreover, he showed that if v is superadditive, then two players who form a new link never lose by it: The two sides of the equation in Axiom 1 are nonnegative. He also established[1] the following practical method for calculating the value: Given v and g, define a coalitional game v^g by

$$v^g(S) := \sum v(S_j^g), \tag{2}$$

where the sum ranges over the connected components S_j^g of the graph $g|S$ (g restricted to S). Then

$$\phi_i^g(v) = \phi_i(v^g), \tag{3}$$

where ϕ_i denotes the ordinary Shapley value for player i.

We illustrate with the game v defined by (1). If P_1 and P_2 happen to meet in the absence of P_3, then the graph g may be represented by

(4)

with only P_1 and P_2 connected. Then $\phi^g(v) = (30,30,0)$; we have already seen that in this situation it is not worthwhile for P_1 and P_2 to bring P_3 into the negotiations, because that would make things entirely symmetric, so P_1 and P_2 would get only 24 each, rather than 30. But P_2, say, might consider offering to form a link with P_3. The immediate result would be the graph

(5)

This graph is not at all symmetric; the central position of P_2 – all communication must pass through him – gives him a decided advantage. This advantage is reflected nicely in the corresponding value, $(14,44,14)$. Thus P_2 stands to gain from forming this link, so it would seem that he should go ahead and do so. But now in this new situation, it would be advantageous for P_1 and P_3 to form a link; this would result in the complete graph

(6)

which is again symmetric and so corresponds to a payoff of $(24,24,24)$. Therefore, whereas it originally seemed worthwhile for P_2 to forge a new link, on closer examination it turns out to lead to a net loss of 6 (he goes from 30 to 24). Thus the original graph, with only P_1 and P_2 linked, would appear to be in some sense "stable" after all.

Can this reasoning be formalized and put into a more general context? It is true that if P_2 offers to link up with P_3, then P_1 also will, but wouldn't P_1 do this anyway? To make sense of the argument, must one assume that P_1 and P_2 explicitly agree not to bring P_3 in? If so, under what conditions would such an agreement come about?

It turns out that no such agreement is necessary to justify the argument. As we shall see in the next section, the argument makes good sense in a framework that is totally noncooperative (as far as link formation is concerned; once the links are formed, enforceable agreements may be negotiated).

3   The formal model

Given a coalitional game v with n players, construct an auxiliary *linking game* as follows: At the beginning of play there are no links between any players. The game consists of pairs of players being offered to form links, the offers being made one after the other according to some definite rule; the rule is common knowledge and will be called the *rule of order*. To form a link, *both* potential partners must agree; once formed, a link cannot be destroyed, and, at any time, the entire history of offers, acceptances, and rejections is known to all players (the game is of perfect information). The only other requirements for the rule of order are that it lead to a finite game, and that after the last link has been formed, each of the $n(n-1)/2$ pairs must be given a final opportunity to form an additional link (as in the bidding stage of bridge). At this point some cooperation graph g has been determined; the payoff to each player i is then defined as $\phi_i^g(v)$.

Most of the analysis in the sequel would not be affected by permitting the rule of order to have random elements as long as perfect information is maintained. It does, however, complicate the analysis, and we prefer to exclude chance moves at this stage.

Note that it does not matter in which order the two players in a pair decide whether to agree to a link; in equilibrium, either order (with perfect information) leads to the same outcome as simultaneous choice.

In practice, the initiative for an offer may come from one of the players rather than from some outside agency. Thus the rule of order might give the initiative to some particular player and have it pass from one player to another in some specified way.

Because the game is of perfect information, it has subgame perfect equilibria (Selten 1965) in pure strategies.[2] Each such equilibrium is associated with a unique cooperation graph g, namely the graph reached at the end of play. Any such g (for any choice of the order on pairs) is called a *natural structure* for v (or a *natural outcome* of the linking game).

Rather than starting from an initial position with no links, one may start from an exogenously given graph g. If all subgame perfect equilibria of the resulting game (for any choice of order) dictate that no additional links form, then g is called *stable*.

4   An illustration

We illustrate with the game defined by (1). To find the subgame perfect equilibria, we use "backwards induction." Suppose we are already at a stage in which there are two links. Then, as we saw in Section 2, it is worthwhile for the two players who have not yet linked up to do so; therefore we may assume that they will. Thus one may assume that an inevitable consequence of going to two links is a graph with three links. Suppose now there is only one link in the graph, say that between P_1 and P_2 [as in (4)]. P_2 might consider offering to link up with P_3 [as in (5)], but we have just seen that this necessarily leads to the full graph [as in (6)]. Because P_2 gets less in (6) than in (4), he will not do so.

Suppose, finally, that we are in the initial position, with no links at all. At this point the way in which the pairs are ordered becomes important;[3] suppose it is 12, 23, 13. Continuing with our backwards induction, suppose the first two pairs have refused. If the pair 13 also refuses, the result will be 0 for all; if, on the other hand, they accept, it will be (30,0,30). Therefore they will certainly accept. Going back one step further, suppose that the pair 12 – the first pair in the order – has refused, and the pair 23 now has an opportunity to form a link. P_2 will certainly wish to do so, as otherwise he will be left in the cold. For P_3, though, there is no difference, because in either case he will get 30; therefore there is a subgame perfect equilibrium at which P_3 turns down this offer. Finally, going back to the first stage, similar considerations lead to the conclusion that the linking game has three natural outcomes, each consisting of a single link between two of the three players.

This argument, especially its first part, is very much in the spirit of the informal story in Section 2. The point is that the formal definition clarifies what lies behind the informal story and shows how this kind of argument may be used in a general situation.

5   Some weighted majority games

Weighted majority games are somewhat more involved than the one considered in the previous section, and we will go into less detail. We start with a fairly typical example. Let v be the five-person weighted majority game [4; 3,1,1,1,1] (4 votes are needed to win; one player has three votes, the other four have one vote each). Let us say that the coalition S has *formed* if g is the complete graph on the members of S (two players are linked if both are members of S). We start by tabulating the values for the complete graphs on various kinds of coalitions, using an obvious notation.

$$\{1,1,1,1\} \quad [0,\tfrac{1}{4},\tfrac{1}{4},\tfrac{1}{4},\tfrac{1}{4}]$$
$$\{3,1\} \quad [\tfrac{1}{2},\tfrac{1}{2},0,0,0]$$
$$\{3,1,1\} \quad [\tfrac{2}{3},\tfrac{1}{6},\tfrac{1}{6},0,0]$$
$$\{3,1,1,1\} \quad [\tfrac{3}{4},\tfrac{1}{12},\tfrac{1}{12},\tfrac{1}{12},0]$$
$$\{3,1,1,1,1\} \quad [\tfrac{3}{5},\tfrac{1}{10},\tfrac{1}{10},\tfrac{1}{10},\tfrac{1}{10}]$$

Intuitively, one may think of a parliament with one large party and four small ones. To form a government, the large party needs only one of the small ones. But it would be foolish actually to strive for such a narrow government, because then it (the large party) would be relatively weak *within* the government, the small party could topple the government at will; it would have veto power within the government. The more small parties join the government, the less the large party depends on each particular one, and so the greater the power of the large party. This continues up to the point where there are so many small parties in the government that the large party itself loses its veto power; at that point the large party's value goes *down*. Thus with only one small party, the large party's value is $\tfrac{1}{2}$; it goes up to $\tfrac{2}{3}$ with two small parties and to $\tfrac{3}{4}$ with three, but then drops to $\tfrac{3}{5}$ with four small parties, because at that point the large party itself loses its veto power within the government. Note, too, that up to a point, the fewer small parties there are in the government, the better for those that are, because there are fewer partners to share in the booty.

We proceed now to an analysis by the method of Section 3. It may be verified that any natural outcome of this game is necessarily the complete graph on some set of players; if a player is linked to another one indirectly, through a "chain" of other linked players, then he must also be linked to him directly. In the analysis, therefore, we may restrict attention to "complete coalitions"–coalitions within which all links have formed.

As before, we use backwards induction. Suppose a coalition of type

{3,1,1,1} has formed. If any of the "small" players in the coalition links up with the single small player who is not yet in, then, as noted earlier, the all-player coalition will form. This is worthwhile both for the small player who was previously "out" and for the one who was previously "in" (the latter's payoff goes up from $\frac{1}{12}$ to $\frac{1}{10}$). Therefore such a link will indeed form, and we conclude that a coalition of type {3,1,1,1} is unstable, in that it leads to {3,1,1,1,1}.

Next, suppose that a coalition of type {3,1,1} has formed. If any player in the coalition forms a link with one of the small players outside it, then this will lead to a coalition of the form {3,1,1,1}, and, as we have just seen, this in turn will lead to the full coalition. This means that the large player will end up with $\frac{3}{5}$ (rather than the $\frac{2}{3}$ he gets in the framework of {3,1,1}) and the small players with $\frac{1}{10}$ (rather than the $\frac{1}{6}$ they get in the framework of {3,1,1}). Therefore none of the players in the coalition will agree to form any link with any player outside it, and we conclude that a coalition of type {3,1,1} is stable.

Suppose next that a coalition of type {3,1} has formed. Then the large player does have an incentive to form a link with a small player outside it. For this will lead to a coalition of type {3,1,1}, which, as we have seen, is stable. Thus the large player can raise his payoff from the $\frac{1}{2}$ he gets in the framework of {3,1} to the $\frac{2}{3}$ he gets in the framework of {3,1,1}. This is certainly worthwhile for him, and therefore {3,1} is unstable.

Finally, suppose no links at all have as yet been formed. If the small players all turn down all offers of linking up with the large player but do link up with each other, then the result is the coalition {1,1,1,1}, and each one will end up with $\frac{1}{4}$. If, on the other hand, one of them links up with the large player, then the immediate consequence is a coalition of type {3,1}; this in turn leads to a coalition of type {3,1,1}, which is stable. Thus for a small player to link up with the large player inevitably leads to a payoff of $\frac{1}{6}$ for him, which is less than the $\frac{1}{4}$ he could get in the framework of {1,1,1,1}. Therefore considerations of subgame perfect equilibrium lead to the conclusion that starting from the initial position (no links), all small players reject all overtures from the large player, and the final result is that the coalition {1,1,1,1} forms.

This conclusion is typical for weighted majority games with one "large" player and several "small" players of equal weight. Indeed, we have the following general result.

Theorem A. In a superadditive weighted majority game of the form $[q; w,1, \ldots ,1]$ with $q > w > 1$ and without veto players, a cooperation structure is natural if and only if it is the complete graph on a minimal winning coalition consisting of "small" players only.

The proof, which will not be given here, consists of a tedious examination of cases. There may be a more direct proof, but we have not found it.

The situation is different if there are two large players and many small ones, as in [4; 2,2,1,1,1,] or [6; 3,3,1,1,1,1,1]. In these cases, either the two large players get together or one large player forms a coalition with *all* the small ones (not minimal winning!). We do not have a general result that covers all games of this type.

Our final example is the game [5; 3,2,2,1,1]. It appears that there are two types of natural coalition structure: one associated with coalitions of type {2,2,1,1}, and one with coalitions of type {3,2,1,1}. Note that neither one is minimal winning.

In all these games some coalition forms; that is, the natural graphs all are "internally complete." As we will see in the next section, that is not the case in general. For simple games, however, and in particular for weighted majority games, we do not know of any counterexample.

6   A natural structure that is not internally complete

Define v as the following sum of three voting games:

$$v := [2; 1,1,1,0] + [3; 1,1,1,0] + [5; 3,1,1,2].$$

That is, v is the sum of a three-person majority game in which P_4 is a dummy, a three-person unanimity game in which P_4 is again a dummy, and a four-person voting game in which the minimal winning coalitions are {1,2,3} and {1,4}. The *sum* of these games is defined as any sum of functions, so the worth $v(S)$ of a coalition S is the number of component games in which S wins. For example, $v(\{2,3\}) = 1$ and $v(\{1,2,4\}) = 2$.

The unique natural structure for this game is

$$4$$

$$2 \underline{\hspace{2cm}} 1 \underline{\hspace{2cm}} 3$$

That is, P_1 links up with P_2 and P_3, but P_2 and P_3 do not link up with each other, and no player links up with P_4. The Myerson value of this game for this cooperation structure is $(\frac{5}{3},\frac{2}{3},\frac{2}{3},0)$.

The Shapley value of this game, which is also the Myerson value for the complete graph on all the players, is $(\frac{5}{4},\frac{3}{4},\frac{3}{4},\frac{1}{4})$. Notice that P_1, P_2, and P_3 all do strictly worse with the Shapley value than with the Myerson value for the natural structure described earlier. It can be verified that for any other graph either the value equals the Shapley value or there is at least one pair of players who are not linked and would do strictly better with the Shapley value. This implies inductively that if any pair of players forms a link that is not in the natural structure, then additional links will continue to form until every player is left with his Shapley value. To avoid this outcome, P_1, P_2, and P_3 will refuse to form any links beyond the two already shown.

For example, consider what happens if P_2 and P_3 add a link so that the graph becomes

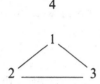

The value for this graph is $(1,1,1,0)$, which is better than the Shapley value for P_2 and P_3, but worse than the Shapley value for P_1. To rebuild his claim to a higher payoff than P_2 and P_3, P_1 then has an incentive to form a link with P_4.

Intuitively, P_1 needs both P_2 and P_3 in order to collect the payoff from the unanimity game $[3; 1,1,1,0]$. They, in turn, would like to keep P_4 out because he is comparatively strong in the weighted voting game $[5; 3,1,1,2]$, whose Shapley value is $(\frac{7}{12},\frac{1}{12},\frac{1}{12},\frac{3}{12})$. With P_4 out, all three remaining players are on the same footing, because all three are then needed to form a winning coalition. Therefore P_1 and P_2 may each expect to get $\frac{1}{3}$ from this game, which is $\frac{1}{4}$ more than the $\frac{1}{12}$ they were getting with P_4 in. On the other hand, excluding P_4 *lowers* P_1's value by $\frac{1}{4}$, from $\frac{7}{12}$ to $\frac{1}{3}$, and P_1 will therefore want P_4 in.

This is where the three-person majority game $[2; 1,1,1,0]$ enters the picture. If P_2 and P_3 refrain from linking up with each other, then P_1's centrality makes him much stronger in *this* game, and his Myerson value in it is then $\frac{2}{3}$ (rather than $\frac{1}{3}$, the Shapley value). This gain of $\frac{1}{3}$ more than makes up for the loss of $\frac{1}{4}$ suffered by P_1 in the game $[5; 3,1,1,2]$, so he is willing to keep P_4 out. On the other hand, P_2 and P_3 also gain thereby, because the $\frac{1}{4}$ each gains in $[5; 3,1,1,2]$ more than makes up for the $\frac{1}{6}$ each loses in the three-person majority game. Thus P_2 and P_3 are motivated to refrain from forming a link with each other, and all are motivated to refrain from forming links with P_4.

In brief, P_2 and P_3 gain by keeping P_4 isolated; but they must give P_1 the central position in the $\{1,2,3\}$ coalition so as to provide an incentive for him to go along with the isolation of P_4, and a credible threat if he doesn't.

7   Natural structures that depend on the rule of order

The natural outcome of the link-forming game may well depend on the rule of order. For example, let u be the majority game $[3; 1,1,1,1]$, let $w := [2; 1,1,0,0]$, and let $w' := [2; 0,0,1,1]$. Let $v := 24u + w + w'$. If the first offer is made to $\{1,2\}$, then either $\{1,2,3\}$ or $\{1,2,4\}$ will form; if it is made to $\{3,4\}$, then either $\{1,3,4\}$ or $\{2,3,4\}$ will form.

The underlying idea here is much like in the game defined by (1). The first two players to link up are willing to admit one more player in order to enjoy the proceeds of the four-person majority game u; but the resulting coalition is not willing to admit the fourth player, who would take a large share of those proceeds and himself contribute comparatively little. The difference between this game and (1) is that here each player in the first pair to get an *opportunity* to link up is positively motivated to seize that opportunity, which was not the case in (1).

The nonuniqueness in this example is robust to small changes in the game. That is, there is an open neighborhood of four-person games around v such that, for all games in this neighborhood, if P_1 and P_2 get the first opportunity to form a link then the natural structures are graphs in which P_1, P_2, and P_3 are connected to each other but not to P_4; but if P_3 and P_4 get the first opportunity to form a link, then the natural structures are graphs in which P_2, P_3, and P_4 are connected to each other but not to P_1. (Here we use the topology that comes from identifying the set of n-person coalitional games with euclidean space of dimension $2^n - 1$.)

Each example in this chapter is also robust in the phenomenon that it is designed to illustrate. That is, for all games in a small open neighborhood of the example in Section 4, the natural outcomes will fail to be Pareto optimal; and for all games in a small open neighborhood of the example in Section 6, the natural outcomes will not be complete graphs on any coalition.

8   Discussion

The theory presented here makes no pretense to being applicable in all circumstances. The situations covered are those in which there is a preliminary period that is devoted to link formation only, during which, for one reason or another, one cannot enter into binding agreements of any kind (such as those relating to subsequent division of the payoff, or even conditional link-forming, or nonforming, deals of the kind "I won't link up with Adams if you don't link up with Brown"). After this preliminary period one carries out negotiations, but then new links can no longer be added.

An example is the formation of a coalition government in a parliamentary democracy in which no single party has a majority (Italy, Germany, Israel, France during the Fifth Republic, even England at times). The point is that a government, once formed, can only be altered at the cost of a considerable upheaval, such as new elections. On the other hand, one cannot really negotiate in a meaningful way on substantive issues before the formation of the government, because one does not know what issues will come up in the future. Perhaps one does know something about some of the issues, but even then one cannot make *binding* deals about them. Such deals, when attempted, are indeed often eventually circumvented or even broken outright; they are to a large extent window dressing, meant to mollify the voter.

An important assumption is that of perfect information. There is nothing to stop us from changing the definition by removing this assumption – something we might well wish to try – but the analysis of the examples would be quite different. Consider, for example, the game [4; 3,1,1,1,1] treated at the beginning of Section 5. Suppose that the rule of order initially gives the initiative to the large player. That is, he may offer links to each of the small players in any order he wants; links are made public once they are forged, but rejected offers do not become known. This is a fairly reasonable description of what may happen in the negotiations for formation of governments in parliamentary democracies of the kind described here. In this situation the small players lose the advantage that was conferred on them by perfect information; formation of a coalition of type {3,1,1} becomes a natural outcome. Intuitively, a small player will refuse an offer from the large player only if he feels reasonably sure that all the small players will refuse. Such a feeling is justified if it is common knowledge that all the others have already refused, and from there one may work one's way backward by induction. But the induction is broken if refused offers do not become known; and then the small players may become suspicious of each other – quite likely rightfully, as under imperfect information, mutual suspicion becomes an equilibrium outcome. We hasten to add that mutual trust – all small players refusing offers from the large

one – remains in equilibrium; but unlike in the case of perfect information, where everything is open and aboveboard, it is no longer the *only*
equilibrium. In short, secrecy breeds mistrust – justifiable mistrust.

Which model is the "right" one (i.e., perfect or imperfect information)
is moot. Needless to say, the perfect information model is not being
suggested as a universal model for all negotiations. But one may feel that
the secrecy in the imperfect information model is a kind of irrelevant
noise that muddies the waters and detracts from our ability properly to
analyze power relationships. On the other hand, one may feel that the
backwards induction in the perfect information model is an artificiality
that overshadows and dominates the analysis, much as in the finitely
repeated Prisoner's Dilemma, and again obscures the "true" power relationships. Moreover, the outcome predicted by the perfect information
model in the game [4; 3,1,1,1,1] (formation of the coalition of all small
players) *is* somewhat strange and anti-intuitive. On the contrary, one
would have thought that the large player has a better chance than each
individual small player to get into the ruling coalition; one might expect
him to "form the government," so to speak.

In brief, there is no single "right" model. Each model has something
going for it and something going against it. You pay your money, and you
take your choice.

We end with an anecdote. This chapter is based on a correspondence
that took place between the authors during the first half of 1977. That
spring, there were elections in Israel, and they brought the right to power
for the first time since the foundation of the state almost thirty years
earlier. After the election, one of us used the perfect information model
proposed here to try to predict which government would form. He was
disappointed when the government that actually did form after about a
month of negotiations did not conform to the prediction of the model, in
that it failed to contain Professor Yigael Yadin's new "Democratic Party
for Change." Imagine his delight when Yadin did after all join the government about four months later!

Appendix

We state and prove here the main result of Myerson (1977).

For any graph g, any set of players S, and any two players j and k in S,
we say that j and k are connected in S by g if and only if there is a path in g
that goes from j to k and stays within S. That is, j and k are connected in S
by g if there exists some sequence of players $i_1, i_2, \ldots, i_M$ such that

$i_1 = j, i_M = k, \{i_1, i_2, \ldots, i_M\} \subseteq S$, and every pair (i_n, i_{n+1}) corresponds to a link in g. Let S/g denote the partition of S into the sets of players that are connected in S by g. That is,

$$S/g = \{\{k \mid j \text{ and } k \text{ are connected in } S \text{ by } g\} \mid j \in S\}.$$

With this notation, the definition of v^g from (2) becomes

$$v^g(S) = \sum_{T \in S/g} v(T) \tag{A1}$$

for any coalition S. Then the main result of Myerson (1977) is as follows.

Theorem. Given a coalitional game v, Axioms 1 and 2 (as stated in Section 2) are satisfied for all graphs if and only if, for every graph g and every player i,

$$\phi_i^g(v) = \phi_i(v^g), \tag{A2}$$

where ϕ_i denotes the ordinary Shapley value for player i. Furthermore, if v is superadditive and if g is a graph obtained from another graph h by adding a single link between players i and j, then $\phi_i(v^g) - \phi_i(v^h) \geq 0$, so the differences in Axiom 1 are nonnegative.

Proof: For any given graph g, Axiom 1 gives us as many equations as there are links in g, and Axiom 2 gives us as many equations as there are connected components of g. When g contains cycles, some of these equations may be redundant, but it is not hard to show that these two axioms give us at least as many independent linear equations in the values ϕ_i^g as there are players in the game. Thus, arguing by induction on the number of links in the graph (starting with the graph that has no links), one can show that there can be at most one value satisfying Axioms 1 and 2 for all graphs.

The usual formula for the Shapley (1953) value implies that

$$\phi_i(v^g) - \phi_j(v^g) = \sum_{S \subseteq N \setminus \{i, j\}} \frac{|S|!(|N| - |S| - 2)!}{(|N| - 1)!} (v^g(S \cup \{i\}) - v^g(S \cup \{j\})).$$

Notice that a coalition's worth in v^g depends only on the links in g that are between two players both of whom are in the coalition. Thus, when S does not contain i or j, the worths $v^g(S \cup \{i\})$ and $v^g(S \cup \{j\})$ would not be changed if we added or deleted a link in g between players i and j. Therefore, $\phi_i(v^g) - \phi_j(v^g)$ would be unchanged if we added or deleted a link in g between players i and j. Thus, (A2) implies Axiom 1.

Given any coalition S and graph g, let the games u^S and w^S be defined by $u^S(T) = v^g(T \cap S)$ and $w^S(T) = v^g(T \backslash S)$ for any $T \subseteq N$. Notice that S is a carrier of u^S, and all players in S are dummies in w^S. Furthermore, if S is a connected component of g, then $v^g = u^S + w^S$. Thus, if S is a connected component of g, then

$$\sum_{i \in S} \phi_i(v^g) = \sum_{i \in S} \phi_i(u^S) = u^S(S) = v^g(S),$$

and so (A2) implies Axiom 2.

Now suppose that the graph g is obtained from the graph h by adding a single link between players i and j. If v is superadditive and $i \in S$, then $v^g(S) \geq v^h(S)$, because S/g is either the same as S/h or a coarser partition than S/h. On the other hand, if $i \notin S$, then $v^g(S) = v^h(S)$. Thus, by the montonicity of the Shapley value, $\phi_i(v^g) \geq \phi_i(v^h)$ if v is superadditive.

Q.E.D.

NOTES

1   These statements are proved in the appendix, and they imply the assertions about the Myerson value that we made in the introduction.
2   Readers unfamiliar with German and the definition of subgame perfection will find the latter repeated, in English, in Selten (1975), though this reference is devoted mainly to the somewhat different concept of "trembling hand" perfection (even in games of perfect information, trembling hand perfect equilibria single out only *some* of the subgame perfect equilibria).
3   For the analysis, not the conclusion.

REFERENCES

Aumann, R. J., and J. H. Dreze (1974), "Cooperative Games with Coalition Structures," *International Journal of Game Theory* 3, 217–37.
Aumann, R. J., and M. Maschler (1964), "The Bargaining Set for Cooperative Games," in Dresher, Shapley, and Tucker (1964), pp. 443–76.
Dresher, M., L. S. Shapley, and A. W. Tucker (1964), editors, *Advances in Game Theory,* Annals of Mathematics Studies No. 52, Princeton: Princeton University Press.
Hart, S., and M. Kurz (1983), "Endogenous Formation of Coalitions," *Econometrica* 51, 1047–64.
Kuhn, H. W., and A. W. Tucker (1953), editors, *Contributions to the Theory of Games,* Volume II, Annals of Mathematics Studies No. 28, Princeton: Princeton University Press.
Myerson, R. B. (1977), "Graphs and Cooperation in Games," *Mathematics of Operations Research* 2, 225–9.

(1980), "Conference Structures and Fair Allocation Rules," *International Journal of Game Theory* 9, 169–82.

von Neumann, J., and O. Morgenstern (1944), *Theory of Games and Economic Behavior,* Princeton: Princeton University Press.

Selten, R. C. (1965), "Spieltheoretische Behandlung eines Oligopolmodells mit Nachfragetraegheit," *Zeitschrift fuer die gesamte Staatswissenschaft* 121, 301–24, 667–89.

(1975), "Reexamination of the Perfectness Concept for Equilibrium Points in Extensive Games," *International Journal of Game Theory* 4, 22–55.

Shapley, L. S. (1953), "A Value for *n*-Person Games," in Kuhn and Tucker (1953), pp. 307–17.

PART IV

Large games

CHAPTER 13

Values of large finite games

Myrna Holtz Wooders and William R. Zame

1   Introduction

The competitive equilibrium, core, and value are solution notions widely used in economics and are based on disparate ideas. The *competitive equilibrium* is a notion of noncooperative equilibrium based on individual optimization. The *core* is a notion of cooperative equilibrium based on what groups of individuals can extract from society. The *value* can be interpreted as a notion of fair division based on what individuals contribute to society. It is a remarkable fact that, under appropriate assumptions, these solution notions (nearly) coincide in large economies. The (near) coincidence of the competitive equilibrium and the core for large exchange economies was first suggested by Edgeworth (1881) and rigorously established by Debreu and Scarf (1963) in the context of replica economies and by Aumann (1964) in the context of continuum economies. This pioneering work has since been extended to much wider contexts; see Hildenbrand (1974) and Anderson (1986) for surveys. The (near) coincidence of the value and the competitive equilibrium (and hence the core) for large exchange economies was first suggested by Shubik[1] and rigorously established by Shapley (1964) in the context of replica economies with money. This pioneering work, too, has since been extended to much wider contexts; see, for example, Shapley and Shubik (1969), Aumann and Shapley (1974), Aumann (1975), Champsaur (1975), Hart (1977), Mas-Colell (1977), and Cheng (1981).

These remarkable and important results deal with (private goods) exchange economies[2] (with divisible goods). Other economic environments, such as ones with indivisibilities, with coalition production possi-

Financial support from the Social Sciences and Humanities Research Council, Canada (Wooders) and the National Science Foundation, United States (Zame) is gratefully acknowledged.

195

bilities, with hedonic coalitions, with (local or pure) public goods are excluded. In some of these other environments, limiting core-equilibrium equivalence results have been obtained (cf. Böhm 1973,1974 and Oddou 1976,1982 on coalition production economies and Wooders 1980,1985 on economies with local public goods). However, no value convergence results have been established in these contexts.[3] (One of the few results in a nonexchange setting is due to Aumann, Gardner, and Rosenthal 1977, who show that the Lindahl equilibrium does *not* coincide with the value in continuum economies with pure public goods.)

This survey reports on two papers (Wooders and Zame 1987a,b), which establish that the value does indeed lie in an approximate core for large economic environments that may include all the aspects listed, with the exception of pure public goods. The framework we use to describe such environments is that of cooperative games. Although we obtain results for both the transferable utility (TU) and nontransferable utility (NTU) settings (corresponding to environments with and without linear money), we describe here only the work in the TU setting. This is the setting in which the results are sharper and easier to describe and in which the economic intuition is most clearly visible.

To model large games, we introduce the notion of a technology.[4] This construction allows us to describe the payoff achievable by any collection of agents in a way that depends continuously on the attributes of the agents (and not on their names). Given such a technology, we describe a game by specifying a set of players and their attributes (in much the same way that an exchange economy is described by specifying a set of consumers and their endowments and utility functions). Players in such a game are near substitutes if they have similar attributes (just as consumers are near substitutes if they have similar endowments and utility functions). A game is large if each player has many near-substitutes.

The ϵ-core of a game (for $\epsilon \geq 0$) is the set of attainable utility vectors that cannot be improved upon by any group by more than ϵ for each member. If we view the core as a set of stable outcomes (i.e., as the set of cooperative equilibria), it is natural to view the ϵ-core as a set of approximately stable outcomes. Our principal result is that, for large games, the value belongs to the ϵ-core (and is thus an approximately stable outcome). (Moreover, ϵ tends to 0 as the game becomes larger.)

This result rests on two economic ideas. The first of these is that if gains to group size are nearly exhausted by relatively small groups,[5] then small groups are effective. The expression of this idea is that small coalitions have almost as much power of improvement as large coalitions. More precisely, any feasible payoff that can be improved upon by any coalition can be improved upon by a small coalition. This observation is by now fairly familiar in the context of exchange economies (cf. Grodal 1972; Schmeidler 1972; Vind 1972; Mas-Colell 1979; Hammond, Kaneko, and Wooders 1985). The idea plays a role in the equivalence results of Böhm (1973, 1974) and Wooders (1980, 1985). The power of the idea emerges perhaps most clearly in large cooperative games (Shubik and Wooders 1983a,b; Wooders 1983; Wooders and Zame 1984, 1988; Kaneko and Wooders 1985, 1986).

The second of these ideas is that small cartels have little monopoly power. The expression of this idea is that in a large game the value confers little benefit (or penalty) on a small syndicate (a group that chooses to act together). More precisely, the sum of the payoffs that the value assigns to the members of a small syndicate is nearly the same as the payoff the value would assign to the syndicate if it were treated as an indivisible unit.

2 Games

By a *game* (in characteristic function form with sidepayments) we mean a pair (N,v), where N is a finite set (the set of *players*) and v is a function (the *characteristic function*) from the set 2^N of subsets of N to the set $\mathbf{R}_+$ of nonnegative real numbers, with the property that $v(\varnothing) = 0$. We usually refer to subsets S of N as *coalitions;* the number $v(S)$ is the *worth* of S. If the player set N is understood, we frequently refer to v itself as the game. We say that v is *superadditive* if for all disjoint subsets S, S' of N we have

$$v(S \cup S') \geq v(S) + v(S')$$

By a *payoff* for (N,v) we mean a vector x in $\mathbf{R}^N$; it is convenient to use functional notation, so for $i \in N$, $x(i)$ is the ith component of x. We say that x is *feasible* if $x(N) \leq v(N)$ (where $x(S) = \Sigma_{i \in S} x(i)$ for each $S \subset N$).

For $\epsilon \geq 0$ a feasible payoff x is in the ϵ-*core* of (N,v) if

(a) $x(N) = v(N)$ *(Pareto optimality)*.
(b) $x(S) \geq v(S) - \epsilon |S|$ for all subsets S of N.

(We use $|S|$ to denote the number of elements of the set S.) We say x is in the *individually rational ϵ-core* if it is in the ϵ-core and

(c) $x(i) \geq v(\{i\})$ for all $i \in N$ *(individually rationality)*.

When $\epsilon = 0$, the ϵ-core (which coincides with the individually rational ϵ-core) is simply the *core*.

Less formally, a feasible Pareto-optimal payoff x belongs to the ϵ-core of (N,v) if no group of players can guarantee for themselves a payoff that each of them finds better than x by more than ϵ. As Shapley and Shubik 1966 point out, such a payoff can be interpreted as stable if players are nearly optimizing, or satisfying, or if there is an organizational or communicational cost to formation of coalitions (proportional to the size of the coalitions).

The *Shapley value* Sh(v) of the game (N,v) is the payoff whose ith component is given by

$$\text{Sh}(v,i) = \frac{1}{|N|} \sum_{J=0}^{|N|-1} \binom{|N|-1}{J}^{-1} \sum_{\substack{S \subset N \setminus \{i\} \\ |S| = J}} [v(S \cup \{i\}) - v(S)].$$

In other words, Sh(v,i) is player i's average marginal contribution to coalitions in N. The Shapley value is a feasible, Pareto-optimal, and individually rational payoff. It is frequently interpreted as representing a "fair" payoff because it yields to each player his expected contribution. It can also be given various other interpretations (as a von Neumann–Morgenstern utility function for example; see Roth 1977 and Chapter 4 this volume).

3　　Technologies

We now describe the framework of a large game for which the worth of a coalition depends in a continuous fashion on the attributes of its members.

Let Ω be a compact metric space. By a *profile* on Ω we mean a function f from Ω to the set $\mathbf{Z}_+$ of nonnegative integers for which the *support* of f,

$$\text{support}(f) = \{\omega \in \Omega: f(\omega) \neq 0\},$$

is finite. We denote the set of profiles on Ω by $P(\Omega)$. Note that the sum of profiles (defined pointwise) is a profile, and that the product of a profile with a nonnegative integer is a profile. We write 0 for the profile that is identically zero. We write $f \leq g$ if $f(\omega) \leq g(\omega)$ for each $\omega \in \Omega$. For ω_0 a point of Ω, we write χ_{ω_0} for the profile given by

$$\begin{aligned}
\chi_{\omega_0}(\omega) &= 0 && \text{if } \omega \neq \omega_0, \\
&= 1 && \text{if } \omega = \omega_0.
\end{aligned}$$

By the *norm* of a profile f we mean

$$\|f\| = \sum_{\omega \in \Omega} f(\omega).$$

(Notice that this is a finite sum, because f has finite support.)

In essence, a profile is simply an (unordered) list of elements of Ω, with each element ω appearing as many times as its multiplicity $f(\omega)$.

By a *technology* we mean a pair (Ω, Λ), where Ω is a compact metric space (the space of *attributes*) and $\Lambda: P(\Omega) \to \mathbf{R}_+$ is a function with the following properties:

(i) $\Lambda(0) = 0$.
(ii) $\Lambda(f + g) \geq \Lambda(f) + \Lambda(g)$ *(superadditivity)*.
(iii) There is a constant M such that $\Lambda(f + \chi_\omega) \leq \Lambda(f) + M$ for each $\omega \in \Omega, f \in P(\Omega)$ (we say M is an *individual marginal bound*).
(iv) For every $\epsilon > 0$ there is a $\delta > 0$ such that $|\Lambda(f + \chi_{\omega_1}) - \Lambda(f + \chi_{\omega_2})| < \epsilon$ whenever $f \in P(\Omega)$ and $\omega_1, \omega_2 \in \Omega$ with $\mathrm{dist}(\omega_1, \omega_2) < \delta$ *(continuity)*.

The interpretation we have in mind is that a technology encompasses all the economic possibilities for every conceivable group of players. A point of Ω represents a complete description of the relevant attributes of players (endowment, utility function, etc.). A profile f represents a group of players of whom $f(\omega)$ are described by the attribute ω; the total number of players in the group is just $\|f\|$. The number $\Lambda(f)$ represents the maximal possible payoff the members of this group could achieve (using their own resources) by cooperation. The requirement that $\Lambda(0) = 0$ means that the group of no players can achieve nothing. Superadditivity has its usual interpretation: One of the possibilities open to the group represented by $f + g$ is to split into the groups represented by f and by g and share the proceeds. (Notice that we do not require the profiles f, g to have disjoint supports. The groups of players represented by the profiles f, g will have no players in common in any case; to require that the profiles f, g have disjoint supports would be to require that these groups have no types of players in common.) The existence of an individual marginal bound simply means that there are no players whose (potential) contributions to society are arbitrarily large. Continuity of Λ means that players with similar attributes are near substitutes (and that players with the same attributes are exact substitutes).

If Ω is finite, we frequently refer to its elements as *types*. (Notice that continuity of Λ is automatic in this case, and that players of the same type are exact substitutes.)

To derive a game from the technology (Ω, Λ), we specify a finite set N and a function $\alpha: N \to \Omega$ (an *attribute function*). We associate with each subset S of N a profile $\mathrm{prof}(\alpha|S)$ given by

$$\mathrm{prof}(\alpha|S)(\omega) = |\alpha^{-1}(\omega) \cap S|.$$

In other words, prof($\alpha|S$)(ω) is the number of players in S possessing the attribute ω. We then define the characteristic function v_α: $2^N \to \mathbf{R}_+$ by

$$v_\alpha(S) = \Lambda(\text{prof}(\alpha|S)).$$

Thus, the worth of a coalition S in a derived game is determined by the technology and depends on the attributes of the players in the coalition. It is easily checked that (N,v_α) is a superadditive game.

4   Results

Having described the framework, we can now state our main result. If the space Ω of attributes is finite (and so consists of a finite number of types), it seems natural to think of a game as large if it has many players of each type; thus each player has many exact substitutes. If Ω is not finite, it thus seems natural to think of a game as large if each player has many near substitutes.

Theorem 1. Let (Ω,Λ) be a technology. For each $\epsilon > 0$ there is a number $\delta(\epsilon) > 0$ and an integer $n(\epsilon)$ with the following property:

> For any game (N,v_α) derived from the technology (Ω,Λ), if for each player i in N there exist $n(\epsilon)$ distinct players $j_1, \ldots, j_{n(\epsilon)}$ in N such that dist($\alpha(i),\alpha(j_k)$) $< \delta(\epsilon)$ for each $k = 1, \ldots,$ $n(\epsilon)$, then the Shapley value of (N,v_α) is in the individually rational ϵ-core of (N,v_α).

As we said earlier, the proof of Theorem 1 rests on the expressions of two economic ideas. The first of these is that (relatively) small coalitions are nearly as effective as large coalitions.

Theorem 2. Let (Ω,Λ) be a technology. For each $\epsilon > 0$, there is an integer $l(\epsilon)$ with the following property:

> For any game (N,v_α) derived from the technology (Ω,Λ), if $x \in \mathbf{R}^N$ is a feasible, Pareto-optimal payoff not in the ϵ-core of (N,v_α), then there is a coalition $S \subset N$ such that $|S| \le l(\epsilon)$ and $v_\alpha(S) > x(S) + (\epsilon/2)|S|$.

Informally: for any derived game, any (feasible, Pareto-optimal) allocation that can be ϵ-improved upon by any coalition whatsoever can be $\epsilon/2$-improved upon by a small coalition.

The expression of the second economic idea is that the value confers little monopoly power on small syndicates. Although we only need such a result in the context of technologies, it is true for individual games, so we give a general formulation.

We consider games (N,v) that are not required to be superadditive. If S is a nonempty subset of N, then by the *syndicate game* (N_S,v_S) we mean the game whose player set is $N_S = (N\backslash S) \cup \{\{S\}\}$ and whose characteristic function is given by

$$v_S(W) = v(W) \qquad \text{if } \{S\} \notin W,$$
$$= v([W\backslash\{\{S\}\}] \cup S) \qquad \text{if } \{S\} \in W.$$

That is, (N_S,v_S) is the game that results if we treat the syndicate S as an indivisible unit. We want to compare $\mathrm{Sh}(v_S,\{S\})$ with $\Sigma_{i \in S}\mathrm{Sh}(v,i)$; the difference between these two numbers might be called the *power* of the syndicate (i.e., the gain or loss resulting from formation of the syndicate).

We need some terminology. We will say that the positive number M is an *individual marginal bound* for the game (N,v) if $|v(W \cup \{j\}) - v(W)| \leq M$ for each $j \in N$ and each $W \subset N$. For $\gamma > 0$, we will say that players i, $j \in N$ are *γ-substitutes* if $|v(W \cup \{i\}) - v(W \cup \{j\})| < \gamma$ for every $W \subset N\backslash\{i,j\}$.

Theorem 3. Let M and γ be positive numbers and let s be a positive integer. Then there is an integer $r(M,\gamma,s)$ with the following property:

> For any game (N,v) with an individual marginal bound of M, and any coalition S of N with $|S| \leq s$, if for each player i in S there are at least $r(M,\gamma,s)$ players not in S who are γ-substitutes for i, then
>
> $$\left|\mathrm{Sh}(v_S,\{S\}) - \sum_{i \in S} \mathrm{Sh}(v,i)\right| \leq \tfrac{3}{2}|S|(|S| + 1)\gamma.$$

We emphasize again that this result is independent of the framework of technologies. It is an assertion about the Shapley value of *every* game. Thus the number $r(M,\gamma,s)$ depends on M, on γ, and on s, but not on any underlying technology – because there isn't one. It is possible to give an explicit bound for $r(M,\gamma,s)$, but it would be very messy.

Theorem 1 follows quite easily from Theorems 2 and 3. If (N,v) is a derived game and the Shapley value does not belong to the ϵ-core, then it can be ϵ-improved upon by some coalition $A \subset N$. According to Theorem 2, it can then be $\epsilon/2$-improved upon by some small coalition $B \subset N$. On the other hand, Theorem 3 tells us that $\Sigma_{b \in B}\mathrm{Sh}(v,b)$ is nearly $\mathrm{Sh}(v_B,\{B\})$, and individual rationality implies that $\mathrm{Sh}(v_B,\{B\}) \geq v_B(\{B\}) = v(B)$. Putting these together yields a contradiction.

The proofs of Theorems 2 and 3 involve complicated combinatorial arguments that are too lengthy to describe here. However, the intuition underlying the proof of Theorem 3 can be exposed in a rather simple example.

5   Example

To expose the intuition underlying Theorem 3, we present a fairly simple but revealing example. We consider a game (N,v) with two types of players. Because players of the same type are exact substitutes, we can describe a coalition by a pair (x,y) of nonnegative integers, representing the numbers of players of types 1 and 2. We suppose that, in total, there are k players of type 1 and l players of type 2, and that the essential coalitions are $(1,0)$, $(0,1)$, $(1,1)$, and $(2,1)$, with $v(1,0) = v(0,1) = 0$, $v(1,1) = 3$, and $v(2,1) = 4$. Other coalitions can obtain only what is achievable by (optimally) subdividing into coalitions of these kinds. Explicitly, this yields

$$v(x,y) = \begin{cases} 4y & \text{if } x \geq 2y, \\ x + 2y & \text{if } 2y > x \geq y, \\ 3x & \text{if } y > x, \\ 0 & \text{if } x = 0 \text{ or } y = 0. \end{cases}$$

Let $\mathrm{Sh}(v,i)$ be the Shapley value for type i ($i = 1,2$), and let $\mathrm{Sh}(v_{(1,1)},\{(1,1)\})$ be the Shapley value of the syndicate $(1,1)$ in the syndicate game $(N_{(1,1)},v_{(1,1)})$. We want to see that if k, l are both large, then

$$\mathrm{Sh}(v_{(1,1)},\{(1,1)\}) \simeq \mathrm{Sh}(v,1) + \mathrm{Sh}(v,2).$$

To see this, we make use of the random-order interpretation of the Shapley value. To compute $\mathrm{Sh}(v,1)$, we fix a player A of type 1 and consider all possible orderings of the total of $k + l$ players. For each of these orderings we assign to player A his marginal contribution to the coalition of all players preceding him. Finally, we sum over all orderings and divide by the number of orderings. Equivalently, we consider all possible coalitions (x,y) of the $k - 1$ other players of type 1 and l players of type 2, multiply A's marginal contribution to (x,y) by the probability that (x,y) occurs, and sum.

Keeping in mind that A's marginal contribution to (x,y) depends only on proportions, we are led to the data in Table 1. The data in Table 2

Table 1. *Marginal contributions of player of type 1*

Proportions in coalition (x,y)	Probability	Marginal contribution of type 1
$x \geq 2y$	p_1	0
$2y > x \geq y$	p_2	1
$y > x$	p_3	3

Table 2. *Marginal contributions of player of type 2*

Proportions in coalition (x,y)	Probability	Marginal contribution of type 2
$x \geq 2y + 2$	q_1	4
$x = 2y + 1$	q_1'	3
$2y \geq x \geq y$	q_2	2
$y > x$	q_3	0

Table 3. *Marginal contributions of player of syndicate (1,1)*

Proportions in coalition (x,y)	Probability	Marginal contribution of syndicate (1,1)
$x \geq 2y$	r_1	4
$2y > x \geq y$	r_2	3
$y > x$	r_3	3

reflect the information necessary to compute $Sh(v,2)$, and the data in Table 3 reflect the information necessary to compute $Sh(v_{(1,1)},\{(1,1)\})$. Thus

$$Sh(v,1) = 0p_1 + 1p_2 + 3p_3,$$

$$Sh(v,2) = 4q_1 + 3q_1' + 2q_2 + 0q_3,$$

$$Sh(v_{(1,1)},\{(1,1)\}) = 4r_1 + 3r_2 + 3r_3.$$

To obtain the result we want, note that p_1 is the probability that a coalition (x,y) drawn at random from $(k-1,l)$ will satisfy $x \geq 2y$, q_1 is the probability that a coalition drawn at random from $(k,l-1)$ will satisfy $x \geq 2y+2$, and r_1 is the probability that a coalition drawn at random from $(k-1,l-1)$ will satisfy $x > 2y$. If k, l are both large, then $p_1 \approx q_1 \approx r_1$. Similarly, if k, l are both large, then $p_2 \approx q_2 \approx r_2$, $p_3 \approx q_3 \approx r_3$, and $q_1' \approx 0$. This yields

$$\text{Sh}(v,1) + \text{Sh}(v,2) \approx \text{Sh}(v_{(1,1)},\{(1,1)\}),$$

as desired.

NOTES

1 See Shapley (1964, pp. 1,7).
2 Champsaur (1975) allows for additive production.
3 Recall that the coincidence of the value allocations and competitive allocations, even in exchange economies, depends on differentiability of the utility functions and is not generally valid without it (see Hart 1977). It is an interesting open question what the analogue of differentiable utility functions would be for large games.
4 The terms *technology* and *pregame* have been used to describe essentially the same structure in Wooders and Zame (1984,1987a,b,c) and Kaneko and Wooders (1985,1986). This framework is, in part, an outgrowth of an NTU types framework introduced in Wooders (1983).
5 This describes economies with private goods or local public goods but typically not, for example, ones with pure public goods.

REFERENCES

R. M. Anderson, Notions of core convergence, in W. Hildenbrand and A. Mas-Colell, eds., *Contribution to Mathematical Economics,* North-Holland, Amsterdam, 1986.

R. J. Aumann, Markets with a continuum of traders, *Econometrica* 32 (1964), 39–50.

Values of markets with a continuum of traders, *Econometrica* 43 (1975), 611–46.

R. J. Aumann, R. J. Gardner, and R. W. Rosenthal, Core and value for a public-goods economy: an example, *J. Econ. Theory* 15 (1977), 363–9.

R. J. Aumann and L. S. Shapley, *Values of Non-Atomic Games,* Princeton Univ. Press, Princeton, N.J., 1974.

V. Böhm, Firms and market equilibria in a private ownership economy, *Zeitschrift fur Nationalokonomie* 33 (1973), 87–102.

V. Böhm, The core of an economy with production, *Rev. Econ. Studies* 41 (1974), 429–36.

P. Champsaur, Cooperation vs. competition, *J. Econ. Theory* 11 (1975), 394–417.

H. C. Cheng, On dual regularity and value convergence theorems, *J. Math. Econ.* 8 (1981), 37–57.

G. Debreu and H. Scarf, A limit theorem on the core of an economy, *Internat. Econ. Rev.* 4 (1963), 235–46.

F. Y. Edgeworth, *Mathematical Psychics,* London: Kegan Paul, 1881.

B. Grodal, A second remark on the core of an atomless economy, *Econometrica* 40 (1972), 581–4.

P. Hammond, M. Kaneko, and M. H. Wooders, Continuum economies with finite coalitions: core, equilibrium, and widespread externalities, *J. Econ. Theory* (forthcoming) (1988).

S. Hart, Values of non-differentiable markets with a continuum of traders, *J. Math. Econ.* 4 (1977), 103–16.

W. Hildenbrand, *Core and Equilibria of a Large Economy,* Princeton Univ. Press, Princeton, N.J., 1974.

M. Kaneko and M. H. Wooders, Nonemptiness of the core of a game with a continuum of players and finite coalitions, Institute of Socio-Economic Planning, University of Tsukuba No. 295, 1985.

The core of a game with a continuum of players and finite coalitions: the model and some results, *Math. Soc. Sci.* 2 (1986), 105–37.

A. Mas-Colell, Competitive and value allocations of large exchange economics, *J. Econ. Theory* 14 (1977), 419–38.

A refinement of the core equivalence theorem, *Econ. Lett.* 3 (1979), 307–10.

C. Oddou, Théorèmes d'existence et d'équivalence pour des économies avec production, *Econometrica* 44 (1976), 265–81.

The core of a coalition production economy, *J. Math Econ* 9 (1982), 1–22.

A. E. Roth, The Shapley value as a von Neumann–Morgenstern utility, *Econometrica* 45 (1977), 657–64.

D. Schmeidler, A remark on the core of an atomless economy, *Econometrica* 40 (1972), 579–80.

L. S. Shapley, Value of large games. VII: A general exchange economy with money, Rand Memorandum RM-4248-PR, 1964.

L. S. Shapley and M. Shubik, Quasi-cores in a monetary economy with nonconvex preferences, *Econometrica* 34 (1966), 805–27.

Pure competition, coalitional power, and fair division, *Internat. Econ. Rev.* 10 (1969), 337–62.

M. Shubik and M. H. Wooders, Approximate cores of replica games and economies. Part I: Replica games, externalities, and approximate cores, *Math. Soc. Sci.* 6 (1983a), 27–48.

Approximate cores of replica games and economies. Part II: Set-up costs and firm formation in coalition production economics, *Math. Soc. Sci.* 6 (1983b), 285–306.

K. Vind, A third comment on the core of an atomless market, *Econometrica* 40 (1972), 585–6.

M. H. Wooders, The Tiebout Hypothesis: Near optimality in local public good economies, *Econometrica* 48 (1980), 1467–85.

The epsilon core of a large replica game, *J. Math. Econ.* 11 (1983), 277–300.

A Tiebout theorem, IMA Preprint #128, Institute for Mathematics and Its Applications, University of Minnesota, 1985.

M. H. Wooders and W. R. Zame, Approximate cores of large games, *Econometrica* 52 (1984), 1327–50.

Large games; fair and stable outcomes, *J. Econ. Theory* 42 (1987a), 59–93.

NTU values of large games, IMSSS Stanford University Technical Report No. 503, 1987b.

Approximate cores of large games without side payments, manuscript, 1988.

CHAPTER 14

Payoffs in nonatomic economies: an axiomatic approach

Pradeep Dubey and Abraham Neyman

1   Introduction

It has been much remarked that different solutions become equivalent in the setting of economies in which there is "perfect competition"; that is, no individual can affect the overall outcome. The conjecture that the core coincides with competitive (Walras) allocations was made as far back as 1881 by Edgeworth [11]. His insight has been confirmed in increasing generality in a series of papers[1] [20,9,2,14,13,7,8,1] over the last three decades. Another line of inquiry originated with the recent introduction of a value for games by Shapley [17]. It was found that this also coincided with the above two [19,6,3].

The equivalence phenomenon is striking in view of the fact that these solutions are posited on entirely different grounds. If we restrict ourselves to smooth, *transferable* utilities, then the result is even sharper: not only do the solutions coincide, but they are also unique (i.e., consist of a single payoff). Our aim here is to give another view of this "coincident payoff" by putting it on an axiomatic foundation. As an upshot of our approach, we get a "metaequivalence" theorem, by way of a categorization: Any solution coincides with this payoff if and only if it satisfies our axioms.

The transferable utility assumption is undoubtedly restrictive. But it has a good track record of being the precursor of the general analysis (e.g., [6] before [3]; [17] before [18], [20] before [9]; indeed, our approach can also be extended to nontransferable utilities [10b]). However, we confine ourselves here to the transferable case, because it makes a cleaner presentation and is, more or less, the heart of the matter.

Denote by *M* the class of nonatomic economies with transferable and differentiable utilities. Any such economy can also be viewed as a produc-

---

But for some minor modifications, this material is taken from [10a].

tive economy with a single consumable output. (See the discussion in Chapter 6 of [6].) We will adopt the production interpretation for most of our discussion. But by thinking of the output as "utiles," everything we say can be translated into the exchange version as well.

The problem of determining payoffs (final distributions of the output) in these economies has been approached from many sides. Let us briefly recount some of them. First there is the classical notion of a competitive payoff that depends on prices that clear all markets (i.e., equate supply and demand). Equally well known is the concept of the core. It is defined by the condition that no coalition of agents in the economy can, on its own, improve what it gets. (See Chapter 6 of [6] for a historical survey and detailed discussion of these concepts.) Other solutions from game theory have also been applied to the economic model. The bargaining set [4,12,15], which contains the core, is based upon a weaker notion of stability: Each "objection" can be ruled out by a "counterobjection." (In this terminology there can be a fortiori no objection to any payoff in the core.) Then there is the concept of the nucleolus [16]. Roughly, what is involved is minimizing the "dissatisfaction" of the most dissatisfied coalition, where dissatisfaction is measured by the difference between what a coalition "could" get and what it is getting. Finally, we have the Shapley value [17], which has been the focus of active, recent research (and was the starting point of this inquiry as well). It is a mapping that assigns to each player of a game a number that purports to represent what he would be willing to pay in order to participate; it is uniquely determined by certain plausible conditions for all finite games [17] and a large class of non-atomic games (pNA) that include the economies in M [6]. The value thus obtained can also be interpreted from a complementary standpoint; it assigns to a player the average of his marginal contributions to coalitions he may join (in a model of random ordering of the players).

These solutions are in general quite different from each other. It is remarkable that they become equivalent on M. The question is: What are the crucial properties that are common across the solutions and on which, at bottom, their equivalence depends? To set the stage for our analysis, we take a map G on M that maps each economy m in M to a subset $G(m)$ of payoffs in m. Then we look for an irreducible list of axioms on G that will uniquely categorize G as the coincident core-value-Walras- . . . -corre-spondence. Four axioms are presented that accomplish the job.

The theorem we will state may be viewed as a metaequivalence theorem. For instance, the equivalence of core and competitive payoffs follows from our result by simply checking that both the map that takes each m in M to its core and the map that takes each m in M to its competitive payoffs satisfy our axioms. That the value also coincides with the core and competitive payoff is immediate, because it satisfies even stronger axioms [6, chap. 1]. In general, if any solution is a candidate for equivalence, it is both necessary and sufficient that it satisfy our axioms.

In our axioms we try to identify the minimal common characteristics of solutions that hold not only on M but also when the set of agents is finite or when utilities are not differentiable (or both). The axioms are therefore cast in as weak a form as possible. They turn out to be categorical (i.e., imply a unique solution) only on M (i.e., only in conjunction with nonatomicity and differentiability). Besides the aesthetic value of the weak form, there is also a pragmatic reason involved. In this form the truth of the axioms can be easily verified for a given solution concept, and thus it provides an effective format for discussing equivalence. Once a solution obeys the axioms, then an implication of our theorem is that on M it coincides with the value and therefore must obey the much stronger axioms of the value. But these strong axioms are often not easy to verify directly. An example is provided by the core for which additivity on M is not obvious (and in fact is not true outside of M) but separability is.

The axioms will be spelled out precisely in Section 3, but we present them at an intuitive level now. Denote the space of agents by $[T,\mathscr{C},\mu]$. Here T is the set of agents, $\mathscr{C}$ the σ-algebra of coalitions, and μ a nonatomic population measure on $[T,\mathscr{C}]$. An economy is a pair of measurable functions (a,u), where $a: T \to R_+^n$ specifies the initial endowment of the n resource commodities, and $u: T \times R_+^n \to R_+$ the production (alternatively, utility) functions. M is the set of all pairs (a,u), subject to certain conditions on a and u (see Section 2). For any m in M we can define an associated characteristic function (or game) $v_m: \mathscr{C} \to R_+$, which assigns to each coalition the maximum output that it could achieve by a reallocation of the resources of its own members; that is,

$$v_m(S) = \max \left\{ \int_S u(t,x(t))\, d\mu(t) : \int_S x(t)\, d\mu = \int_S a(t)\, d\mu,\ x: T \to R_+^n \right\}.$$

Payoffs in $m \in M$ can be thought of as integrable functions from T to R_+, and in turn can be identified with nonnegative countably additive measures on $(T,\mathscr{C})$ that are absolutely continuous with respect to μ. But let us make only the assumptions that they lie in FA, the collection of functions from $\mathscr{C}$ to R that are finitely additive and bounded. Let $P(\text{FA})$ be the set of all subsets of FA. Then any assignment of payoffs to economies may be represented by a map $\phi: M \to P(\text{FA})$.

We will impose four axioms on ϕ: inessential economy, anonymity, separability, and continuity. Our main result is that there is one, and only one, map that satisfies these axioms: It maps m into the (unique) coincident payoff of m. An immediate corollary to this is useful to keep in mind for the metaequivalence aspect of the result. Given two solutions ϕ_1: $M \to P(\text{FA})$ and ϕ_2: $M \to P(\text{FA})$, call ϕ_2 a *cover* of ϕ_1 if $\phi_1(m) \subset \phi_2(m)$ for all m in M. Our result implies that if a solution is nonempty-valued and has a cover that satisfies the axioms, then it must also agree on M with the coincident payoff. Thus even though competitive payoffs, in general, violate continuity and the nucleolus violates separability (when the agent space is finite), their equivalence on M is ensured because the core is readily seen to be a satisfactory cover for both.

The inessential economy axiom has to do with economies in which agents have no motivation to collude in order to increase the output. Indeed, suppose that m in M is such that each coalition $S \in \mathscr{C}$ achieves its maximum $v_m(S)$ *uniquely* by sticking to its allocation of resources. Then one would expect that no exchange, either of the inputs or the output, will occur. And this is just what the axiom says.

The anonymity axiom asserts that the labels of the agents do not matter. If we were to relabel them, this would have the effect of relabeling their payoffs accordingly.

These two axioms hold widely for most solutions, not only on M, but in general.

The separability axiom considers an economy made up of two separate, noninteracting parts. Take m' and m'' in M. Let us construct the economy m by, as it were, "collating" m' and m''. Each agent in m possesses the same initial resources that he had in m' and in m''; also he has access to both his production functions from m' and m''. However, suppose that the input commodities of m' and m'' are completely disjoint: Those in m' cannot be used for production in m'', and vice versa (though the two economies produce the same output). Now consider any coalition S that forms in m. Each agent in s can send his black-hatted (white-hatted) representative to m' (m''). If these two types of representatives separately maximize the output in m' and m'', then the sum of what they get back is precisely what S can obtain in m; that is, $v_m(S) = v_{m'}(S) + v_{m''}(S)$ for all $S \in \mathscr{C}$. Thus m, in essence, consists of operating in m' and in m'' independently of each other. We require that in this case if we put together a payoff in m' with one in m'', the outcome should be feasible in m. However, we do not exclude the possibility that other payoffs may also be obtained in m. In symbols, $\phi(m') + \phi(m'') \subset \phi(m)$. This is related to the additivity axiom for the value, but it is so watered down as to apply to the core even when the economy is finite (in which case additivity, $\phi(m) = \phi(m') + \phi(m'')$, no longer holds). Clearly it applies always to the value and to competitive payoffs; indeed, both of these satisfy additivity.

The continuity axioms say that if the distance between two economies is small, then so is that between their sets of payoffs. It is intimately bound up with the notion of distance. The one we employ declares the distance between two economies to be zero if they yield the same characteristic function. Thus the payoffs depend on the characteristic function alone; in other words, they depend on the data (a,u) of the economy only insofar as it shows up in the net production of the coalitions [if $v_m = v_{m'}$, $\phi(m) = \phi(m')$]. Modulo this, however, our continuity requirement is weak. We choose a "large" norm on the characteristic functions (the bounded variation norm) and a "small" one on $P(\mathrm{FA})$ (the Hausdorff distance in the bounded variation norm, which is equivalent in FA to the maximum norm).

Our axiomatic approach is akin to that of [6] and invites immediate comparison. We begin with a point-to-set map (from M to FA). That $\phi(m)$ is a nonempty one-element set of FA is a deduction, not a postulate, in our case. Also note that we do not require that $\phi(m)$ consist of efficient payoffs; this, too, is deduced. Separability reduces to additivity if the solution is single-valued but not otherwise. Clearly separability is weaker than the additivity required in [6]. Continuity is closely related to the positivity axioms of [6]. Finally, we emphasize that the axioms are invoked on the set of games that arise from M alone. This set is much smaller than the general space $p\mathrm{NA}$ of [6]. (Its complement in $p\mathrm{NA}$ is open and dense.) Thus the uniqueness of ϕ does become an issue. (Existence, on the other hand, is no problem: Simply restrict the value on $p\mathrm{NA}$ to our domain.) The very question we set out with, "What are payoffs in nonatomic economies?" makes it desirable that we exclude any reference to games that do not arise from M. Thus we stay within M throughout and give a self-contained analysis of it. Each axiom is cast in an economic framework and can be interpreted therein. It is fortunate that even though the scope of the axioms is diminished by this restriction of the domain, they nevertheless are sufficiently far-reaching to determine a unique map.

Our result also sheds new light on the nature of competitive (Walras) equilibrium itself. The direct definition of this (see the next section, and Chapter 6 of [6]) is "local." It is based on a model of individualistic optimization of trade in the presence of complete markets with fixed prices, and it refers only to the data $(a,\mathbf{u})$ of a single, given economy. But because our axioms categorize it, they also serve as a definition of the Walras correspondence on M. Here a space of economies is needed, and the axioms express "global" properties in which two or more markets are compared with each other. In this sense our theorem provides a dual, global view of Walras equilibrium. The spirit of our axioms is quite different from the Walrasian. Nowhere is the existence of prices "put into" the axioms. Nor is it postulated that traders behave like individual optimizers. Nor indeed is any notion of equilibrium or stability invoked.

What we do is tantamount to value theory on M. It is just that, given the special economic structure of M, one can water down the value axioms in such a way as to bring within their ambit various other solution concepts. This, in turn, gives insight into the equivalence phenomenon on M.

2   Nonatomic economies with transferable, differentiable utilities

Let us recall more precisely the economic model presented in Chapter 6 of [6]. We begin with a measure space $[T,\mathscr{C},\mu]$. T is the set of agents, $\mathscr{C}$ the σ-algebra of coalitions, and μ the population measure. $[T,\mathscr{C}]$ is assumed to be isomorphic to the closed unit interval $[0,1]$ with its Borel sets, μ is a finite, σ-additive, nonnegative, and nonatomic measure, and we assume (w.l.o.g.) that $\mu(T) = 1$.

Each agent $t \in T$ is characterized by an initial endowment of resources, $a^t \in R_+^n$ and a production (utility) function $u^t: R_+^n \to R$. Here R_+^n is the nonnegative orthant of the euclidean space R^n, and n is the number of (resource) commodities. Denoting the jth component of $x \in R^n$ by x_j, a_j^t is the quantity of the jth commodity held by agent t, and $u^t(x)$ is the amount of output he can produce using x. Thus, the economy consists of the pair of functions (a,u), where $a: T \to R_+^n$, $u: T \times R_+^n \to R$ [note the identifications $a(t) \equiv a^t$; $u(t,x) \equiv u^t(x)$].

To spell out the conditions on (a,u), we need some additional notation. For x, y in R_+^n, say $x = y(x \geqq y, x > y)$ when $x_j = y_j(x_j \geqq y_j, x_j > y_j)$ for all $1 \leq j \leq n$; $x \geq y$ when $x \geqq y$, but not $x = y$. Put $\|x\| = \max\{|x_j|: 1 \leq j \leq n\}$. Also note that R_+^n can be regarded as a measurable space with its Borel sets. We will require that (a,u) satisfy the following:

(1) $a: T \to R_+^n$ is integrable.
(2) $u: T \times R_+^n \to R$ is measurable, where $T \times R_+^n$ is equipped with the product σ-field $\mathscr{C} \times B$, where B denotes the Borel sets of R_+^n.

(3)　$u(x) = o(\|x\|)$, as $\|x\| \to \infty$, integrably in t; that is, for every $\epsilon > 0$ there is an integrable function $\eta: T \to R$ such that $|u^t(x)| \le \epsilon \|x\|$ whenever $\|x\| \ge \eta(t)$.

For almost all[2] $t \in T$:

(4)　$a^t > 0$ (where, without confusion, 0 also stands for the origin of R^n_+).

(5)　x^t is continuous and increasing [i.e., $x \ge y$ implies $u^t(x) > u^t(y)$].

(6)　$u^t(0) = 0$.

(7)　The partial derivative $\partial u^t / \partial x_j$ exists and is continuous at each point where $x_j > 0$.

The collection of all pairs (a,u) that satisfy (1)–(7) will be called M; that is, we keep the space $[T,\mathscr{C},\mu]$ of agents fixed but vary their characteristics (a,u); in particular, the number n of resource commodities can be any positive integer 1, 2, 3, ... As we said in the introduction, to each $m = (a,u) \in M$, we associate a game or characteristic function $v_m: \mathscr{C} \to R$ by

$$v_m(S) = \max \left\{ \int_S u^t(x^t)\, d\mu(t): x: T \to R^n_+,\, x(S) = a(S) \right\}. \quad (8)$$

(For an integrable function $y: T \to R^n_+$, $y(S)$ abbreviates $\int_S y\, d\mu$.) That this max is attained is essentially the main theorem in [5].

FA is the collection of all functions from $\mathscr{C}$ to R that are finitely additive and bounded, and $P(\text{FA})$ is the set of all subsets of FA. We are going to characterize a map $\phi: M \to P(\text{FA})$ via axioms. It will turn out that, for any $m \in M$, $\phi(m)$ is the set of competitive payoffs in m. Recall that a pair (p,x), where $x: T \to R^n_+$ is an integrable function with $x(T) = a(T)$ and p a price vector in R^n_+, is called a transferable utility competitive equilibrium (t.u.c.e.) of the economy (a,u) if, for almost all $t \in T$,

$$u^t(y) - p(y - a^t) \le u^t(x^t) - p(x^t - a^t)$$

for any y in R^n_+; the corresponding competitive payoff is the measure $v_{p,x}$ defined by

$$v_{p,x}(S) = \int_S [u^t(x^t) - p(x^t - a^t)]\, d\mu$$

for $S \in \mathscr{C}$. If we denote by $\psi(m)$ the set of competitive payoffs in m, then under assumptions (1)–(7), $\psi(m)$ is a singleton for any $m \in M$. (See Proposition 32.3 in [6].)

3   Statement of the theorem

In this section we prepare for and state the four axioms and our main result.

Axiom 1 (Inessential economy). Suppose $m = (a,u)$ in M is such that, for each nonnull set $S \in \mathscr{C}$, $v_m(S)$ is achieved uniquely by $a: S \to R_+^n$ [i.e., $a: S \to R_+^n$ is the unique solution to the maximization problem (8)]. Then $\phi(m)$ consists of just the payoff γ given by $\gamma(S) = \int_S u^t(a^t)\, d\mu(t)$ for $S \in \mathscr{C}$.

Let Q_μ be the set of all automorphisms of $[T,\mathscr{C}]$ that preserve the measure μ; that is, Q_μ consists of bimeasurable bijections $\theta: T \to T$ such that $\mu(\theta(S)) = \mu(S)$ for all $S \in \mathscr{C}$. For $m = (a,u) \in M$ and $\theta \in Q_\mu$, define $\theta m = (\theta a, \theta u)$ by $(\theta a)(t) = a(\theta(t))$, $(\theta u)(t,x) = u(\theta(t),x)$. Also, for $v \in BV$ and $\theta \in Q_\mu$ define $\theta v: \mathscr{C} \to R$ by $(\theta v)(S) = v(\theta(S))$; and for $A \subset BV$ define $\theta A = \{\theta v: v \in A\}$.

Axiom 2 (Anonymity). For any m in M and θ in Q_μ, $\phi(\theta m) = \theta\phi(m)$.

Because $A \subset FA$ implies $\theta A \subset FA$ and $m \in M$ implies $\theta m \in M$, the axiom makes sense.

For the separability axiom we need to define the disjoint sum of two economies. Let $m = (a,u)$ and $m' = (a',u')$, where $a: T \to R_+^l$ and $a': T \to R_+^k$. Put $m \oplus m' = (a \oplus a', u \oplus u')$, where $(a \oplus a'): T \to R_+^{l+k}$ and $(u \oplus u'): T \times R_+^{l+k} \to R$ are given by

$$(a \oplus a')(t) = (a(t),a'(t)),$$

$$(u \oplus u')(t,(x,y)) = u(t,x) + u'(t,y).$$

(For $x \in R_+^l$ and $y \in R_+^k$, (x,y) is the vector R_+^{l+k} whose first l components are according to x, and the last k are according to y.) Note that $m \oplus m' \in M$ if $m \in M$ and $m' \in M$. Also note that $A + B \in P(FA)$ if $A \in P(FA)$ and $B \in P(FA)$, where we define $A + B = \{\alpha + \beta: \alpha \in A, \beta \in B\}$.

Axiom 3 (Separability). For any m and m' in M, $\phi(m) + \phi(m') \subset \phi(m \oplus m')$.

The continuity axiom is stated in terms of the bounded variation norm on set functions. A set function v is a map from $\mathscr{C}$ to R such that $v(\varnothing) = 0$.

It is called *monotonic* if $T \subset S$ implies $v(S) \geq v(T)$. The difference between two monotonic set functions is said to be of bounded variation. Let BV be the real vector space of all set functions of bounded variation. For $v \in$ BV define the norm $\|v\|$ of v by

$$\|v\| = \inf\{u(T) + w(T)\},$$

where the infimum ranges over all monotonic functions u and w such that $v = u - w$.

Each characteristic function v_m of an economy m in M is monotonic and thus is in BV. Hence, we can introduce the distance d on M by $d(m,m') = \|v_m - v_{m'}\|$. Also observe that FA $\subset$ BV. For A and B in $P(\text{FA})$, let $h(A,B)$ be the Hausdorff distance between A and B; that is, $h(A,B) = \inf\{\epsilon \in R_+ : A \subset B^\epsilon \text{ and } B \subset A^\epsilon\}$, where A^ϵ is the set $\{\alpha' \in \text{FA}: \|\alpha - \alpha'\| < \epsilon \text{ for some } \alpha \in A\}$, and $\inf \emptyset = \infty$. We are ready for Axiom 4.

Axiom 4 (Continuity). There is a constant K such that $h(\phi(m),\phi(m')) < Kd(m,m')$.

Our main result is the next theorem.

Theorem. There is one, and only one, map $\phi: M \to P(\text{FA})$ that satisfies Axioms 1–4. It assigns to each m in M the set consisting of the competitive payoff of m.

For the proof and other details see [10a].

NOTES

1 This list is by no means exhaustive.
2 This is true for all, except perhaps a μ-null set of agents.

REFERENCES

1. Anderson, R. M., "An Elementary Core Equivalence Theorem," *Econometrica*, 46 (1978), 1483–7.
2. Aumann, R. J., "Markets with a Continuum of Traders," *Econometrica*, 34 (1966), 1–7.
3. "Values of Markets with a Continuum of Traders," *Econometrica*, 43 (1975), 611–46.
4. Aumann, R. J. and M. Maschler, "The Bargaining Set for Cooperative Games," in *Advances in Game Theory* (M. Dresher, L. S. Shapley, and

A. W. Tucker, eds.), *Annals of Mathematics Studies,* 52, Princeton: Princeton University Press, pp. 443–7, 1964.

5. Aumann, R. J. and M. Perles, "A Variational Problem Arising in Economics," *J. Math. Anal. Appl.,* 12 (1965), 488–503.

6. Aumann, R. J. and L. S. Shapley, *Values of Nonatomic Games,* Princeton: Princeton University Press, 1974.

7. Bewley, T. F., "Edgeworth's Conjecture," *Econometrica,* 41 (1973), 425–54.

8. Brown, D. J. and A. Robinson, "Nonstandard Exchange Economies," *Econometrica,* 43 (1975), 41–55.

9. Debreu, G. and H. E. Scarf, "A Limit Theorem on the Core of an Economy," *International Economic Review,* 4 (1963), 235–69.

10a. Dubey, P. and A. Neyman, "Payoffs in Non-Atomic Economics: An Axiomatic Approach," *Econometrica,* 52 (1984), 1129–50.

10b. "An Equivalence Principle for Perfectly Competitive Economies," Technical Report, forthcoming.

11. Edgeworth, F. Y., *Mathematical Psychics,* London: Kegan Paul, 1881.

12. Geanakoplos, J., "The Bargaining Set and Non-standard Analysis," Technical Report No. 1, Center on Decision and Conflict in Complex Organizations, Harvard University, 1978.

13. Hildenbrand, W., *Core and Equilibria of a Large Economy,* Princeton: Princeton University Press, 1974.

14. Kannai, Y., "Continuity Properties of the Core of a Market," *Econometrica,* 38 (1970), 791–815.

15. Mas-Collel, A. "An Equivalent Theorem for a Bargaining Set," forthcoming in *Journal of Mathematical Economics.*

16. Schmeidler, D., "The Nucleolus of a Characteristic Function Game," *SIAM J. Appl. Math.,* 17 (1969), 1163–70.

17. Shapley, L. S., "A Value for *n*-Person Games," *Annals of Mathematics Studies,* 28 (1953), 308–17.

18. "Utility Comparison and the Theory of Games," in *La Decision: Aggregation et Dynamique des Ordres de Preference,* Paris: Editions du Centre National de la Recherche Scientifique, 1969, pp. 251–63.

19. "Values of Large Games. VII: A General Exchange Economy with Money," RM-4248, The Rand Corporation, Santa Monica, California, 1964.

20. Shubik, M., "Edgeworth Market Games," *Annals of Mathematics Studies,* 40 (1959), 267–78.

CHAPTER 15

Values of smooth nonatomic games: the method of multilinear approximation

Dov Monderer and Abraham Neyman

1   Introduction

In their book *Values of Non-Atomic Games,* Aumann and Shapley [1] define the value for spaces of nonatomic games as a map from the space of games into bounded finitely additive games that satisfies a list of plausible axioms: linearity, symmetry, positivity, and efficiency. One of the themes of the theory of values is to demonstrate that on given spaces of games this list of plausible axioms determines the value uniquely. One of the spaces of games that have been extensively studied is pNA, which is the closure of the linear space generated by the polynomials of nonatomic measures. Theorem B of [1] asserts that a unique value ϕ exists on pNA and that $\|\phi\| = 1$. This chapter introduces a canonical way to approximate games in pNA by games in pNA that are "identified" with finite games. These are the multilinear nonatomic games–that is, games v of the form $v = F \circ (\mu_1, \mu_2, \ldots, \mu_n)$, where F is a multilinear function and $\mu_1, \mu_2, \ldots, \mu_n$ are mutually singular nonatomic measures.

The approximation theorem yields short proofs to classic results, such as the uniqueness of the Aumann–Shapley value on pNA and the existence of the asymptotic value on pNA (see [1, Theorem F]), as well as short proofs for some newer results such as the uniqueness of the μ value on $pNA(\mu)$ (see [4]). We also demonstrate the usefulness of our method by proving a generalization to pNA of Young's characterization [6 and Chapter 17 this volume] of the Shapley value without the linearity axiom, and by generalizing Young's characterization [7] of the Aumann-Shapley price mechanism. In the last chapter we use the ideas behind the multilinear approximation in order to supply an elementary proof to a classic result in analysis: the Weierstrass approximation theorem.

This work was supported by National Science Foundation Grant DMS 8705294, and by Israel–US Binational Science Foundation Grant 8400201.

2   Preliminaries

We follow basically the terminology and notations of Aumann and Shapley [1]. Let $(I,\mathscr{C})$ be a fixed standard measurable space (i.e., a measurable space isomorphic to $([0,1],\mathscr{B})$, where $\mathscr{B}$ denotes the Borel field in $[0,1]$). A *game* is a real-valued function v on $\mathscr{C}$ with $v(\varnothing) = 0$. A game v is *monotonic* if $v(S \cup T) \geq v(S)$ for all S and T in $\mathscr{C}$. A game v has a *bounded variation* if it is the difference of two monotonic games. The variation $\|v\|$ of such game is $\|v\| = \inf\{w(I) + u(I)\}$, where the infimum ranges over all monotonic games u and w for which $v = w - u$. The space BV of all games with bounded variation is a Banach algebra (see [1, sect. 4]). The space of all finitely additive games in BV is denoted by FA, and the subspace of all nonatomic measures in FA is denoted by NA. The closed Banach algebra generated by NA is denoted by pNA. Equivalently, pNA is the closed linear subspace of BV generated by the powers of the nonatomic probability measures. Let Q be a subset of BV. The set of monotonic games in Q is denoted by Q^+. A map of Q into BV is called *positive* if it maps Q^+ into BV^+. An *automorphism* of $(I,\mathscr{C})$ is a 1-1 map θ of I onto itself such that for every $S \subseteq I$, $S \in \mathscr{C}$ iff $\theta(S) \in \mathscr{C}$. The group of all automorphisms is denoted by $\mathscr{G}$. Each θ in $\mathscr{G}$ induces a linear map θ_* of BV onto itself, defined by $(\theta_* v)(S) = v(\theta S)$. A subset Q of BV is called *symmetric* if $\theta_* Q \subseteq Q$ for all $\theta \in \mathscr{G}$. A map ϕ of a symmetric subset Q of BV into BV is called *symmetric* if, for every $\theta \in \mathscr{G}$, $\theta_* \circ \phi = \phi \circ \theta_*$. A map ϕ of a subset Q of BV into BV is called *efficient* if, for every $v \in Q$, $(\phi v)(I) = v(I)$. Let Q be a symmetric subspace of BV. A *value* on Q is a linear, positive, efficient, and symmetric map of Q into FA. Let Q be a subspace of BV. Q is an *internal space* if for every $v \in Q$ and every $\epsilon > 0$ there exist u, $w \in Q^+$ with $v = w - u$ and $\|v\| \geq w(I) + u(I) - \epsilon$. The importance of internal spaces in the theory of values follows from [1, Propositions 4.7,4.12], where it was proven that every linear, positive, efficient map of an internal subspace of BV into FA is continuous and that the closure of an internal space is internal. These results provide a very efficient tool for deriving uniqueness theorems. One of the fundamental results of the theory of values of nonatomic games [1, Theorem B] is the existence of a unique value on pNA. The uniqueness of the value on a dense subspace of pNA follows from [1, Proposition 6.1], and the uniqueness on pNA is obtained by showing that pNA is an internal space.

Let Π be a finite subfield of $\mathscr{C}$. The set of all atoms of Π is denoted by π. The power set 2^π of π is identified naturally with Π, and thus a finite game on the players' set π is identified with a function $w: \Pi \to R$, with $w(\varnothing) = 0$. The restriction of $v \in \mathrm{BV}$ to Π is denoted by v_Π. An *admissible sequence* of finite fields is an increasing sequence $(\Pi_n)_{n=1}^\infty$ of finite sub-fields of $\mathscr{C}$ such that $\cup_{n=1}^\infty \Pi_n$ generates $\mathscr{C}$. For every game w of finitely many players, we denote by ψw the Shapley value of w considered as a measure on the set of players. A game v has an asymptotic value if there exists a game ϕv such that, for every admissible sequence of finite fields $(\Pi_n)_{n=1}^\infty$ and every S in Π_1, $\lim_{n\to\infty} \psi v_{\Pi_n}(S)$ exists and equals $\phi v(S)$. It follows that ϕv is finitely additive, and it is called the *asymptotic value* of v. The set of all games in BV having an asymptotic value is denoted by ASYMP. Aumann and Shapley [1, Theorem F] have shown that ASYMP is a linear, symmetric, closed subspace of BV, and that the operator ϕ that associates to each v its asymptotic value is a value on ASYMP with norm 1.

3 Multilinear nonatomic games and finite games

For every finite field $\Pi \subset \mathscr{C}$ we denote by π the set of atoms of Π. Let $G(\Pi)$ be the space of all finite games on the players' set π. The power set 2^π of π is naturally identified with Π. Thus, a game w in $G(\Pi)$ is identified with a function $w: \Pi \to R$ satisfying $w(\varnothing) = 0$. The space of all additive games in $G(\Pi)$ is denoted by $AG(\Pi)$. The set of all monotonic games in a subset H of $G(\Pi)$ is denoted by H^+. Let $w \in G(\Pi)$. Define w^+ and w^- in $G(\Pi)^+$ such that $w = w^+ - w^-$ in the following way:

$$w^+(S) = \max \sum_{i=1}^n \max\{w(S_0 \cup S_1 \cup \cdots \cup S_i)$$
$$- w(S_0 \cup S_1 \cup \cdots \cup S_{i-1}),0\},$$

where n is the number of elements in π, $S_0 = \varnothing$, and the outer maximum ranges over all possible orders $S_1, S_2, \ldots, S_n$ of $\{T \in n : T \subseteq S\}$. The variation norm of $w \in G(\Pi)$ is given by $\|w\| = \inf\{w_2(I) + w_1(I)\}$, where the infimum ranges over all $w_1, w_2 \in G(\Pi)^+$ for which $w = w_2 - w_1$. Actually, $\|w\| = w^+(I) + w^-(I)$. Let T_Π be the map from the set of all games into $G(\Pi)$ given by $T_\Pi v = v_\Pi$, where v_Π is the restriction to Π of v. Note that T_Π is linear, efficient, positive, and $\|T_\Pi v\| \leq \|v\|$ for every $v \in$ BV.

A *carrier* of a game v is a set I' in $\mathscr{C}$ such that $v(S) = v(S \cap I')$ for every $S \in \mathscr{C}$. Let λ be a probability measure in NA. The set of all games v in pNA having the property that every carrier of λ is a carrier of v is denoted by pNA(λ). Equivalently, pNA(λ) is the closed algebra generated by NA(λ), where NA(λ) denotes the space of all measures in NA that are absolutely continuous with respect to λ.

Given a nonatomic probability measure λ and a finite field $\Pi \subset \mathscr{C}$ with the set of atoms $\pi = \{S_1, S_2, \ldots, S_n\}$ $(1 \le i < j \le n \Rightarrow S_i \ne S_j)$, denote the restriction of λ to S_i, $1 \le i \le n$, by $\lambda_{S_i} = \lambda_i$. Let $ML(\lambda, \Pi)$ be the set of all games v having the form $v = F \circ (\lambda_1, \lambda_2, \ldots, \lambda_n)$, where F is a multilinear function (see [3, and Owen Chapter 10 this volume]) on $\Pi_{i=1}^n [0, \lambda(S_i)]$ – the range of the vector measure $(\lambda_1, \lambda_2, \ldots, \lambda_n)$. Note that $ML(\lambda, \Pi)$ is a linear space of games and that every game $v \in ML(\lambda, \Pi)$ is a polynomial in the λ_i's; therefore $ML(\lambda, \Pi) \subset pNA(\lambda) \subset pNA$. Also note that, for every $u, v \in ML(\lambda, \Pi)$, $u = v$ iff $T_\Pi u = T_\Pi v$. That is, T_Π is 1-1 on $ML(\lambda, \Pi)$. Let $G_\lambda(\Pi)$ be the set of all games w in $G(\Pi)$ having the property that $w(S) = w(T)$ whenever $\lambda(S \triangle T) = 0$, that is, every atom in π that is a null set for λ is a null player for w. The space of all additive games in $G_\lambda(\Pi)$ is denoted by $AG_\lambda(\Pi)$. For every game w in $G_\lambda(\Pi)$ there exists a unique game $v \in ML(\lambda, \Pi)$ with $T_\Pi v = w$ (just take F to be the multilinear function for which $F(\lambda_1(S), \ldots, \lambda_n(S)) = w(S)$ for all $S \in \Pi$). Thus, the map T_Π from $ML(\lambda, \Pi)$ onto $G_\lambda(\Pi)$ has an inverse $T^\lambda : G_\lambda(\Pi) \to ML(\lambda, \Pi)$. Moreover, $v \in ML(\lambda, \Pi)^+$ iff $T_\Pi v \in G_\lambda(\Pi)^+$. Therefore T^λ is also positive. Thus, both T_Π and T^λ are linear, positive, efficient operators. Let $v \in ML(\lambda, \Pi)$ and set $w = T_\Pi v$. Because $w = w^+ - w^-$ with $\|w\| = w^+(I) + w^-(I)$, we have $v = T^\lambda(w^+) - T^\lambda(w^-)$, which implies that

$$\|v\| \le T^\lambda(w^+)(I) + T^\lambda(w^-)(I) = w^+(I) + w^-(I) = \|w\| = \|T_\Pi v\|.$$

Because we also have $\|T_\Pi v\| \le \|v\|$, we get that T_Π, and therefore, T^λ, is an isometry. Finally, because we have shown that $\|v\| = T^\lambda(w^+)(I) + T^\lambda(w^-)(I)$, $ML(\lambda, \Pi)$ is an internal space.

Altogether, the following proposition holds.

Proposition 1.

  (i) $ML(\lambda, \Pi) \subset pNA(\lambda)$.
  (ii) $T_\Pi : ML(\lambda, \Pi) \to G_\lambda(\Pi)$ is a linear, efficient, positive isometry.
  (iii) $T^\lambda : G_\lambda(\Pi) \to ML(\lambda, \Pi)$ is a linear, efficient, positive isometry.
  (iv) $T_\Pi \circ T^\lambda$ is the identity map on $G_\lambda(\Pi)$, and $T^\lambda \circ T_\Pi$ is the identity map on $ML(\lambda, \Pi)$.
  (v) $ML(\lambda, \Pi)$ is internal. Moreover, every $v \in ML(\lambda, \Pi)$ is the difference of two monotonic games v_1 and v_2 in $ML(\lambda, \Pi)$ with $\|v\| = v_1(I) + v_2(I)$.

Observe that T^λ maps $AG_\lambda(\Pi)$ into $NA \cap ML(\lambda, \Pi)$. Therefore for every function $f : ML(\lambda, \Pi) \to NA \cap ML(\lambda, \Pi)$ there exists a unique function $g : G_\lambda(\Pi) \to AG_\lambda(\Pi)$ that makes diagram (D1) commutative:

$$\begin{array}{ccc}
\mathrm{ML}(\lambda,\Pi) & \xrightarrow{\;f\;} & \mathrm{NA} \cap \mathrm{ML}(\lambda,\Pi) \\
{\scriptstyle T^\lambda}\big\uparrow & & \big\downarrow{\scriptstyle T_\Pi} \\
G_\lambda(\Pi) & \xrightarrow{\;g\;} & AG_\lambda(\Pi)
\end{array} \qquad\qquad (\mathrm{D1})$$

That is, $g = T_\Pi \circ f \circ T^\lambda$.

By (iv) we also get that for every $g: G_\lambda(\Pi) \to AG_\lambda(\Pi)$ there exists a unique $f: \mathrm{ML}(\lambda,\Pi) \to \mathrm{NA} \cap \mathrm{ML}(\lambda,\Pi)$ that makes (D1) commutative. That is, $f = T^\lambda \circ g \circ T_\Pi$. Alternatively, f is the unique function that makes diagram (D2) commutative:

$$\begin{array}{ccc}
\mathrm{ML}(\lambda,\Pi) & \xrightarrow{\;f\;} & \mathrm{NA} \cap \mathrm{ML}(\lambda,\Pi) \\
{\scriptstyle T_\Pi}\big\downarrow & & \big\uparrow{\scriptstyle T^\lambda} \\
G_\lambda(\Pi) & \xrightarrow{\;g\;} & AG_\lambda(\Pi)
\end{array} \qquad\qquad (\mathrm{D2})$$

Let ϕ denote the Aumann–Shapley value on $p\mathrm{NA}$, and let ψ denote the Shapley value for finite games. It is easy to verify that ϕ maps $\mathrm{ML}(\lambda,\Pi)$ into $\mathrm{NA} \cap \mathrm{ML}(\lambda,\Pi)$, that ψ maps $G_\lambda(\Pi)$ into $AG_\lambda(\Pi)$, and that the diagrams (D1) and (D2) are commutative with $f = \phi$ and $g = \psi$ (e.g., use [5] and [1, note 1 on p. 166]). This gives us a very efficient tool to derive uniqueness theorems.

Proposition 2. Let $\hat{\phi}: p\mathrm{NA} \to \mathrm{FA}$ be a function that maps $\mathrm{ML}(\lambda,\Pi)$ into $\mathrm{NA} \cap \mathrm{ML}(\lambda,\Pi)$, where λ is a nonatomic probability measure and $\Pi \subset \mathscr{C}$ is a finite field. Define $\hat{\psi}: G_\lambda(\Pi) \to AG_\lambda(\Pi)$ such that (D1) will be commutative with $f = \hat{\phi}$ and $g = \hat{\psi}$. Then if $\hat{\psi}$ is the Shapley value on $G_\lambda(\Pi)$, $\hat{\phi}$ equals the Aumann–Shapley value on $\mathrm{ML}(\lambda,\Pi)$.

Given any finite field $\Pi \subset \mathscr{C}$ and a nonatomic probability measure λ, we denote by E_Π^λ the map from $p\mathrm{NA}(\lambda)$ onto $\mathrm{ML}(\lambda,\Pi)$ given by $E_\Pi^\lambda v = T^\lambda(T_\Pi v)$. Note that E_Π^λ is a linear, efficient, positive projection onto $\mathrm{ML}(\lambda,\Pi)$, and $\|E_\Pi^\lambda\| = 1$. In particular, diagram (D3) (in which i denotes the identity map) is commutative:

$$\begin{array}{ccc}
p\mathrm{NA}(\lambda) & \xrightarrow{\;T_\Pi\;} & G_\lambda(\Pi) \\
{\scriptstyle E_\Pi^\lambda}\big\downarrow & & \big\downarrow{\scriptstyle T^\lambda} \\
\mathrm{ML}(\lambda,\Pi) & \xrightarrow{\;i\;} & \mathrm{ML}(\lambda,\Pi)
\end{array} \qquad\qquad (\mathrm{D3})$$

4   The approximation theorem

We start with an inequality that holds in any normed algebra $(X, \| \, \|)$; that is, $\|xy\| \leq \|x\| \, \|y\|$ for every $x, y, \in X$. Let $x_1, x_2, \ldots, x_n$ be fixed elements in X. For every $J = (j_1, j_2, \ldots, j_k) \in \{1, 2, \ldots, n\}^k$ denote the product $\Pi_{i=1}^k x_{j_i} = x_{j_1} x_{j_2}, \ldots, x_{j_k}$ by $x(J)$. It follows that

$$(x_1 + x_2 + \cdots + x_n)^k = \sum_{J \in \{1,2, \ldots, n\}^k} x(J).$$

Let D be the set of all $J \in \{1, 2, \ldots, n\}^k$ such that for every $1 \leq i < m \leq k, j_i \neq j_m$, and let B be the set of all $J \in \{1, 2, \ldots, n\}^k$ that are not in D.

Lemma 3. For every $x_1, x_2, \ldots, x_n$ in a normed algebra and for every integer $k > 1$ the following holds:

$$\left\| \sum_{J \in B} x(J) \right\| = \left\| \left(\sum_{i=1}^n x_i \right)^k - \sum_{J \in D} x(J) \right\|$$

$$\leq \binom{k}{2} \left(\max_{i=1, \ldots, n} \|x_i\| \right) \left(\sum_{i=1}^n \|x_i\| \right)^{k-1}.$$

Proof: For every $1 \leq l \leq n$ let

$$B_l = \{ J \in B : \exists \, 1 \leq i < m \leq k \text{ s.t. } j_i = j_m = l \}.$$

Then $B = \cup_{l=1}^n B_l$. For every $1 \leq i < m \leq k$ let $B_l^{i,m} = \{ J \in B_l : j_i = j_m = l \}$. Then

$$\left\| \sum_{J \in B_l^{i,m}} x(J) \right\| \leq \|x_l\|^2 \left\| \sum_{i=1}^n x_i \right\|^{k-2}.$$

Therefore,

$$\left\| \sum_{J \in B_l} x(J) \right\| \leq \binom{k}{2} \|x_l\|^2 \left\| \sum_{i=1}^n x_i \right\|^{k-2}.$$

Hence,

$$\left\| \sum_{J \in B} x(J) \right\| \leq \sum_{l=1}^n \left\| \sum_{J \in B_l} x(J) \right\| \leq \binom{k}{2} \left\| \sum_{i=1}^n x_i \right\|^{k-2} \sum_{l=1}^n \|x_l\|^2.$$

Because

$$\sum_{i=1}^{n} \|x_i\|^2 \le (\max_{i=1,\ldots,n} \|x_i\|) \sum_{i=1}^{n} \|x_i\| \quad \text{and} \quad \left\| \sum_{i=1}^{n} x_i \right\|^{k-2} \le \left(\sum_{i=1}^{n} \|x_i\| \right)^{k-2}$$

The result follows. ∎

Theorem 4. Let $(\Pi_n)_{n=1}^{\infty}$ be an admissible sequence of finite fields. Then for every $v \in p\text{NA}(\lambda)$, $\lim_{n \to \infty} E_{\Pi_n}^{\lambda} v = v$ (in the bounded variation norm).

Proof: Because all operators $E_{\Pi_n}^{\lambda}$ are linear with norm 1, the space Q consisting of all games $v \in p\text{NA}(\lambda)$ for which $E_{\Pi_n}^{\lambda} v \xrightarrow[n \to \infty]{} v$ is a closed subspace of $p\text{NA}(\lambda)$. Let γ be a probability measure in $\text{ML}(\lambda, \Pi_m)$. We will show that for every $k \ge 1$, $\gamma^k \in Q$.

Because $\text{ML}(\lambda, \Pi_m) \subseteq \text{ML}(\lambda, \Pi_n)$ for every $n > m$, $\gamma \in \text{ML}(\lambda, \Pi_n)$ for every $n > m$, so $E_{\Pi_n}^{\lambda} \gamma = \gamma$ for every $n > m$, which proves our claim for $k = 1$. As for $k > 1$, for every $n > m$ and every $J = (A_1, A_2, \ldots, A_k) \in \pi_n^k$ let $\gamma(J) = \Pi_{i=1}^{k} \gamma_{A_i}$, where γ_A denotes the restriction of γ to A. Obviously, $\gamma(J) \in \text{ML}(\lambda, \Pi_n)$ whenever $A_i \ne A_j$ for every $1 \le i < j \le k$. Because $\gamma = \Sigma_{A \in \pi_n} \gamma_A$, we can use Lemma 3 to prove the existence of $u_n \in \text{ML}(\lambda, \Pi_n)$ such that

$$\|\gamma^k - u_n\| \le \binom{k}{2} (\max_{A \in \pi_n} \|\gamma_A\|) \left(\sum_{A \in \pi_n} \|\gamma_A\| \right)^{k-1} = \binom{k}{2} \max_{A \in \pi_n} \gamma(A) \xrightarrow[n \to \infty]{} 0,$$

because γ is a nonatomic probability measure on a standard measurable space.

Obviously $u_n \in Q$ for every $n > m$ (because $E_{\Pi_p}^{\lambda} u_n = u_n$ for every $p \ge n$). Therefore $\gamma^k \in Q$ for every $k \ge 1$.

Finally, since $\cup_{n=1}^{\infty} \Pi_n$ is dense in $\mathscr{C}$, then $\text{NA} \cap (\cup_{n=1}^{\infty} \text{ML}(\lambda, \Pi_n))$ is dense in the space of all measures which are absolutely continuous w.r.t. λ, and since $p\text{NA}(\lambda)$ is a Banach algebra it is the closed algebra generated by $\text{NA} \cap (\cup_{n=1}^{\infty} \text{ML}(\lambda, \Pi_n))$. This completes the proof. ∎

5   Internality

Let λ be a probability measure in NA, and let $(\Pi_n)_{n=1}^{\infty}$ be an admissible sequence of finite fields. By (v) $\text{ML}(\lambda, \Pi_n)$ is internal for every $n \ge 1$. Because $\text{ML}(\lambda, \Pi_n) \supseteq \text{ML}(\lambda, \Pi_m)$ for every $n > m$, $\cup_{n=1}^{\infty} \text{ML}(\lambda, \Pi)_n$ is a linear space; and because the union of internal spaces is an internal space (if it is linear), $\cup_{n=1}^{\infty} \text{ML}(\lambda, \Pi_n)$ is an internal space [moreover, for every v in $\cup_{n=1}^{\infty} \text{ML}(\lambda, \Pi_n)$ there exist u, $w \in (\cup_{n=1}^{\infty} \text{ML}(\lambda, \Pi_n))^+$ such that $v = w - u$ and $\|v\| = w(I) + u(I)$]. Theorem 4 implies that $p\text{NA}(\lambda)$ is the closure of $\cup_{n=1}^{\infty} \text{ML}(\lambda, \Pi_n)$, and therefore $p\text{NA}(\lambda)$ is internal by [1, Proposition 4.12]. Alternatively, for every $v \in p\text{NA}(\lambda)$ and every $\epsilon > 0$ construct a sequence of games $(v_k)_{k=1}^{\infty}$ in $\text{ML}(\lambda, \Pi_{n_k})$ (where (n_k) is an increasing sequence) with $\|v - v_k\| < \epsilon 2^{-k-1}$ for every $k \geq 1$. Let $v_0 = 0$. For every $k \geq 1$ let $v_k - v_{k-1} = w_k - u_k$, where u_k and w_k are monotonic games in $\text{ML}(\lambda, \Pi_{n_k})$ with $\|v_k - v_{k-1}\| = w_k(I) + u_k(I)$. Let $w = \Sigma_{k=1}^{\infty} w_k$ and $u = \Sigma_{k=1}^{\infty} u_k$. Then u, $w \in p\text{NA}(\lambda)^+$ (because for every $k > 1$, $u_k(I) + w_k(I) < \epsilon 2^{-k} + \epsilon 2^{-(k+1)}$), $v = w - u$, and

$$u(I) + w(I) = \sum_{k=1}^{\infty} (u_k(I) + w_k(I))$$

$$= u_1(I) + w_1(I) + \sum_{k=2}^{\infty} (u_k(I) + w_k(I)) \leq \|v\| + \epsilon.$$

Because $p\text{NA} = \cup_{\lambda} p\text{NA}(\lambda)$, it is also internal.

6   The uniqueness of the value

The uniqueness of the Aumann–Shapley value on $p\text{NA}$ is mainly the consequence of the internality of $p\text{NA}$ that was proved in the previous section. However, the uniqueness of the λ value on $p\text{NA}(\lambda)$, which cannot be based on internality observations alone, can also be derived by the methods developed here.

Let λ be a nonatomic probability measure. A set Q of games is λ-symmetric if $\theta_* Q \subseteq Q$ for every automorphism θ with $\theta_* \lambda = \lambda$. Let Q be a λ-symmetric set of games. A map ϕ from Q into BV is λ-symmetric if $\theta_* \circ \phi = \phi \circ \theta_*$ for every automorphism θ that preserves λ. It satisfies the *dummy axiom* if $\phi v(S^c) = 0$ whenever S is a carrier of v.

Theorem (Monderer [4]). There exists a unique linear λ-symmetric positive efficient operator $\phi : p\text{NA}(\lambda) \to \text{FA}$ that satisfies the dummy axiom. It is the restriction to $p\text{NA}(\lambda)$ of the Aumann–Shapley value ϕ on $p\text{NA}$.

Proof: Let $\Pi \subset \mathcal{C}$ be a finite field with $\lambda(A) = \lambda(B) = 1/\#\pi$ for every two atoms A, $B \in \pi$. Note that for every $v \in \text{ML}(\lambda, \Pi)$, $\theta_* v = v$ for every automorphism θ of $(I, \mathscr{C})$ that preserves the measure λ and satisfies $\theta S = S$ for every $S \in \pi$. Therefore, by a slight change in the proof of [1, Proposition 6.1] (using the λ-symmetry of $\hat{\phi}$), we get that, for every $v \in \text{ML}(\lambda, \Pi)$, $\hat{\phi}v$ is a linear combination of the measures λ_A, $A \in \pi$. Hence, $\hat{\phi}v \in$ NA $\cap$ ML(λ, Π). Let $\hat{\psi} : G_\lambda(\Pi) \to AG_\lambda(\Pi)$ be the function that makes the diagram D4 commutative:

$$
\begin{array}{ccc}
\text{ML}(\lambda, \Pi) & \overset{\hat{\phi}}{\longrightarrow} & \text{NA} \cap \text{ML}(\lambda, \Pi) \\[2pt]
{\scriptstyle T^\lambda} \Big\uparrow & & \Big\downarrow {\scriptstyle T_\Pi} \\[2pt]
G_\lambda(\Pi) & \overset{\hat{\psi}}{\longrightarrow} & AG_\lambda(\Pi)
\end{array}
\qquad\qquad \text{(D4)}
$$

Note that $\hat{\psi}$ satisfies the Shapley value axioms on $G_\lambda(\Pi)$, so, by Proposition 2, $\hat{\phi} = \phi$ on ML(λ, Π). Therefore, $\hat{\phi} = \phi$ on $\cup_{n=1}^\infty \text{ML}(\lambda, \Pi_n)$, where $(\Pi_n)_{n=1}^\infty$ is any admissible sequence of finite fields with $\lambda(A) = 1/\#\pi_n$ for every atom A of Π_n. That is, $\hat{\phi}$ and ϕ coincide on a dense subset of pNA(λ). Because pNA(λ) is internal and $\hat{\phi}$ is linear and positive, $\hat{\phi}$ is continuous and thus coincides with ϕ on all of pNA(λ). ∎

7   The asymptotic value on pNA

In this section we will show that the asymptotic value exists in pNA. We will show that the asymptotic value of each $v \in p$NA equals its Aumann–Shapley value. Let $v \in p$NA, let $(\Pi_n)_{n=1}^\infty$ be an admissible sequence of finite fields, and let $T \in \Pi_1$. We have to show that

$$
\lim_{m \to \infty} (\psi v_{\Pi_m}(T) - \phi v(T)) = 0.
$$

Note that there exists a probability measure $\lambda \in$ NA for which $v \in p$NA(λ). Also note that for every $u \in \text{ML}(\lambda, \Pi_n)$, $\psi u_{\Pi_n}(S) = \phi u(S)$ for every $S \in \Pi_n$. In particular, $\psi u_{\Pi_n}(T) = \phi u(T)$. Finally, recall that $E_{\Pi_m}^\lambda$ maps pNA(λ) into ML(λ, Π_m). Hence,

$$
|\psi v_{\Pi_m}(T) - \phi v(T)| \le |\psi v_{\Pi_m}(T) \\
- \psi(E_{\Pi_m}^\lambda v)_{\Pi_m}(T) + |\phi(E_{\Pi_m}^\lambda v)(T) - \phi v(T)|.
$$

Because for every $w \in$ BV, $\|w_{\Pi_m}\| \le \|w\|$ and $\|\psi\| = \|\phi\| = 1$, we deduce from the approximation theorem that

$$
|\psi v_{\Pi_m}(T) - \phi v(T)| \le 2\|v - E_{\Pi_m}^\lambda v\| \xrightarrow[m \to \infty]{} 0.
$$

8   Characterization of the Aumann–Shapley value without the linearity axiom

The Aumann–Shapley value ϕ on pNA is the unique linear, positive, efficient, and symmetric map from pNA to FA. It turns out that the value satisfies additional desirable properties like continuity, $\phi\mu = \mu$ for every $\mu \in$ NA, and stronger versions of positivity. One of the stronger versions of positivity will be called strong positivity: Let $Q \subseteq$ BV. A map $\bar{\phi}: Q \to$ FA is *strongly positive* if $\bar{\phi}v(S) \geq \bar{\phi}u(S)$ whenever $u, v \in Q$ and

$$v(T \cup S') - v(T) \geq u(T \cup S') - u(T)$$

for every $S' \subseteq S$ and T in $\mathscr{C}$. Strong positivity is a desirable property for values, and it is satisfied by the value on pNA as well as by any other known nonpathological value. The following theorem asserts that strong positivity and continuity can replace positivity and linearity in the characterization of the value on pNA.

Theorem 5. Any symmetric, efficient, strongly positive, and continuous map from pNA to FA is the Aumann–Shapley value.

Proof: Let $\hat{\phi}: p$NA $\to$ FA be a map satisfying the conditions of the theorem. Denote by ϕ the Aumann–Shapley value on pNA. In order to prove that $\hat{\phi} = \phi$ it suffices to prove that they coincide on pNA(λ) for every probability measure $\lambda \in$ NA. Let then λ be a fixed arbitrary measure in NA. Because $\hat{\phi}$ and ϕ are continuous, it suffices to prove that $\hat{\phi} = \phi$ on ML(λ,Π) for every finite field $\Pi \subset \mathscr{C}$. Because $\hat{\phi}$ is symmetric, it maps ML(λ,Π) into NA $\cap$ ML(λ,Π) (we have already proved a similar claim in the proof of the theorem in Section 6). Let $\hat{\psi}: G_\lambda(\Pi) \to AG_\lambda(\Pi)$ be the function that makes diagram (D4) commutative. Obviously, $\hat{\psi}$ is a symmetric and efficient map. We will show that

$$\hat{\psi}u(A) \geq \hat{\psi}w(A) \tag{5.1}$$

for every atom A of Π for which

$$u(S \cup A) - u(S) \geq w(S \cup A) - w(S) \tag{5.2}$$

for every $S \in \Pi$. Therefore, $\hat{\psi}$ is strongly positive, and by Young's characterization [6, Theorem 2] it is the Shapley value ψ. By Theorem 2 we get that $\hat{\phi} = \phi$ on ML(λ,Π).

Let then $u, w \in \mathrm{ML}(\lambda,\Pi)$ satisfy (5.2). Note that for every $v \in G_\lambda(\Pi)$ and every $R \in \mathscr{C}$,

$$T^\lambda v(R) = \sum_{S \in \Pi} v(S) \left[\prod_{B \in \pi; \, B \subseteq S} \lambda^B(R) \right] \left[\prod_{B \in \pi; \, B \subseteq S^c} (1 - \lambda^B(R)) \right],$$

where $\lambda^B(R) = \lambda(R \cap B)/\lambda(B)$ if $\lambda(B) > 0$, and $\lambda^B(R) = 0$ if $\lambda(B) = 0$. Therefore, for every $A' \in \mathscr{C}$, $A' \subseteq A$,

$$T^\lambda v(R \cup A') - T^\lambda v(R) = (\lambda^A(R \cup A') - \lambda^A(R)) \sum_{T \in \Pi; \, A \subseteq T^c} \left[\prod_{B \in \pi, \, B \subseteq T} \kappa^B(R) \right]$$
$$\cdot \left[\prod_{B \in \pi, \, B \subseteq T^c; \, B \neq A} (1 - \lambda^B(R)) \right] (v(T \cup A) - v(T)).$$

Thus (2) implies that

$$T^\lambda u(R \cup A') - T^\lambda u(R) \geq T^\lambda w(R \cup A') - T^\lambda w(R)$$

for every $A' \subseteq A$ and R in $\mathscr{C}$.

Hence, by the strong positivity of $\hat{\phi}$, we have

$$\hat{\psi} u(A) = \hat{\phi}(T^\lambda u)(A) \geq \hat{\phi}(T^\lambda w)(A) = \hat{\psi} w(A). \qquad \blacksquare$$

Corollary 6. Any λ-symmetric, efficient, strongly positive, continuous map from $p\mathrm{NA}(\lambda)$ to FA is the Aumann–Shapley value.

Proof: Let $\hat{\phi}: p\mathrm{NA}(\lambda) \to \mathrm{FA}$ be a map satisfying the conditions of the theorem. As in the proof Theorem 5, one can show that $\hat{\phi} = \phi$ on every $\mathrm{ML}(\lambda,\Pi)$ for which $\lambda(A) = 1/|\pi|$ for every atom $A \in \pi$.

Because for every probability measure $\lambda \in \mathrm{NA}^+$ there exists an admissible sequence of finite fields, each of them has the above property, the proof of the theorem follows from the continuity of $\hat{\phi}$. $\qquad \blacksquare$

9 Characterizations of the value on $p\mathrm{NA}\infty$

For every two games u and v, we say that $v \geq u$ if $v - u$ is a monotonic game. Note that $v \geq u$ iff $v(T \cup S) - v(T) \geq u(T \cup S) - u(T)$ for every $S, T \in \mathscr{C}$. Also note that for any two additive games μ and $\gamma, \mu \geq \gamma$ iff $\mu \geq \gamma$. The set of all games v for which there exists $\mu \in \mathrm{NA}^+$ such that $-\mu \leq v \leq \mu$ is denoted by AC_∞. AC_∞ is a linear symmetric subspace of BV that contains NA. For every $v \in \mathrm{AC}_\infty$ let

$$\|v\|_\infty = \inf\{\mu(I): \mu \in \mathrm{NA}^+, -\mu \leq v \leq \mu\} + \max\{|v(S)|: S \in \mathscr{C}\}.$$

It can be easily verified that $(\text{AC}_\infty, \| \ \|_\infty)$ is a Banach algebra and that $\| \ \| \leq \| \ \|_\infty$ on AC_∞. Also, for $\mu \in \text{NA}, \|\mu\|_\infty \leq 2\|\mu\|$, which implies that the two norms are equivalent on NA.

Lemma. Let $Q \supseteq \text{NA}$ be a subspace of AC_∞ and let $\overline{\phi} : Q \to \text{FA}$ be a positive map satisfying $\overline{\phi}(v + \mu) = \overline{\phi}(v) + \mu$ for every $u \in Q$ and every $\mu \in \text{NA}$. Then $\|\overline{\phi}v - \overline{\phi}u\| \leq \|v - u\|_\infty$ for every $u, v \in Q$.

Proof: For every $\mu \in \text{NA}^+$ for which $-\mu \leq v - u \leq \mu$, we have $u - \mu \leq v \leq u + \mu$. Therefore, by the properties of $\overline{\phi}$, $\overline{\phi}u - \mu \leq \overline{\phi}v \leq \overline{\phi}u + \mu$. Hence, $-\mu \leq \overline{\phi}v - \overline{\phi}u \leq \mu$, which implies that $\|\overline{\phi}v - \overline{\phi}u\| \leq \mu(I)$. Because the last inequality holds for every μ for which $-\mu \leq v - u \leq \mu$, we get $\|\overline{\phi}v - \overline{\phi}u\| \leq \|v - u\|_\infty$.   ∎

Let $p\text{NA}_\infty$ be the $\| \ \|_\infty$-closed algebra generated by NA. $p\text{NA}_\infty$ is a $\| \ \|$-dense subspace of $p\text{NA}$ that contains NA as well as any game $v = F \circ (\mu_1, \ldots, \mu_n)$, where $\mu_i \in \text{NA}$ and F is continuously differentiable on the range of $(\mu_1, \ldots, \mu_n)$.

Theorem 7. There exists a unique value on $p\text{NA}_\infty$. It is the restriction to $p\text{NA}_\infty$ of the Aumann–Shapley value on $p\text{NA}$.

Proof: Let $\hat{\phi}$ be a value on $p\text{NA}_\infty$. Because $\hat{\phi}$ is symmetric and efficient, $\hat{\phi}\mu = \mu$ for every $\mu \in \text{NA}$. Because $\hat{\phi}$ is linear, the previous lemma implies that it is $\| \ \|_\infty$-continuous. By [1, Note 2 on p. 54] $\hat{\phi}$ coincides with the Aumann–Shapley value on the algebra generated by NA. Because $\hat{\phi}$ and the Aumann–Shapley value are $\| \ \|_\infty$-continuous, they coincide on all of $p\text{NA}_\infty$.   ∎

We now turn to characterize the value on $p\text{NA}_\infty$ without the linearity and positivity axioms. Both axioms will be replaced by the strong positivity axiom. We will not need any continuity assumption (compare with the analogous result in the previous chapter). Note that because Lemma 3 holds in any normed algebra, we can mimic the proof of Theorem 4 to get $\lim_{n \to \infty} E^\lambda_{\Pi_n} v = v$ (in the $\| \ \|_\infty$ norm) for every probability measure $\lambda \in \text{NA}$, every admissible sequence of finite fields, and every $v \in p\text{NA}_\infty(\lambda)$, where $p\text{NA}_\infty(\lambda)$ is the $\| \ \|_\infty$-closed algebra generated by $\text{NA}(\lambda)$. Therefore if $\hat{\phi} : p\text{NA}_\infty \to \text{FA}$ is a symmetric, efficient, strongly positive map that satisfies $\hat{\phi}(v + \mu) = \hat{\phi}(v) + \hat{\phi}(\mu)$ for every $v \in p\text{NA}_\infty$ and for every $\mu \in \text{NA}$, then it coincides with ϕ (the Aumann–Shapley value) on a $\| \ \|_\infty$-dense subspace of $p\text{NA}_\infty$, and it is $\| \ \|_\infty$-continuous (by the lemma in this chapter); therefore, it coincides with ϕ on $p\mathrm{NA}_\infty$. As claimed, we have a stronger result.

Theorem 8. Any symmetric, efficient, strongly positive map from $p\mathrm{NA}_\infty$ to FA is the Aumann–Shapley value.

Proof: Let $\hat{\phi}:p\mathrm{NA}_\infty \to \mathrm{FA}$ be a symmetric, efficient, strongly positive map. As we have already mentioned, it suffices to prove that $\hat{\phi}(v + \mu) = \hat{\phi}(v) + \mu$ for all $v \in p\mathrm{NA}_\infty$ and for all $\mu \in \mathrm{NA}$.

Let $v \in p\mathrm{NA}_\infty$. The map $G(\mu) = \hat{\phi}(v + \mu) - \hat{\phi}(v)$ is a strongly positive map of NA into FA. Therefore, $G(\mu)(S) = G(\mu_S)(S)$ for all $S \in \mathscr{C}$. As $(\mu_S)_{S^c} = 0_{S^c}$ and $G(0) = 0$, $G(\mu_S)(S^c) = G(0)(S^c) = 0$. Hence, by the efficiency axiom $G(\mu_S(S)) = \mu(S)$. Therefore $\hat{\phi}(v + \mu) = \hat{\phi}(v) + \mu$. ∎

10   Application to cost allocation

A *cost problem* is a pair (f,a), where $a \in R^n_{++}$ and f is a real valued function on $D_a = \{x \in R^n_+ : 0 \leq x \leq a\}$ with $f(0) = 0$. For each $x \in D_a$ $f(x)$ is interpreted as the cost of producing the bundle $x = (x_1, \ldots, x_n)$ of commodities or services and a is interpreted as the vector of quantities actually produced.

Let $n \geq 1$. The set of all cost problems (f,a) for which $a \in R^n_{++}$ and f is continuously differentiable on D_a is denoted by $\mathscr{F}_n$. Let $\mathscr{F} = \cup_{n=1}^\infty \mathscr{F}_n$. A *price mechanism* is a function $\psi : \mathscr{F} \to \cup_{n=1}^\infty R^n$ such that $\psi(f,a) \in R^n$ for every $(f,a) \in \mathscr{F}_n$. The i-th coordinate of $\psi(f,a)$ will be denoted by $\psi_i(f,a)$.

A price mechanism ψ is *cost sharing* if

$$\sum_{i=1}^n \psi_i(f,a)a_i = f(a). \tag{1}$$

for every $n \geq 1$ and for every $(f,a) \in \mathscr{F}_n$.

Let $m \geq n \geq 1$ and let $\pi = (S_1, S_2, \ldots, S_n)$ be an ordered partition of $\{1, 2, \ldots, m\}$. We define $\pi^* : R^m \to R^n$ by $\pi_i^*(x) = \Sigma_{j \in S_i} x_j$ for every $x \in R^m$ and for every $1 \leq i \leq n$.

A price mechanism ψ is *consistent* if for every $m \geq n \geq 1$, for every $b \in R^m_{++}$, for every ordered partition $\pi = (S_1, S_2, \ldots, S_n)$ of $\{1, 2, \ldots, m\}$ and for every $(f, \pi^*(b)) \in \mathscr{F}_n$

$$\psi_i(f \circ \pi^*, b) = \psi_j(f, \pi^*(b)) \tag{2}$$

for every $1 \leq j \leq n$ and for every $i \in S_j$.

For each $x, y \in R^n$ denote $x * y = (x_1 y_1, \ldots, x_n y_n)$ and for each $\lambda \in R^n_{++}$ denote $\lambda^{-1} = (1/\lambda_1, \ldots, 1/\lambda_n)$. Also, for each function f on R^n define $(\lambda * f)(x) = f(\lambda * x)$ for all $x \in R^n$.

A price mechanism ψ is *rescaling invariant* if

$$\psi(\lambda * f, \lambda^{-1} * a) = \lambda * \psi(f,a) \tag{3}$$

for all $\lambda, a \in R_{++}^n$ and $(f,a) \in \mathscr{F}_n$.

A price mechanism ψ is *strongly monotone* if

$$\frac{\partial f}{\partial x_i}(x) \geq \frac{\partial g}{\partial x_i}(x) \ \forall x \in D_a \Rightarrow \psi_i(f,a) \geq \psi_i(g,a) \tag{4}$$

for every $n \geq 1$, for every $(f,a), (g,a) \in \mathscr{F}_n$ and for every $1 \leq i \leq n$.

The Aumann-Shapley price mechanism ϕ was defined in [2] and [3] by:

$$\phi_i(f,a) = \int_0^1 \frac{\partial f}{\partial x_i}(ta)dt$$

for every $n \geq 1$, for every $(f,a) \in \mathscr{F}_n$ and for every $1 \leq i \leq n$.

Theorem 9. There exists a unique price mechanism on $\mathscr{F}$ which is cost sharing, consistent, rescaling invariant and strongly monotone. It is the Aumann–Shapley price mechanism. ■

Theorem 9 is a generalization of a result of Young [7], who proved that the Aumann–Shapley price mechanism is the unique price mechanism which is cost sharing, strongly monotone and aggregation invariant, where aggregation invariance means that the price mechanism is covariant under linear transformations. The following example shows that consistency and rescaling invariance are weaker than aggregation invariance even in the presence of the cost sharing axiom.

Example 10. For every $n \geq 1$, for every $a \in R_{++}^n$, for every $(f,a) \in \mathscr{F}_n$, and for every $1 \leq j \leq n$ denote $s_j^a(f) = \max_{x \in D_a} \partial f/\partial x_j(x)$. Define

$$\psi_i(f,a) = s_i^a(f)f(a) \Big/ \sum_{j=1}^n a_j s_j^a(f)$$

whenever $\Sigma_{j=1}^n a_j s_j^a(f) \neq 0$, and

$$\psi_i(f,a) = \phi_i(f,a)$$

otherwise.

It is easily verified that ψ is cost sharing, consistent, rescaling invariant and not aggregation invariant.

Proof of Theorem 9: We start with some definitions. Let $n \geq 1$. The space of all games on $\{1, \ldots, n\}$ will be denoted by $G(n)$. Let $a \in R_{++}^n$. The set of all (f,a) in $\mathscr{F}$ will be denoted by $\mathscr{F}(a)$. The set of all $(f,a) \in \mathscr{F}(a)$ for which f is a multilinear function on D_a will be denoted by $ML(a)$. Let $T^a : \mathscr{F}(a) \to G(n)$ be defined as follows: For every $S \subseteq \{1, \ldots, n\}$.

$$T^a(f,a)(S) = f(1_S * a),$$

where $(1_S)_i = 1 \; \forall i \in S$ and $(1_S)_i = 0 \; \forall i \notin S$.

It is easily verified that the restriction to $ML(a)$ of T^a is a $1-1$ function onto $G(n)$. Let $T^{-a} : G(n) \to ML(a)$ be the inverse function of $T_{|ML(a)}^a$. We now turn to the proof.

Let ψ be a cost sharing, consistent, rescaling invariant, strongly monotone price mechanism on $\mathscr{F}$. For each $n \geq 1$ and for each $a \in R_{++}^n$ define $\psi^a : G(n) \to R^n$ such that the following diagram will be commutative:

$$
\begin{array}{ccc}
ML(a) & \xrightarrow{\; a * \psi \;} & R^n \\
{\scriptstyle T^{-a}} \uparrow & & \downarrow {\scriptstyle i} \\
G(n) & \xrightarrow{\; \psi^a \;} & R^n,
\end{array}
$$

where i is the identity map of R^n, and $(a * \psi)(f,a) = a * (\psi(f,a))$.

ψ^a is efficient, symmetric, and strongly positive since ψ is cost sharing, consistent and rescaling invariant, and strongly monotone respectively. Therefore, by [6], ψ^a is the Shapley value. Hence by [5] ψ coincides with the Aumann–Shapley price mechanism ϕ on $ML(a)$. Thus we have proven that ψ and ϕ coincide on $\bigcup_{n \geq 1, a \in R_{++}^n} ML(a)$.

Let then $n \geq 1$ and let $a \in R_{++}^n$. We show that $\psi = \phi$ on $\mathscr{F}(a)$. For every $k \geq 1$ let $\pi(k) = (S_1, \ldots, S_n)$ be the ordered partition of $\{1, 2, \ldots, kn\}$, where for each $1 \leq p \leq n$

$$S_p = \{(p-1)k + 1, (p-1)k + 2, \ldots, pk\}.$$

Also, denote $a(k) = (a_1(k), a_2(k), \ldots, a_{kn}(k))$, where $a_j(k) = a_p/k$ for every $j \in S_p$, and let $f(k) = f \circ \pi(k)$.

As ψ is consistent, for every $1 \leq p \leq n$ and every $j \in S_p$,

$$\psi_j(f(k), a(k)) = \psi_p(f,a). \tag{9.1}$$

For each fixed $m \geq 1$ and for each $b \in R_{++}^m$, the space $C_0^1(D_b)$ of all continuously differentiable functions g on D_b with $g(0) = 0$ is a normed algebra with the norm

$$\|g\| = \max_{x \in D_b} |g(x)| + \sum_{l=1}^m \max_{x \in D_b} \left| \frac{\partial g}{\partial x_l}(x) \right| b_l,$$

and the polynomials that vanish at 0 are dense in $C_0^1(D_b)$. Note that the mapping $f \to f(k)$ is a linear isometry from $C_0^1(D_a)$ into $C_0^1(D_{a(k)})$.

Let $f \in C_0^1(D_a)$ and $\epsilon > 0$. Let g be a polynomial on D_a with $g(0) = 0$ such that $\|f - g\| < \epsilon$. Applying Lemma 3 to $C_0^1(D_{a(k)})$ we deduce that for a sufficiently large k, there exists a multilinear function γ on $D_{a(k)}$ such that $\|\gamma - g(k)\| < \epsilon$. As $\|g(k) - f(k)\| < \|g - f\|$, it follows that

$$\|\gamma - f(k)\| < 2\epsilon. \tag{9.2}$$

Let L be the linear function in $C_0^1(D_{a(k)})$ that is given by,

$$L(z) = \sum_{l=1}^{kn} \max_{x \in D_{a(k)}} \left| \frac{\partial(\gamma - f(k))}{\partial x_l}(x) \right| z_l. \tag{9.3}$$

As $\gamma + L$ and $\gamma - L$ are multilinear functions on $D_{a(k)}$,

$$\psi(\gamma \pm L, a(k)) = \phi(\gamma \pm L, a(k)). \tag{9.4}$$

It follows from (9.3) that for every $1 \le l \le kn$,

$$\frac{\partial(\gamma - L)}{\partial x_l} \le \frac{\partial f(k)}{\partial x_l} \le \frac{\partial(\gamma + L)}{\partial x_l}$$

on $D_{a(k)}$. Therefore, by (9.4), the consistency of both ψ and ϕ, and the linearity of ϕ, we have:

$$a_p|\psi_p(f,a) - \phi_p(f,a)| = \left| \sum_{l \in S_p} a_l(k)(\psi_l(f(k),a(k)) - \phi_l(f(k),a(k))) \right|$$

$$\le \sum_{l \in S_p} \phi_l(2L,a(k))a_l(k) \le 4\epsilon.$$

Thus for every $1 \le p \le n$ and for every $\epsilon > 0$

$$a_p|\psi_p(f,a) - \phi_p(f,a)| < 4\epsilon.$$

As $a_p > 0$ it follows that $\psi(f,a) = \phi(f,a)$. ∎

11   Bernstein's polynomials

Let f be a continuous function on $[0,1]$. Bernstein's theorem asserts that the sequence of polynomials $(B_n(t))_{n \ge 1}$ converges to $f(t)$ uniformly on $[0,1]$, where

$$B_n(t) = \sum_{k=0}^{n} \binom{n}{k} t^k(1 - t)^{n-k} f(k/n).$$

It is easily verified that it suffices to prove the theorem for continuously differentiable functions f. Let then f be a continuously differentiable function on $[0,1]$. For every $n > 1$ define f_n on $D_n = \{x \in R^n : 0 \le x_i \le 1 \ \forall 1 \le i \le n\}$ by $f_n(x) = f((x_1 + x_2 + \cdots + x_n)/n)$. Let g_n be the multi-linear function on D_n whose values on the vertices 1_S, $S \subseteq \{1,2, \ldots ,n\}$ of D_n are $f_n(1_S)$.

Let $\epsilon > 0$ and let n be an integer large enough such that $|f'(t_2) - f'(t_1)| < \epsilon$ whenever $|t_2 - t_1| \le 1/n$. We will show that

$$|g_n(x) - f_n(x)| \le \epsilon \ \forall x \in D_n. \tag{1}$$

The theorem will follow by substituting $x = (t,t, \ldots ,t)$ in the last inequality.

We now prove (1). For each $x \in D_n$ let $N(x)$ be the number of the indices i for which $0 < x_i < 1$. Obviously $0 \le N(x) \le n$. We will prove by induction on k that

$$|g_n(x) - f_n(x)| \le k\epsilon/n$$

whenever $N(x) = k$.

For $x \in D_n$ with $N(x) = 0$, $x = 1_S$ for some $S \subseteq \{1,2, \ldots ,n\}$ and therefore $g_n(x) = f_n(x)$. Assume the claim has been proven for $0 \le k < n$. We now prove it for $k + 1$. Let $x \in D_n$ with $N(x) = k + 1$. Let $l \in \{1,2, \ldots ,n\}$ with $0 < x_l < 1$. Since g_n is a multilinear function,

$$g_n(x) = x_l g_n(z^1) + (1 - x_l)g_n(z^0),$$

where $z^0 = (x_1, \ldots ,x_{l-1},0,x_{l+1}, \ldots ,x_n)$ and $z^1 = (x_1, \ldots ,x_{l-1},1,x_{l+1}, \ldots ,x_n)$.

Observe that for $i = 0, 1$, $N(z^i) = k$, and therefore by the induction hypothesis

$$|g_n(z^i) - f_n(z^i)| \le k\epsilon/n.$$

Hence,

$$|g_n(x) - f_n(x)| \le k\epsilon/n + |x_l(f_n(z^1) - f_n(x)) - (1 - x_l)(f_n(x) - f_n(z^0))].$$

By the intermediate value theorem:

$$(f_n(z^1) - f_n(x)) - f'(a)((1 - x_l)/n)$$

and

$$(f_n(x) - f_n(z^0)) = f'(b)(x_l/n),$$

where $|a - b| \le 1/n$. Hence,

$$|g_n(x) - f_n(x)| \le k\epsilon/n + (x_l(1 - x_l))\epsilon/n \le (k + 1)\epsilon/n$$

since $x_l(1 - x_l) \le 1$. ∎

REFERENCES

[1] Aumann, R. J., and Shapley, L. S., *Values of Non-Atomic Games,* Princeton University Press, Princeton NJ, 1974.
[2] Billera, L. J. and Heath, D. C., *Allocation of Shared Costs: A Set of Axioms Yielding a Unique Procedure,* Math. Oper. Res. 7 (1981), 32–39.
[3] Mirman, L. J. and Tauman, Y., *Demand Compatible Equitable Cost Sharing Prices,* Math. Oper. Res. 7 (1981), 40–56.
[4] Monderer, D., *Measure-Based Values of Nonatomic Games,* Math. Oper. Res. 11 (1986), 321–335.
[5] Owen, G., *Multilinear Extensions of Games,* Manag. Sci. 18 (1972), 64–79.
[6] Young, H. P., *Monotonic Solutions of Cooperative Games,* Int. J. Game Th. 14 (1985), 65–72.
[7] Young, H. P., *Producer Incentives in Cost Allocation,* Econometrica 53 (1985), 757–765.

CHAPTER 16

Nondifferentiable TU markets: the value

Jean-François Mertens

Abstract

TU economies with private production are shown to have a value, as defined in Mertens (1988), without any differentiability or interiority or other restriction. An explicit formula is given, describing the value as a barycenter of the core, for a probability distribution depending only on the set of net trades at equilibrium.

1 Introduction

We prove existence and exhibit the formula for the value of transferable utility markets, getting rid of differentiability assumptions and allowing for private production (as a first step toward removing the Aumann–Perles assumptions and the monotonicity assumptions). Under differentiability assumptions, the treatment by Aumann and Shapley yielded equivalence with the core. In the nondifferentiable case the more powerful value constructed in Mertens (1988) is required. In particular, whereas the differentiable case uses the symmetry axiom only in a "first-order" sense – comparable to the strong law of large numbers – in the nondifferentiable case it is used in its full force, in a "second-order" sense – comparable to the central limit theorem. But contrary to the case of the central limit theorem, no normal distribution appears here. Indeed, as shown in Hart (1980), the formulas involving those would satisfy only a restricted symmetry property (and are not characterized by it), so no value would be obtained. Instead a Cauchy-type distribution was obtained in Mertens (1988) as being uniquely characterized by symmetry. In our case of markets the averaging with respect to this Cauchy distribution disappears from utility space, where it was originally defined, to reemerge much more naturally in the linear spaces of prices and commodities, and the value appears thus as a barycenter of the core.

2   The model

1. A nonatomic probability space $(T, \mathscr{C}, \mu)$ of traders is given.

2. Consumption sets are $\mathbf{R}^n_+$, and a Borel-measurable utility function $u: T \times \mathbf{R}^n_+ \to \mathbf{R}_+$ is given, such that, for each t, $u_t(0) = 0$ and u_t is monotonic (i.e., nondecreasing) and uppersemicontinuous.

3. The Aumann–Perles assumption: $u_t(x)$ is $o(\|x\|)$ integrably in t; that is, $\forall \epsilon > 0$, $\exists \eta(t) \in L_1(\mu): \forall x \in \mathbf{R}^n_+$, $\|x\| \geq \eta(t) \Rightarrow u_t(x) \leq \epsilon \cdot \|x\|$.

4. A production correspondence Y_t is given – a Borel subset of $T \times \mathbf{R}^n$ – such that $Y_t \cap \mathbf{R}^n_+ \neq \varnothing$ for all t and $\int Y_t \mu(dt)$ is closed and has a bounded nonempty intersection with $\mathbf{R}^n_+$.

Remark 1: Utility functions could be of the type $u_t(x) = 1$ if $x \geq d_t$, and 0 otherwise, as for cost allocation problems, where individual demands are considered as given.

Remark 2: Initial allocations are put in the production sets, and it is not necessary to impose free disposal, because we have monotonic utilities. Private production sets represent each trader's own productivity; coalitional production sets could not be introduced without changing the whole nature of the analysis (loss of homogeneity). They can also be taken as a proxy for general consumption sets: We could define the consumption set of a trader t as his set of feasible trades $\mathbf{R}^n_+ - Y_t$, with utility for a trade $\max_{\text{prod} \in Y_t} u_t$ (trade + prod), thus reducing our model to a model with general consumption sets and no production. (This reduction remains true even in an "incomplete markets" setting, where some commodities, such as own leisure time, cannot be bought and sold, so trades are restricted to a subspace V or $\mathbf{R}^n_+$.) The only reason for using the present formulation is that it permits more explicit treatment of production, as required, for example, for cost allocation problems, and that it lets us use existing results on the demand side (Aumann and Perles 1965; Aumann and Shapley 1974) without having to rebuild from scratch.

Remark 3: Y_t to intersect $\mathbf{R}^n_+$ is the minimum for the model to make sense – the player has at least one action on his own to which he can attach utility. It is also the minimum for individual rationality and cooperative theory to be usable. The other condition too is extremely weak; still it ensures that, for at least one strictly positive price vector p, one has $\int \sup_{y \in Y_t} \langle p, y \rangle \, \mu(dt) < 1$:

We write Y instead of $\int Y_t \, \mu(dt)$, and fix y_0 in $Y \cap \mathbf{R}_+^n$. We show first that $\forall M$, $X_M = Y \cap (-(M,M,M, \ldots) + \mathbf{R}_+^n)$ is bounded. Otherwise, choose y_k in this set, with $\|y_k\| \to \infty$. Extract a subsequence such that $y_k/\|y_k\|$ converges, say to y_∞. We have $y_\infty \in \mathbf{R}_+^n$ because of the lower bound. By convexity of Y (Lyapunov's theorem), the line segments joining y_0 to y_k belong to this set, and they converge to the half-line starting from y_0 in the direction y_∞. By closedness, this half-line belongs to the set; hence $Y \cap \mathbf{R}_+^n$ would be unbounded, because y_0 belongs to it and $y_\infty \geq 0$. The compactness of X_M implies the closedness of $X_M - \mathbf{R}_+^n$, hence of $(Y - \mathbf{R}_+^n) \cap (-(M,M,M, \ldots) + \mathbf{R}_+^n)$, hence of $Y - \mathbf{R}_+^n$.

Now choose K sufficiently large that $Y \cap \{x \in \mathbf{R}_+^n | \Sigma \, x_i \geq K\} = \varnothing$ (possible because $Y \cap \mathbf{R}_+^n$ is bounded). Both sets are closed and convex, and, from what we have shown, the shortest distance between both is achieved (i.e., at infinity the distance would go to infinity) and thus strictly positive. Thus both sets can be strictly separated: We have a linear functional p such that $\min_{x \geq 0; \, \Sigma x_i \geq K} \langle p, x \rangle > \sup_{y \in Y} \langle p, y \rangle$. The left-hand member being bounded below implies $p \in \mathbf{R}_+^n$; hence, because $Y \cap \mathbf{R}_+^n \neq \varnothing$, the right-hand member is nonnegative; the left-hand member being strictly positive implies that p is strictly positive. It can then be normalized to have the right-hand member < 1.

Finally, it is easy to show that, for any measurable correspondence Y_t with nonempty integral Y ($y_0 \in Y$), one has $\int \sup_{y \in Y_t} \langle p, y \rangle \, \mu(dt) = \sup_{y \in Y} \langle p, y \rangle$ for any linear function p. [Let y_t be an integrable selection from Y_t, and let $Y_t^n = \{y \in Y_t | \|y - y_t\| \leq n\}$. Any measurable selection from Y_t^n is integrable, and $\sup \langle p, Y_t^n \rangle$ converges monotonically to $\sup \langle p, Y_t \rangle$. Because there exist measurable selections y_t^n from Y_t^n such that $\langle p, y_t^n \rangle \geq \sup \langle p, Y_t^n \rangle - \epsilon$, the result follows.] In particular, any measurable selection from $Y_t \cap \mathbf{R}_+^n$ is integrable.

In addition, this implies also that the closed set $Y - \mathbf{R}_+^n$ equals $\int (Y_t - \mathbf{R}_+^n) \, \mu(dt)$. Indeed, denote by z_t an integrable selection from $Y_t - \mathbf{R}_+^n$. There exists a measurable selection y_t from Y_t such that $y_t \geq z_t$. Hence, y_t^- is integrable. Because $\langle p, y_t \rangle$ is majorized by the integrable function $\sup_{y \in Y_t} \langle p, y \rangle$, and because p is strictly positive, integrability of y_t follows. Hence our claim is established.

Remark 4 : An equivalent formulation of the Aumann–Perles assumption is to require that for some (and then for every) strictly positive vector of total initial resources ω, the set of utility vectors achievable by redistribution be weakly relatively compact in L_1 (uniformly integrable); it is then even weakly compact if u is concave.

Indeed, assume u_t satisfies the Aumann–Perles assumption. Then $u_t(x) \leq \epsilon\|x\|$ for $\|x\| \geq f_\epsilon(t)$; hence, by monotonicity $u_t(x) \leq \epsilon \max(\|x\|,$ $f_\epsilon(t))$ for all x, with $f_\epsilon(t)$ integrable. Hence, for every redistribution x_t and all $\lambda > 0$ we have

$$\int_{u_t(x_t) \geq \lambda} u_t(x_t)\,\mu(dt) \leq \epsilon \int \|x_t\|\,\mu(dt) + \int_{(\epsilon f_\epsilon(t) \geq \lambda)} \epsilon f_\epsilon(t)\,\mu(dt)$$

$$= \epsilon\|\omega\| + \int_{(\epsilon f_\epsilon(t) \geq \lambda)} \epsilon f_\epsilon(t)\,\mu(dt)$$

(using for convenience $\|x\| = \Sigma |x_i|$).

Hence, for any $\delta > 0$ and any ω, we can first choose $\epsilon > 0$ sufficiently small such that $\epsilon\|\omega\| \leq \delta/2$. Next, given this ϵ, choose λ sufficiently large such that $\int_{(\epsilon f_\epsilon(t) \geq \lambda)} \epsilon f_\epsilon(t)\,\mu(dt) \leq \delta/2$, because $\epsilon f_\epsilon(t)$ is integrable.

Thus we obtain $\int_{(u_t(x_t) \geq \lambda)} u_t(x_t)\,\mu(dt) \leq \delta$. Uniform integrability of $\{u_t(x_t)|x_t \geq 0, \int x_t \leq \omega\}$ is proved, which is equivalent to its weak relative compactness in L_1, by the Dunford–Pettis criterion.

Conversely, if this set H is uniformly integrable for some strictly positive ω_0, there exists by the de la Vallée-Poussin criterion a convex, continuous function F on $\mathbf{R}_+$ such that $F(0) = 0$, $F(x)/x \geq 1$, $\lim F(x)/x = +\infty$, and $\sup \{\int F(|u_t|)\,\mu(dt)|u_t \in \lambda H\} < +\infty$ for all λ. Let $v_t(x) = F(\lambda u_t(x))$ for $\lambda > 0$. We have

$$H(\omega) = \sup \{\int v_t(x_t)\,\mu(dt)|\int x_t\,\mu(dt) \leq \omega, x_t \geq 0\}$$

is finite at some interior ω_0. Being nonnegative for all $\omega \geq 0$ and being concave by Lyapunov's theorem, it is finite for all $\omega \geq 0$ and clearly monotonic. Concavity then implies $H(\omega) \leq A + \langle p,\omega \rangle$, where p belongs to the supergradient of H (e.g., at ω_0); choosing $B > \max_i p_i$, we obtain $H(\omega) \leq A + B\|\omega\|$. Hence for all integrable x_t and all $\omega \geq \int x_t\,\mu(dt)$, we have

$$\int v_t(x_t)\,\mu(dt) \leq A + B \Sigma \omega_i;$$

that is,

$$\int [v_t(x_t) - B \Sigma_i x_t^i]\,\mu(dt) \leq A$$

for all integrable x_t. In other words, the function $g(t) = \sup_{x \geq 0} v_t(x) - B \Sigma_i x^i$ is integrable, and $v_t \leq g(t) + B \Sigma x^i$, or $u_t(x) \leq (1/\lambda) F^{-1}[g(t) + B\|x\|]$ for all t and x. This inequality obviously implies the Aumann–

Perles condition. It can be further improved. Consider the formula with $\lambda = 1$. Correct g and F so that $B = 1$.

We could have chosen a smaller F, for example, to satisfy $xF'(x)/F(x) \rightarrow 1$ when $x \rightarrow \infty$. Then $F(\lambda x) \leq \lambda^c F(x)$ for some c and for all x and all $\lambda \geq 1$. Now choose a convex monotonic function H satisfying $H(0) = 0$, $H(x)/x \geq 1$, $\lim_{x \rightarrow \infty} H(x)/x = +\infty$, and $\lim H(F^{-1}(x))/x = 0$. Then for $y = F^{-1}(x)$ and $\lambda \geq 1$,

$$\frac{H(\lambda F^{-1}(x))}{x} = \frac{H(\lambda y)}{F(y)} \leq \lambda^c \frac{H(\lambda y)}{F(\lambda y)}$$

$$= \lambda^c \frac{H(F^{-1}(z))}{z} \qquad \text{with } z = F(\lambda y).$$

Hence,

$$\lim_{x \rightarrow \infty} \frac{H(\lambda F^{-1}(x))}{x} = 0 \qquad \text{for all } \lambda > 0.$$

Thus $H[\epsilon^{-1} F^{-1}(x)] - \epsilon x$ attains a finite maximum, say $h(\epsilon)$, for all $\epsilon > 0$. Further, the convexity of H implies $H(A/\epsilon)$ is convex in ϵ; thus $h(\epsilon)$ is a convex, decreasing function of ϵ, as a supremum of such functions. Then

$$H[\epsilon^{-1} u_t(x)] - \epsilon \|x\| \leq H[\epsilon^{-1} F^{-1}(g(t) + \|x\|)] - \epsilon \|x\|$$
$$= H[\epsilon^{-1} F^{-1}(\alpha)] - \epsilon \alpha + \epsilon g(t),$$

for $\alpha = g(t) + \|x\|$. Hence

$$\sup_{x \geq 0} H\left[\frac{1}{\epsilon} u_t(x)\right] - \epsilon \|x\| \leq \sup_{\alpha \geq g(t)} \left[H\left(\frac{1}{\epsilon} F^{-1}(\alpha)\right) - \epsilon \alpha + \epsilon g(t)\right]$$

$$\leq \epsilon g(t) + \sup_{\alpha \geq 0} \left[H\left(\frac{1}{\epsilon} F^{-1}(\alpha)\right) - \epsilon \alpha\right] \leq h(\epsilon) + \epsilon g(t).$$

Thus, letting $H^{-1} = U$, we obtain that

$$u_t(x) \leq \epsilon U[h(\epsilon) + \epsilon(g(t) + \|x\|)] \qquad \text{for all } t, x \geq 0, \epsilon > 0.$$

Here U is an increasing, concave, Lipschitz function satisfying $U(0) = 0 = \lim_{x \rightarrow \infty} U(x)/x$, h is a convex, decreasing function, and g is a positive integrable function.

Thus we obtain even more precise bounds for $u_t(x)$ than do the Aumann–Perles conditions; they involve only functions of one variable $h(\epsilon)$ and $g(t)$ (and U) instead of the function of two variables $f_\epsilon(t)$.

There only remains to show that, if u is, in addition, concave, then the set $H = \{u_t(x_t) | \int x_t\, \mu(dt) \leq \omega\}$ is weakly closed in L_1. Because H is convex, it is sufficient to prove strong closure. Consider then a sequence $x_t^n \geq 0$ s.t. $\int x_t^n \mu(dt) \leq \omega$ and $u_t(x_t^n)$ converges in L_1, say to $f(t)$. Extracting a subsequence, we can also assume $u_t(x_t^n) \rightarrow f(t)$ a.e. By Hildenbrand and Mertens (1971), there exists a measurable function x_t s.t. μ-a.e. x_t is a limit point of x_t^n [hence $u_t(x_t) = f(t)$] and s.t. $\int x_t\, \mu(dt) \leq \omega$. Thus $f \in H$, and our claim is proved.

This characterization removes the apparently ad hoc aspect of the Aumann–Perles condition and "explains" why it is the natural condition to impose for all relevant maxima in the computation of the characteristic function to be finite and attained. (For this last point, in case of nonconcave u_t, a last use of Lyapunov's theorem is still required.) It also yields, in the NTU framework, an easy characterization of those functions u_t that satisfy the Aumann–Perles conditions after multiplication by some positive λ_t. Up to such a multiplication, they are those that satisfy

$$\lim_{r \to \infty} \frac{1}{r} \sup_{\|x\|=r} \sup_t u_t(x) = 0.$$

Indeed, if $\lambda_t u_t(x) \leq U(g(t) + \|x\|) \leq U(g(t)) + U(\|x\|)$ (concavity of U), then

$$\frac{\lambda_t}{1 + U(g(t))} u_t(x) \leq 1 + U(\|x\|).$$

Thus our condition is established, taking $\lambda_t/[1 + U(g(t))]$ as a positive multiple. Conversely, let $h(r) = \sup_{\|x\|=r} \sup_t u_t(x)$. If $h(r)/r$ converges to zero, then, by monotonicity, the concavification U of h will also satisfy $U(r)/r \rightarrow 0$, and we will have for all t and x that $u_t(x) \leq U(\|x\|)$, which implies the Aumann–Perles condition.

In addition, for such u, the condition for $\lambda_t u_t(x)$ to satisfy the Aumann–Perles condition is, letting $v_t(\alpha) = \sup_{x \geq 0}[\alpha u_t(x) - \|x\|]$ (v_t is convex, monotonic, with $v_t(0) = 0$, and even $v_t'(0) = 0$, and $\sup_t v_t < +\infty$), that $\int v_t(K\lambda_t)\, \mu(dt) < +\infty$ for all $K \geq 0$.

3   The characteristic function

Definition. Let

$$u(\chi,\alpha) = \sup\{\int \chi(t) u_t(x(t))\, \mu(dt) | \int \chi(t) x(t)\, \mu(dt) = \alpha, x(t) \geq 0\}.$$

Lemma 1

(a) The sup in the definition of u(χ,α) is attained;
(b) u is monotonic, positively homogeneous of degree 1, concave, and continuous over the product with $\mathbf{R}^n_+$ of the space of all $\chi \geq 0$, endowed with the NA-topology [or the $\sigma(L_\infty(\mu), L_1\mu))$-topology].

Proof: This follows basically from the results of Aumann and Shapley (1974, chap. VI; hereafter A.S.) and through them from those of Aumann and Perles (1965).

Note first that the concavification u_t^* of u_t is achieved, that it also satisfies our assumptions, and is furthermore continuous (A.S., 36.2 – uppersemicontinuity of u is sufficient). Similarly (A.S., 36.1) yields point (a), and (A.S., 36.3) implies that $u(\chi,\alpha)$ will not be affected if u is replaced by u^*. Thus we can assume u is concave and continuous. Note that it is sufficient to prove (b) when u is replaced by a uniform (in t and x) approximand. Thus, first add $\epsilon \Sigma_i x_i/(x_i + 1)$ to each u_t, which are now strictly concave and strictly monotonic. Replace them by a uniform smoothing to obtain the differentiability assumptions of A.S., if so desired. Concavity now follows from a straightforward and well-known computation: If x^i achieves the maximum at χ^i, α^i, let then for $\lambda^i \geq 0$, $\lambda^1 + \lambda^2 = 1$,

$$\chi(t) = \lambda^1\chi^1(t) + \lambda^2\chi^2(t), \quad \alpha = \lambda^1\alpha^1 + \lambda^2\alpha^2,$$

and

$$x(t) = \frac{\lambda^1\chi^1(t)x^1(t) + \lambda^2\chi^2(t)x^2(t)}{\chi(t)}$$

(only t: $\chi(t) > 0$ are interesting). Then $\int \chi(t)x(t)\,\mu(dt) = \alpha$, $x(t) \geq 0$, and

$$u_t(x(t)) \geq \frac{\lambda^1\chi^1(t)u_t(x^1(t)) + \lambda^2\chi^2(t)u_t(x^2(t))}{\chi(t)}$$

by the concavity of u_t, so

$$\int \chi(t)u_t(x(t))\,\mu(dt) \geq \lambda^1 u(\chi^1,\alpha^1) + \lambda^2 u(\chi^2,\alpha^2).$$

Positive homogeneity of degree 1 is obvious, and monotonicity follows from positivity and concavity (e.g., as in Lemma 39.9 of A.S.).

For the continuity, we remark first that it is sufficient to prove continuity in each variable separately. Indeed, in the space of continuous, concave functions over a compact, convex polyhedron, pointwise convergence implies uniform convergence (e.g., use induction over the dimensions of the faces), so, if $\chi_\beta \to \chi$ in the NA-topology, $u(\chi_\beta,\alpha)$ still converge uniformly to $u(\chi,\alpha)$ on every simplex $\{\alpha | \Sigma \alpha_i \leq M\}$ (continuity in χ). Thus if also $\alpha_n \to \alpha$ in this simplex, we have $u(\chi_\beta,\alpha_n) \to u(\chi,\alpha)$. Continuity of $u(\chi,\cdot)$ in α is established in Proposition 37.13 in A.S. (replace $\chi\, d\mu$ by $d\mu$ and use $S = I$). For fixed α we can assume $\alpha > 0$ and neglect the other coordinates. For the uppersemicontinuity, use A.S. proposition 36.4 with χ_0 instead of S: Choose an arbitrary $y(t) \in \mathbf{R}_+^n$ such that $\int \chi(t) y(t)\, \mu(dt) = \alpha$ for some χ. Integrating the result of 36.4 with $y(s)$ instead of x yields

$$u(\chi,\alpha) \leq \langle p,\alpha \rangle + \int \chi(t) f(t)\, \mu(dt) \qquad \text{for all } \alpha \text{ and } \chi,$$

with $f(t) = u_t(x(t)) - \langle p,x(t) \rangle$, where x achieves the maximum at (χ_0,α_0). Hence $f(t) \geq 0$, and x_t is integrable by the Aumann–Perles condition on u, because p is strictly positive. It follows that f is integrable, so the right-hand member is $\sigma(L_\infty(\mu),L_1(\mu))$-continuous and lies everywhere above u. Because we have equality at χ_0, it follows that $u(\chi,\alpha)$ is uppersemicontinuous at any χ_0. The $\sigma(L_\infty(\mu),L_1(\mu))$-lowersemicontinuity is established directly: Let the maximum at (χ,α) be achieved at x_t. Replace x_t by $\min(x_t,(M,M,M,\cdot))$ for some large constant M. It is now integrable, and certainly feasible at (χ,α), and achieves approximately the maximum there. Now let $v_t(x)$ be utility functions of finite type, satisfying our assumptions, such that $v_t \leq u_t$ everywhere and $v_t(x_t)$ is close to $u_t(x_t)$. The function v derived from the v_t lies everywhere below u and approximates it at (χ,α). Because v_t is of finite type, v is a continuous function of the integrals of χ for finitely many measures in $L_1(\mu)$, and thus is $\sigma(L_\infty(\mu), L_1(\mu))$-continuous. Therefore the lowersemicontinuity is established. This proves Lemma 1. ∎

For all $\chi \geq 0$, χ bounded, let

$$V_\chi = \int [\chi_t Y_t]\, d\mu(t) = \int Y_t(\chi_t\, d\mu(t)),$$

$$\underline{V}_\chi = \left\{ \int \chi_t y_t\, d\mu(t) \,\middle|\, y_t \text{ integrable selection from } Y_t \right\}.$$

Also let Y_χ (resp. $\underline{Y}_\chi$) denote $V_\chi \cap \mathbf{R}_+^n$ (resp. $\underline{V}_\chi \cap \mathbf{R}_+^n$).

Lemma 2. $\underline{V}_\chi$ (resp. $\underline{Y}_\chi$) is dense in V_χ (resp. Y_χ): For any $(\chi_t\, d\mu(t))$- integrable selection y_t from Y_t, there exists a sequence y_t^n of μ-integrable selections from Y_t converging in $L_1(\chi_t\, d\mu_t)$ to y such that $\int \chi_t y_t^n\, d\mu_t \geq 0$ if $\int \chi_t y_t\, d\mu(t) \geq 0$.

Proof: We clearly have inclusion. Let y_t denote a $(\chi(t)\, d\mu(t))$-integrable selection of Y_t. Let $A_n = \{t | \chi_t \geq 1/n$ and $\|y_t\| \leq n\}$, and let $v(B) = (\int_B \chi_t\, d\mu_t, \int_B \chi_t y_t\, d\mu_t)$. Let z_t denote a measurable selection from $Y_t \cap \mathbf{R}^n_+ : z_t$ is integrable (§2, Remark 3). We want to show that $\forall \theta < 1, \exists n, \exists C \subseteq A_n$ s.t. $v(C) = \theta v(I)$. Indeed, if we then put $\tilde{y}_t = y_t I_C + z_t(1 - I_C)$, then $\tilde{y}_t$ will be an integrable selection from Y_t, because y_t is integrable on A_n. Also, if $\int y_t \chi_t\, d\mu_t \geq 0$, then $\int \tilde{y}_t \chi_t\, d\mu_t \geq v(C) = \theta \int \chi_t y_t\, d\mu_t \geq 0$; and $\int |\tilde{y}_t - y_t| \chi_t\, d\mu_t = \int_{T \setminus C} |z_t - y_t| \chi_t\, d\mu_t$ can be made arbitrarily small, because the integrand is integrable $(\chi_t\, d\mu_t)$ and the measure of $T \setminus C$ can be made arbitrarily small. Thus the lemma will follow. We will show this to be true for any nonatomic vector measure v and for any sequence A_n increasing to I. For this purpose we can separate each coordinate of v into its positive and negative parts and normalize everything; hence we may further assume v is a vector of nonatomic probabilities. Also if one of the coordinates of v could be written as a linear combination of the other coordinates, this coordinate can be deleted w.l.o.g.: in addition, v is full-dimensional. This is well known to imply immediately that the range of v is full-dimensional. Thus by convexity and by symmetry around $\frac{1}{2}$, $(\frac{1}{2}, \frac{1}{2}, \cdots, \frac{1}{2})$ is an interior point of the range; again by convexity, $(\theta, \theta, \cdots, \theta)$ $(0 < \theta < 1)$ is an interior point.

Therefore let $(z_i)^n_{i=0}$ denote the vertices of a small simplex containing θ into its interior, with $z_i = v(B_i)$. Let $z_{i,k} = v(B_i \cap A_k) : z_{i,k} \to z_i$, so, for $k \geq k_0$, θ is a convex combination of the $z_{i,k}$. By Lyapunov's theorem this implies that $\exists C \subseteq A_{k_0}$, with $v(C) = \theta$. This proves the lemma. ∎

Corollary 1. Let $\overline{V}_\chi$ denote the closure of V_χ. Thus $\underline{V}_\chi$ is dense in $\overline{V}_\chi$.

Definition.

$$w(\chi,x) = \sup\{u(\chi,\alpha) | \alpha \in V_\chi + x, \alpha \geq 0\} \qquad (\sup \varnothing = -\infty.)$$

$$v(\chi) = w(\chi,0).$$

$$\bar{v}(\chi) = \sup_{\alpha \in \overline{V}_\chi \cap \mathbf{R}_+ - \overline{Y}_\chi} u(\chi,\alpha).$$

Corollary 2.

(1) $0 \leq v \leq \bar{v}.$

(2) $w, v,$ and $\bar{v}$ are concave, positively homogeneous of degree 1, and monotone.

Proof: The inequalities are obvious. $w(\chi_1 + \chi_2, x_1 + x_2) \geq w(\chi_1, x_1) + w(\chi_2, x_2)$ follows from $V_{\chi_1} + V_{\chi_2} = V_{\chi_1 + \chi_2}$ (see Lemma 1 in the appendix), and $u(\chi_1 + \chi_2, \alpha_1 + \alpha_2) \geq u(\chi_2, \alpha_2) + u(\chi_1, \alpha_1)$ (Lemma 1). Positive homogeneity of degree 1 follows similarly.

We only used $Y_{\chi_1 + \chi_2} \supseteq Y_{\chi_1} + Y_{\chi_2}$ from Appendix Lemma 1. But it yields $V_{\chi_1} + V_{\chi_2} \subseteq V_{\chi_1 + \chi_2}$; hence, $\bar{V}_{\chi_1} + \bar{V}_{\chi_2} \subseteq \bar{V}_{\chi_1 + \chi_2}$ and the proof yields also the concavity of $\bar{v}$.

Note that $w(\chi_1, x_1) > -\infty$ and $\chi_2 \geq \chi_1$, $x_2 \geq x_1$ imply $w(\chi_2, x_2) > -\infty$ (hence both ≥ 0). Thus along the whole half-line going from point 1 to point 2 and further, the function w is concave and remains ≥ 0. It must be monotonic, so w is monotonic (because there is nothing to prove when $w(\chi_1, x_1) = -\infty$). The same argument applies for $\bar{v}$. This proves Corollary 2. ∎

Corollary 3. $v(\chi) = \bar{v}(\chi)$ for $\chi \geq \epsilon > 0$.

Proof: Follows immediately from Lemma 2 of the appendix.

Lemma 3. Let v be a nonatomic vector measure, $\sigma = \Sigma_i |v_i|$. For any vector measure μ denote the range of μ, $\{\mu(C) | C \in \mathscr{C}\}$, by $R(\mu)$, and for any $f \in L_1(\sigma)$ denote by $f \cdot v$ the vector measure $(f \cdot v)(C) = \int_C f \, dv$. Then for any vector x the set of $f \in L_1(\sigma)$ s.t. $R(f \cdot v)$ intersects $\{\lambda x | \lambda > 1\}$ is weakly open in $L_1(\sigma)$.

Proof: Only $x \neq 0$ is interesting. Then let f_0 be in the set; that is, $\exists C: \int_C f_0 \, dv = (1 + \epsilon)x$. If f_α converges to f_0, then $f_\alpha \cdot I_C$ converges to $f_0 \cdot I_C$, and $R(f_\alpha I_C \cdot v) \subseteq R(f_\alpha \cdot v)$. Because we can clearly assume that $f_0(t) \neq 0$ for $t \in C$, we can assume C is the whole space and $f_0 \neq 0$ everywhere. We can then replace v by $f_0 \cdot v$ and f_α by f_α / f_0 and reduce ourselves to the case where $f_0 = 1$ identically. Note also that the vector space V spanned by $R(v)$ contains all $R(f_\alpha \cdot v)$. [If λ is a linear functional vanishing on V, the measure $\Sigma \lambda_i v_i$ is zero, so its Radon–Nikodým derivative w.r.t. σ, $\Sigma \lambda_i g_i$ ($g_i = dv_i / d\sigma$), is zero a.s.; hence $\Sigma \lambda_i \int_S f_\alpha \cdot g_i \, d\sigma$ is zero for any S.] We can thus assume w.l.o.g. that $R(v)$ is full-dimensional: x is an interior point of $R(v)$ [by convexity (Lyapunov) and symmetry around $v(\frac{1}{2})$]. Because for each $v(S) \in R(v)$ we have $v(S) = \lim[(f_\alpha \cdot v)(S)]$ (convergence of f_α to 1), the convexity of $R(f_\alpha \cdot v)$ will immediately imply that $x \in R(f_\alpha \cdot v)$ for all sufficiently large α. This proves the lemma. ∎

Proposition A. v is $\sigma(L_\infty(\mu), L_1(\mu))$-lowersemicontinuous on $(L_\infty(\mu))^+$.

Proof: We show lowersemicontinuity at χ_0. Let $\alpha = \int \chi_0(t) y(t) \mu(dt)$, with y_t an integrable selection of Y_t, be such that $u(\chi_0, \alpha)$ approximates $v(\chi)$ (cf.

Corollary 1 and the definition of v). We have seen that v was not affected by adding free disposal to the sets Y_t, and, clearly, reducing the sets Y_t will only decrease v. Thus we can assume $Y_t = \{y_t, 0\}$ for all t. By Lemma 3, the total production set $R(\chi \cdot \mathbf{y} \cdot \mu)$ of any coalition χ in the neighborhood of χ_0 will contain $(1 - \epsilon)\alpha$. Thus we will have $v(\chi) \geq u(\chi, (1 - \epsilon)\alpha)$ in this neighborhood. By Lemma 1,

$$u(\chi, (1 - \epsilon)\alpha) \geq u((1 - \epsilon)\chi, (1 - \epsilon)\alpha) = (1 - \epsilon)u(\chi, \alpha),$$

and for χ in the neighborhood of χ_0, $u(\chi, \alpha)$ is close to $u(\chi_0, \alpha)$, which is close to $v(\chi_0)$, so the proof is finished. ∎

Proposition B. At every χ_0 that is bounded away from zero, $\bar{v} = v$ and is $\sigma(L_\infty(\mu), L_1(\mu))$-uppersemicontinuous at χ_0 as a function on $\{\chi | 0 \leq \chi \leq M\}$.

Proof: By Corollary 3, we have to show that any χ_∞ in the weak*-closure of $\{\chi | 0 \leq \chi \leq 1, \bar{v}(\chi) \geq \alpha\}$ and that is bounded away from zero belongs to the set. By Corollary 2 those sets are convex, so it is sufficient to consider their $\tau(L_\infty, L_1)$-closure. Because the Mackey topology coincides on $\{\chi | 0 \leq \chi \leq 1\}$ with the topology of convergence in measure, we have to show that, if $\chi_i \to \chi_\infty$ in μ-measure, $0 \leq \chi_i \leq 1$, then lim sup $\bar{v}(\chi_i) \leq \bar{v}(\chi_\infty)$.

We can first extract a subsequence of the χ_i such that the $\bar{v}(\chi_i)$ converge [to the previous lim sup $\bar{v}(\chi_i)$]. Next we can extract a further subsequence χ_i converging μ-a.e. to χ_∞ (and even everywhere by changing on a null set).

Now let $\tilde{\chi}_i(t) = \sup_{j \geq i} \chi_j(t)$. The χ_i form a sequence of ideal set functions decreasing to χ_∞. Now $\tilde{\chi}_i \geq \chi_i$, so the monotonicity of $\bar{v}$ (Corollary 2) implies $\bar{v}(\tilde{\chi}_i) \geq \bar{v}(\chi_i)$, and similarly $\bar{v}(\tilde{\chi}_i)$ is decreasing, with $\bar{v}(\tilde{\chi}_i) \geq \bar{v}(\chi_\infty)$: We can further assume that the original sequence χ_i is decreasing. Utilities are monotonic, so there is no loss in assuming free disposal in the Y_i's for the computation of v. Our assumptions remain true with the modified Y's.

Let us first add the vector ϵ of length $\epsilon > 0$ along the main diagonal to every production set Y_t, and let V_χ^ϵ denote the corresponding coalitional production sets. We have $V_\chi^\epsilon = V_\chi + \epsilon \int \chi \, d\mu$. Therefore if $v \in \cap_{\epsilon > 0} V_\chi^\epsilon$, then $v \in \bar{V}_\chi$. Therefore $\cap_{\epsilon > 0} \bar{Y}_\chi^\epsilon = \bar{Y}_\chi$.

Also, because Y_1 is compact, Y_1^ϵ is also compact and $\bar{Y}_\chi^\epsilon$ are compact. It then follows that $\bar{Y}_\chi^\epsilon$ decreases to $\bar{Y}_\chi$ in the Hausdorff topology.

Further, $u(\chi, \cdot)$, being continuous, is uniformly continuous on compact sets, and therefore $\bar{v}^\epsilon(\chi)$ decreases to $\bar{v}(\chi)$. Thus it suffices to show the uppersemicontinuity of $\bar{v}^\epsilon$. We can assume that for some $\epsilon > 0$, $\epsilon \in Y_t$ for all t. It follows immediately under this assumption that Y_χ is dense in $\bar{Y}_\chi$ for all χ, and hence that $\bar{v} = v$ everywhere.

Further, the continuity of $u(\chi,\alpha)$ implies that, when $\chi_i \to \chi$, $u(\chi_i \cdot)$ converges uniformly to $u(\chi, \cdot)$ on bounded subsets of R^n. Hence to show that $v(\chi_i) \to v(\chi)$, it is sufficient to show that $Y_{\chi_i} \to Y_\chi$ in the Hausdorff topology, for decreasing sequences χ_i (i.e., that $\cap_i \overline{Y}_{\chi_i} \subseteq \overline{Y}_\chi$). Finally, because our χ_i are all bounded from below, we only have to show that $\cap_i Y_{\chi_i} \subseteq \overline{V}_\chi$. Otherwise, choose $y \in (\cap_i Y_{\chi_i}) \setminus \overline{V}_\chi$. We have that $\epsilon\mu(\chi)$ is in Y_χ, and hence in all Y_{χ_i}, and that the Y_χ are convex, so we can replace y by $(1 - \delta)y + \delta \cdot \epsilon\mu(\chi)$ for $\delta > 0$ small enough and still have the same properties: We can assume that y is in the interior of the positive orthant. Also, denote by C_M the convex hull of y and $\{z \mid z \geq 0,\ \Sigma\ z_i = M\}$: For M sufficiently large, $C_M \cap \overline{V}_\chi = \varnothing$; otherwise we would have $(y + R_+^n) \cap \overline{V}_\chi \neq \varnothing$, so $y \in \overline{V}_\chi$. For a separating functional λ we then obtain, as in §2 Remark 3,

$$\lambda_i > 0 \quad \forall\ i \quad \text{and} \quad \sup_{z \in V_\chi} \sum \lambda_i z_i < \sum \lambda_i y_i.$$

Note that $\sup_{z \in V_1} \langle \lambda, z \rangle = \epsilon^{-1} \sup_{z \in V_\epsilon} \langle \lambda, z \rangle \leq \epsilon^{-1} \sup_{z \in V_\chi} \langle \lambda, z \rangle < \infty$ for $\chi \geq \epsilon > 0$.

Let y_t^ϵ be an integrable selection from Y_t such that $\epsilon + \int \langle \lambda, y_t^\epsilon \rangle \mu(dt) \geq \int \sup_{y \in Y_t} \langle \lambda, y \rangle \mu(dt)$ (cf. §2 Remark 3). Then $0 \leq \chi(t) \leq 1$ implies $\sup_{z \in V_\chi} \langle \lambda, z \rangle - \langle \lambda, \int \chi(t)y^\epsilon(t)\ \mu(dt) \rangle \leq \epsilon$. Choose ϵ such that $\sup_{z \in \overline{V}_\chi} \langle \lambda, z \rangle + \epsilon < \langle \lambda, y \rangle$; then

$$\langle \lambda, y \rangle \leq \sup_{z \in V_{\chi_i}} \langle \lambda, z \rangle \leq \langle \lambda, \int \chi_i(t)y^\epsilon(t)\ \mu(dt) \rangle + \epsilon$$

Hence, going to the limit over the decreasing sequence χ_i, we get (since $y^\epsilon(t)$ is integrable)

$$\langle \lambda, y \rangle \leq \langle \lambda, \int \chi(t)y^\epsilon(t)\ \mu(dt) \rangle + \epsilon \leq \sup_{z \in \overline{V}_\chi} \langle \lambda, z \rangle + \epsilon,$$

contradicting our previous inequality.

This proves Proposition B. ■

Theorem 1. v and $\bar{v}$ are monotonic, positively homogeneous of degree 1, concave, and at every χ_0 bounded away from zero, they coincide and are $\sigma(L_\infty(\mu),L_1(\mu))$-continuous. v is attained at those points and is $\sigma(L_\infty(\mu),L_1(\mu))$-lowersemicontinuous everywhere.

Proof: The function v is attained because, at those χ, $\underline{V}_\chi = V_\chi = \overline{V}_\chi$ by Appendix Lemma 2. The rest was shown before, except for the fact that M could be taken as $+\infty$ in Proposition B. This will follow from later results and will not be used before. ■

4 The core

This section is basically an adaption of the classical treatment in S. Hart (1977a,b) and of course in Aumann and Shapley further up the tree (cf. also P. Dubey 1975 for the finite type case with production).

Proposition 1. Let

$$\tilde{v}(\chi) = \lim_{\substack{\tau \geq 0 \\ \rightarrow}} \frac{v(t + \tau\chi) - v(t)}{\tau}$$

$[t > 0$ arbitrary, $\chi \in B(T,\mathscr{C})]$. Then

(a) The limit always exists and is independent of t. It is uniform over bounded subsets of $B(T,\mathscr{C})$ and $t \geq t_0 > 0$.

(b) $\tilde{v}$ is a Lipshitz function of finitely many measures in $L_1(\mu)$, monotonic, concave, and satisfies $\tilde{v}(a \cdot 1 + b \cdot \chi) = av(1) + b\tilde{v}(\chi)$ for $b \geq 0$.

(c) $\tilde{v}(\chi) = \min\{v(\chi)|v \in \text{Core}(v)\}$ $\forall \chi \in B(T,\mathscr{C})$, and $\tilde{v} \geq \bar{v}$ on $B^+(T,\mathscr{C})$.

(d) $\text{Core}(v)$ is a finite-dimensional, compact convex subset of $L_1(\mu)$.

Remarks:

1. $\text{Core}(v)$ is the set of all additive set functions ϕ defined on $\mathscr{C}$ and that satisfy $\phi(S) \geq v(S)$ $\forall S \in \mathscr{C}$, $\phi(T) = v(T)$.

2. As seen in the previous paragraph, there is possibly some degree of arbitrariness in the definition of the characteristic function v – maybe $\bar{v}$ or even the uppersemicontinuous regularization of $\bar{v}$ would be preferred. But certainly v is the most conservative choice, thus yielding the biggest core and the smallest function $\tilde{v}$. Proposition 1(b) then implies $\tilde{v}$ is $\sigma(L_\infty(\mu),L_1(\mu))$-continuous and, being larger than $\bar{v}$ on $B^+(T,\mathscr{C})$ (c), it is even larger than its uppersemicontinuous regularization. Hence (by (c) again), any element of the core is larger even than this regularization, and even on all $\chi \geq 0$.

Thus the definition of the core is completely independent of this arbitrariness, and for the same reason so is the definition of $\tilde{v}$. Therefore, as we will see, so is the Shapley value.

Proof: The finite dimensionality of the core will be proved only in Proposition 4. By (c) it will imply that $\tilde{v}$ is a function of finitely many measures, and even Lipshitz, although this would also follow from the general result in Mertens (1988, Theorem 2). We now prove the remaining points.

(a) (cf. Mertens 1980, prop. 11, p. 550.) Homogeneity of degree 1 yields

$$\frac{v(t + \tau\chi) - v(t)}{\tau} = \frac{v(1 + \epsilon\chi) - v(1)}{\epsilon} \qquad \text{with } \epsilon = \frac{\tau}{t} \leq \frac{\tau}{t_0}.$$

Thus it is sufficient to prove that $(v(1 + \epsilon\chi) - v(1)/\epsilon$ converges uniformly on bounded subsets of $B(T,\mathscr{C})$. Note that concavity implies that, for $\epsilon < \epsilon_0$ and $\|\chi\| \leq \epsilon_0^{-1}$, the ratio is an increasing function of ϵ, thus establishing convergence. By Theorem 1, the ratios are then $\sigma(L_\infty,L_1)$-continuous on this $\sigma(L_\infty,L_1)$-compact subset of L_∞. Thus uniformity of the convergence will follow by Dini's theorem if we prove that the limit $\tilde{v}$ is $\sigma(L_\infty,L_1)$-up-persemicontinuous on this bounded subset. But this will follow from (c) and Core$(v) \subseteq L_1(\mu)$ (d), and uniformity of the convergence will not be used before.

(b) $\tilde{v}$ is concave and monotonic as a limit of such functions, and the equality was proved in Mertens (1988), after Mertens 1980.

(d) Let v be an element of the core of v. Monotonicity of v implies $v \geq 0$; because $v(T) < \infty$, this implies v is bounded. Let S_i be an increasing sequence of coalitions, with $\mu(S_i)$ converging to $\mu(T)$. By Theorem 1, $v(S_i)$ converges to $v(T)$. Hence, $v(S_i) \geq v(S_i)$ implies $\lim v(S_i) \geq v(T) = v(T)$. Positivity of v and $S_i \subseteq S_{i+1}$ ensures the existence of the limit; it also implies $v(S_i) \leq v(T)$. Thus, $v(S_i)$ converges to $v(T)$. It follows first that v is countably additive, hence a measure, and next that it is absolutely continuous w.r.t. μ. Thus Core$(v) \subseteq L_1(\mu)$ (Radon–Nikodým theorem). Weak-compactness and convexity follow from the fact that we just proved that it could have been defined as those v in the dual L_∞^* of L_∞ satisfying our weak inequalities–which involve $\sigma(L_\infty^*,L_\infty)$-continuous linear functionals–and from its boundedness in L_∞^*, [a $\sigma(L_\infty^*,L_\infty)$-compact convex set that happens to be included in L_1 is obviously $\sigma(L_1,L_\infty)$-compact convex].

(c) Concavity and homogeneity of degree 1 of v imply $v(1 + \epsilon\chi) \geq v(1) + \epsilon v(\chi)$; hence $\tilde{v}(\chi) \geq v(\chi)$ for all $\chi \geq 0$. For $v \in$ Core(v), v being continuous and v lowersemicontinuous $(\sigma(L_\infty,L_1))$ at any $\chi \geq 0$ (above for v and Theorem 1 for v), and the indicator functions being dense in the set of all $0 \leq \chi \leq 1$ for this topology (Lyapunov), the inequalities $v(S) \geq v(S)$ yield in the limit $v(\chi) \geq v(\chi)$ for $0 \leq \chi \leq 1$, and, hence, by homogeneity, for all $\chi \geq 0$. Therefore

$$v(\chi) = \frac{v(1 + \epsilon\chi) - v(1)}{\epsilon} \geq \frac{v(1 + \epsilon\chi) - v(1)}{\epsilon} \qquad \text{for all } \chi \text{ with } \|\chi\| \leq \epsilon^{-1}$$

[because $v(1) = v(1)$]. Going to the limit yields $v(\chi) \geq \tilde{v}(\chi)$ for all χ. Thus $\min\{v \in$ Core$(v)\} \geq \tilde{v}$.

To prove equality, consider a fixed χ_0. Define v on the space spanned by χ_0 and the constants by $v(\chi_0) = \tilde{v}(\chi_0)$, $v(1) = v(1)$. For $b \geq 0$ we have $\tilde{v}(a \cdot 1 + b \cdot \chi_0) = av(1) + b\tilde{v}(\chi_0) = v(a \cdot 1 + b \cdot \chi_0)$, so concavity of $\tilde{v}$ implies $\tilde{v}(a \cdot 1 - b \cdot \chi_0) \leq v(a \cdot 1 - b \cdot \chi_0)$: we have $v \geq \tilde{v}$ on the whole plane generated by χ_0 and the constants. Because $\tilde{v}$ is concave and positively homogeneous of degree 1 on $B(T,\mathscr{C})$, the Hahn–Banach theorem yields a linear extension of v to all of $B(T,\mathscr{C})$ satisfying everywhere the same inequality. In particular, $v(S) \geq \tilde{v}(S) \geq v(S)$, so the restriction of v to $\mathscr{C}$ coincides with a measure [cf(d)] $\bar{v}$ in the core of v. By linearity, both coincide on all step functions, and we have seen that $\bar{v}$ is monotonic, and the monotonicity of v follows from $v(\chi) \geq \tilde{v}(\chi) \geq 0$ for all $\chi \geq 0$. Because they coincide on step functions and are monotonic, v and $\bar{v}$ coincide everywhere. Thus the v we constructed is a measure in Core (v), satisfying $v(\chi_0) = \tilde{v}(\chi_0)$. This proves equality. Finally, $\tilde{v}(\chi) \geq v(\chi)$ for $\chi \geq 0$ implies by Theorem 1 that $\tilde{v}(\chi) \geq \bar{v}(\chi)$ for χ bounded below; hence, for $\chi \geq 0$, $\epsilon > 0$, and for any $v \in \text{Core}(v)$ we obtain $v(\chi + \epsilon) \geq \tilde{v}(\chi + \epsilon) \geq \bar{v}(\chi + \epsilon) \geq \bar{v}(\chi)$ (the last by monotonicity). Therefore $v(\chi) \geq \bar{v}(\chi)$ (letting ϵ go to zero). Hence, finally, $\tilde{v}(\chi) = \min\{v(\chi)|v \in \text{Core}(v)\} \geq \bar{v}(\chi)$. This finishes the proof of (c) and of the theorem. ■

Remark: This also finishes the proof of Theorem 1: there only remains to show the uppersemicontinuity of $\bar{v}$ at all χ bounded below (this will indeed imply that of v, because $v \leq \bar{v}$ everywhere and $v(\chi) = \bar{v}(\chi)$ at those χ). Proposition 1(c) and (d) imply the uppersemicontinuity $(\sigma(L_\infty(\mu),L_1(\mu)))$ of $\tilde{v}$ at 1 because $v(1) = v(1) = \tilde{v}(1)$ for $v \in \text{Core}(v)$. Hence, $\tilde{v} \geq \bar{v}$ and $\tilde{v}(1) = v(1)$ imply the uppersemicontinuity of $\bar{v}$ at 1. But if we replaced the measure $\mu(dt)$ by the measure $\chi_0(t)\, \mu(dt)$ for some $\chi_0(t)$ bounded away from zero, the new economy would (by Lemma 2 of the appendix) satisfy all properties of our economy and would have as characteristic function $\bar{w}(\chi) = \bar{v}(\chi \cdot \chi_0)$. Hence $\bar{v}(\chi \cdot \chi_0)$ is uppersemicontinuous at $\chi = 1$. But if χ_α converges $\sigma(L_\infty,L_1)$ to χ_0, then χ_α/χ_0 converges $\sigma(L_\infty,L_1)$ to 1, because χ_0 is bounded away from zero [for the same reason, we do not have to distinguish $\sigma(L_\infty(\chi_0 \cdot \mu),L_1(\chi_0 \cdot \mu))$ from $\sigma(L_\infty(\mu),L_1(\mu))$]. Thus $\bar{v}(\chi_\alpha) = \bar{v}((\chi_\alpha/\chi_0) \cdot \chi_0)$ has a lim sup $\leq \bar{v}(1 \cdot \chi_0)$: $\bar{v}$ is uppersemicontinuous at any χ_0 bounded away from zero.

Now we turn to a description of Core(v): the core-equivalence theorem. First we need some vocabulary.

Definitions

(1) A *feasible plan* (for a coalition χ_t) is a pair (y_t,x_t) of $(\chi_t\, d\mu(t))$-integrable functions to $\mathbf{R}^n$ such that for all t, $x_t \in \mathbf{R}^n_+$ and $y_t \in Y_t$ and

such that $\int \chi_t x_t\, \mu(dt) = \int \chi_t y_t\, \mu(dt)$, which is called the *corresponding output*. A feasible plan for the total coalition T will be called simply a feasible plan.

(2) A *price system* is a (nonnegative) linear functional p on $\mathbf{R}^n$.

(3) A *transferable utility competitive equilibrium* (t.u.c.e.) consists of a feasible plan (y,x) and a price system p such that $\mu(dt)$-a.e. $u_t(x_t) - \langle p,x_t \rangle = \sup_{x\in\mathbf{R}_+^n}(u_t(x) - \langle p,x \rangle)$ and $\langle p,y_t \rangle = \sup_{y\in Y_t}\langle p,y \rangle$. (Note that $p \geq 0$ would thus follow even if it was not imposed).

(4) An *efficient plan* is a feasible plan (y,x) such that $\int u_t(x_t)\,\mu(dt) = v(T)$ (i.e., is maximal). The efficient outputs are the outputs of efficient plans.

(5) The *competitive payoff* (c.p.) corresponding to some t.u.c.e. (y,x,p) is the payoff function $h_p(t) = u_t(x_t) - \langle p,x_t \rangle + \langle p,y_t \rangle$.

(6) The *set P of competitive prices* is the set of price vectors arising from some t.u.c.e.

Proposition 2

(a) The c.p. h_p corresponding to a t.u.c.e. (y,x,p) depends only on p and is given by

$$h_p(t) = \sup_{x\in\mathbf{R}_+^n} [u_t(x) - \langle p,x \rangle] + \sup_{y\in Y_t} \langle p,y \rangle.$$

We can use this to define h_p for any p.

(b) For any linear functional p and any $\chi \geq 0$, set $h_p(\chi) = \int \chi(t)h_p(t)\, \mu(dt)$ (note the integrand is ≥ 0). h_p is convex and $\langle p,x \rangle + h_p(\chi) \geq w(\chi,x)$ for all p, χ, and x. $p \in P$ iff $h_p(T) \leq v(T)$-i.e., iff $h_p \in \mathrm{core}(v)$.

(c) (y,x,p) is a t.u.c.e. iff p is a competitive price and (y,x) an efficient plan.

Proof: (a) is obvious from the definition of a t.u.c.e. It is clear that h_p is ≥ 0 (choose $x = y \in Y_t \cap \mathbf{R}_+^n$) and convex.

(b) For $p \in P$, (p,x,y) a t.u.c.e., we have

$$h_p(T) = \int_T h_p(t)\, \mu(dt) = \int_T u_t(x_t)\, \mu(dt) - \langle p, \int_T (x_t - y_t)\, \mu(dt) \rangle$$

$$= \int_T u_t(x_t)\, \mu(dt) \leq v(T)$$

because feasibility implies both $\int(x_t - y_t)\,\mu(dt) = 0$ and the last inequality (definition of v). For the inequality, let y_t denote a production plan and x_t a consumption plan for χ that yield approximately $w(\chi,x)$. Then integrating

$\chi_t h_p(t) \geq \chi_t u_t(x_t) - \langle p, \chi_t(x_t - y_t) \rangle$ yields $h_p(\chi) \geq u(\chi, \alpha) - \langle p, \alpha - y \rangle$, with $\alpha = \int \chi_t x_t$ and $y = \int \chi_t y_t$. Hence, $\alpha = y + x \geq 0$ with $y \in Y_\chi$. Because they were chosen optimally, we get $h_p(\chi) \geq w(\chi, x) - \langle p, x \rangle$. Finally, the implication $h_p(T) \leq v(T) \Rightarrow p \in P$ will be done together with (c).

(c) Efficiency of (y, x) for a t.u.c.e. (p, y, x) follows from (b), which implies

$$v(T) \leq \int_T h_p(t)\,\mu(dt) = \int_T u_t(x_t)\,\mu(dt) \leq v(T) \qquad \text{(cf. supra).}$$

Conversely, assume (y, x) is an efficient plan (those exist by Theorem 1) and $h_p(T) \leq v(T)$. Integrating both terms of $h_p(t) \geq u_t(x_t) - \langle p, x_t \rangle + \langle p, y_t \rangle$ yields $v(T)$ on both sides, for $h_p(t)$ because $v(T) \geq h_p(T)$ and for the right-hand member because $\int (x_t - y_t)\,\mu(dt) = 0$ (feasibility) and $\int u_t(x_t)\,\mu(dt) = v(T)$ (efficiency). Hence, we have equality a.e. and (p, x, y) is a t.u.c.e. ∎

Proposition 3. Denote by E the subspace spanned by $(Y_1 - \mathbf{R}_+^n) \cap \mathbf{R}_+^n$, and neglect some null set of traders. Then, for some subspace V of $\mathbf{R}^n$:

(a) $V \cap \mathbf{R}_+^n = V^+ = E^+ = E \cap \mathbf{R}_+^n$ (note that E^+ is a face $\mathbf{R}_+^n$) (hence $E \subseteq V$).

(b) For any ideal coalition $\chi_t \geq 0$, every feasible plan (y_t, x_t) for χ_t can be modified on a $(\chi_t \mu(dt))$-negligible set to yield $y_t \in \tilde{Y}_t = Y_t \cap V$ and $x_t \in E^+$ everywhere.

(c) There exists a finite sequence of price systems p_i of which V is the set of zeros and such that, for all t, $\tilde{Y}_t$ is the set of lexicographic maximizers in Y_t of the p^i, and E^+ is their set of lexicographic minimizers (or joint . . .) in $\mathbf{R}_+^n$.

(d) $\int \tilde{Y}_t\,\mu(dt) - E^+$ is a neighborhood of zero in V.

(e) $E, E^+,$ and V are uniquely determined by (a)–(d). More precisely, (d) implies that V is the smallest space satisfying (b), even just for the all-player coalition T; that is, $\chi_t = 1$.

(f) Let $\tilde{u}_t(x, x') = u_t(x, 0)$ for $(x, x') \in \mathbf{R}_+^n$, $x \in E$, x' orthogonal to E. Then the economy $\tilde{\mathscr{E}} = (\tilde{Y}, \tilde{u})$ satisfies all our assumptions and has the same possible feasible plans and the same characteristic function v as the original economy $\mathscr{E} = (Y, u)$.

Proof: Denote $\mathbf{R}^n$ by V^0. If 0 is not an interior point of $Y_1 - \mathbf{R}_+^n$ in V^0, it can be separated: there exists a nonzero linear functional p_1 which is ≤ 0 on $Y_1 - \mathbf{R}_n^+$. Let $V^1 = \{x \in V^0 | \langle p_1, x \rangle = 0\}$. p_1 is a positive linear functional because it is nonzero and bounded above on $Y_1 - \mathbf{R}_n^+$. Thus p_1 should be both positive and negative on $(Y_1 - \mathbf{R}_n^+) \cap \mathbf{R}_+^n$ and therefore zero on the subspace E spanned by this subset: $E \subset V^1$. From §2, Remark 3, $\sup_{y \in Y_t} \langle p_1, y \rangle = \int \sup_{y \in Y_t} \langle p_1, y \rangle \, \mu(dt)$, and since the integrand is everywhere ≥ 0 (because Y_t intersect $\mathbf{R}_+^n$ and $p_1 \geq 0$), p_1 being negative on Y_1 implies that μ-a.e. $\sup_{y \in Y_t} \langle p_1, y \rangle = 0$. Neglect the remaining set. Hence, for any feasible plan (y_t, x_t) for an ideal coalition χ_t we get $\langle p_1, y_t \rangle \leq 0$ and $\langle p_1, x_t \rangle \geq 0$ (because $p_1 \geq 0$, $x_t \geq 0$); so feasibility $- \int \chi_t y_t \, \mu(dt) = \int \chi_t x_t$ $\mu(dt)$ - yields $\langle p_1, y_t \rangle = \langle p_1, x_t \rangle = 0$, $(\chi_t \mu(dt))$-a.e. On the exceptional set, change x_t to zero and y_t to some measurable selection from $Y_t \cap \mathbf{R}_+^n$. Then $\langle p_1, y_t \rangle = \langle p_1, x_t \rangle = 0$ everywhere (because we had $\sup_{y \in Y_t} \langle p_1, y \rangle = 0$ everywhere): any feasible plan can be modified on a negligible set to yield a feasible plan with y_t and x_t everywhere in V^1. Thus set $Y_t^1 = Y_t \cap V^1$. We then have $Y_t^1 \cap \mathbf{R}_+^n = Y_t \cap \mathbf{R}_+^n \neq \varnothing$ for all t, because $p_1 \geq 0$ on $\mathbf{R}_+^n$ and ≤ 0 on Y_t, and the same use as before of §2, Remark 3 yields that $\int Y_t^1$ $\mu(dt) = Y_1 \cap V^1$, and so is closed. Thus replacing the Y_t by the Y_t^1 preserves all our assumptions and all feasible plans.

Continue thus, as long as 0 is not an interior point of $Y_1^k - V_+^k$ in V^k, to separate it by a linear functional p_{k+1} on V^k (which will be ≥ 0 on V_+^k ($= V^k \cap \mathbf{R}_+^n$), hence extendable as a price system p_{k+1} on $\mathbf{R}^n$) and to construct new subspaces V^{k+1} of V^k and subsets Y_t^{k+1} of Y_t^k. The dimension of V decreases by 1 at every stage, so after finitely many iterations we will stop with a subspace V, a finite sequence of price systems p_i, and subsets $\tilde{Y}_t$ of Y_t. For those, (b), (c), and (d) are already proved with V^+ instead of E^+ [(d) is the criterion to stop the iteration]. Note that (a) just asserts $V^+ = E^+$, and that (b) will then also imply (f), since we have already shown that $\tilde{\mathscr{E}}$ satisfies all our assumptions and has the same feasible plans as $\mathscr{E}$, because (b) implies that $\tilde{u}_t(x_t) = u_t(x_t)$ for any feasible plan. Thus we need only prove that $V^+ = E^+$, and then (e). Because $\tilde{\mathscr{E}}$ has the same feasible plans as $\mathscr{E}$, we have $\tilde{Y}_1 \cap \mathbf{R}_+^n = Y_1 \cap \mathbf{R}_+^n$. Therefore E is still the vector space spanned by $(\tilde{Y}_1 - \mathbf{R}_+^n) \cap \mathbf{R}_+^n$. In particular, any vector in this set lies in E^+, so this set is still the same as $(\tilde{Y}_1 - E^+) \cap E^+$. We have also seen that $E \subset V^1$, so inductively $E \subseteq V$. Because $E^+ \subseteq V^+ \subseteq \mathbf{R}_+^n$, it follows that this set is still equal to $(\tilde{Y}_1 - V^+) \cap V^+$. But $\tilde{Y}_1 - V^+$ is a neighborhood of zero in V (stopping criterion), so it follows that its intersection $(\tilde{Y}_1 - E^+) \cap E^+$ with V^+ is a neighborhood of zero in V^+. A fortiori E^+ is a neighborhood of zero in V^+, and both are cones, so equality follows.

There only remains to prove (e). This is obvious for E and E^+. By (d), there exist integrable selections y_t^i from the $\tilde{Y}_t$ whose integrals form the vertices of a full-dimensional simplex containing a point x of E^+ in its interior, say $x = \Sigma \alpha_i \int y^i \, d\mu$ with $\alpha_i > 0$, $\Sigma \alpha_i = 1$. By a version of

Lyapunov's theorem (Mertens 1981), there exists a finite set of measurable selections z_t^j from $\cup_i\{y_t^i\}$ such that $\int z^j \, d\mu = x \; \forall j$ and such that some convex combination of them is uniformly close to $\Sigma \alpha^i y^i$. Because $\alpha_i > 0$, this implies that, for all t, the z_t^j and the y_t^i span the same affine space. Because the z^j are integrable selections from $\tilde{Y}$ with $\int z^j \, d\mu \in E^+$, any space $\tilde{V}$ satisfying (b) will contain almost all z_t^j, hence almost all y_t^i, hence all integrals $\int y_t^i \, \mu(dt)$. Because those integrals span a full-dimensional simplex in V, $\tilde{V}$ will contain V. We have shown that any space $\tilde{V}$ satisfying (b) contains every space V satisfying (d), hence (e).

This proves Proposition 3. ■

Note that this characterization of the feasible space V is not at all sensitive to any form of pathology in the sets Y_t. In §2, Remark 3 we have seen that $Y_1 - \mathbf{R}_+^n$ was still closed and the integral of the $Y_t - \mathbf{R}_+^n$, of their convexification (by Lyapunov's theorem), and of their closed convex hulls (by closedness of the integral). V was constructed only in terms of $Y_1 - \mathbf{R}_+^n$ (or even the cone generated), so it would still be the same if the Y_t were replaced by their closed, convex, comprehensive hulls (or even the cones generated by them, because the integral of those is the cone generated by $Y_1 - \mathbf{R}_+^n$; thus V also does not depend on μ but only on its null sets, this being so for an integral of convex cones).

Note also that $\mathscr{E}$ and $\tilde{\mathscr{E}}$ have the same efficient plans and efficient outputs.

Proposition 4

(a) The core of v is the set of competitive payoffs of the economy $\tilde{\mathscr{E}}$.

(b) Denote by A the set of efficient outputs: $A = \{\alpha | \alpha \text{ is a maximizer of } u(1,\alpha) \text{ over } Y_1\}$ is compact convex $\subseteq E^+$, and (y,x) is an efficient plan iff, for some $\alpha \in A$, y is a feasible production plan for α and x is an efficient redistribution of α.

(c) Then the set P of competitive prices of $\tilde{\mathscr{E}}$ is the compact, convex set of linear functionals p on V – or, equivalently, of price systems p on $\mathbf{R}^n$ – such that some $\alpha \in A$ (and then every such α) maximizes $\langle p,y \rangle$ on $\tilde{Y}_1$ and $u(1,x) - \langle p,x \rangle$ on $V^+ (= E^+)$; that is, p is a "supergradient" of $u(1,x)$ and a supporting hyperplane of $\tilde{Y}_1$ at $\alpha \in A$.

(d) Equivalently, P can be characterized as the set of supergradients on V of $w(1,x)$ at $x = 0$.

(e) The set of supergradients of $w(\chi,x) \, (x \in V)$ at $(1,0)$ is exactly the set of functionals $h_p(\chi) + \langle p,x \rangle$ for $p \in P$.

Proof: (a) We know already (Proposition 2) that competitive payoffs are in the core. By Proposition 1, Core(v) is a subset of $L_1(\mu)$. Thus let $c(t)$ be an element of the core and write $c(\chi)$ for $\int c(t)\chi(t)\,\mu(dt)$. Let $F(x) = \sup_{\chi \geq 0}[w(\chi,x) - c(\chi)]$ for $x \in V$. Clearly F is monotonic, concave, and positively homogeneous of degree 1 because w is (§3, Corollary 2; the projection of a convex set is convex). Further, by Proposition 3(d), $w(1,x) > -\infty$ in a neighborhood of zero in V. Hence, $F(x) > -\infty$ there and, thus, on V by homogeneity. Finally, c being in the core implies that $F(0) = 0$, by Proposition 1(c). It follows that $F(x) < +\infty$ for $x \in V$; indeed, because $F(-x) > -\infty$, $F(x) = +\infty$ would by concavity imply $F(0) = +\infty$. Thus F is real-valued on V. Hence, by the separation theorem there exists a linear functional p on V such that $F(x) \leq \langle p,x \rangle$ on V. F is monotonic so $p \geq 0$ (i.e., $\langle p,x \rangle \geq 0$ for $x \in E^+ = V^+$). This implies that p can be extended, if desired, to a price system on $\mathbf{R}^n$ [hence the "equivalently" sub (c)]. It follows that, for all $\chi \geq 0$, $w(\chi,x) \leq \langle p,x \rangle + c(\chi)$; that is, for all $\alpha \in E^+$ and $y \in V_\chi$ we have $u(\chi,\alpha) + \langle p,y - \alpha \rangle \leq c(\chi)$. Thus for all integrable selections x_t from E^+ and y_t from $\tilde{Y}_t$,

$$\int \chi_t[u_t(x_t) + \langle p,y_t - x_t \rangle - c(t)]\,\mu(dt) \leq 0$$

for all χ_t; hence

$$c(t) \geq u_t(x_t) - \langle p,x_t \rangle + \langle p,y_t \rangle \quad \mu\text{-a.e.}$$

for all integrable x_t and y_t, so

$$c(t) \geq \sup_{x \in E^+} [u_t(x) - \langle p,x \rangle] + \sup_{y \in \tilde{Y}_t} \langle p,y \rangle = h_p(t) \quad \mu\text{-a.e.}$$

and the feasibility of c [$c(T) = v(T)$] and $h_p(T) \geq v(T)$ [Proposition 2(b)] imply $c(t) = h_p(t)$ a.e. and $h_p(T) = v(T)$. Therefore $p \in P$ by Proposition 2(b).

(a) is proved, (b) is obvious, and the characterization in (c) follows easily by integration from the definition of a t.u.c.e. [for the "and then every such α," one may use, for example, Proposition 2(c)]. Closedness and convexity of P follow immediately, and boundedness (hence compactness) in the dual of V (obviously not in the dual of $\mathbf{R}^n$) follows from $u(1,\alpha) - \langle p,\alpha \rangle \geq u(1,0) - \langle p,0 \rangle = 0$ (by maximization), and

$$\langle p,\alpha \rangle = \max\{\langle p,y \rangle | y \in \tilde{Y}_1\} = \max\{\langle p,y \rangle \mid y \in \tilde{Y}_1 - E^+\}$$

(the last equation because we have seen that p must be nonnegative on E^+); hence

$$\max\{\langle p,y \rangle | y \in \tilde{Y}_1 - E^+, p \in P\} \leq u(1,\alpha) = v(T) < +\infty.$$

The boundedness of P follows because $\tilde{Y}_1 - E^+$ is a neighborhood of zero [Proposition 3(d)] in V.

For (e), note that for any supergradient $c(\chi) + \langle p, x \rangle$ of $w(\chi, x)$ at $(1,0)$, $c(\chi)$ must be a supergradient of $v(\chi) = w(\chi, 0)$ at $\chi = 1$ – that is, c must be in the core. Hence, we can use the proof of (a), where we deduced from $c \in \text{Core}(v)$ and $w(\chi, x) \leq c(\chi) + \langle p, x \rangle$, that $c = h_p$ and $p \in P$. Any supergradient has the required form. The converse follows from Proposition 2(b).

Finally for (d), (e) implies that all $p \in P$ are supergradients. Conversely, let p be a supergradient of $w(1, x)$ at zero: even if the economy is allowed to trade commodities with the auctioneer at prices p, it cannot do better than $w(1,0) = v(T)$. Hence, if players are individually authorized to trade this way and thus obtain $h_p(t)$, they will not do better than $v(T)$ in total: $h_p(T) \leq v(T)$, so $p \in P$ by Proposition 2(b).

Definition. Denote by X the set of vector measures $\xi = (\xi_0, \tilde{\xi})$, with ξ_0 real-valued and $\tilde{\xi}$ V-valued, that are obtained as $\xi_0(S) = \int_S u_t(x_t) \, \mu(dt)$, $\tilde{\xi}(S) = \int_S (y_t - x_t) \, \mu(dt)$ for efficient plans (x, y). Also let $[p, \xi] = \xi_0 + \langle p, \tilde{\xi} \rangle$ for $\xi \in X$, p in the dual of V.

Define $F: V \to \mathbf{R}$ by $F(v) = \min_{p \in P} \langle p, v \rangle$.

Corollary.

  (a) $h_p = [p, \xi]$ is an affine function on the compact convex set P, independent of $\xi \in X$.
  (b) $\text{core}(v) = \{h_p | p \in P\}$ is a finite-dimensional, compact, convex set.
  (c) $\tilde{v}(\chi) = \xi_0(\chi) + F(\tilde{\xi}(\chi))$ for any $\xi \in X$ and all χ.

Proof: (a) restates Proposition 2(a) and (c) [affinity is obvious from the definition of $[p, \xi]$, and compactness and convexity come from Proposition 4(c)]; (b) follows from (a) and Proposition 4(a); and similarly (c) follows from (a) and (b) and Proposition 1(c).

Remarks:
  1. With (b), the proof of Proposition 1 is also finished.
  2. Proposition 3(c) allows us to interpret Proposition 4 as an equivalence theorem for the original economy $\mathcal{E}$ too, under the "lexicographic price system" $(p_1, p_2, p_3, \ldots ; p)$, where the p_i's come from Proposition 3(c) and p from Proposition 4. Such infinite prices can be interpreted not only as those consumers may have in mind for objects that cannot be produced – but that are in the model, for example, because they

might be producible tomorrow or in another state of nature due to techno-
logical progress–but also as constraints (of the "zero-discharge" form:
$\langle p_i,y \rangle \geq 0$) put on producers to prevent them from adopting production
plans that would put consumers outside their consumption sets. (Think of
the safety regulations imposed on the nuclear electricity generating industry, and of the total cleanup exacted after the Harrisburg incident.)
Alternatively, one may just interpret V as an "incomplete markets" limitation. Observe finally that, in many cases, high finite prices will be
sufficient, and the infinite ones just a convenience in the proof.

   3. Because the dimension of V may be higher than that of its positive
orthant $V^+ = E^+$, studying the markets $\tilde{\xi}$ restricted to V is also a way to
model situations where there are more primary inputs and intermediate
goods than there are final consumption goods.

5   The value

Definition. For $\tilde{\xi} = (\xi_0, \xi) \in X$, define the range of ξ as the ball

$$R_\xi = \{\xi(S)|S \in G\} = \tfrac{1}{2}\{\xi(\chi)| \|\chi\| \leq 1\}$$

[using Lyapunov's theorem and the fact that ξ has total mass zero ($\int (y - x)\, d\mu = 0$)]. R_ξ is the set of net trades at the efficient plan ξ.

   The relevant concept of value for the next theorem was defined in
Mertens (1988). Otherwise, the result is reminiscent of Hart (1980).

Theorem.

   (a)   Let $P^* = \int p(z)\, dC(z)$, where $p(z)$ denotes the set of minimizers of
         $\langle p,z \rangle$ on P, and $dC(z)$ denotes the distribution on $\mathbf{R}^n$ with Fourier
         transform $\exp(-N(q))$, where the pseudonorm N is the support
         function of the ball R_ξ; that is, $N(q) = \|\langle q,\xi \rangle\| = \sup_{z \in R_\xi} \langle q,z \rangle$.
         Then P^* is a well-defined compact convex subset of P, indepen-
         dent of $\xi \in X$.
   (b)   The game v has a value $\phi(v)$ given by $\phi(v) = h_p$ for any $p \in P^*$.

Proof: We start with (b). Note that the extension, say $w(\chi)$, of the characteristic function is not necessarily well defined for ideal set functions χ that
are not bounded away from zero. It could, at worst, be anything between
$v(\chi)$ (which is lowersemicontinuous) and the uppersemicontinuous regularization of $\bar{v}$, and [§4, Proposition 1(b), (c)] this is smaller than $\tilde{v}(\chi)$.

Literally speaking, we could therefore not use the operator "ϕ_3" as defined in Mertens (1988). We should either resort to the generalization mentioned in Section 4 of that paper (e.g., operator ψ of 4.3), or just note that a trivial modification in the definition of the domain of ϕ_3 will already suffice to include our games. We therefore use the second route, which shows better how little is at issue and which deals better at the same time with the margin of uncertainty about the true characteristic function [$v(S)$ or $\bar{v}(S)$?].

Note that all specifications of w agree on constant functions. Thus for any specification and any $\tau > 0$,

$$\frac{v(t + \tau\chi) - v(t)}{\tau} \leq \frac{w(t + \tau\chi) - w(t)}{\tau} \leq \frac{\bar{v}(t + \tau\chi) - \bar{v}(t)}{\tau}.$$

Let us show that

$$\int_0^1 \frac{v[1 \wedge (t + \tau\chi)^+] - v(t)}{\tau} \, dt$$

converges to $\tilde{v}(\chi)$ uniformly on bounded subsets of $B(T,C)$. This will also imply the corresponding statement with $\tilde{v}$ instead of v and, hence, with an arbitrary specification w (with the uniform convergence independent of the choice of w). This follows, as noted in Mertens (1980, Proposition 11), from §4, Proposition 1(a) using Lebesgue's dominated convergence theorem, because the integrand is uniformly bounded by $\|\chi\| \cdot v(1)$ (loc. cit. Proposition 4).

As one immediately checks, the entire first section of Mertens (1988) goes through as soon as any specification w of the extension of v – with w between the DNA uppersemicontinuous and the DNA lowersemicontinuous extensions of v – the same ϕ_3 yields after integration. Here we have even more, because we prove convergence for the unsymmetrized version, but only the symmetrized version – convergence of $\int_0^1 [[w(t + \tau\chi) - w(t - \tau\chi)]/(2\tau)] dt$ to $\frac{1}{2}[\tilde{v}(\chi) - \tilde{v}(-\chi)]$ – is required.

Because $\frac{1}{2}(\tilde{v}(\chi) - \tilde{v}(-\chi))$ is a function of finitely many measures [§4, Corollary, part (c)], Section 2 (Theorem 2) of Mertens (1988) implies the game has a value, independent of the exact specification of v (such as: $v(S)$ or $\bar{v}(S)$?). This value $\phi(v)$ is obtained by averaging the gradient of $\frac{1}{2}(\tilde{v}(\chi) - \tilde{v}(-\chi))$ with a certain Cauchy distribution. This distribution is symmetric, and the gradient of $\tilde{v}$ exists a.e. w.r.t. this distribution [using the fact that $\tilde{v}$ is either a concave or a Lipshitz function of finitely many measures; the Lipshitz case is known as Rademacher's theorem and was essentially rediscovered in the proof of loc. cit., Theorem 2], so we obtain that equivalently $\phi(v)$ is the Cauchy average of the gradient of $\tilde{v}$.

By the corollary of §4, we have $\tilde{v}(\chi) = \xi^0(\chi) + F(\xi(\chi))$, with $F(z) = \min_{p \in P} \langle p, z \rangle = \langle p(z), z \rangle$, and $p(z)$ is an uppersemicontinuous correspondence with nonempty, compact, convex values in the compact, convex set P (hence P^* is a compact, convex subset of P).

It follows by an elementary computation that the directional derivative $F_z(z')$ of F at z in the direction z' is

$$F_z(z') = \min_{q \in p(z)} \langle q, z' \rangle.$$

Hence, in the notation of Section 2 of Mertens (1988) (with the aforementioned proviso),

$$D_\chi(\tilde{\chi}) = \lim_{\substack{\tau \to 0 \\ >}} \frac{\tilde{v}(\chi + \tau\tilde{\chi}) - \tilde{v}(\chi)}{\tau} = \xi_0(\tilde{\chi}) + \lim_{q \in p(\xi(\chi))} \langle q, \xi(\tilde{\chi}) \rangle.$$

By Theorem 2 (loc. cit.) we have therefore

$$[\phi(v)](\tilde{\chi}) = \xi^0(\tilde{\chi}) + \int F_z(\xi(\tilde{\chi})) \, dC(z),$$

where C is the distribution of $\xi(\chi)$ under the cylinder probability on $B(T,C)$ having Fourier transform $\exp(-\|\mu\|)$. Thus the Fourier transform of C is

$$\int \exp(i\langle q, z \rangle) \, dC(z) = \int \exp i(\langle q, \xi \rangle(\chi)) \, d\chi = \exp(-\|\langle q, \xi \rangle\|)$$
$$= \exp(-N(q)).$$

The proof of Theorem 2 in Mertens (1988) showed that, for any z' in the space spanned by $R(\xi)$, F had $dC(z)$ a.e. two-sided directional derivatives in the direction z'; that is, $F_z(z') + F_z(-z') = 0$, or $\langle p(z), z' \rangle$ is $C(dz)$ a.e. single-valued. Thus $C(dz)$ a.e., $F_z(z') = \langle p(z), z' \rangle$, and hence $[\phi(v)](\tilde{\chi}) = \xi^0(\tilde{\chi}) + \langle \int p(z) \, dC(z), \xi(\tilde{\chi}) \rangle$, which proves (b).

To prove (a), we need only show that P^* is independent of $\tilde{\xi} \in X$. We know that P is a canonically defined, compact, convex set in the dual of V. Denote by A the vector space of all affine real-valued functions defined on P, and let $P' = A/\mathbf{R}$ be the quotient by the subspace of constant functions. P' can be identified with the dual of the affine subspace spanned by P. Any $\tilde{\xi} \in X$, being a V-valued measure, induces canonically an A-valued measure $h : p \to [p, \tilde{\xi}] = h_p$, which is independent of $\tilde{\xi} \in X$ (§4, corollary). For $z \in V$ the set $p(z)$ depends only on z viewed as an element of P', so only the image distribution of $C(dz)$ on P' is relevant for the computation of P^*. But this is the canonical image in P' of the distribution of $h(\chi)$ on A, where χ has our cylinder probability on $B(T,C)$. Thus it is canonical; hence (a) is proved.

Appendix

Let U_t denote an integrable correspondence (i.e., measurable graph with an integrable selection). Let $V_\chi = \int \chi(t) U_t \, d\mu(t)$ ($\chi \geq 0$ bounded measurable).

Lemma 1. $\forall \chi$ V_χ is convex nonempty and $V_{\lambda_1 \chi_1 + \lambda_2 \chi_2} = \lambda_1 V_{\chi_1} + \lambda_2 V_{\chi_2}$ ($\lambda_i \in \mathbf{R}_+$).

Proof: Note first that $V_\chi \neq \varnothing$ because U_t is integrable. $V_{\lambda\chi} = \lambda V_\chi$ and the inclusion $V_{\chi_1 + \chi_2} \subseteq V_{\chi_1} + V_{\chi_2}$ are obvious from the definitions. For the reverse inclusion let $v = v_1 + v_2$, $v_i \in V_{\chi_i}$ with

$$v_i = \int \chi_i(t) y_i(t) \, d\mu(t), \qquad \chi_i(t) y_i(t) \in L_1(\mu), \quad y_i(t) \in U_t.$$

We want to show that $v = \int (\chi_1(t) + \chi_2(t)) y(t) \, d\mu(t)$, with $(\chi_1(t) + \chi_2(t)) y(t) \in L_1(\mu)$, and $y(t) \in \{y_1(t), y_2(t)\}$. Hence, let $\sigma(t) = \chi_1(t) / [\chi_1(t) + \chi_2(t)]$ $[= \frac{1}{2}$ if $\chi_1(t) = \chi_2(t)]$, and let $z_i(t) = (\chi_1(t) + \chi_2(t)) y_i(t)$. We have $\sigma(t) z_1(t)$ and $(1 - \sigma(t)) z_2(t)$ μ-integrable, and we look for a μ-integrable $z(t) \in \{z_1(t), z_2(t)\}$ with

$$\int z_t \, d\mu(t) = \int [\sigma(t) z_1(t) + (1 - \sigma(t)) z_2(t)] \, d\mu(t).$$

It is sufficient to construct this on $\{\sigma \leq \frac{1}{2}\}$. On the complement, permute the two indices 1 and 2. Then we have, in addition, $z_2(t)$ μ-integrable, and we look for a measurable set A such that $I_A z_1(t)$ is μ-integrable and

$$\int [I_A z_1(t) + I_{A^c} z_2(t)] \, d\mu(t) = \int [\sigma(t) z_1(t) + (1 - \sigma(t)) z_2(t)] \, d\mu(t);$$

or, because $z_2(t)$ is μ-integrable,

$$\int_A (z_1(t) - z_2(t)) \, d\mu(t) = \int \sigma(t)[z_1(t) - z_2(t)] \, d\mu(t)$$

with $I_A(z_1(t) - z_2(t))$ μ-integrable. We can also w.l.o.g. assume $\sigma(t) > 0$ everywhere (on the complement, $A = \varnothing$). We have $\sigma(t)[z_1(t) - z_2(t)]$ is μ-integrable, so we denote by v the vector measure $(\sigma(t)[\mathbf{z}_1(t) - \mathbf{z}_2(t)]^+ \, d\mu(t), \sigma(t)[\mathbf{z}_1(t) - \mathbf{z}_2(t)]^- \, d\mu(t))$ and let $f(t) = 1/\sigma(t)$ (≥ 2).

The problem is then as follows: Given a nonnegative nonatomic vector measure v and a measurable function $f(t) \geq 2$, find a measurable set A

such that $\int_A f(t)\, dv(t) = v(I)$ [v is nonnegative and bounded, so this will automatically ensure the μ-integrability of $I_A(\mathbf{z}_1(t) - \mathbf{z}_2(t))$].

Let $I_n = \{n \leq f < n + 1\}$ $(n = 2,3,4, \ldots)$ and use Lyapunov's theorem to choose $A_n \subseteq I_n$ so that $\int_{A_n} f(t)\, dv(t) = v(I_n)$. Then $A = \cup_n A_n$ satisfies our requirements, by the monotone convergence theorem. This proves our formula. The same formula, with $\chi_1 = \chi_2$ and $\lambda_1 + \lambda_2 = 1$ shows the convexity of V_χ. ∎

For the next lemma, call a set Ξ an *archimedean cone* when

(1) it is an abelian semigroup (i.e., endowed with an associative and commutative addition) having the archimedean property $\forall \chi_1,$ $\chi_2 \in \Xi,\ \exists \chi_3 \in \Xi,\ \exists n: n\chi_1 = \chi_2 + \chi_3$, and

(2) it is endowed with a multiplication by the positive real numbers satisfying $(\lambda\mu)(\chi) = \lambda(\mu\chi)$, $1 \cdot \chi = \chi$, $(\lambda + \mu)\chi = \lambda\chi + \mu\chi$, $\lambda(\chi_1 + \chi_2) = \lambda\chi_1 + \lambda\chi_2$ $(\lambda,\mu \in \mathbf{R}_+,\ \chi,\chi_i \in \Xi)$.

Remark: The set $\Xi = \{\chi \in B(I,C)\,|\,\inf \chi > 0\}$ is an archimedean cone. The convex subsets of $\mathbf{R}^n$ also form a (not necessarily archimedean) cone.

Lemma 2. Let Ξ denote an archimedean cone and $\forall \chi \in \Xi$ let V_χ denote a subset of $\mathbf{R}^n$ such that ("linearity") $V_{\lambda_1\chi_1 + \lambda_2\chi_2} = \lambda_1 V_{\chi_1} + \lambda_2 V_{\chi_2}$. Then

(a) All sets V_χ are convex.

(b) $(V_\chi \neq \emptyset\ \forall \chi \in \Xi) \cdot \equiv \cdot (\exists \chi \in \Xi: V_\chi \neq \emptyset)$.

(c) $(V_\chi$ is closed $\forall \chi \in \Xi) \cdot \equiv \cdot (\exists \chi \in \Xi: V_\chi$ is closed$)$.

Proof:

(a) follows by taking $\chi_1 = \chi_2 = \chi$, $\lambda_1 + \lambda_2 = 1$.

(b) follows because otherwise let $V_{\chi_1} \neq \emptyset$, $V_{\chi_2} = \emptyset$, and choose n and χ_3 such that $n\chi_1 = \chi_2 + \chi_3$. We get $\emptyset \neq nV_{\chi_1} = V_{n\chi_1} = V_{\chi_2} + V_{\chi_3} = \emptyset + V_{\chi_3}$, which is impossible.

(c) By (b), (c) is obviously true if $\exists \chi \in \Xi: V_\chi = \emptyset$. So we can assume that V_{χ_0} is closed and nonempty. We know then, because of (a) and (b), that all sets V_χ are nonempty convex sets and thus have a dimension d_χ. Again, the linearity and the archimedean property imply immediately $d_{\chi_1} = d_{\chi_2} \forall \chi_1, \chi_2 \in \Xi$: for some $d \geq 0$, all sets V_χ are d-dimensional convex sets.

We prove (c) by induction on the dimension d. Clearly for $d = 0$ there is no problem, because zero-dimensional convex sets are points and hence closed. Thus we can assume (c) is proved for all dimensions $d < d_0$.

Let us first show that we can further assume $d_0 = n$. If not, for each χ let

v_χ denote the projection of zero on the d_0-dimensional affine subspace generated by V_χ. Because all those subspaces are parallel (d_0 being independent of χ), it follows that v_χ depends linearly on χ. Hence, $\tilde{V}_\chi = V_\chi - v_\chi$ would be another linear correspondence, with values in a fixed d_0-dimensional subspace of $\mathbf{R}^n$ and having the same closedness properties as V_χ. Hence, it would be sufficient to do the proof for $\tilde{V}_\chi$, which takes values in a d_0-dimensional space.

In short, we can assume each V_χ is a full-dimensional convex set in $\mathbf{R}^n$, and (c) is proved for all correspondences V_χ of dimension $d < n$.

For the induction step, we introduce some notation:

1    $\overline{V}_\chi$ is the closure of V_χ.
2   ϕ_χ is the support function of V_χ (and of $\overline{V}_\chi$): $\phi_\chi(p) = \sup_{v \in V_\chi}\langle p,v \rangle = \sup_{v \in \overline{V}_\chi}\langle p,v \rangle$. Then
     a. ϕ has values in $\mathbf{R} \cup \{+\infty\}$.
     b. ϕ_χ is, $\forall \chi$, convex and positively homogeneous of degree 1 in p.
     c. $\phi_{\lambda_1\chi_1+\lambda_2\chi_2} = \lambda_1\phi_{\chi_1} + \lambda_2\phi_{\chi_2}$ from   the   linearity   (using $0 \cdot (+\infty) = 0$).
     d.   This last equation and the archimedean property imply that the convex cone $\overline{\overline{\Pi}} = \{p | \phi_\chi(p) < +\infty\}$ is independent of χ.
3    $F_{p\chi} = \{v \in V_\chi | \langle p,v \rangle = \phi_\chi(p)\}$; $\overline{F}_{p\chi} = \{v \in \overline{V}_\chi | \langle p,v \rangle = \phi_\chi(p)\}$. Clearly for each p, the linearity in χ of V_χ carries over to $F_{p\chi}$.
4    $\Pi = \{p | F_{p\chi} \neq \varnothing\}$; $\overline{\Pi}_\chi = \{p | \overline{F}_{p\chi} \neq \varnothing\}$ [by (b) and the linearity of $F_{p\chi}$, Π does not depend on the choice of χ].

Our first step will be to show

Claim 1. For $p \neq 0$, $F_{p\chi} \neq \varnothing \Rightarrow F_{p\chi} = \overline{F}_{p\chi}$ (i.e., $p \in \Pi \Rightarrow F_{p\chi} = \overline{F}_{p\chi}$).

Proof: By the induction hypothesis, $F_{p\chi}$ is closed for $p \neq 0$, because $F_{p\chi_0}$ is closed and not of full dimension. Thus we will only have to prove that, for $p \in \Pi$, $F_{p\chi}$ and $\overline{F}_{p\chi}$ have the same support function. Hence, let $\psi_{p\chi}(q) = \sup_{y \in F_{p\chi}}\langle q,y \rangle$, $\overline{\psi}_{p\chi}(q) = \sup_{y \in \overline{F}_{p\chi}}\langle q,y \rangle$: $\overline{\psi} \geq \psi$, and, for $p \in \Pi$, both have values in $\mathbf{R} \cup \{+\infty\}$. Further, $\psi_{p,\lambda_1\chi_1+\lambda_2\chi_2} = \lambda_1\psi_{p,\chi_1} + \lambda_2\psi_{p,\chi_2}$ by the linearity of $F_{p\chi}$ and $\overline{\psi}_{p,\lambda_1\chi_1+\lambda_2\chi_2} \geq \lambda_1\overline{\psi}_{p,\chi_1} + \lambda_2\overline{\psi}_{p,\chi_2}$ because the linearity of V implies $\overline{V}_{\lambda_1\chi_1+\lambda_2\chi_2} \supseteq \lambda_1\overline{V}_{\chi_1} + \lambda_2\overline{V}_{\chi_2}$, hence $\overline{F}_{p,\lambda_1\chi_1+\lambda_2\chi_2} \supseteq \lambda_1\overline{F}_{p,\chi_2} + \lambda_2\overline{F}_{p,\chi_2}$.

It follows first that $\psi_{p\chi}(q) < \infty$ for some χ implies $\psi_{p\chi}(q) < \infty$ for all χ, and then that if we set for such pairs (p,q) $h_{p,q}(\chi) = \overline{\psi}_{p\chi}(q) - \psi_{p\chi}(q)$, then $h_{p,q}$ is nonnegative, concave, and positively homogeneous of degree 1 in χ. Further, $V_{\chi_0} = \overline{V}_{\chi_0}$ implies $h_{p,q}(\chi_0) = 0$. For χ arbitrary, choose n and $\tilde{\chi}$

such that $n\chi_0 = \chi + \tilde{\chi}$, and consider $f(\theta) = h_{p,q}(\chi + \theta\tilde{\chi})$: f is a nonnegative concave function of $\theta \geq 0$ satisfying $f(1) = 0$. Therefore $f(\theta) = 0$ for all θ; i.e., $(\theta = 0)$ $h_{p,q}(\chi) = 0$ for all χ.

Thus, for $p \in \Pi$, we have shown that for all $\chi \in \Xi$ either $\psi_{p,\chi}(q) < \infty$ and then $\bar{\psi}_{p,\chi}(q) = \psi_{p,\chi}(q)$ or $\psi_{p,\chi}(q) = +\infty$ and then also $\bar{\psi}_{p,\chi}(q) = \psi_{p,\chi}(q)$. Thus, for $p \in \Pi$, $F_{p,\chi}$ and $\bar{F}_{p,\chi}$ indeed have the same support function, and therefore are equal. This proves Claim 1.

To finish the induction step, and thereby the proof of Lemma 2, there only remains to show that $p \notin \Pi \Rightarrow \bar{F}_{p,\chi} = F_{p,\chi} = \varnothing$. Indeed, it will then follow that, $\forall \chi$, $F_{p,\chi} = \bar{F}_{p,\chi} \forall p \neq 0$, and hence $V_\chi = \bar{V}_\chi$ (V_χ being convex). Thus we have

Claim 2. $F_{p,\chi} = \varnothing \Rightarrow \bar{F}_{p,\chi} = \varnothing$ (i.e., $\bar{\Pi}_\chi = \Pi$).

Proof: We start the proof of Claim 2 by a sublemma.

Sublemma. Let C_k denote a decreasing sequence of closed convex sets in R^n, with $\cap_k C_k = \varnothing$. Then $\exists q : \inf_{c \in C_k}\langle q,c\rangle \xrightarrow[k \to \infty]{} +\infty$.

Proof: The lemma should be well known. For instance, we can take for q any element of the relative interior of the polar of the intersection of the asymptotic cones of the C_k. For the sake of completeness, we give an easy, direct proof of the sublemma.

Let $\phi_k(q) = \inf\{\langle q,c\rangle | c \in C_k\}$. The ϕ_k are increasing with k and are concave and positively homogeneous of degree 1 in q, with values in $\mathbf{R} \cup \{-\infty\}$. If the sublemma were not true, we would have $\phi = \lim_{k \to \infty}\phi_k < +\infty$, and ϕ also would be concave and positively homogeneous of degree 1. Let $D = \{(\alpha,q) \in \mathbf{R} \times \mathbf{R}^n | \alpha \leq \phi(q)\}$, and $\bar{D}$ denote the closure of D. I claim ϕ is uppersemicontinuous at any point $\tilde{q}$ of the relative interior of the convex cone $V = \{q | \phi(q) > -\infty\}$. Indeed, there would otherwise exist a sequence q_i converging to $\tilde{q}$ with $\lim\phi(q_i) > \phi(\tilde{q}) > -\infty$. Hence, we can assume $\phi(q_i) > -\infty$ for all i (i.e., $q_i \in V$). Thus, because $\tilde{q}$ is in the relative interior of V, the contradiction would follow from the continuity of concave functions in the interior of their domain.

This uppersemicontinuity implies in particular that $\exists \alpha_0$ such that $(\alpha_0,\tilde{q}) \notin \bar{D}$. Denote by (λ,x) a linear functional that strictly separates $(\alpha_0,\tilde{q})$ from $\bar{D}$. We have $v = \lambda\alpha_0 + \langle \tilde{q},x\rangle > \lambda\alpha + \langle q,x\rangle \ \forall(\alpha,q): \alpha \leq \phi(q)$. It follows immediately (from $\alpha \leq \phi(q)$) that $\lambda \geq 0$, and from the strict inequality that $\lambda \neq 0$ (otherwise let $q = \tilde{q}$). Hence, by renormalizing we can assume $\lambda = 1$. Therefore, changing the sign of x, we get that $\phi(q) - \langle q, x \rangle$ is bounded from above (by v); because it is positively homogeneous of degree 1, we get zero as the upper bound: $\exists\, x : \forall k, \forall q, \phi_k(q) \leq \langle q, x \rangle$; in other words, because C_k is closed and convex, $x \in C_k$: the sets C_k have a nonempty intersection. This proves the sublemma.

Now we prove Claim 2.

Proof of Claim 2: If the claim were not true, let $\|\bar{p}\| = 1$, $\bar{v} \in F_{\bar{p},\bar{\chi}}$, $\psi(\chi) = \phi_\chi(\bar{p})$, and $F_{\bar{p},\chi} = \varnothing\ \forall \chi \in \Xi$. Choose $\epsilon > 0$ and $\chi_1 \in \Xi$ (archimedean property) such that $\bar{\chi} = \epsilon\chi_0 + \chi_1$. We have $\varnothing = F_{\bar{p},\chi_0} = \overline{F}_{\bar{p},\chi_0}$, so if we let $C_\delta^i = \{v \in V_{\chi_i} | \langle \bar{p}, v \rangle \geq \psi(\chi_i) - \delta\}$, then the C_δ^0 form a decreasing sequence of closed convex sets with empty intersection. Thus by the sublemma, $\exists \bar{q} : \inf_{v \in C_\delta^0} \langle \bar{q}, v \rangle \xrightarrow[\delta \to 0]{} +\infty$ (and $\|\bar{q}\| = 1$).

Now choose $v \in V_{\bar{\chi}}$ such that $\|v - \bar{v}\| \leq \eta$, $v = \epsilon v_0 + v_1$, $v_i \in V_{\chi_i}$. Then

$$\epsilon\langle \bar{p}, v_0 \rangle + \langle \bar{p}, v_1 \rangle = \langle \bar{p}, v \rangle \geq \langle \bar{p}, \bar{v} \rangle - \eta = \psi(\bar{\chi}) - \eta$$
$$= \epsilon\psi(\chi_0) + \psi(\chi_1) - \eta,$$

and because $\langle \bar{p}, v_i \rangle \leq \psi(\chi_i)$, we obtain $\langle \bar{p}, v_0 \rangle \geq \psi(\chi_0) - \eta\epsilon^{-1}$ and $\langle \bar{p}, v_1 \rangle \geq \psi(\chi_1) - \eta$.

In particular, given η_0 and δ, choose $\eta = \min(\eta_0, \epsilon\delta, 1)$. We then get the existence of $v_0 \in C_\delta^0$ and $v_1 \in C_\eta^1$ such that $\|(\epsilon v_0 + v_1) - \bar{v}\| \leq 1$.

If we had chosen δ sufficiently small such that $\inf_{v \in C_\delta^0} \langle \bar{q}, v \rangle \geq M\epsilon^{-1}$, then we would have $M + \langle \bar{q}, v_1 \rangle - \langle \bar{q}, \bar{v} \rangle \leq 1$ (i.e., $\langle \bar{q}, v_1 \rangle \leq \langle \bar{q}, \bar{v} \rangle + 1 - M$). Therefore $\inf_{v \in C_\eta^1} \langle \bar{q}, v \rangle = -\infty$. In particular, we can choose $v_i^1 \in V_{\chi_1}$ such that $\langle \bar{q}, v_i^1 \rangle \leq -i^2$ and $\langle \bar{p}, v_i^1 \rangle \to \psi(\chi_1)$.

Now choose n and χ_2 such that $n\chi_0 = \chi_1 + \chi_2$ (archimedean property) and choose a sequence $v_i^2 \in V_{\chi_2}$ with $\langle \bar{q}, v_i^2 \rangle \leq i$ and $\langle \bar{p}, v_i^2 \rangle \to \psi(\chi_2)$. Then for $v_i = (1/n)[v_i^1 + v_i^2]$ we obtain $v_i \in V_{\chi_0}$, $\langle \bar{q}, v_i \rangle \to -\infty$ and $\langle \bar{p}, v_i \rangle \to \psi(\chi_0)$ $(= [\psi(\chi_1) + \psi(\chi_2)]/n)$, which contradicts the definition of $\bar{q}$. This proves Claim 2, and thus Lemma 2.

REFERENCES

Aumann, R. J. (1965), "Integrals of set-valued functions," *Journal of Mathematical Analysis and Applications*, **12**, 1–12.
   (1975), "Values of markets with a continuum of traders," *Econometrica*, **43**(4), 611–46.
Aumann, R. J. and M. Perles (1965), "A variational problem arising in economics," *Journal of Mathematical Analysis and Applications*, **11**, 488–503.

Aumann, R. J. and L. S. Shapley (1974), *Values of Non-Atomic Games*, Princeton: Princeton University Press.

Champsaur, P. (1975), "Cooperation versus Competition," *Journal of Economic Theory*, **11**(3), 394–417.

Debreu, G. (1966), "Integration of correspondences," *Proceedings of the Fifth Berkeley Symposium on Mathematical Statistics and Probability*, pp. 351–72.

Dubey, P. (1975), Ph.D. Thesis.

Hart, S. (1977a), "Asymptotic value of games with a continuum of players," *Journal of Mathematical Economics*, **4**, 57–80.

(1977b), "Values of non-differentiable markets with a continuum of traders," *Journal of Mathematical Economics*, **4**, 103–16.

(1980), "Measure-based values of market games," *Mathematics of Operations Research*, **5**, 197–228.

Hildenbrand, W. and J. F. Mertens (1971), "On Fatou's lemma in several dimensions," *Zeitschrift fur Wahrscheinlichkeitstheorie und verwandte Gebiete*, **17**, 151–5.

Mertens, J. F. (1980), "Values and derivatives," *Mathematics of Operations Research*, **5**, 523–52.

(1981), "On the density of the extreme points in the unit ball of spaces of type *C(K)*." CORE Discussion Paper 8123, Université Catholique de Louvain, Louvain-la-Neuve, Belgium.

(1988), "The Shapley value in the non-differentiable case," *International Journal of Game Theory*, **17**(1), 1–65.

Taumann, Y. (1981), "Value on a class of non-differentiable market games," *International Journal of Game Theory*, **10**, 155–82.

PART V

Cost allocation and fair division

CHAPTER 17

Individual contribution and just compensation

H. P. Young

Abstract

The "marginality principle" states that the share of joint output atrributable to any single factor of production should depend only on that factor's own contribution to output. This property, together with symmetry and efficiency, uniquely determines the Shapley value. A similar result characterizes Aumann–Shapley pricing for smooth production functions with variable input levels.

1   Introduction

In a perfectly competitive market, the wage of a laborer equals his marginal product. No ethical judgment need be made as to whether marginal productivity is a "just" rule of compensation so long as competitive markets are accepted as the correct form of economic organization. Nevertheless, the idea that rewards should be in proportion to contributions has considerable ethical appeal in itself, and appears to reflect widely held views about what constitutes "just compensation" without any reference to the theory of perfect competition.

In this paper we shall ask what "compensation in accordance with contribution" means in the *absence* of competition. How does the marginality principle translate into a rule of distributive justice when cooperation rather than competition is the mode of economic organization?

Unfortunately, if we attempt to translate marginalism directly into a

This research was supported by the Office of Naval Research under contract N00014-86-K-0586.

267

cooperative sharing rule, difficulties arise. For, except in very special cases, the sum of individuals' marginal contributions to output will not equal total output. If there are increasing returns from cooperation, the sum of marginal contributions will be too great; if there are decreasing returns, it will be too small.

One seemingly innocuous remedy is to compute the marginal product of all factor inputs and then adjust them by some common proportion so that total output is fully distributed. This *proportional to marginal product* principle is the basis of several classical allocation schemes, including the "separable costs remaining benefits" method in cost-benefit analysis [3,6]. We show by example, however, that the proportional to marginal product principle does not resolve the "adding up" problem in a satisfactory way. The reason is that the rule does not base the share of a factor solely on that factor's *own* contribution to output, but on all factors' contribution to output. For example, if one factor's marginal contribution to output increases while another's decreases, the share attributed to the first factor may actually decrease; that is, it may bear some of the decrease in productivity associated with the second factor.

We show that there is essentially only one cooperative sharing rule that avoids this difficulty – the Shapley value. More particularly, the Shapley value is the unique sharing rule with the following three properties:

(i)   Output is fully distributed.
(ii)   Factors that enter into the productive function in a symmetric way receive equal shares.
(iii) A factor's share depends only on its own contribution to output.

This result holds for all production functions with discrete factor inputs (i.e., all cooperative games). A similar result characterizes the Aumann–Shapley sharing rule on the class of smooth production functions with variable levels of input. In this sense it can be said that the Shapley value (and Aumann–Shapley prices in the continuous case) are the natural interpretations of marginalism in problems of pure cooperation.

2   Sharing as a cooperative game

Consider n agents $N = \{1, 2, \ldots, n\}$ who can cooperate to produce a single joint product. The product is assumed to be perfectly divisible. The agents have different skills, so some agents may contribute more to production than others. For each subset of agents $S \subseteq N$, let $v(S)$ be the total amount produced by S when the agents in S pool their skills. We assume that nothing is produced for free; that is, $v(\varnothing) = 0$. The set function v defines a cooperative game on the fixed set N of agents. A *sharing rule* (or "solution concept") is a function ϕ, defined for every cooperative game on the fixed set N, such that $\phi(v) = (a_1, \ldots, a_n) \in R^n$. Here a_i is interpreted to be i's "share" of the total output $v(N)$.

We shall be interested in sharing rules ϕ that obey three properties. First, the output $v(N)$ should be *fully distributed:*

$$\Sigma \phi_i(v) = v(N). \tag{1}$$

This property is also known as *efficiency* [5].

Second, an agent's share should depend only on his structural role in the function v, not on his name. We say that ϕ is *symmetric* if for every permutation π of N, $\phi_{\pi(i)}(\pi v) = \phi_i(v)$.

A third important property is that each agent's share should depend only on his own contribution to output. The problem immediately arises of how to define "own contribution" unambiguously. Consider the following example. Two agents, 1, 2, each working by himself can produce two units per period; working together they can produce ten units per period. Thus $v(1) = v(2) = 2$, $v(1,2) = 10$ (and $v(\varnothing) = 0$). What is i's contribution? Relative to the state of full cooperation (i.e., the set $\{1,2\}$), each agent contributes eight units at the margin. But relative to the state of noncooperation, each agent contributes only two units at the margin. The meaning of "marginal contribution" is ambiguous because one cannot say a priori which of the coalitions will actually form.

One way around this impasse is the following idea, due to Shapley [5]. Imagine that the agents arrive on the scene of cooperation in some random order. If, say, agent 1 arrives first, then 1 is credited with a marginal contribution of $v(1) - v(\varnothing) = 2$ units. Agent 2 arrives next and is credited with a marginal contribution of $v(1,2) - v(1) = 8$ units. In this case, there is a premium on arriving last. To place all of the agents on the same footing, we can average the agents' expected marginal contributions over all $n!$ orderings. The result is the Shapley value

$$\phi_i^*(v) = \sum_{S \subseteq N-i} \frac{|S|!(|N-S|-1)!}{|N|!} [v(S+i) - v(S)]. \tag{2}$$

Instead of determining contributions according to a random ordering of the players, let us postulate merely that each agent's share should depend *in some fashion* on his own contributions. A full description of agent *i*'s marginal contributions, at all possible levels of output, is contained in the *partial derivative* of *v* with respect to *i*, namely, the function v_i defined as follows:

$$v_i(S) = v(S + i) - v(S) \qquad \text{if } i \notin S,$$
$$= v(S) - v(S - i) \qquad \text{if } i \in S. \tag{3}$$

The sharing rule ϕ satisfies the *marginality principle* if $\phi_i(v)$ is solely a function of v_i: in other words, if for every $i \in N$ and every two games v, w on N,

$$v_i \equiv w_i \Rightarrow \phi_i(v) = \phi_i(w). \tag{4}$$

If a sharing rule does *not* satisfy the marginality principle, it is subject to serious distortions. For, if one agent's share depends on another's contributions, the first agent can be rewarded (or punished) for actions undertaken by the second. Such rules force dependencies among agents that are not at all necessary for cooperation, and may penalize individual initiative.

Consider the proportional to marginal product rule:

$$\phi_i(v) = \left[\frac{v_i(N)}{\Sigma_N v_j(N)} \right] v(N). \tag{5}$$

This rule does not satisfy the marginality principle because $\phi_i(v)$ depends on $v(N)/\Sigma_{j \in N} v_j(N)$, which involves other agents' marginal contributions. This dependence can lead to unfortunate results, as shown by the following example. Suppose that two agents can pool their labor and resources to produce grain. Agent A alone can produce 20 bushels per year by his own labor on his own land (net of his own subsistence requirements). Agent B alone can grow 60 bushels per year (net of subsistence). Working together they can produce 100 bushels per year (net of subsistence). The marginal contributions to the grand coalition are 40 for A and 80 for B. Hence, the proportional to marginal product rule implies that A's share of net output is 33⅓ and B's is 66⅔. Now suppose that A works more efficiently than before: for example, A tightens his belt and eats 1 bushel per year less. Thus A adds 1 bushel a year to net output whether working alone or with B. Simultaneously, suppose that B uses up 21 bushels per year more, either through waste or self-indulgence. Combining both effects, the new output function will be

ϕ: 0

A: 21

B: 39

A, B: 80

A's marginal contribution to every coalition of which it is a member has increased by 1, and B's has decreased by 21. Yet the proportional to marginal product rule now gives A 32.8 bushels and B 47.2 bushels. Thus, even though A becomes more efficient, A is penalized for B's becoming less efficient.

The following result [7] shows that this sort of injustice can be avoided in essentially only one way. (This generalizes a result of Loehman and Winston [4], who showed it for a special class of cooperative games.)

Theorem 1. The Shapley value is the unique sharing rule that is symmetric, fully distributes all gains, and satisfies the marginality principle.

Proof: Fix a set of agents $N = \{1,2, \ldots ,n\}$. For every game v defined on N, it is clear that the Shapley value (2) satisfies the properties of symmetry (S), full distribution (D), and marginality (M).

Conversely, let ϕ be a sharing rule defined for all games v on N such that S, D, and M hold. First we shall show that an agent whose marginal contribution to *every* coalition is zero (i.e., a *dummy*) gets nothing. Consider the game w that is identically zero for all $S \subseteq N$. This game is symmetric in all agents, so all agents receive equal shares. Because $\Sigma_{i \in N}\phi_i(w) = 0$, it follows that $\phi_i(w) = 0$ for all $i \in N$. Now suppose that i is a dummy in an arbitrary game v on N. Then v_i is identically zero. Hence $v_i \equiv w_i$, so marginality implies that $\phi_i(v) = \phi_i(w) = 0$. Thus dummies get nothing under ϕ.

Next we show that $\phi(v)$ must be the Shapley value for every game v on N. Consider first the case where v is a *unanimity game*: For some nonempty subset $R \subseteq N$, $v = v_R$, where

$$v_R(S) = \begin{cases} 1 & \text{if } R \subseteq S, \\ 0 & \text{if } R \nsubseteq S. \end{cases}$$

It is easy to see that every $i \notin R$ is a dummy in v_R. Hence, the preceding implies that $\phi_i(v_R) = 0$ for all $i \notin R$. Because v_R is symmetric with respect to all agents $i \in R$, symmetry implies that $\phi_i(v_R) = \phi_j(v_R)$ for all $i, j \in R$. This, together with full distribution, implies that $\phi_i(v_R) = 1/|R|$ for all

$i \in R$. This argument shows that $\phi(v)$ is the Shapley value whenever v_R is a unanimity game. A similar argument shows that $\phi(cv)$ is the Shapley value whenever c is a constant and v is a unanimity game.

For a general game v on N, we may write

$$v = \sum_{\substack{R \subseteq N \\ R \neq \varnothing}} c_R v_R, \qquad (6)$$

where each v_R is a unanimity game and the coefficients c_R are real numbers. Let $I(v)$ be the least number of nonzero terms in such an expression for v. (If v is identically zero, $I(v) = 0$.) The proof that $\phi(v)$ is the Shapley value for v is by induction on $I(v)$. We have already shown that this is the case when $I(v) = 0$ or $I(v) = 1$.

Assume now that $\phi(v)$ is the Shapley value whenever the index of v is at most I, and let v have index $I + 1$ with expression

$$v = \sum_{k=1}^{I+1} c_{R_k} v_{R_k}, \qquad \text{all } c_{R_k} \neq 0.$$

Let $R = \cap_{k=1}^{I+1} R_k$ and choose $i \notin R$. If i is a dummy, then $\phi_i(v) = 0$, which is also the Shapley value of i. If i is not a dummy, consider the game

$$w = \sum_{k: i \in R_k} c_{R_k} v_{R_k}.$$

Since $i \notin R$, the index of w is at most I. Furthermore, $w_i(S) = v_i(S)$ for all $S \subseteq N$, so marginality implies that $\phi_i(v) = \phi_i(w)$. By the induction hypothesis,

$$\phi_i(v) = \phi_i(w) = \sum_{k: i \in R_k} \frac{c_{R_k}}{|R_k|},$$

which is the Shapley value of i.

It remains to show that $\phi_i(v)$ is the Shapley value when $i \in R = \cap_{k=1}^{I+1} R_k$. By symmetry, $\phi_i(v)$ is a constant c for all members of R; likewise the Shapley value is some constant c' for all members of R. Because both allocations sum to $v(N)$ and are equal for all $i \notin R$, it follows that $c = c'$.

Q.E.D.

If it is desired to stay entirely within the class of superadditive games, the foregoing proof may be modified as follows. Every superadditive game v may be written in the form $v = u - \Sigma c_R v_R$, where all $c_R > 0$, u is superadditive, and u is *symmetric* in the sense that $u(S)$ depends only on the cardinality of S. (Every unanimity game v_R is also superadditive.) Proceed by induction on the minimum number of nonzero terms in such an expression, observing that the deletion of any term $c_R v_R$ leaves a superadditive game. The result holds in the base case $v = u$, because symmetry and full distribution imply that $\phi_i(u) = u(N)/|N|$, which accords with the Shapley value.

3   Aumann–Shapley pricing

In this section we show that a similar set of axioms characterizes the Aumann–Shapley pricing mechanism. Consider a firm that produces a single homogeneous product as a function of several resource inputs. Let $y = f(x_1, x_2, \ldots, x_n)$ be the maximum quantity of output that can be produced with x_i units of each resource i ($i = 1, 2, \ldots, n$). Assume that $f(\mathbf{x})$ is defined for all $\mathbf{x}$ on some bounded domain of the form $D = D(\overline{\mathbf{x}}) = \{\mathbf{x} \in \mathbf{R}^n : 0 \leq \mathbf{x} \leq \overline{\mathbf{x}}\}$, where $\overline{\mathbf{x}} > 0$. The *target level* of production is $f(\overline{\mathbf{x}})$. Assume that f has continuous first partial derivatives on D (the one-sided derivative applies on the boundary of D). Assume further that there are no fixed costs–that is, $f(0) = 0$. A pair $(f, \overline{\mathbf{x}})$ satisfying these conditions will be called a *variable-input production problem*.

How much product should be attributed to each of the n inputs? This question arises in a firm that wants to allocate profit to different inputs for purposes of internal accounting and control. Assume for simplicity that output is measured in terms of revenues, and inputs are measured in terms of costs. The firm wants to allocate total revenue $\overline{y} = f(\overline{\mathbf{x}})$ among the various inputs $i = 1, 2, \ldots, n$ so that a net profit can be imputed to each input (or groups of inputs that constitute "profit centers"). In other words, the firm wishes to find a vector of unit prices $(p_1, \ldots, p_n)$ such that $\Sigma_{i \in N} p_i \overline{x}_i = f(\overline{\mathbf{x}})$.

A *pricing rule* is a function ψ defined for all production problems $(f, \overline{\mathbf{x}})$ on some fixed set of inputs $N = \{1, 2, \ldots, n\}$ such that $\psi_i(f, \overline{\mathbf{x}}) = p_i$ is the unit price associated with i. *Full distribution* requires that

$$\sum_{i \in N} \overline{x}_i \psi_i(f, \overline{\mathbf{x}}) = f(\overline{\mathbf{x}}). \tag{7}$$

If $f(\overline{\mathbf{x}})$ is the total revenue from production and $\overline{x}_i$ is the total cost of input i, then $\psi_i(f, \overline{\mathbf{x}})$ may be interpreted as the imputed revenue per unit cost of i, and $\psi_i(f, \overline{\mathbf{x}}) - 1$ is i's *imputed rate of profit*. A pricing rule might be used as part of a compensation or bonus scheme to reward different profit centers according to their imputed profitability. Alternatively, management might treat the rule as an internal accounting method for monitoring the performance of profit centers or divisions over time. In either case it is reasonable to require that the unit price imputed to i depends only on i's *own* contribution to revenue or product. That is, $\psi_i(f,\overline{\mathbf{x}})$ should be a function only of the partial derivative $f_i(\mathbf{x}) = \partial f(\mathbf{x})/\partial x_i$, $\mathbf{0} \le \mathbf{x} \le \overline{\mathbf{x}}$ (and possibly of i itself).

The function ψ satisfies the *marginality principle* if and only if for every $i \in N$ and for every two production functions f and g defined on the same domain $D = \{\mathbf{x} \in R^n: \mathbf{0} \le \mathbf{x} \le \overline{\mathbf{x}}\}$,

$$f_i(\mathbf{x}) = g_i(\mathbf{x}) \text{ for all } \mathbf{x} \in D \quad \text{implies} \quad \psi_i(f,\overline{\mathbf{x}}) = \psi_i(g,\overline{\mathbf{x}}). \tag{8}$$

A method that does *not* have this property is the proportional to marginal product pricing rule:

$$\psi_i(f,\overline{\mathbf{x}}) = \lambda f_i(\overline{\mathbf{x}}) \quad \text{where } \lambda = \frac{f(\overline{\mathbf{x}})}{\Sigma_{j \in N} \overline{x}_j f_j(\overline{x})}.$$

Like its relative in the finite case, this method behaves in an unsatisfactory way when the production function shifts. In particular, it may impute a lower unit revenue to i even though i's marginal revenue product increases over all possible levels of output. The reason is that i's imputed revenue may be dragged down through its dependence on the other factors' marginal revenue products.

We claim that there is only one plausible pricing mechanism that is fully distributive and satisfies (8), namely, Aumann–Shapley pricing:

$$\psi_i^{\text{AS}}(f,\overline{\mathbf{x}}) = \int_0^1 \frac{\partial f(t\overline{\mathbf{x}})}{\partial x_i} \, dt. \tag{9}$$

To establish this fact, we need continuity plus a condition analogous to symmetry. One natural formulation of symmetry is the following: If f is symmetric in the two factors i and j, that is, if

$$f(x_1, \ldots, x_i, \ldots, x_j, \ldots, x_n)$$
$$= f(x_1, \ldots, x_j, \ldots, x_i, \ldots, x_n) \text{ for all } \mathbf{x}, \mathbf{0} \le \mathbf{x} \le \overline{\mathbf{x}},$$

then $\psi_i(f,x) = \psi_j(f,x)$. In fact, we need a somewhat stronger condition that identifies inputs which are essentially the same. Consider the case where two inputs represent the same item expressed in different units. For example, let x_1 be the number of quarts of gasoline and x_2 the number of pints of gasoline used in production. The number of gallons of gasoline is therefore $y = x_1/4 + x_2/8$. If the imputed price per gallon is p, then it is natural to assign a unit price of $p/4$ to x, and $p/8$ to x_2.

In general, define a *linear aggregate* of the input factors $x_1, \ldots, x_n$ to be an input of the form $y_i = \sum_{j=1}^{n} a_{ij} x_j$, where all $a_{ij} \geq 0$. Let $g(\mathbf{y})$ be a production function of m aggregate inputs $y_1, \ldots, y_m$, each of which is a linear combination of inputs $x_1, \ldots, x_n$. Thus $\mathbf{y} = A\mathbf{x}$, where A is a nonnegative matrix. Consider the production function f defined directly on $\mathbf{x}$ as follows: $f(\mathbf{x}) = g(A\mathbf{x})$. The pricing rule ψ is *aggregation invariant* if whenever $A \geq \mathbf{0}$ and $A\bar{\mathbf{x}} = \bar{\mathbf{y}} > \mathbf{0}$, $f = g \circ A$ implies $\psi(f, \bar{\mathbf{x}}) = [\psi(g, A\bar{\mathbf{x}})]A$. In other words, the prices to the $\mathbf{y}$ inputs are imputed to the $\mathbf{x}$ inputs via the linear system A. (A similar property was defined by Billera and Heath [2]). Notice that symmetry follows from aggregation invariance by taking A to be a transposition matrix.

For every $\bar{\mathbf{x}} \in \mathbf{R}^N$, $\bar{\mathbf{x}} > \mathbf{0}$, let $C^1(\bar{\mathbf{x}})$ be the Banach space of all continuously differentiable, real-valued functions f defined on $D = D(\bar{\mathbf{x}})$ such that $f(\mathbf{0}) = 0$, with norm

$$\|f\| = \sup_{\mathbf{x} \in D} |f(\mathbf{x})| + \sum_{i=1}^{n} \sup_{\mathbf{x} \in D} \left| \frac{\partial f(\mathbf{x})}{\partial x_i} \right|.$$

The pricing rule ψ is *continuous* if for every fixed $\bar{\mathbf{x}} > \mathbf{0}$ $\psi(f, \bar{\mathbf{x}})$ is continuous in f in the topology of $C^1(\bar{\mathbf{x}})$.

Theorem 2. Aumann–Shapley pricing is the unique pricing rule that is continuous, aggregation invariant, fully distributive, and satisfies the marginality principle.

Proof: The reader may verify that the Aumann–Shapley pricing rule has the required properties. (Aggregation invariance follows from Corollary 4 in [2].)

Conversely, let ψ be a pricing rule with these properties. Consider first the case where the production function f is a polynomial in $x_1, \ldots, x_n$ and $f(\mathbf{0}) = 0$. Aumann and Shapley [1] showed that in this instance $f(\mathbf{x})$ can be written in the form

$$f(\mathbf{x}) = \sum_{k=1}^{I} c_k P_k(\mathbf{x}), \quad \text{where } P_k(\mathbf{x}) = \left(\sum_{j=1}^{n} b_{kj} x_j \right)^{r_k}, \tag{10}$$

r_k is a positive integer for all k, and all $b_{kj} \geq 0$.

Let the *index I* of f be the least number of nonzero terms in any expression for $f(\mathbf{x})$ of form (10). (If f is identically zero, let $I = 0$.) Assume that the theorem is false for polynomial f and we shall derive a contradiction. Let I^* be the least index ($I^* \geq 0$) for which there exists a problem $(f, \bar{\mathbf{x}})$, such that $\bar{\mathbf{x}} > \mathbf{0}$, f is polynomial with index I^*, and $\psi(f, \bar{\mathbf{x}}) \neq \psi^{AS}(f, \bar{\mathbf{x}})$.

If $I^* = 0$, then f is identically zero. Let $y = \Sigma_{i-1}^n x_i$ and $g(y) = f(x)$. Then g is identically zero, and, by full distribution, $y\phi(g,y) = g(y) = 0$. Since $y > 0$, it follows that $\psi(g,y) = 0$. By aggregation invariance, it follows that for all i, $\psi_i(f,\overline{x}) = 0 = \psi_i^{AS}(f,\overline{x})$, a contradiction.

Assume then that $I^* > 0$. Consider an expression of form (10) for f. Let J^+ be the subset of indices i for which x_i has a positive coefficient $b_{ki} > 0$ in *every* term $c_k P_k(x)$, and let J^0 be the set of all other indices. If $i \in J^0$, then by deleting the terms $c_k P_k(x)$ in which x_i has a zero coefficient, we obtain a polynomial function $g(x)$ with index less than I^* such that, for this particular i,

$$g_i(x) = f_i(x) \qquad \text{for all } x \in D(\overline{x}).$$

Thus by the induction assumption $\psi_i(g,\overline{x}) = \psi_i^{AS}(g,\overline{x})$. From the marginality principle it follows that

$$\psi_i(f,\overline{x}) = \psi_i(g,\overline{x}) = \psi_i^{AS}(g,\overline{x}) = \psi_i^{AS}(f,\overline{x}).$$

If J^+ is empty, it follows that $\psi(f,\overline{x}) = \psi^{AS}(f,\overline{x})$, contrary to assumption. If J^+ consists of a single index, say i, then the fact that ψ and ψ^{AS} must both satisfy (7) implies (because $\overline{x}_i > 0$) that $\psi_i(f,\overline{x}) = \psi_i^{AS}(f,\overline{x})$.

The case $J^+ \geq 2$ remains. Without loss of generality let $1 \in J^+$, so $b_{k1} > 0$ for all k, $1 \leq k \leq I^*$. Define an aggregate product y_1 as follows:

$$y_1 = x_1 + \sum_{j-2}^n a_{1j}x_j, \qquad \text{where } a_{1j} = \min_{1 \leq k \leq I^*} \left\{\frac{b_{kj}}{b_{k1}}\right\} \geq 0.$$

Let $y_j = x_j$ for $2 \leq j \leq n$, and let A be the nonnegative, $n \times n$ matrix such that $y = Ax$. Let

$$g(y) = \sum_{k=1}^{I^*} c_k Q_k(y), \qquad (11)$$

where

$$Q_k(y) = \left[b_{k1}y_1 + \sum_{j-2}^n (b_{kj} - b_{k1}a_{1j})y_j\right]^{r_k} \qquad \text{for } 1 \leq k \leq I^*.$$

Then $g(Ax) = f(x)$. By choice of the coefficients a_{1j}, y_1 is the only variable that has positive coefficients in every term of (11). By the preceding argument, we can conclude that for all $\overline{y} > 0$ and all i,

$$\psi_i(g,\overline{y}) = \psi_i^{AS}(g,\overline{y}).$$

For all $\bar{x} > 0$ let $\bar{y} = A\bar{x} > 0$ and conclude by aggregation invariance for ψ and ψ^{AS} that

$$\psi(f,\bar{x}) = \psi(g,\bar{y})A = \psi^{AS}(g,\bar{y})A = \psi^{AS}(f,\bar{x}),$$

a contradiction. This establishes that ψ is identical with Aumann–Shapley pricing for all problems $(f,\bar{x})$ in which f is a polynomial in $C^1(\bar{x})$. Since the polynomials are dense in $C^1(\bar{x})$ and both $\psi(f,\bar{x})$ and $\psi^{AS}(f,\bar{x})$ are continuous in f, it follows that $\psi(f,\bar{x}) = \psi^{AS}(f,\bar{x})$ for all f in $C^1(\bar{x})$. This concludes the proof of Theorem 2.

Several variants of Theorem 2 can be obtained by strengthening the marginality principle. One natural variation is to require that the unit price of each product i be monotone nondecreasing with respect to i's marginal contributions. We say that a pricing rule ψ is *monotonic* if for every $i \in N$, every positive $\bar{x} \in \mathbf{R}^N$, and every $f, g \in C^1(\bar{x})$,

$$\frac{\partial f(x)}{\partial x_i} \geq \frac{\partial g(x)}{\partial x_i} \text{ for all } x \in D(\bar{x}) \text{ implies } \psi_i(f,\bar{x}) \geq \psi_i(g,\bar{x}). \quad (12)$$

If we assume monotonicity instead of marginality, then the continuity assumption may be dropped in Theorem 2 (see [8] Theorem 2). The reason is that every f in $C^1(\bar{x})$ may be sandwiched between two sequences of polynomials in $C^1(\bar{x})$ that converge to f from above and below in the topology of $C^1(\bar{x})$.

The marginality principle may be strengthened in another way to incorporate symmetry. We say that ψ satisfies the *symmetric marginality principle* if every two inputs with equal partial derivatives are priced equally. That is, for every $i, j \in N$, every positive $\bar{x} \in \mathbf{R}^N$, and every $f, g \in C^1(\bar{x})$

$$\frac{\partial f(x)}{\partial x_i} = \frac{\partial g(x)}{\partial x_j} \text{ for all } x \in D(\bar{x}) \text{ implies } \psi_i(f,\bar{x}) = \psi_j(g,\bar{x}). \quad (13)$$

The symmetric marginality principle, together with continuity and full distribution, uniquely characterizes Aumann–Shapley pricing. The method of proof is different than that used to derive Theorem 2 (see [8], Theorem 1).

Finally, we may combine (12) and (13) into the following single condition: for every $i, j \in N$, every positive $\bar{x} \in \mathbf{R}^N$, and every $f, g \in C^1(\bar{x})$

$$\frac{\partial f(x)}{\partial x_i} \geq \frac{\partial g(x)}{\partial x_j} \text{ for all } x \in D(\bar{x}) \text{ implies } \psi_i(f,\bar{x}) \geq \psi_j(g,\bar{x}). \quad (14)$$

This allows us to drop both aggregation invariance and continuity. That is, (14) and full distribution uniquely characterize Aumann–Shapley pricing on $C^1(\bar{x})$ (see [8], Theorem 1).

REFERENCES

1. R. J. Aumann and L. S. Shapley, *Values of Non-Atomic Games,* Princeton, N.J.: Princeton University Press, 1974.
2. L. J. Billera and D. C. Heath, "Allocation of shared costs: a set of axioms yielding a unique procedure," *Mathematics of Operations Research 7* (1982), 32–39.
3. L. D. James and R. R. Lee, *Economics of Water Resources Planning,* New York: McGraw-Hill, 1971.
4. E. Loehman and A. Winston, "An axiomatic approach to cost allocation for public investment," *Public Finance Quarterly* (1974), 236–51.
5. L. S. Shapley, "A value for n-person games," in H. W. Kuhn and A. W. Tucker (eds.), *Contributions to the Theory of Games,* Vol. II, Annals of Mathematics Studies No. 28, Princeton, N.J.: Princeton University Press, 1953. (reprinted as Chapter 2 of this volume)
6. P. Straffin and J. P. Heaney, "Game theory and the Tennessee Valley Authority," *International Journal of Game Theory 10* (1981), 35–43.
7. H. P. Young, "Monotonic solutions of cooperative games," *International Journal of Game Theory 14* (1985), 65–72.
8. H. P. Young, "Producer incentives in cost allocation," *Econometrica 53* (1985), 757–65.

CHAPTER 18

The Aumann–Shapley prices: a survey

Yair Tauman

1   Introduction

The theory of values of nonatomic games as developed by Aumann and Shapley was first applied by Billera, Heath, and Raanan (1978) to set equitable telephone billing rates that share the cost of service among users. Billera and Heath (1982) and Mirman and Tauman (1982a) "translated" the axiomatic approach of Aumann and Shapley from values of nonatom games to a price mechanism on the class of differentiable cost functions and hence provided a normative justification, using economic terms only, for the application of the theory of nonatomic games to cost allocation problems. New developments in the theory of games inspired parallel developments to cost allocation applications. For instance, the theory of semi-values by Dubey, Neyman, and Weber (1981) inspired the work of Samet and Tauman (1982), which characterized the class of all "semi-price" mechanisms (i.e., price mechanisms that do not necessarily satisfy the break-even requirement) and led to an axiomatic characterization of the marginal cost prices. The theory of Dubey and Neyman (1984) of nonatomic economies inspired the work by Mirman and Neyman (1983) in which they characterized the marginal cost prices on the class of cost functions that arise from long-run production technologies. Young's (1984) characterization of the Shapley value by the monotonicity axiom inspired his characterization (Young 1985a) of the Aumann–Shapley price mechanism on the class of differentiable cost functions. Hart and Mas-Colell (1987) used their characterization of the Shapley value via the potential function approach to characterize the Aumann–Shapley prices of differentiable cost functions. Recently, Monderer and Neyman (Chapter 15 this volume) applied Owen's multilinear extension to provide a simple alternative proof to the existence and the uniqueness of the value on the class pNA of nonatomic games as well as to characterize the Aumann–Shapley prices. Finally, Mirman and Neyman (1984) proved the diagonal property of cost allocation prices in a way analogous to

279

Neyman's (1977) result, which asserts that continuous values of non-atomic games are diagonal.

Some developments, however, in the theory of Aumann–Shapley prices cannot be identified with a parallel development in game theory. In this category we have, for example, the application of the Aumann–Shapley prices for cost allocation in transportation models (Samet, Tauman, and Zang 1984), the extension of the Aumann–Shapley prices to cost functions that include a fixed-cost component (Mirman, Samet, and Tauman 1983), and the use of the Aumann–Shapley prices as sustainable prices in the theory of contestable markets (Mirman, Tauman, and Zang 1985a, 1986).

This chapter surveys the works related to the Aumann–Shapley prices.

The axiomatic approach to cost-sharing prices as discussed by Billera and Heath (1982) and by Mirman and Tauman (1982a) can be regarded as an extension of the average cost pricing to the multiproduct case (Mirman et al. 1986). Let $AC(F,\alpha) = F(\alpha)/\alpha$ be the average cost pricing rule for the single-product case, where F is a differentiable cost function and $\alpha \neq 0$ is a specific production level. Consider the following four properties of $AC(\cdot,\cdot)$.

I   *Cost sharing.* $\alpha AC(F,\alpha) = F(\alpha)$ for each $\alpha > 0$.

II   *Additivity.* $AC(F + G,\alpha) = AC(F,\alpha) + AC(G,\alpha)$.

III   *Rescaling.* If $G(x) = F(\lambda x)$, then $AC(G,\alpha) = \lambda AC(F,\lambda \alpha)$.

IV   *Continuity.* $AC(\cdot,\alpha)$ is continuous with respect to the C^1 norm (i.e., if $F_n \to F$ in the C^1 norm on $[0,\alpha]$, then $AC(F_n,\alpha) \to AC(F,\alpha)$ as $n \to \infty$).

These four properties of the average cost pricing rule for the single-product case are used as the basis of the multiproduct extension.

Let $\mathcal{F}$ be a family of functions F defined for some M on a full-dimensional comprehensive subset C^F of E^M_+ (i.e., $\alpha \in C^F$ implies $C_\alpha \subseteq C^F$, where $C_\alpha = \{x \in E^M_+ | x \leq \alpha\}$). By a *price mechanism* on $\mathcal{F}$ we mean a function $P(\cdot,\cdot)$ that assigns to each cost function F in $\mathcal{F}$ and each vector α in C^F with $\alpha \gg 0$ a price vector,

$$P(F,\alpha) = (P_1(F,\alpha), \ldots , P_M(F,\alpha)).$$

We impose the four properties of the average cost pricing on $P(\cdot,\cdot)$.

Axiom 1 (Cost sharing). For every $F \in \mathcal{F}$ and every $\alpha \in C^F$,

$$\alpha \cdot P(F,\alpha) = F(\alpha)$$

(i.e., total cost equals total revenue).

Axiom 2 (Additivity). If F and G are in $\mathcal{F}$ and $\alpha \in C^{F+G}$, then

$$P(F + G, \alpha) = P(F, \alpha) + P(G, \alpha),$$

where $C^{F+G} = C^F \cap C^G$. [If the cost is broken into two components (e.g., management and production), then the prices are the sum of the prices determined by the two components separately.]

Axiom 3 (Rescaling). Let F be in $\mathcal{F}$ with $C^F \subseteq E^M_+$. Let $\lambda_1, \ldots, \lambda_M$ be M positive real numbers. Define $C = \{(x_1, \ldots, x_M) | (\lambda_1 x_1, \ldots, \lambda_M x_M) \in C^F\}$, and let G be the function defined on $C^G = C$ by

$$G(x_1, \ldots, x_M) = F(\lambda_1 x_1, \ldots, \lambda_M x_M).$$

Then for each $\alpha \in C^G$ and each m, $1 \le m \le M$,

$$P_m(G, \alpha) = \lambda_m P_m(F, (\lambda_1 \alpha_1, \ldots, \lambda_M \alpha_M)).$$

(A change in the scale of the commodities should yield an equivalent change in the prices.)

Axiom 4′ (Continuity). Let $F \in \mathcal{F}$ be defined on C^F, and let $(F_n)_{n=1}^\infty$ be a sequence of functions in $\mathcal{F}$ s.t. for each n $C^{F_n} = C^F$ and suppose that $F_n \to F$, as $n \to \infty$, in the C^1 norm on C_α. Then $P(F_n, \alpha) \to P(F, \alpha)$ as $n \to \infty$.

The continuity axiom can be replaced by the following positivity axiom.

Axiom 4 (Positivity). If $F \in \mathcal{F}$ is nondecreasing on C_α for some $\alpha \in C^F$, then $P(F, \alpha) \ge 0$.

To connect the multiproduct case with the single-product case, we require that two (or more) commodities that are "the same commodity" should have the same average cost. Because average cost prices depend only on the cost structure, being "the same commodity" means playing the same role in the production cost. As an illustration, consider the production of a specific car with n different colors. The cost of producing $x = \sum_{m=1}^M x_m$ cars, where x_m is the number of cars of the mth color, can be represented by an M-variable function F as $F(x_1, \ldots, x_M)$. However, if $G(x)$ is the cost of producing a total of x cars, regardless of their colors, then

$$F(x_1, \ldots, x_M) = G\left(\sum_{m=1}^M x_m\right).$$

In this case it is required that the average cost of a blue car be the same as the average cost of a red car, and so on.

Axiom 5 (Weak consistency). Let $F \in \mathcal{F}$ and assume that $C^F \subseteq E_+^M$. Let C be the subset of E_+^1 defined by $C = \{y \in E^1 | y = \Sigma_{m=1}^M x_m, x \in C^F\}$, and let G be a function on C such that $F(x_1, x_2, \ldots, x_M) = G(\Sigma_{m=1}^M x_m)$. Then for each m, $1 \leq m \leq M$, and for each $\alpha \in C^F$,

$$P_m(F,\alpha) = P\left(G, \sum_{m=1}^M \alpha_m\right).$$

Definition. Let $\mathcal{F}_0$ be the subclass of $\mathcal{F}$ that consists of all functions F such that

   (a) $F(0) = 0$; that is, F does not contain a fixed-cost component.
   (b) F is continuously differentiable on C_α for each $\alpha \in C^F$.

Theorem 1 (Mirman and Tauman 1982a). There exists one and only one price mechanism $P(\cdot,\cdot)$ on $\mathcal{F}_0$ that satisfies Axioms 1–5. This is the Aumann–Shapley price mechanism; that is,

$$P_m(F,\alpha) = \int_0^1 \frac{\partial F}{\partial x_m}(t\alpha)\, dt, \qquad m = 1, \ldots, M,$$

for each $F \in \mathcal{F}_0$ and $\alpha \in C^F (\subseteq E_+^M)$. Furthermore, the theorem holds if Axiom 4 is replaced by Axiom 4'.

Theorem 1 is Theorem 1.2 of Mirman and Tauman (1982a). The Aumann–Shapley price mechanism (ASPM) is therefore considered to be a natural extension of the average cost pricing from the single-product case to the multiproduct case. A similar axiomatic approach to ASPM was independently obtained by Billera and Heath (1982).

Billera et al. (1978) were the first to introduce the AS prices as an application of the theory of values of nonatomic games developed by Aumann and Shapley (1974). They proposed equitable telephone billing rates that share the cost of service. One can use their idea to allocate costs through prices when a finite number of any infinitely divisible commodities are produced. Their idea can be roughly described as follows. Suppose that $F(x_1, \ldots, x_M)$ is a cost function satisfying $F(0) = 0$. The variables x_m denote nonnegative quantities of the commodities produced. Let $\alpha = (\alpha_1, \ldots, \alpha_M)$ be a vector of quantities of these commodities. Suppose that these are various types of corn that are piled together into one heap. Identify this heap with a continuum of players and associate with it a cooperative game v_α defined as follows: For each subset S of the heap let $v_\alpha(S)$ be the cost of producing S. The Aumann–Shapley value for this nonatomic game is a measure defined on the space of players (the heap) that assigns to each coalition its contribution to the total production cost of the heap (i.e., to the cost of producing α). The AS price of the mth commodity is the value of a unit of this commodity (i.e., the contribution of this unit to the total cost). The existence of a value for the game v_α described here is guaranteed whenever v_α belongs to the class pNAD of nonatomic games. Moreover, on this class of games, there is only one continuous value (this follows from Propositions 43.13 and 44.22 of Aumann and Shapley together with Neyman 1977). Using the value formula on pNAD, the value of the game v_α assigns to a unit of the mth commodity the magnitude

$$P_m(F,\alpha) = \int_0^1 \frac{\partial F}{\partial x_m}(t\alpha)\,dt,$$

which is the AS price of the mth commodity.

2   Other characterizations of the Aumann–Shapley price mechanism

Since the works of Billera and Heath (1982) and Mirman and Tauman (1982a), other alternative characterizations of the AS pricing rule have been obtained. Samet and Tauman (1982) suggested two alternative requirements to replace the additivity axiom. Young (1985a) offered a characterization based on a monotonicity axiom. Hart and Mas-Colell (1987) offered to use their concept of potential functions to characterize the ASPM and Monderer and Neyman (Chapter 15 this volume) made use of the multiextension function (see Owen 1972) to relax Young's result.

We start with Samet and Tauman (1982). They showed that the additivity axiom can be replaced by the assembling and the separability axioms. The first one asserts that if two commodities are combined to one (i.e., a unit of the "new" commodity consists of a unit of the first commodity and a unit of the second commodity), then the price of the new commodity should be the sum of the prices of the two original commodities.

Axiom 6 (Assembling). Let F be a function on $C^F \subseteq E^k_+$, where $k = \Sigma^M_{m=1} n_m$. Any $x \in C^F$ is of the form $x = (x_{11}, \ldots, x_{1n_1}, x_{21}, \ldots, x_{2n_2}, \ldots, x_{M1}, \ldots, x_{Mn_M})$. Define

$$G(x_1, \ldots, x_M) = F(\underbrace{x_1, \ldots, x_1}_{n_1}, \underbrace{x_2, \ldots, x_2}_{n_2}, \underbrace{x_M, \ldots, x_M}_{n_M}).$$

Then for each m, $1 \le m \le M$, and for each $\alpha \in C^G$,

$$P_m(G, (\alpha_1, \ldots, \alpha_M)) =$$
$$\sum^{n_m}_{j=1} P_{m,j}(F, (\alpha_1, \ldots, \alpha_1, \alpha_2, \ldots, \alpha_2, \alpha_M, \ldots, \alpha_M)).$$

The second axiom deals with the case where the set of commodities consists of two independent subsets (i.e., the production processes of the two groups of commodities are independent). Then it is required that the price of each commodity depend only on the part of the production cost that it affects. To state it formally, we need the following notations. Let $N = \{i_1, \ldots, i_n\}$, where $i_1 < i_2 < \cdots < i_n$ is a subset of $\{1, 2, \ldots, M\}$, and let $x \in E^M$. Denote by x_N the element in E^n defined by $x_N = (x_{i_1}, \ldots, x_{i_n})$.

Axiom 7 (Separability). Let N_1 and N_2 be two disjoint sets with M_1 and M_2 elements, respectively, such that $N_1 \cup N_2 = \{1, \ldots, M\}$. Let F, G, and H be defined on C^F, C^G, and C^H, respectively, where $C^F \subseteq E^M_+$, $C^G \subseteq E^{M_1}_+$, and $C^H \subseteq E^{M_2}_+$. Suppose that $C^F_{N_1} = C^G$, $C^F_{N_2} = C^H$, and, for each $x \in C^F$,

$$F(x_N) = G(x_{N_1}) + H(x_{N_2}).$$

Then, for each $\alpha \in C^F$,

$$P_{N_1}(F, \alpha) = P(G, \alpha_{N_1}) \quad \text{and} \quad P_{N_2}(F, \alpha) = P(H, \alpha_{N_2}).$$

Proposition 1 (Samet and Tauman 1982). Axioms 6 and 7 imply the additivity axiom.

The proof of this proposition is stated in Samet and Tauman (1982) for the case where the functions are defined on E^M_+ (for some M), but it can be directly extended to functions with any comprehensive domains.

Young (1985a) introduced the monotonicity requirement and showed that this together with a stronger version of the weak consistency axiom and the cost-sharing requirement are sufficient for the characterization of the ASPM.

Axiom 8 (Monotonicity). Let F and G be two functions in $\mathcal{F}_0$ s.t. $C^F = C^G \subseteq E^M_+$. Let $\alpha \in C^F$ and suppose that for any x, $0 \leq x \leq \alpha$, and for any m, $1 \leq m \leq M$, $\partial F(x)/\partial x_m \geq \partial G(x)/\partial x_m$. Then $P_m(F,\alpha) \geq P_m(G,\alpha)$.

The next axiom used by Young was first introduced by Billera and Heath (1982). This is the aggregation invariance requirement. Consider a function G defined on a comprehensive set C^G. Suppose that $G(y_1, \ldots, y_n)$ is the joint cost of producing n types of gasoline where the quantity y_i of each type is a blend of M refinery grades $x_1, \ldots, x_M$, $y_i = \Sigma^M_{m=1} a_{im} x_m$, where $a_{im} \geq 0$. Let $A = (a_{im})$ and define

$$F(x_1, \ldots, x_M) = G(Ax).$$

That is, $F(x_1, \ldots, x_M)$ is the cost of producing $\Sigma^M_{m=1} a_{im} x_m$ units of the ith type of gasoline for all i, $1 \leq i \leq n$. A price mechanism satisfies the aggregation invariance property if costs are aggregated in the same manner as product quantities. We state this formally as follows:

Axiom 9 (Aggregation invariance). Let $C^F \subseteq E^M_+$ and $C^G \subseteq E^n_+$ be the domains of F and G, respectively. Let A be a nonnegative matrix of dimension $n \cdot M$. Suppose that $C^G = A \cdot C^F$ and that, for any $x \in C^F$, $F(x) = G(Ax)$. Then, for any $\alpha \in C^F$,

$$P(F,\alpha) = (P(G,A\alpha)) \cdot A.$$

Theorem 2 (Young 1985a). The Aumann–Shapley price mechanism is the unique mechanism on $\mathcal{F}_0$ that satisfies Axioms 1 (cost-sharing), 8 (monotonicity), and 9 (aggregation invariance).

Monderer and Neyman (Chapter 15 this volume) proved Young's result with a requirement weaker than aggregation invariance. They require the rescaling axiom and the consistency axiom, first introduced by Mirman and Neyman (1983). To state this axiom, we need the following notations. Let $T = (T_1, \ldots, T_n)$ be an ordered partition of $\{1, \ldots, M\}$. That is, T is an ordered n-tuple of nonempty disjoint subsets of $\{1, \ldots, M\}$ such that $\cup_{i=1}^{n} T_i = \{1, \ldots, M\}$. The ordered partition T induces a mapping $T: E^n \to E^M$ defined by

$$Tx = (x(T_1), x(T_2), \ldots, x(T_M)),$$

where $x(T_i) = \Sigma_{j \in T_i} x_j$.

Axiom 5′ (Consistency). Let $C^F \subseteq E_+^n$ and $C^G \subseteq E_+^M$ be the domains of F and G, respectively. Let $T = (T_1, \ldots, T_n)$ be an ordered partition of $\{1, \ldots, M\}$ such that $TC^F = C^G$. If, for any $x \in C^G$, $G(x) = F(Tx)$, then for any $\alpha \in C^G$,

$$P_m(G, \alpha) = P_i(F, T\alpha) \qquad \text{where } m \in T_i.$$

For a better understanding of Axiom 5′, notice that it is equivalent to the following two requirements.

Axiom 5″. Let $C^F \subseteq E_+^{M-1}$ and $C^G \subseteq E_+^M$ be the domains of F and G, respectively. Suppose that $C^F = \{y \in E_+^{M-1} | y = (x_1 + x_2, x_3, \ldots, x_M), x \in C^G\}$ and that $G(x) = F(x_1 + x_2, x_3, \ldots, x_M)$, $x \in C^G$. Then for any $\alpha \in C^G$,

$$P_1(G, \alpha) = P_2(G, \alpha) = P_1(F, (\alpha_1 + \alpha_2, \alpha_3, \ldots, \alpha_M)).$$

Axiom 5″ differs from Axiom 5 (weak consistency) in only a technical manner. Axiom 5 allows for irrelevant split of one commodity in the production of a single good, whereas Axiom 5″ allows a split of one commodity in the production of any number of goods.

Axiom 10 (Symmetry). Let $C^F \subseteq E_+^M$ and $C^G \subseteq E_+^M$ be the domains of F and G, respectively. Let π be a permutation of $\{1, \ldots, M\}$. For $x \in E^M$ let $\pi x \in E^M$ be defined by $\pi x_m = x_{\pi(m)}$. Suppose that $C^G = \pi C^F$ and, for any $x \in C^F$, $F(x) = G(\pi x)$. Then for any $\alpha \in C^F$,

$$P(F, \alpha) = \pi P(G, \pi \alpha).$$

The following is an easy observation.

Proposition 2. Axioms 5″ and 10 are equivalent to Axiom 5′.

Observe that Axiom 9 is stronger than Axiom 5′, because it implies Axioms 5″ and 10. In addition, Axiom 9 implies Axiom 3, but it is not equivalent to Axioms 3, 5″, and 10 (see Monderer and Neyman chapter 15 this volume).

Theorem 3 (Monderer and Neyman 1987, Chapter 15 this volume). The Aumann–Shapley price mechanism is the unique mechanism on $\mathscr{F}_0$ that satisfies Axioms 1, 3, 8, and 5′.

A different characterization of the ASPM is via the potential approach due to Hart and Mas-Colell (1987). A *potential* of a cost function $F \in \mathscr{F}_0$, which is defined on C^F, is a differentiable function $P^F: C^F \to E^1$ such that $x\nabla P^F(x) = F(x)$ for each $x \in C^F$, where $\nabla P^F(x)$ is the gradient of P^F at x. It can be shown that any cost function $F \in \mathscr{F}_0$ is associated with a unique potential P^F, defined by

$$P^F(x) = \int_0^1 \frac{1}{t} F(tx) \, dt, \qquad x \in C^F.$$

Furthermore, among all price mechanisms on $\mathscr{F}_0$ that satisfy the cost-sharing requirement (Axiom 1) the unique solution to the functional equation $P(F,\alpha) = \nabla P^F(\alpha)$ is the ASPM.

3   Price mechanisms without the break-even assumption

In this section we review the characterization of Samet and Tauman (1982) of price mechanisms that satisfy Axioms 2–5 (i.e., price mechanisms that satisfy additivity, rescaling, positivity, and weak consistency but not cost-sharing). This characterization stems from that of Dubey et al. (1981) of semivalues on pNA.

Theorem 4 (Samet and Tauman 1982). $P(\cdot,\cdot)$ is a price mechanism of $\mathscr{F}_0$ that satisfies Axioms 2–5 if and only if there is a nonnegative measure μ on $([0,1],\mathscr{B})$ ($\mathscr{B}$ is the set of all Borel subsets of $[0,1]$) such that for each $F \in \mathscr{F}_0$ with a domain $C^F \subseteq E_+^M$ and for each $\alpha \in C^F$,

(*) $$P_m(F,\alpha) = \int_0^1 \frac{\partial F}{\partial x_m}(t\alpha) \, d\mu(t), \qquad m = 1, \ldots, M.$$

Moreover, for a given price mechanism $P(\cdot,\cdot)$ that satisfies Axioms 2–5 there is a unique measure μ that satisfies (*). In other words, (*) defines a one-to-one mapping from the set of all nonnegative measures on $([0,1],\mathscr{B})$ onto the set of all price mechanisms on $\mathscr{F}_0$ satisfying Axioms 2–5.

If μ is the Lebesgue measure on $[0,1]$, then the corresponding price mechanism is the ASPM. If μ is the atomic probability measure whose whole mass is concentrated at the point $t = 1$, then the corresponding price mechanism is the marginal cost pricing. The next goal is to use Theorem 4 for the characterization of the marginal cost pricing rule. For this purpose we introduce a stronger version of the positivity axiom.

Axiom 4″. Let $C^F \subseteq E_+^M$ be the domain of F and let $\alpha \in C^F$. If F is nondecreasing at each $x \leq \alpha$ in a neighborhood of α, then $P(F,\alpha) \geq 0$.

Theorem 5 (Samet and Tauman 1982). A price mechanism $P(\cdot,\cdot)$ on $\mathscr{F}_0$ satisfies Axioms 2, 3, 4″, and 5 if and only if there is a constant $c \geq 0$ such that for each $F \in \mathscr{F}_0$ with $C^F \subseteq E_+^M$ and for each $\alpha \in C^F$,

$$P_m(F,\alpha) = c\,\frac{\partial F}{\partial x_m}(x). \qquad m = 1, \ldots, M.$$

If in addition to Axioms 2, 3, 4″, and 5 we impose a normalization condition, [e.g., for the identity (one-variable) function $H(x) = x$, $P(H,1) = 1$], then $c = 1$ (i.e., the marginal cost pricing is the only price mechanism that satisfies these requirements).

4   The Aumann–Shapley price mechanism on classes of nondifferentiable cost functions

We have discussed various characterizations of the ASPM on the class $\mathscr{F}_0$ of differentiable functions. This analysis was extended to cost functions that are not necessarily differentiable. Mirman and Neyman (1983) characterized the ASPM on the class H^c of cost functions that arise from long-run production technologies. These are cost functions that are nondecreasing, homogeneous of degree 1, and convex and do not include a fixed-cost component. Notice that the ASPM coincides with the marginal cost price mechanism on cost functions that are homogeneous of degree 1. Thus, the characterization of the ASPM on H^c is equivalent to that of MC prices on H^c. In their study, Mirman and Neyman extended the definition of price mechanism to be a map ψ that associates with each (F,α), $F \in H^c$

and $\alpha \in C^F$, a *set* of prices. The axioms were adjusted accordingly. For example, additivity was replaced by superadditivity, which asserts that

$$\psi(F + G,\alpha) \supseteq \psi(F,\alpha) + \psi(G,\alpha).$$

They defined a certain topology on the set of problems (F,α), where $F \in H^c$ and $\alpha \in C^F$, and showed that the ASPM is the unique price mechanism that satisfies (i) superadditivity, (ii) consistency, (iii) continuity, (iv) rescaling, and the following normalization condition (v). If F is linear, then $\psi(F,\alpha) = \nabla F(\alpha)$. Their work was inspired by a parallel development of Dubey and Neyman (1984) in the theory of nonatomic economies.

The next work by Samet et al. (1984) applied the ASPM to cost allocation problems in transportation models. To motivate this work, consider the following example.

Example. Suppose there are two destinations A_1 and A_2 and two origins B_1 and B_2, and a certain commodity available at the origins is shipped to the destinations. The following 2×2 matrix $C = (C_{nm})$ represents the cost of shipping a unit from origin n to destination m:

	A_1	A_2	
B_1	$C_{11} = 10$	$C_{12} = 15$	$b_1 = 20$
B_2	$C_{21} = 1000$	$C_{22} = 1500$	$b_2 = 20$
	$x_1 = 20$	$x_2 = 20$	

Each origin has 20 units of available resources, and each destination demands 20 units. It is easy to verify that the optimal solution is obtained by transporting 20 units from B_2 to A_1 with associated cost of $20 \cdot 1000 = 20{,}000$, and by transporting 20 units from B_1 to A_2 with costs $20 \cdot 15 = 300$. However, destination A_1 should not be allocated 20,000 out of the total cost of 20,300.

The solution turns out to be optimal because the penalty paid, once A_2 is not supplied from its cheapest origin, is much higher than the penalty paid if case A_1 is not supplied from its cheapest origin. Therefore, A_1 should be supplied from the more expensive origin for him, namely from

B_2, in order to achieve overall minimization of cost. Hence, destination A_2 subsidizes destination A_1. But this cannot be a reason to charge A_1 a price higher than A_2 is charged. On the contrary, transportation from each of the origins to A_1 is cheaper than to A_2, so it is expected that the price per unit charged at A_1 should be less than the one charged at A_2.

It is suggested (and later on will be axiomatically justified) to use here the AS prices for the allocation of the total cost of 20,300 between the destinations. To that end, we consider the cost function that associates with each feasible demand vector $x = (x_1, x_2)$, $x_1 + x_2 \le 40$, $x_1 \ge 0$, and $x_2 \ge 0$, the minimum cost $F(x_1, x_2)$ of shipping x_1 units to the first destination and x_2 units to the second destination. In this case

$$C^F = \{(x_1, x_2) | x_1 + x_2 \le 40, x_1 \ge 0, x_2 \ge 0\},$$

and it is easy to check that

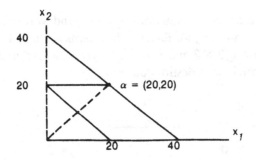

$$F(x_1, x_2) = \begin{cases} 10x_1 + 15x_2, & x_1 \ge 0, x_2 \ge 0, x_1 + x_2 \le 20, \\ 1000x_1 + 1005x_2 - 19,800, & \\ & 0 \le x_2 \le 20, 20 \le x_1 + x_2 \le 40, \\ 1000x_1 + 1500x_2 - 29,700, & \\ & x_1 \ge 0, x_2 \ge 20, x_1 + x_2 \le 40. \end{cases}$$

Consequently, for $\alpha = (20,20)$,

$$\nabla F(t\alpha) = (10,15) \qquad \text{for } 0 \le t < \tfrac{1}{2},$$
$$= (1000,1005) \qquad \text{for } \tfrac{1}{2} < t \le 1,$$

and thus the AS prices are given by

$$P(F, \alpha) = \frac{1}{2}\binom{10}{15} + \frac{1}{2}\binom{1000}{1005} = \binom{505}{510}.$$

The general transportation model under consideration consists of N origins $B_1, \ldots, B_N$ and M destinations $A_1, \ldots, A_M$, an $N \times M$ matrix

$C = (C_{nm})$, where C_{nm} is the cost of shipping a unit from the origin B_n to the destination A_m, a vector $b = (b_1, \ldots, b_N)$ of the available resources in the N origins (b_n in B_n) that is assumed to be fixed, and a vector of quantities $x = (x_1, \ldots, x_M)$, where x_m is the demand at A_m satisfying the condition $\Sigma_m^M = x_m \leq \Sigma_{n-1}^N b_n$. Let $F(x_1, \ldots, x_M)$ be the minimal cost of supplying x. Formally,

$$F(x_1, \ldots, x_M) = \min \sum_{n,m} C_{nm} y_{nm}$$

$$\text{subject to } \sum_{n=1}^{N} y_{nm} = x_m, \qquad m = 1, \ldots, M,$$

$$\sum_{m=1}^{M} y_{nm} \leq b_n, \qquad n = 1, \ldots, N,$$

$$y_{nm} \geq 0.$$

It is well known that the cost function F, which is defined on the simplex $\{x \in E_+^M | \Sigma_{m-1}^M x_m \leq \Sigma_{n-1}^N b_n\}$, is piecewise linear and convex.

Cost functions derived from the solution of general linear programming (LP) problems are piecewise linear. In many cases, however, one may have an LP cost function F together with a vector α in its domain such that the linear segment $[0,\alpha]$ contains a continuum of kinks (of F). For example, let

$$F(x_1, x_2) = \min y$$
$$\text{s.t. } y \geq x_1, y \geq x_2, \qquad \text{(TP)}$$

and let $\alpha = (1,1)$. Then $F(x_1, x_2) = \max(x_1, x_2)$, and F is not differentiable along the line segment $[0,\alpha]$. Thus, one cannot apply the AS formula to obtain prices for these F and α. Fortunately, this is not the case for TP cost functions or for the generalized TP cost functions (as shown later). The latter are cost functions of the form

$$F(x) = \min \sum_{n=1}^{N} \sum_{m=1}^{M} C_{nm} y_{nm}$$

$$\text{subject to } \sum_{n=1}^{N} a_{nm} y_{nm} = x_m, \qquad 1 \leq m \leq M,$$

$$\sum_{m=1}^{M} d_{nm} y_{nm} \leq b_n, \qquad 1 \leq n \leq N,$$

$$y_{nm} \geq 0, \qquad \text{(WDP)}$$

where a_{nm}, d_{nm}, and C_{nm} are nonnegative for all n and m. In addition, it is required that each y_{nm} have a nonzero coefficient in at least one equation.

We also assume, without loss of generality, that the rank of the constraints matrix is $M + N$. This LP problem is known in the literature as the weighted distribution problem (WDP) or as the generalized transportation problem (Dantzig 1963, chap. 21). The first result applies to WDP problems for which all constraints are equalities. We denote this problem by WDPE. Note that a WDP problem can be transformed into an equivalent WDPE problem by the addition of slack variables to the nonequality constraints. Thus, the next theorem applies to WDP cost functions as a special case.

Theorem 6. Let F be a WDPE cost function. Then F is a piecewise linear function, and there is a finite number of hyperplanes $H_1, \ldots, H_k$ of the form

$$H_j = \left\{ x \in E^M \;\middle|\; \sum_{m=1}^{M} \lambda_m^j x_m = \beta^j \right\},$$

where $\lambda_m^j \geq 0$ and $\beta^j \geq 0$ such that F is continuously differentiable off $U_{j=1}^k H_j$.

Corollary. If $F(x_1, \ldots, x_m)$ is a WDP cost function defined on a comprehensive domain C^F, then for each α in C^F, F is continuously differentiable along the line segment $[0, \alpha]$, except perhaps for finitely many points. Thus, the AS formula can be applied to any WDP cost function.

The next goal is to characterize the ASPM on the class of cost functions spanned by all WDP cost functions (this is the class $\mathcal{F}_3$ defined later). This characterization uses exactly the same set of axioms used by Mirman and Tauman (1982a) for the class of all differentiable cost functions. To state the results, we need some notation.

Let C be a subset of E^M, and let $H_1, \ldots, H_k$ be k hyperplanes in E^M. Each hyperplane H_j defines two closed half-spaces, which we denote by H_j^+ and H_j^-. We call each nonempty subset of the form $C \cap H_1^{\epsilon_1} \cap \cdots \cap H_k^{\epsilon_k}$, where ϵ_j stands for $+$ or $-$, a region.

Definition. A function F defined on a subset C of E^M is piecewise continuously differentiable (p.c.d.) if it is continuous and there are k hyperplanes $H_1, \ldots, H_k$ in E^M and r continuously differentiable function $F^1, \ldots, F^r$ on E^M such that F coincides on each of the regions of C (determined by $H_1, \ldots, H_k$) with some F^j, $1 \leq j \leq r$.

Definition. Let $\mathscr{F}_1^M$ be the family of all functions F such that

(a) F is defined on a full-dimensional comprehensive subset C^F of E_+^M.
(b) $F(0) = 0$.
(c) F is p.c.d.
(d) The hyperplanes $H_1, \ldots, H_k$ involved in the definition of F are defined by positive functionals; that is,

$$H_j = \{x \mid \lambda^j x = a^j\}$$
$$\text{where } \lambda_m^j \geq 0,\ \lambda^j \neq 0,\quad j = 1, \ldots, k, m = 1, \ldots, M.$$

Notice that $\mathscr{F}_1^M$ is a linear space when $F + G$ is taken to be the function on $C_F \cap C_G$ defined by

$$(F + G)(x) = F(x) + G(x), \qquad x \in C_f \cap C_G.$$

Now set $\mathscr{F}_1 = \cup_{M=1}^{\infty} \mathscr{F}_1^M$. Note that $\mathscr{F}_1$ contains $\mathscr{F}_0$ and, in view of the preceding corollary, all WDP cost functions. In particular, all TP cost functions are in $\mathscr{F}_1$.

Let $\mathscr{F}_2^M$ be the linear space consisting of the piecewise linear functions in $\mathscr{F}_1^M$, and let $\mathscr{F}_2 = \cup_{M=1}^{\infty} \mathscr{F}_2^M$. By $\mathscr{F}_3^M$ we denote the linear space spanned by all WDP cost functions with M variables. Again, let $\mathscr{F}_3 = \cup_{M=1}^{\infty} \mathscr{F}_3^M$. Notice that $\mathscr{F}_1 \supseteq \mathscr{F}_0$ and that $\mathscr{F}_1 \supseteq \mathscr{F}_2 \supseteq \mathscr{F}_3$.

Theorem 7 (Samet et al. 1984). For each of the spaces $\mathscr{F}_0, \mathscr{F}_1, \mathscr{F}_2$, and $\mathscr{F}_3$ there exists one and only one price mechanism $P(\,\cdot\,,\,\cdot\,)$ that obeys Axioms 1–5. This is the Aumann–Shapley price mechanism; that is, for each $F \in \mathscr{F}_i^M$ ($i = 0, 1, 2, 3$) and $\alpha \in C^F,\ \alpha \gg 0$,

$$P_m(F, \alpha) = \int_0^1 \frac{\partial F}{\partial x_m}(t\alpha)\, dt, \qquad m = 1, \ldots, M.$$

5 The extension of the Aumann–Shapley prices to cost functions with fixed-cost component

The ASPM has been defined only for cost functions without a fixed-cost component. Mirman et al. (1983) extended the analysis to the class $\mathscr{F}^{FC}$ of functions of the form $F + c$, where $F \in \mathscr{F}_0$ [i.e., a differentiable function on a comprehensive subset C^F of E_+^M s.t. $F(0) = 0$] and c is the fixed-cost component, a nonnegative real number. It is easy to verify that the three axioms of cost-sharing, additivity, and weak consistency are incompatible. For example, let $x_1 + x_2 + c$ be the cost function and suppose that $\alpha = (1,1)$. By the consistency axiom the prices of the two commodities should be the same. But if we decompose this cost function into x_1 and $x_2 + c$ and apply the additivity and the cost-sharing axioms, we find that the price of the first commodity covers only the variable cost of producing one unit, which is 1. The price of the second commodity is $1 + c$, and it covers all of the fixed cost. This contradicts the consistency axiom. Mirman et al. (1983) suggested modifying the additivity axiom in order to extend the ASPM to $\mathscr{F}^{FC}$.

Axiom 2′. Let F be a function in $\mathscr{F}_0$ defined on C^F, and let c be a nonnegative number. Then for each G in $\mathscr{F}_0$ for which $C^G = C^F$ and $G \leq F$, there is a nonnegative number c_G such that if $F = \Sigma^n_{i=1} G_i$ then $c = \Sigma^n_{i=1} c_{G_i}$ and

$$P(F + c, \alpha) = \sum_{i=1}^{n} P_i(G_i + c_{G_i}, \alpha).$$

That is, it is not necessary to specify a priori how the fixed cost is split between different variable-cost components. It is only required that there be a way to do it.

The second axiom asserts that the part c_{G_i} of the fixed cost c that is associated with the component G_i should be at least as large as c_{G_j} whenever the part $G_i(\alpha)$ in the total variable cost $F(\alpha)$ is at least as large as $G_j(\alpha)$.

Axiom 11. Let $F, G_1, \ldots, G_n$, and c be as stated in Axiom 2′. Then $G_i(\alpha) \geq G_j(\alpha)$ implies $c_{G_i} \geq c_{G_j}$.

Theorem 8 (Mirman et al. 1983). There exists a unique price mechanism $\hat{P}(\cdot , \cdot)$ on $\mathscr{F}^{FC}$ that satisfies Axioms 1, 2′, 3–5, and 11. This mechanism is defined as follows: For each (F, α) s.t. $F(\alpha) \neq 0$

$$\hat{P}(F + c, \alpha) = \left(1 + \frac{c}{F(\alpha)}\right) P(F, \alpha),$$

where $P(F, \alpha)$ is the AS price vector associated with (F, α); that is,

$$\hat{P}_m(F + c, \alpha) = \left(1 + \frac{c}{F(\alpha)}\right) \int_0^1 \frac{\partial F}{\partial x_m}(t\alpha)\, dt, \qquad m = 1, \ldots, M.$$

For further discussion, see also Mirman, Tauman, and Zang (1985b).

6   The Aumann–Shapley price mechanism as an incentive compatible scheme

Recently, Schmeidler and Tauman (1987) considered a transportation model, like that described before, with one additional characteristic – that the destinations can self-produce their demands (possibly at higher costs than offered by the origins). Consequently, depending on the cost-sharing mechanism used, it may be to their advantage to misreport their true demands and to self-produce (or to dispose) the difference. An interesting problem in this model is to characterize the cost-sharing schemes that are incentive compatible. Schmeidler and Tauman showed that the ASPM is an incentive-compatible cost-sharing scheme. That is, to report the true demands is a dominant strategy for each destination, if the ASPM is used to share the production and the transportation costs of the reporting demands. Also, it was shown that the second-best Ramsey price scheme (defined later) and the price mechanism $P(\,\cdot\,,\,\cdot\,)$ that allocates the costs proportional to the marginal cost [i.e., $P(F,\alpha) = c \cdot \nabla F(\alpha)$, where c satisfies $c \cdot \nabla F(\alpha) = F(\alpha)$] are not incentive compatible. That is, the Nash equilibrium of the strategic game played by the destinations (where the levels of reported demands are their strategies) can result, under these two schemes, in strategies where some of the destinations will not report their true demands.

7   The Aumann–Shapley price mechanism as a demand-compatible scheme

We have shown that the ASPM is uniquely determined by a set of axioms formulated in purely economic terms. A natural question arises: If the ASPM is used to regulate a public firm or a monopoly, would these prices be compatible with demands and, in the case of a natural monopoly, could they deter undesirable entry. Mirman and Tauman (1981, 1982a) considered a partial equilibrium model consisting of n consumers and one firm that produces several commodities jointly, using only one input. The monopoly is regulated through the AS prices. It was shown that under standard assumptions on preferences and weak assumptions on the cost structure there exists a supply decision such that the corresponding AS prices lead to demands that match supply. The equilibrium depends on both supply (or costs) and demand. This result is independent of the returns to scale properties of production. In the case of constant returns to scale, AS prices and MC prices coincide and the standard competitive equilibrium is obtained.

The assumptions on the cost function F that guarantee the existence of an equilibrium in the Mirman–Tauman model are (1) $F(0) = 0$, (2) $\partial F/\partial x_i$ exists on $x_i > 0$ and is continuous there, and (3) F is continuous and nondecreasing on C^F, and for each $\alpha \in C^F, \alpha \in E^M_+$, the line segment $\{t\alpha\}, 0 \leq t \leq 1$, contains at most a finite number of points at which F is not continuously differentiable. The last assumption describes the case in which the means of production is not infinitely divisible. Enlarging the quantities produced along some nondecreasing path starting at zero and ending at α yields changes in the configuration of the means of production that may change the slope of the cost function (noncontinuously). It is natural to assume that on each such path only a finite number of changes occur. This implies that on each such path there may exist a finite number of kinks. Assumption (3) requires even less: Only intervals $[0,\alpha], \alpha \in E^M_+$, are assumed to contain a finite number of kinks, whereas general paths may contain an infinite number of kinks. The main difficulty in the existence proof was to prove that under the three assumptions the ASPM, $P(F,\alpha)$, is continuous in α. This result was shown in Mirman and Tauman (1982b). In fact, their result is more general. Suppose that, for each $\alpha \in E^M_+, \mu^\alpha$ is the vector measure defined on the interval $[0,M]$ by

$$\mu^\alpha(S) = (\alpha_1\lambda(S \cap [0,1]), \ . \ . \ . \ , \alpha_M \lambda(S \cap [M-1,M]))),$$

where $\alpha = (\alpha_1, \ . \ . \ . \ , \alpha_M)$, λ is the Lebesgue measure on $[0,M]$, and S is a Borel subset of $[0,M]$. Let v_α be the nonatomic game defined by

$$v_\alpha(S) = (F \cdot \mu^\alpha)(S) = F(\mu^\alpha(S)).$$

The interval $[m-1,m]$ represents the mth commodity, and S is a coalition that represents a vector $x = \mu^\alpha(S)$ of quantities of consumption goods.

Theorem 9 (Mirman and Tauman 1982b). Let $F: E^M_+ \rightarrow R$ be such that $F \cdot \mu^\alpha \in p\text{NAD}$ for each $\alpha \in E^M_{++}$. Then the ASPM $P(F, \cdot)$ is continuous on E^M_{++}.

As shown in Mirman, Raanan, and Tauman (1982), if the cost function F satisfies our three assumptions, then for any $\alpha \in C^F$ $F \cdot \mu^\alpha \in p\text{NAD}$ and, thus by Theorem 9, $P(F, \cdot)$ is continuous on C^F.

Boss and Tillmann (1983) extend the existence result of Mirman and

Tauman (1981, 1982a) to include all price mechanisms that satisfy Axioms 2–5. By Theorem 4 these are prices of the form

$$P_m(F,\alpha) = \int_0^1 \frac{\partial F}{\partial x_m}(t\alpha)\, d\mu(t), \qquad m = 1, \ldots, M,$$

for some nonnegative measure μ. They proved that these price schemes are compatible with demand if the financing of deficits or the distribution of profits of the regulated public firm is made via lump-sum transfers that are specified in advance. Their assumption on the cost structure is stronger than the three assumptions given here because they assumed that the cost functions are continuously differentiable on E_+^M.

Dierker, Guesnerie, and Neuefeind (1985) and, independently, Böhm (1983) have substantially extended the aforementioned existence results. Dierker et al. prove the existence of an equilibrium in a general setting. They consider an economy in which there are two sectors, the private sector and the public sector. The firms in the private sector behave competitively (price takers), whereas the firms of the public sector follow special pricing rules (possibly different pricing rules for different firms). These firms consider the output levels of their own products as well as the prices of the inputs as given, minimize their cost, and set prices for their products according to a specific abstract pricing scheme (e.g., one that satisfies (*) or the second-best price scheme). Böhm has a similar setup but somewhat less general. He does not allow for more than one price-setting firm and requires the public firm to charge break-even prices.

8   Aumann–Shapley prices and contestable market theory

The theory of contestable markets (Baumol, Panzar, and Willig 1982) has focused on the idea that potential entry has the effect of self-regulation, so in a natural monopoly industry only a single firm, making normal profits, will survive. The issue remains, however, whether there exist prices that do not yield an incentive for entry by a potential entrant and that generate normal profits for the monopolist. This question is particularly relevant for a multiproduct monopoly because a potential entrant need not necessarily enter all markets but may enter any subset of the markets. These questions have led to the development of a theory of sustainable prices (Baumol et al. 1977; Panzar and Willig 1977).

The conditions under which a multiproduct natural monopoly may be sustained by prices, in the sense that no profitable entry will occur in any of the markets, are less understood. Because it is clear that for prices to be sustainable one good should not cross-subsidize another, the concept of sustainability is closely related to various concepts of nonsubsidizing prices that are discussed in the literature. These are the notions of subsidy-free prices (Faulhaber 1975), anonymously equitable prices (Faulhaber and Levinson 1981), and supportability (Sharkey and Telser 1978). Generally speaking, these are core concepts in various relevant cost games, and they play a crucial part in characterizing sustainable prices.

Consider a firm producing M infinitely divisible goods with a technology, expressed by a nondecreasing joint cost function $C: E_+^M \to R$, where $C(y)$ is the minimum cost of producing the output vector $y \in E_+^M$. Let $Q(p)$ be the inverse demand function; that is, for each $p \in E_+^M$,

$$Q(p) = (Q_1(p), \ldots, Q_M(p))$$

denotes the vector of quantities demanded at prices p.

Denote by $N = \{1, \ldots, M\}$ the set of all goods, and let $S \subseteq N$ be a subset of N. Let s denote the number of goods in S (or the cardinality of S). Then for a given $S \subseteq N$, y^S [or similarly $Q^S(p)$] and p^S are vectors in E_+^s denoting quantities and prices, respectively, of goods in S. For $S = N$ the superscript is omitted. Thus, y^S and p^S are the projections of y and p, respectively, on E_+^s.

The first concept of nonsubsidizing prices is due to Faulhaber (1975) and Faulhaber and Levinson (1981).

Definition. A price vector p is *subsidy-free* if (i) $py = C(y)$, (ii) $p^S y^S \le C(y^S)$ for each $S \subseteq N$, and (iii) $y = Q(p)$.

That is, p is subsidy-free if the cost of producing the entire market demand at p is covered by the total revenue and, furthermore, the revenue generated from each subset of the goods is not greater than the stand-alone production cost for this subset. Hence, in a market in which a subsidy-free price vector prevails (through regulation or competition), there is no profitable way of producing the entire demands of any subset of the goods.

The second concept of nonsubsidizing prices is due to Sharkey and Telser (1978).

Definition. The cost function C is *supportable* at y_0 if there exists a $p \in E_+^M$ such that (i) $py_0 = C(y_0)$ and (ii) $pz \le C(z)$ for any $z \in E_+^M$ such that $z \le y_0$.

Faulhaber and Levinson (1981) introduced the third concept of anonymous equity.

Definition. The price vector p is *anonymously equitable* if (i) $py = C(y)$, (ii) $pz \leq C(z)$ for any $z \in E_+^M$ such that $z \leq y$, and (iii) $y = Q(p)$.

Thus, if for some $p \in E_+^M$, C is supportable at $Q(p)$ by p, then p is an anonymously equitable price vector. Also, notice that any anonymously equitable price vector is subsidy-free. In a market in which an anonymously equitable price prevails, no attempt to produce a portion of market demand at the prevailing price can be profitable. In such cases entry can occur only if prices are lowered. Prices that prevent entry by making it nonprofitable are called *sustainable prices*.

Definition. The price vector $\bar{p}$ with the property $\bar{p}Q(p) - C(Q(\bar{p})) \geq 0$ is *sustainable* if every triple $(S, \hat{y}^S, \hat{p}^S)$ satisfying (i) $\hat{p}^S \leq \bar{p}^S$ and (ii) $\hat{y}^S \leq Q^S(\hat{p}^S, \bar{y}^{N/S})$ also satisfies $\hat{p}^S \hat{y}^S - C(\hat{y}^S) \leq 0$, where $Q^S(\hat{p}^S, \bar{p}^{N/S})$ is the demand vector for the goods in S under the entrant prices $\hat{p}^S$ for the goods in S and the monopoly prices vector $\bar{p}^{N/S}$ for the goods in N/S.

Conditions (i) and (ii) describe the behavior of an entrant: For the goods in S, prices are offered that are no greater than those already prevailing in the market [condition (i)]. At these prices any quantities up to those determined by the market demand functions evaluated at the new (lower) prices $\hat{p}^S$ for goods in S and at the prevailing prices $\bar{p}^{N/S}$ for the rest of the goods [condition (ii)] may be sold. Thus, $\bar{p}$ is sustainable if a potential entrant cannot anticipate positive profits by lowering some or all of the prices.

Let v_C be the cost game associated with the cost function C. [This game was defined in the previous section as v_α for $\alpha = (1, \ldots, 1)$.] Thus, $v_C(S) = C(z)$, where z is the vector of quantities associated with the coalition S. An imputation of $C(\alpha)$ is a price vector $p = (p_1, \ldots, p_M) \in E_+^M$ such that

$$\sum_{m=1}^{M} p_m \alpha_m = C(\alpha).$$

The set of all imputations of $C(\alpha)$ is denoted by $P(\alpha)$. The core $H(\alpha)$ of v_C is defined by

$$H(\alpha) = \{p \in P(\alpha) | pz \leq C(z) \text{ for all } z \leq \alpha\}.$$

The set $H(\alpha)$ is related to the concept of anonymous equity. A price vector p is anonymously equitable iff $p \in H(\alpha)$, where $\alpha = Q(p)$. Note that supportability at α is equivalent to the nonemptiness of $H(\alpha)$.

Mirman, Tauman, and Zang (1985a) provided sufficient conditions under which the cost function is supportable under AS prices and for the existence of an AS price vector that is anonymously equitable and sustainable. To state their results, we need three assumptions.

Assumption 1 (Cost complementarity). The cost function C is twice differentiable and

$$C_{mj} = \frac{\partial^2 C}{\partial y_m \partial y_j} \leq 0 \quad \text{on } E_+^M \backslash \{0\}.$$

Assumption 2 (Weak gross substitutability). For $j \in N$, $Q_j(\cdot)$ is differentiable on $E_+^M \backslash \{0\}$ and $\partial Q_j / \partial p_m \geq 0$ for each $m \neq j$.

The assumption that all goods are cost complements implies that the cost function is subadditive – the usual definition of a natural monopoly. Moreover, this assumption means that the marginal and average cost functions are downward sloping.

Assumption 3. The demands are inelastic with respect to prices below $\bar{p}$; that is,

$$\frac{\partial Q_m(p)/Q_m(p)}{\partial p_m/p_m} \geq -1 \quad \text{for each } m \in N \text{ and } p \leq \bar{p}.$$

Proposition 3. Suppose that C is a nondecreasing function on E_+^M. Then under cost complementarities (Assumption 1) the cost function C is supportable by AS prices.

Proposition 4. Under cost complementarities (Assumption 1) and upper semicontinuity of demands, there exists an Aumann–Shapley price vector $\bar{p}$ that is anonymously equitable; that is, there exists $\bar{p} \in E_+^M$, such that

(i) $\bar{p} \in H(Q(\bar{p}))$,

(ii) $\bar{p}_m = \int_0^1 \frac{\partial C}{\partial y_m} (tQ(\bar{p})) \, dt, \quad m = 1, \ldots, M.$

If, in addition, the assumptions of weak gross substitutability and inelasticity of demand (Assumptions 2 and 3) hold, then $\bar{p}$ is sustainable.

It can be shown that Assumption 3 can be replaced either by the assumption of nonnegative marginal profitability on E^M_+ or by both nonnegative marginal profitability at $\bar{p}$ and pseudoconcavity of the profit function (see Mirman et al. 1985a).

9 Aumann–Shapley prices and Ramsey prices

In this section we define the Ramsey prices and discuss their relationship with AS prices. Consider a model of one input (labor) and $M + 1$ outputs (one which is leisure). Suppose that $\bar{L}$ is the total labor market allocated to production. Then

$$C(Q(p)) + R = \bar{L}, \tag{*}$$

where $Q(p) \in E^M_+$ is the demand vector for the M outputs, $C(Q(p))$ is the cost of producing $Q(p)$ (in units of labor), and R is the amount of leisure. The Ramsey problem is to maximize, over output prices, an indirect social welfare function $v(p_1, \ldots, p_n, R)$ subject to the constraint (*) and subject to a cost-sharing (or fixed profit) constraint

$$\Pi(p) = pQ(p) - C(Q(p)) = 0.$$

Under the assumption of redistribution of income, a Ramsey price vector p^* obeys, for some $\lambda \geq 0$,

$$p_j^* - MC_j = -\lambda(MR_j - MC_j) \quad \text{if } y_j^* > 0,$$
$$\leq -\lambda(MR_j - MC_j) \quad \text{if } y_j^* = 0.$$

Thus, if for example the labor supply has zero elasticity, namely just a fixed quantity of labor is offered in exchange for the monopoly's products, then $MR_j = 0$, and it follows that a Ramsey price vector is proportional to marginal cost prices. Namely, p^* satisfies

$$\alpha MC_j(Q_j(p^*)) = p_j^*, \quad Q_j(p^*) > 0,$$

where α is determined by the cost-sharing constraint

$$\alpha Q(p^*)MC(Q(p^*)) = C(Q(p^*)).$$

For further discussion see Mirman et al. (1986) and Young (1985b).

The Ramsey prices are named after Frank Ramsey (1927), who suggested using them to determine optimal methods of taxation. Since then they have been discussed extensively in the economic literature, especially by Boiteux (1971). (The Ramsey prices are sometimes called the Ramsey–Boiteux prices.) By definition, the Ramsey prices are most efficient among all cost-sharing prices, because they maximize the total welfare of consumers. Nevertheless, they are debatable in some aspects. The first one is the fairness aspect. For example, low-income families who need telephones for emergencies may, under the Ramsey prices, subsidize long-distance usage by businesses. From the practical aspect, Ramsey prices may be difficult to compute, because they rely on demand elasticities that may not be known. A third aspect is that Ramsey prices in general are cross-subsidizing prices and thus cannot sustain a natural monopoly. Even in the separable-cost case they differ from the average cost pricing, which are, in this case, necessary to sustain a natural monopoly against undesirable entry. (For further discussion see Mirman et al. 1986.) Nevertheless, Baumol et al. (1977) have shown that the Ramsey prices sustain a natural monopoly. However, to obtain their result, they assumed, among few other conditions, the following two assumptions: strictly decreasing ray average cost, which means that

$$C(\delta y) < \delta C(y), \qquad \delta > 1.$$

The other condition is the transray convexity, namely,

$$C(\lambda y^1 + (1 - \lambda)y^2) \leq \lambda C(y^1) + (1 - \lambda)C(y^2), \qquad 0 < \lambda < 1.$$

These two conditions, when stated globally, are contradictory. Therefore, Baumol et al. required that the transray convexity of $C(\cdot)$ held only on a hyperplane defined by the marginal profits at the Ramsey optimal price vector and not on E^M_+.

Because sustainable prices cannot be cross-subsidized and must coincide with the average cost prices when the cost function is separable, the AS prices seem to be a more natural candidate to sustain a monopoly. Also, to compute AS prices, we need only the cost structure and the aggregate demand. Finally, as a closing remark on the difference between AS prices and Ramsey prices, we mention that in contrast to the Ramsey prices, AS prices are incentive compatible in strategic transportation models. This is discussed in Section 6.

REFERENCES

Aumann, R. J. and Shapley, L. S. (1974). *Values of Non-Atomic Games.* Princeton University Press, Princeton, N.J.

Baumol, W. J., Bailey, E. E., and Willig, R. D. (1977). "Weak Invisible Hand Theorems on the Sustainability of Multiproduct Natural Monopoly." American Economic Review, Vol. 67, pp. 350–65.

Baumol, W. J., Panzar, J. C., and Willig, R. D. (1982). *Contestable Markets and the Theory of Industry Structure.* New York: Harcourt Brace Jovanovich.

Billera, L. J. and Heath, D. C. (1982). "Allocation of Shared Costs: A Set of Axioms Yielding a Unique Procedure." Mathematics of Operations Research, Vol. 7, pp. 32–39.

Billera, L. J., Heath, D. C., and Raanan, J. (1978). "Internal Telephone Billing Rates–A Novel Application of Non-Atomic Game Theory," Operations Research, Vol. 26, pp. 956–65.

Billera, L. J., Heath, D. C., and Verrecchia, R. E. (1981). "A Unique Procedure for Allocating Common Costs from a Production Process." Journal of Accounting Research, Vol. 19, pp. 185–96.

Boiteux, M. (1971). "On the Management of Public Monopolies Subject to Budgetary Constraint." Journal of Economic Theory, Vol. 3, pp. 219–40.

Böhm, V. (1985). "Existence and Optimality of Equilibria with Price Regulation." Mimeo, Universitat Maunheim.

Bös, D. and Tillmann, G. (1983). "Cost-Axiomatic Regulatory Pricing" Journal of Public Economics, Vol. 22, pp. 243–56.

Dantzig, G. B. (1963). *Linear Programming and Extensions.* Princeton University Press, Princeton, N.J.

Dierker, E., Guesnerie, R., and Neufeind, W. (1985). "General Equilibrium When Some Firms Follow Special Pricing Rule." Econometrica, Vol. 53, pp. 1369–93.

Dubey, P. and Neyman, A. (1984). Payoffs in Nonatomic Economies: An Axiomatic Approach." Econometrica, Vol. 52, pp. 1129–50.

Dubey, P., Neyman, A., and Weber, R. J. (1981). "Value Theory without Efficiency." Mathematics of Operations Research, Vol. 6, pp. 122–8.

Faulhaber, G. R. (1975). "Cross-Subsidization: Pricing in Public Enterprises." American Economic Review, Vol. 65, pp. 966–77.

Faulhaber, G. R. and Levinson, S. B. (1981). "Subsidy-Free Prices and Anonymous Equity." American Economic Review, Vol. 71, pp. 1083–91.

Hart, S. and Mas-Colell, A. (1987). "Potential, Value and Consistency." Preprint.

Mirman, L. J. and Neyman, A. (1983). "Diagonality of Cost Allocation Prices." Mathematics of Operations Research, Vol. 9, pp. 66–74.

(1984). "Prices for Homogeneous Cost Functions." Journal of Mathematical Economics, Vol. 12, pp. 257–73.

Mirman, L. J., Raanan, J., and Tauman, Y. (1982). "A Sufficient Condition on f for $f \cdot \mu$ to be in pNAD." Journal of Mathematical Economics, Vol. 9, pp. 251–7.

Mirman, L. J., Samet, D., and Tauman, Y. (1983). An Axiomatic Approach to the Allocation of a Fixed Cost through Prices." Bell Journal of Economics, Vol. 14, pp. 139–51.

Mirman, L. J. and Tauman, Y. (1981). "Valuer de Shapley et Repartition Equitable des Couts de Production." Cahiers du Seminare d'Econometrie, Vol. 23, pp. 121–51.

(1982a). "Demand Compatible Equitable Cost Sharing Prices." Mathematics of Operations Research, Vol. 7, pp. 40–56.

(1982b). "The Continuity of the Aumann–Shapley Price Mechanism." Journal of Mathematical Economics, Vol. 9, pp. 235–49.

Mirman, L. S., Tauman, Y., and Zang, I. (1985a). "Supportability, Sustainability and Subsidy Free Prices." The Rand Journal of Economics, Vol. 16 (Spring), pp. 114–26.

(1985b). "On the Use of Game Theoretic Concepts in Cost Accounting." *Cost Allocation Methods, Principles and Applications,* H. Peyton Young (Ed.), North-Holland.

(1986). "Ramsey Prices, Average Cost Prices and Price Sustainability." International Journal of Industrial Organization, Vol. 4, pp. 123–40.

Neyman, A. (1977). "Continuous Values Are Diagonal." Mathematics of Operations Research, Vol. 2, pp. 338–42.

Owen, G. (1972). "Multilinear Extensions of Games." Management Science, Vol. 5, pp. 64–79.

Panzar, J. C. and Willig, R. D. (1977). "Free Entry and the Sustainability of Natural Monopoly." Bell Journal of Economics, Vol. 8, pp. 1–22.

Ramsey, F. (1927). "A Contribution to the Theory of Taxation." Economic Journal, Vol. 37, pp. 47–61.

Samet, D. and Tauman, Y. (1982). "The Determination of Marginal Cost Prices under a Set of Axioms." Econometrica, Vol. 50, pp. 895–909.

Samet, D., Tauman, Y. and Zang, I. (1984). "An Application of the Aumann–Shapley Prices to Transportation Problem." Mathematics of Operations Research, Vol. 10, pp. 25–42.

Schmeidler, D. and Tauman, Y. (1987). "Non Manipulable Cost Allocation Schemes." OSU Discussion Paper.

Sharkey, W. W. and Telser, L. G. (1978). "Supportable Cost Functions for the Multiproduct Firm." Journal of Economic Theory, Vol. 18, pp. 23–37.

Young, H. P. (1985). "Monotonicity in Cooperative Games." International Journal of Game Theory, Vol. 13, pp. 65–72.

(1985a). "Producer Incentives in Cost Allocation." Econometrica, Vol. 53, pp. 757–66.

(1985b). *Methods and Principles of Cost Allocation: Methods, Principles, Applications.* H. Peyton Young (ed.), North-Holland.

PART VI

NTU games

CHAPTER 19

Utility comparison and the theory of games

Lloyd S. Shapley

1. Interpersonal comparability of utility is generally regarded as an unsound basis on which to erect theories of multipersonal behavior. Nevertheless, it enters naturally – and, I believe, properly – as a nonbasic, derivative concept playing an important if sometimes hidden role in the theories of bargaining, group decisionmaking, and social welfare. The formal and conceptual framework of game theory is well adapted for a broad and unified approach to this group of theories, though it tends to slight the psychological aspects of group interaction in favor of the structural aspects – e.g., complementary physical resources, the channels of information and control, the threats and other strategic options open to the participants, etc. In this note I shall discuss two related topics in which game theory becomes creatively involved with questions of interpersonal utility comparison.

The first topic concerns the nature of the utility functions that are admissible in a bargaining theory that satisfies certain minimal requirements. I shall show, by a simple argument, that while cardinal utilities are admissible, purely ordinal utilities are not. Some intriguing intermediate systems are not excluded. The argument does not depend on the injection of probabilities or uncertainty into the theory.

The second topic concerns a method of solving general n-person games by making use of the interpersonal comparisons of utility that are implicit in the solution. After two complementary modes of comparison have been distinguished, a "principle of equivalence" points the way to an attractively direct extension of the definition of the value of a game, from the "transferable" case to the "nontransferable" case.

Reprinted from *La Decision: Aggregation et Dynamique des Ordres de Preference* (Paris: Editions du Centre National de la Recherche Scientifique, 1969), pp. 251–63. The views expressed in this paper are those of the author, and should not be interpreted as reflecting the views of the RAND Corporation or the official opinion or policy of its governmental or private research sponsors.

2. A number of qualitatively different definitions of "solution" exist in the literature of n-person game theory. An explanation for this multiplicity may be found in the essential ambiguity of decision making in the presence of several independent "free wills". Simple rationality (utility maximization) is not a sufficient determinant of behavior when one ventures beyond simple cases like the one-person decision problem or the two-person game with directly opposed interests. Determinateness (i.e., uniqueness of outcome) may be desirable in a solution, but it can generally be obtained only at the price of oversimplifying or ignoring the observed tendencies toward organized cooperation (e.g., markets, political parties, cartels, etc.) when real people cope with the indeterminacy of real-life multilateral competition. Such social, political, or economic institutions, often highly abstracted, are at the heart of many of the best-known solution concepts.

In this note, however, we shall be dealing only with the simplest kind of solution concept, which seeks to reduce each game to a single vector of payoffs, known as the *value* of the game. From what has just been said, it should be clear that a "value" concept is not the only possible capstone to a well-built theory of games. Hence conclusions (such as those in this paper) that are based on the assumed existence of a self-consistent method of game valuation can be rejected without necessarily demolishing the entire theory. From some plausible standpoints, in fact, it can be demonstrated that a valuation theory free from contradiction is unattainable.

But there are other standpoints from which it can be argued that a valuation theory is virtually indispensible. The most compelling argument, perhaps, is one that takes us back to the basics of utility theory. Let an individual be confronted with the prospect of entering some sort of multilateral game situation, e.g., a partnership, an oligopolistic industry, a political office. What is the utility to him of that prospect?

3. For our first topic, we consider a two-sided negotiation. The "rules of the game" are simple: If the parties agree, they can have any outcome in an "agreement set" A, but if they fail to agree, they must take the "disagreement point" D. A and D are construed in the cartesian product of the two bargainers' utility spaces, which we take to be real numbers scales, and A is assumed to be a continuous, strictly monotonic curve with endpoints aligned with D, as shown in Figure 1.

Let us postulate a valuation theory for cooperative games that is powerful enough to resolve at least this elementary kind of bargaining game (hopefully more), and that gives some interior point of A, say V, as the solution. Let us further postulate:

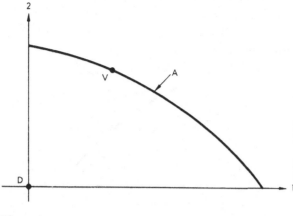

Figure 1

(I) The solution depends only on the configuration (A,D) in the joint utility space, and not on any nonutilitarian attributes (e.g., physical symmetry, numerical quantities) of the actual subject of negotiation.

(II) The solution is covariant (i.e., the physical outcome is invariant) under some group G of order-preserving transformations, applied separately to the two utility scales.

What do these postulates imply about the nature of the group G?

First, let us test the ordinalist assumption. Let G be the group of *all* continuous order-preserving transformations on the real line R. We soon run into trouble. Let us apply to the first player's utility scale any continuous order-preserving transformation that leaves the endpoints of A fixed, but moves V. A curve like A' might result (Figure 2), the points of A having been displaced horizontally. But now we can immediately construct a transformation of the *second* player's scale that restores the curve A, by displacing the points of A' vertically. Since the point D has not moved, our first postulate plainly requires that V be the solution of the twice-transformed problem. But since the outcome originally at V is now at V'', our second postulate just as plainly requires that V'' be the solution. Since $V \neq V''$, we are forced to conclude that purely ordinal utilities are inadmissible.

4. This kind of contradiction is always present so long as there is any element of G that has two fixed points with a nonfixed point in between. Indeed, if g is such an element, we can arrange (A,D) so that g^{-1} applied to the second scale restores the displacement of A caused by g applied to the

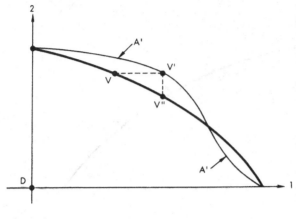

Figure 2

first scale, and in such a way that every interior point of *A* is shifted in the process. Conversely, if *G* contains no such element, then postulates (I) and (II) can never be brought into conflict. Let us call such a group – characterized by the property that the set of fixed points of each element is convex – an *unwavering* group.

Of course, a complete valuation theory will have other postulates, which may further restrict the admissible utilities. Nevertheless, it is of some interest to explore the class of unwavering groups, to discover just how far (I) and (II) force us to go in our retreat (advance?) from purely ordinal utility. The group of all positive linear transformations, which characterizes the usual "cardinal" or "linear" utility, is certainly unwavering, as are its subgroups. But there are various other possibilities, qualitatively different; the least strange among them is the group that leaves some point, say 0, fixed (the status quo?) while operating separately in a linear fashion on the positive and negative half lines. Our most interesting result, in the context of the present discussion, is the following

Theorem. If *G* is an unwavering group of order-preserving transformations of the real line *R*, and if *G* is *transitive*[1], then there exists a continuous order-preserving recoordinatization of *R* such that, in the new coordinate system, every element of *G* is a positive linear transformation.

Our main conclusion is that if we want a value theory for bargaining games that is based on utility considerations alone, then we cannot use ordinal utilities, but are driven to cardinal utilities or some even more stringent system. This can perhaps be made more palatable to the intuition if we reflect that bargaining, by its very nature, tests the *intensities* of the desires of the contending parties. In other words, *utility differences* become comparable, between persons. By repetition, utility differences may also become comparable between different parts of the same person's scale of values. Thus, speaking intuitively, experience in bargaining forces an individual to "straighten out" his value system – makes him decide not only what he wants but how badly he wants it. A nonlinear transformation of such a man's utility scale would represent a real change in his bargaining attitudes.

5. We now turn to our second topic. The interpersonal utility comparisons that figure in negotiatory processes can be divided into two classes. The distinction is one of relative direction. At times, a person may compare his projected gain against another's loss, or his loss against another's gain. Thus: "Do me a favor! It would only be a little bother for you, and would help me a lot." The comparison is implicit in the words "a little . . . a lot"; and the point of the comparison is that society as a whole would be better off if the request were granted.

At other times, a person may compare his gain against another's gain, or loss against loss. "This is going to hurt me more than it hurts you!", the classic slogan of parental discipline, has its counterpart in the language of negotiation. The criterion in this form of comparison is not total welfare, as above, but "fair division," or "equity." It must be stressed that the utility comparison implicit in our use of these terms is not of an absolute or universal nature, but is relative to the realities of the particular bargaining positions, i.e., to the *competitive* rules of the game. In the previous type of comparison, only the *cooperative* rules, which determine feasibility, were relevant.

Given a game and its outcome, we can make separate estimates regarding the two types of interpersonal comparison we have described. On the one hand, we can measure the given outcome against other possible outcomes – for example, nearby points on the Pareto surface, and base a utility comparison on the exchanges that could have occurred, but did not. On the other hand, we can measure the given outcome against the initial prospects and opportunities of the players, and base a comparison on the presumption that each player "got what he deserved" – i.e., that the outcome was in some sense *equitable*. (In contrast, we might say that the first comparison was based on the presumption that the given outcome was *efficient*). If the comparisons are expressed as sets of weights, or scaling factors, to apply to the players' (cardinal) utility scales, then the first set of weights becomes a guide to the *maximization of social welfare,* the second to the *sharing of social profit.*

6. Having thus sketched a qualitative distinction between two modes of interpersonal comparison that may be detectable in the outcome of a cooperative multiperson game, we now proceed to declare their *equivalence,* as a central prerequisite for a value theory.

(III) An outcome is acceptable as a "value of the game" only if there exist scaling factors for the individual (cardinal) utilities under which the outcome is *both* equitable *and* efficient.

As it stands, (III) is a guiding principle rather than an exact postulate, since there remain several questions of interpretation, particularly regarding the meaning of "equitable." Before continuing, however, it may be helpful to show how this principle works in a special case: the familiar two-person pure bargaining game.

In Figure 3, the point X implies "efficiency weights" in the ratio $1:3$, since the slope of the tangent at X is $-\frac{1}{3}$. (That is, in order for X to maximize the sum of utilities, the second player's nominal, numerical payoffs must be tripled). At the same time, X implies "equity weights" in the ratio $2:1$, since the line joining D to X has slope 2. (That is, in order for the players to be sharing equally at X, the first player's payoffs must be doubled). Since the two sets of comparison weights are not proportional, X cannot be the value of the game, according to (III).

It is well known that a pure bargaining situation of this kind has a unique solution satisfying (III), namely the "Zeuthen–Nash" outcome that maximizes the product of the utility gains (the point V in the figure). It can be given a much more solid derivation than we have given here; the only virtue we claim for our present method is that it can be generalized, as we shall now proceed to demonstrate, to the more complex models of general game theory, where strategies and coalitions play essential roles.

7. We must first become more explicit about the notion of "equitable" (with respect to a given set of comparison weights), when used in a multiperson, strategically rich context. The simple idea of "sharing equally" no longer works; it may not even be well defined.

Our procedure, in the present note, will be to assume that we have a notion of equitable value for games where utility is *transferable,* at stated rates of exchange, so as to concentrate on the extension to the more general, nontransferable case. Our nominee for this "transfer value" is the value for games with sidepayments, discovered by Harsanyi[2] and axiomatized by Selten,[3] but our method of extension will be independent of

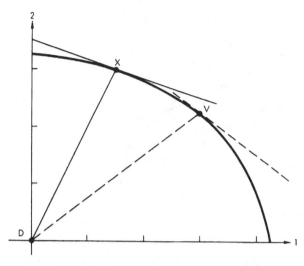

Figure 3

this particular choice. We shall require merely that the transfer value be unique, Pareto optimal, individually rational, and continuous as a function of the game's payoffs.

Consider now an n-person game in which there is no vehicle for the direct, unrestricted transfer of utility, but in which utility is nevertheless assumed to be interpersonally comparable according to some definite system of weighting factors. For convenience, assume that the weights are all equal. In this case, the *efficient* outcomes are simply those that maximize the sum of utilities. But which are the *equitable* outcomes?

A first candidate would be the transfer value, which by assumption is equitable if utility sidepayments are admitted. In general, however, the transfer value will not be a feasible outcome in the nontransferable game. To be sure, one might propose as equitable all outcomes of the form

$$(\phi_1 - x, \phi_2 - x, \ldots, \phi_n - x),$$

where ϕ is the transfer value and x is large enough to make the result feasible (or subfeasible). (This rule would pick out the outcomes along the line DX in Figure 3, if the first player's payoff is doubled). However, "equal taxation to overcome the deficit" is a dubious principle of fair division, and we do not insist on it. Instead, we shall make only the more modest claim that any outcome giving some player *more* than his transfer value, while giving some other player less, is certainly inequitable. This is illustrated schematically in Figure 4.

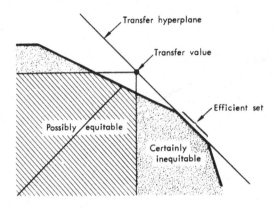

Figure 4

As already intimated, we shall also claim that the transfer value itself, if it is feasible, is certainly equitable. This may be regarded as an application of the "principle of irrelevant alternatives": If restricting the feasible set by eliminating sidepayments does not eliminate some solution point, then that point remains a solution.[4]

A glance at Figure 4 may now convince the reader that an outcome can be both efficient and equitable, as required by the principle of equivalence (III), if and only if *it is the transfer value and the transfer value is feasible.* To prove this, we merely note that the transfer value and all the efficient points lie on the hyperplane representing the maximum feasible utility sum. Hence, if the transfer value is feasible, then it is efficient as well as equitable, while if it is not feasible then the efficient points all lie in the "certainly inequitable" zone.

8. To complete the picture, we must of course allow for different sets of weights. Varying the weights will in general move the set of efficient points, since it changes the slope of the transfer hyperplane. Also, it will in general move the transfer value. (Under our assumptions the second motion will be continuous, the first semi-continuous). We shall therefore speak of "λ-efficiency" and the "λ-transfer value," where $\lambda = (\lambda_1, \ldots, \lambda_n)$ is an arbitrary vector of nonnegative weights, not all zero.

In view of the preceding discussion linking feasibility and efficiency, our goal is to choose λ in such a way that the λ-transfer value is feasible and hence λ-efficient. By the principle of equivalence (III), no other outcomes are acceptable as value solutions of the nontransferable game.

It may be noted that we can put $\Sigma \lambda_i = 1$ without loss of generality, since only ratios matter in the end. Hence there are really only $n - 1$ "degrees of freedom" in the choice of λ. On the other hand, there are essentially $n - 1$ conditions involved in requiring the λ-transfer value to be feasible, since the transfer hyperplane is $n - 1$ dimensional. This naive "equation counting" suggests that there may be a unique λ such that the λ-transfer value is feasible, or at worst, a 0-dimensional set of such λ. Thus encouraged, we propose (III) as a sufficient as well as necessary condition, and *define* a value of the nontransferable game to be any λ-transfer value that is feasible. As a companion to each value vector, ϕ, obtained under this definition, there will be a vector, λ, of intrinsic utility-comparison weights.

9. Our fundamental existence theorem states that every game (of a suitably wide class of games) has a value. Since the present account has so far been free from complicated mathematical argumentation, we have put the formal proof (previously unpublished) in an appendix. However, an outline of the proof can be given in a few words, as follows:

For each λ we consider the possible sidepayment vectors that could take us from the λ-efficient set to the λ-transfer value, which we denote $\phi(\lambda)$. The set of all such vectors, denoted $P(\lambda)$, is nonempty, convex, and compact under the hypotheses of the theorem, and it varies uppersemi-continuously with λ. If $P(\lambda)$ contains the zero vector, then $\phi(\lambda)$ is feasible and we are through. Restricting λ to the hyperplane $\Sigma\lambda_i = 1$, we define a point-to-convex set mapping $\lambda \to \lambda + P(\lambda)$. After an extension, which is needed to make this mapping go from points of a simplex to subsets of the same simplex, we apply the Kakutani fixed-point theorem to show that the mapping has a fixed point. The individual rationality of the λ-transfer value is then invoked, to ensure that the fixed point belongs to the original mapping rather than the extension, and we conclude that for at least one λ, $0 \in P(\lambda)$.

10. The value definition developed here was first contrived in an attempt to approximate Harsanyi's 1963 bargaining value[5] by something that might prove analytically more tractable in dealing with economic models having large numbers of participants.[6] We then perceived that the "approximation" had virtues of its own. Despite the rather different approach we have adopted (deductive rather than constructive), the influence of Harsanyi's work remains considerable — particularly his key idea of using intrinsically defined utility weights.

The two values have the following common features: (1) Zero weights can occur, and must be allowed if the existence theorem is to hold in general. (2) Nonunique solutions can occur, even in games (with three or more players) that are not noticeably exceptional. But different solutions never have the same comparison weights. (3) If utility is transferable, then the solution is unique and agrees with the "Harsanyi – Selten" value (or "modified Shapley" value). In fact, uniqueness holds whenever the Pareto surface is a hyperplane, or coincides with a hyperplane over a sufficiently large compact set.[7] (4) In the two-person case the solution is "almost always" unique, even without transferable utility, and agrees with the Nash cooperative solution for such games.[8]

We have no results indicating how well or poorly the two solutions approximate to each other, nor have we discovered any concrete example where the numerical contrast between them seems especially significant. But we can state two general properties of our present solution that are not satisfied by the other; either one, in fact, could be used (with suitable technical adjustments) in place of the principle of equivalence (III) in the derivation of our definition:

(IV) If two games have the same solution (payoffs *and* comparison weights), then any probability mixture of the two games – i.e., a game in which the first move decides by chance which of the two given games is to be played – also has that solution.

(V) If a game is modified by allowing side payments (restricted or unrestricted in amount), at exchange ratios corresponding to the comparison weights associated with a solution of the original game, then that solution remains a solution of the modified game.

(The latter will be recognized as a converse of the "irrelevant alternatives" condition that we invoked earlier).

Finally, for those familiar with the Harsanyi model, we might briefly describe the modification that would be required to obtain the present value. In effect, one must permit each syndicate, after maximizing its potential as measured by the weighted sum of the members' utilities, to pay dividends in "utility scrip," written in the utility units of any or all of its members, without regard to who receives it. One would then require, as an additional equilibrium condition, that all the scrip so issued be redeemed in the end – i.e., traded back to the players named on the face of the scrip, at the rates of exchange corresponding to the weights of the game. While the immediate effects of this modification (which can be expressed in other ways) seem to complicate the bargaining model, there is indirect compensation in the new ability of the syndicates to transfer utility internally, which removes some of the modeling difficulties associated with variable threats.

Appendix: the existence theorem

The mathematical formulation of the game Γ in normal, extensive, or characteristic function form is not relevant for our purpose; our only assumption is that the set F of payoff vectors that are feasible for the all-player coalition without the use of side payments is compact and convex. Let $\Gamma(\lambda)$ denote the same game with the payoffs to players 1, 2, . . . , n multiplied by $\lambda_1, \lambda_2, \ldots , \lambda_n$, respectively, where λ is a point in the simplex $\Lambda = \{\lambda \geq 0 | \Sigma \lambda_i = 1\}$. Let $F(\lambda)$ denote the feasible set for $\Gamma(\lambda)$, and let $\phi(\lambda)$ denote the sidepayment value of $\Gamma(\lambda)$—i.e., the λ-transfer value of Γ. We assume that $\phi(\lambda)$ is continuous in λ, Pareto optimal, and individually rational. From the latter it follows that $\lambda_i = 0$ implies $\phi_i(\lambda) \geq 0$; this is the only use we make of individual rationality.

Theorem. Under the stated assumptions, there exists $\lambda \in \Lambda$ such that $\phi(\lambda) \in F(\lambda)$.

Proof: Let $P(\lambda)$ be the set of vectors π such that $\Sigma \pi_i = 0$ and $\phi(\lambda) - \pi \in F(\lambda)$. $P(\lambda)$ is nonempty, convex, and compact, for each $\lambda \in \Lambda$, and is an uppersemicontinuous function of λ. Define the set-valued function T by

$$T(\lambda) = \lambda + P(\lambda) = \{\lambda + \pi | \pi \in P(\lambda)\}.$$

Let A be a simplex in the hyperplane $\{\alpha | \Sigma \alpha_i = 1\}$, large enough to contain all sets $T(\lambda)$, $\lambda \in \Lambda$, as well as Λ itself; the upper-continuity of T makes this possible – i.e., makes $T(\Lambda)$ compact. Extend the definition of T to A by

$$T(\alpha) = T(f(\alpha)), \quad \text{where } f_i(\alpha) = \frac{\max(0, \alpha_i)}{\Sigma_j \max(0, \alpha_j)}.$$

According to Kakutani's theorem, there is a "fixed point" α^* satisfying $\alpha^* \in T(\alpha^*)$. Denote $f(\alpha^*)$ by λ^*. Suppose first that $\alpha^* \neq \lambda^*$. Then $\alpha^* \in A - \Lambda$, and for some i $\lambda_i^* = 0 > \alpha_i^*$. But $\alpha^* \in T(\lambda^*) = \lambda^* + P(\lambda^*)$, hence $\pi_i^* < 0$ for some $\pi^* \in P(\lambda^*)$. Since $\phi_i(\lambda^*) \geq 0$ by individual rationality, the feasible payoff vector $\phi(\lambda^*) - \pi^* \in F(\lambda^*)$ gives player i a positive amount. But this is impossible without sidepayments, since all his payoffs in $\Gamma(\lambda^*)$ are zero. We conclude that $\alpha^* = \lambda^*$; hence that $0 \in P(\lambda^*)$; hence that

$$\phi(\lambda^*) \in F(\lambda^*).$$

Discussion

M. Dreze à M. Shapley

Question. – Given a complete preordering $\mathscr{L}$ of points (x,y) in $\mathbb{R}^2$, and two monotonic transformations $f(x)$, $g(y)$, there will under fairly general conditions exist a derived ordering $\underset{D}{\succeq}$ such that $(x,y) \succeq (x',y') \Leftrightarrow$ $[f(x),g(y)] \underset{D}{\succeq} [f(x'),g(y')]$. In what respects is your problem different from the one just mentioned?

Does your theorem bear upon the conditions under which $\underset{D}{\succeq}$ does indeed exist?

(Please feel free to disregard this question if you do not particularly care to answer it).

Réponse. – I believe there is no formal connection between the two problems. [I might add that by requiring the monotonic transformations to form a group, we *a fortiori* require them to be invertible and hence strictly monotonic and continuous.]

M. Rapoport à M. Shapley

Question. – Do you agree that while the negotiation set is naturally determined by the set of payoffs, the point of disagreement is not uniquely determined without further assumptions?

Réponse. – I regard the Nash (two-person cooperative) solution, or something in the absence of a fixed disagreement point equivalent to it, as probably the only satisfactory way to proceed here.

M. Barbut à M. Shapley

Question. – Avez-vous étudié le groupe G (unwavering group) dans le cas où la condition II est modifiée de sorte que les transformations monotones n'agissent plus séparément sur les deux composantes?

$$(x_1,x_2) \rightsquigarrow (\phi_1(x_1 x_2),\phi_2(x_1,x_2))$$

au lieu de:

$$(x_1,x_2) \rightsquigarrow (\psi_1(x_1),\psi_2(x_2))$$

Réponse. – I have no immediate comments to make on this mathematically very interesting idea, except to agree that it seems to merit further study. [Later, in conversation, M. Barbut suggested the possibility of certain physical applications for a theory of "unwavering" group on higher-dimensional spaces.]

NOTES

1 Transitivity is equivalent to the assertion that the orbit of any point of R is R itself. The theorem remains valid if this is weakened to the assertion that the orbit of each point of R is dense in R.

2 *Ann. Math. Study 40* (1959), pp. 325–355.

3 *Ann. Math. Study 52* (1964), pp. 577–626.

4 In thinking about these claims concerning "fair division," it is well to remember that they are being made in reference to a never-never land in which utility has been *assumed* to be extrinsically comparable. This assumption is a technical expedient with no standing in the final theory, introduced merely to aid in uncovering a possible *intrinsic* comparability.

5 J. C. Harsanyi, "A simplified bargaining model for the n-person cooperative game," *International Economic Review 4* (1963), pp. 194–220.

6 The author and Martin Shubik have calculated explicit values, as functions of n, for an "Edgeworth" market game (i.e., bilateral exchange economy) with $2n$ players. Interestingly, as n tends to ∞ the value payoffs (which are covariant only under positive linear transformations) and the competitive equilibrium payoffs (covariant under arbitary order-preserving transformations) converge to the same limit. See "Pure competition, coalitional power, and fair division", *International Economic Review 10* (1969), pp. 337–62; also the RAND Corporation, Memorandum RM-4917-1.

7 For our present value, which can easily be shown to be individually rational, it is sufficient that the Pareto surface coincide with a hyperplane within the individually rational zone. I do not know of any proof that Harsanyi's 1963 value is necessarily individually rational (but see Harsanyi, *op. cit.,* p. 194, footnote 4).

8 J. F. Nash, "Two-person cooperative games," *Econometrica 21* (1953), pp. 128–140.

CHAPTER 20

Paths leading to the Nash set

Michael Maschler, Guillermo Owen, and Bezalel Peleg

Abstract

A dynamic system is constructed to model a possible negotiation process for players facing a (not necessarily convex) pure bargaining game. The critical points of this system are the points where the "Nash product" is stationary. All accumulation points of the solutions of this system are critical points. It turns out that the asymptotically stable critical points of the system are precisely the isolated critical points where the Nash product has a local maximum.

1   Introduction

J. F. Nash (1950) introduced his famous solution for the class of two-person pure bargaining convex games. His solution was defined by a system of axioms that were meant to reflect intuitive considerations and judgments. The axioms produced a unique one-point solution that turned out to be that point at which the "Nash product" is maximized. Harsanyi (1959) extended Nash's ideas and obtained a similar solution for the class of *n*-person pure bargaining convex games. (See also Harsanyi 1977, chap. 10.)

Harsanyi (1956) also suggested a procedure, based on the Zeuthen principle, that modeled a possible bargaining process that leads the players to the Nash–Harsanyi point. (See also Harsanyi 1977, chap. 8.)

Recently, in an elegant paper, T. Lensberg (1981) (see also Lensberg 1985) demonstrated that the Nash–Harsanyi point could be characterized by another system of axioms. His main axiom was a *consistency requirement.* Lensberg's axioms are an important contribution because they offer a justification of the Nash solution in those cases where Nash's axiom of independence of irrelevant alternatives can be criticized.

321

Consistency means, essentially, that if some of the players gather together and inspect what they received at a solution point, they will have no motivation to move away, because what they received was precisely the solution point for their "reduced game."[1]

If consistency requirement is an appealing concept, then it should also guide us when viewing these games more dynamically: Suppose the players negotiate at a Pareto optimal point that is *not* a Nash point. Then surely there will be some players – in fact, even a pair of players – who will realize that they are not getting their Nash point in their reduced game. They will therefore ask for shifts in the payments in a direction of decreasing the "unfairness." Unfortunately, if such shifts are taken simultaneously, the players, in general, will arrive either at an infeasible point or at a non-Pareto-optimal point. One way to overcome this difficulty is to perform shifts only within tangent hyperplanes[2] and make them infinitesimal. In other words, one has to consider *a system of differential equations.*

In this chapter we construct such a system, which models simultaneous requests of bilateral shifts, and show, among other things, that every solution of this system converges to the Nash point.

While doing this research, we realized that a great part of it does not require the feasible set to be convex. We therefore consider a general pure bargaining game. In this generality one loses uniqueness of the Nash point. We define the *Nash set* to be essentially the set of individually rational and Pareto-optimal points for which the Nash product is stationary (see Section 2). In general, this set may contain many or even a continuum of points, and it is easy to see that it coincides with the set of Shapley's NTU values (see 1969[3]). In Section 3 we derive the dynamic system whose critical points are the points of the Nash set. We show that each accumulation point of any of its solutions belongs to the Nash set. It follows that if the Nash set consists of discrete points, then each solution converges.

Section 4 is devoted to stability properties of the critical points of the system. It turns out that the points in the Nash set are not going to occur "equally likely." The asymptotically stable points of the system are precisely those points of the Nash set that are isolated and whose Nash product is a local maximum.

To avoid complications, we have assumed that the Pareto set in our games is C^1-smooth. If this is not the case and the game is convex, then presumably one could replace the tangent hyperplane by all supporting hyperplanes and replace the system of differential equations that represent our dynamic system by a system of differential inclusions. If the feasible set is neither smooth nor convex, it is not clear how a generalization should proceed. At any rate, it would be interesting to learn to what extent our results can be generalized when one relaxes the smoothness conditions on the feasible set.

2   Notation, definitions, and preliminary results

We shall be concerned with a pure bargaining game S on a set N of n players, with a conflict point normalized to be the origin and a feasibility set[4] S in the utility space R^N of the players. On S we impose the following conditions:

(i) S is comprehensive; namely, if $x \in S$, then $x - R^N_+ \subseteq S$.

(ii) $S \cap R^N_{++}$ is nonempty and $S \cap R^N_+$ is compact. Here, $R^N_{++} = \{x \in R^N : x_i > 0$ for all $i \in N\}$ and $R^N_+ = \mathrm{cl}\ R^N_{++}$.

(iii)   The northeast boundary ∂S of S can be represented as a graph of an equation $g(x) = 0$, where g is a C^1 function.

(iv)   The partial derivatives $p_i \equiv \partial g(x)/\partial x_i$ are positive on $\partial S_+ \equiv \partial S \cap R^N_+$.

Note that we do not require S to be convex.

The *Nash set* of a game S is defined to be the set of points x in $\partial S_{++} \equiv \partial S \cap R^N_{++}$ for which the product $V(x) \equiv x_1 x_2 \cdots x_n$ is stationary. Points of this set will be called *Nash points*.

Theorem 1. Let x be a Nash point of a game S and let $H(x)$ be the tangent hyperplane to ∂S at x. With this notation, x is the center of gravity of the simplex $\Delta \equiv H(x) \cap R^N_+$. Moreover, the Nash points are characterized by this property. Thus, the Nash set is the set of Shapley's NTU values of the game S (see Shapley 1969).

Proof: Using the method of Lagrange multipliers, we characterize a stationary point of $V(x)$ by the system

$$\begin{cases} \dfrac{\partial}{\partial x_i} [x_1 x_2 \cdots x_n - \lambda g(x)] = 0, & \forall i \in N, \\ g(x) = 0, \quad x \in R^N_{++}; \end{cases} \tag{1}$$

that is,

$$\begin{cases} \dfrac{V(x)}{x_i} - \lambda p_i(x) = 0, \qquad \forall i \in N, \\ g(x) = 0, \qquad x \in R_{++}^N. \end{cases} \tag{2}$$

So, the stationary point x is characterized by

$$p_1(x)x_1 = p_2(x)x_2 = \cdots = p_n(x)x_n, \qquad x \in \partial S_{++}. \tag{3}$$

The hyperplane $H(x)$ is given by

$$\{y : p(x) \cdot y = r(x)\}, \qquad \text{where } r(x) = p(x) \cdot x,$$
$$p(x) = (p_1(x), p_2(x), \ldots, p_n(x)), \tag{4}$$

so the vertices of Δ are

$$\frac{r(x)}{p_1(x)} \mathbf{e}_1, \frac{r(x)}{p_2(x)} \mathbf{e}_2, \ldots, \frac{r(x)}{p_n(x)} \mathbf{e}_n,$$

where $\mathbf{e}_j$ is the jth unit vector, $j = 1, 2, \ldots, n$.

By (3) and (4), $p_j(x)x_j$ are all equal to $r(x)/n$, so x is indeed the center of gravity of Δ.

The proof of the second part reverses the above arguments.

Corollary 1. The Nash points are characterized by (3).

Proof: Proof of Theorem 1.

Remark 1: Because the $p_i(x)$ are all positive and $0 \notin \partial S$, it follows that (3) cannot be satisfied at a point where some x_i's are zero; consequently, the Nash set is closed.

Corollary 2. A point x is a Nash point if it remains a Nash point when S is replaced by the half-space bounded by the hyperplane through x that is tangent to S.

3 The dynamic system

Suppose the players find themselves at a point x is ∂S_+ that is not a Nash point. Using the idea of consistency, we wish to model their tendency to move away from x along a path that hopefully will lead them to a Nash point. This path should make intuitive sense.

Consider a pair of players i, j for which, say, $p_i(x)x_i < p_j(x)x_j$; then the players may reason as follows: At x there is a natural rate of exchange between their utilities, given by the coefficients $p_i(x)$, $p_j(x)$. Thus, in "common" units, player j is receiving $p_j(x)x_j$, which is more than $p_i(x)x_i$. Player i therefore claims that j is getting "too much"; hence, j should transfer (in the common units) an amount of $\epsilon(p_j(x)x_j - p_i(x)x_i)$. Doing these transfers simultaneously for all players j, player i is actually demanding (in the common units) the sum[5] $\Sigma\{\epsilon(p_j(x)x_j - p_i(x)x_i): j \in N\setminus\{i\}\}$. But the players can only move on ∂S, so ϵ must be infinitesimal, and we are thus led to the *system of differential equations*

$$p_i(x)\dot{x}_i = \sum_{j \in N\setminus(i)} [p_j(x)x_j - p_i(x)x_i], \qquad i = 1, 2, \ldots, n; \quad (5)$$

here, dot means time derivative.

Note that $\Sigma\{p_i(x)\dot{x}_i: i \in N\} = 0$, so solutions to this equation lie on ∂S. From the continuity of the $p_i(x)$ and their positiveness, it follows that through each point x of ∂S_+ there passes at least one trajectory.

In particular, in view of Corollary 1, the critical points of this system are precisely the Nash points.

Definition 1. Let $x = \phi(t)$ be a solution of (5). A point x is called *an accumulation point* of the solution if there exists a sequence (t_n) that tends to infinity such that

$$\lim_{n \to \infty} \phi(t_n) = x. \tag{6}$$

Obviously, every Nash point is a limit point of some solution $\phi(t)$ (e.g., a solution passing through such a point). The next theorem will show that the converse is also true.

Theorem 2. Each solution $x = \phi(t)$ of (5) that at some time passes through ∂S_+ has an accumulation point; and each such accumulation point is a Nash point.

Proof: Let $x = \phi(t)$ be a solution of (5), satisfying, say, $\phi(0) \in \partial S_+$. If $\phi_i(0) = 0$ for one or several i's, we see from (5) that $\phi(t)$ moves in the direction of increasing ϕ_i for these i's. Thus, for convenience, we "start" our time count when $\phi(0)$ is already in ∂S_{++}. We shall later see that $\phi(t)$ will remain in ∂S_{++}.

We introduce the *Lyapunov function*

$$L(x) = \ln V(x) = \sum_{j=1}^{n} \ln x_j, \tag{7}$$

whose domain is ∂S_{++}, and study its behavior along the path $x = \partial(t)$ as long as $\partial(t) \in \partial S_{++}$. Clearly, by (7),

$$\dot{L}(x) = \sum_{j=1}^{n} \frac{\dot{x}_j}{x_j}. \tag{8}$$

However, by (5),

$$p_j(x_j)\dot{x}_j = \sum_{v:v\neq j} (p_v(x)x_v - p_j(x)x_j) = \sum_{v=1}^{n} p_v(x)x_v - np_j(x)x_j; \tag{9}$$

therefore,

$$\frac{\dot{x}_j}{x_j} = \frac{1}{p_j(x)x_j} \sum_{v=1}^{n} p_v(x)x_v - n, \tag{10}$$

and (8) becomes

$$\dot{L}(x) = \sum_{j=1}^{n} \frac{1}{p_j(x)x_j} \cdot \sum_{v=1}^{n} p_v(x)x_v - n^2. \tag{11}$$

Let $H(x)$ be the harmonic mean of the $p_v(x)x_v$'s and $A(x)$ their arithmetic mean; with this notation, (11) becomes

$$\dot{L}(x) = \frac{n}{H(x)} nA(x) - n^2 = n^2 \left(\frac{A(x)}{H(x)} - 1 \right). \tag{12}$$

As is well known, $A(x) \geq H(x)$, with equality holding only when all the $p_v x_v$'s are equal, namely, only if our solution has reached a Nash point. Thus, for $x = \phi(t)$, $L(x(t))$, and therefore $V(x(t))$, strictly increases at all times unless a Nash point has been reached. In particular, this implies that if $\phi(0) \in R_{++}^N$, then $\phi(t) \in R_{++}^N$ for every $t > 0$, because $V(x)$ is continuous, positive at points of R_{++}^N, and vanishes in $R_+^N \backslash R_{++}^N$. Thus, the discussion is valid throughout $t \in R_+$, and $\phi(t)$ remains in the compact set ∂S_+. Thus, $\phi(t)$ must have accumulation points.

Let z be one of them. It remains to show that z is a Nash point. Indeed, otherwise, the $p_j(z)z_j$'s are not all equal and so $A(z) > H(z)$. Thus,[6] $\dot{L}(x) > 0$ at $x = z$, and we may write

$$\dot{L}(z) = \epsilon > 0. \tag{13}$$

By continuity, there exists $r > 0$ such that $\dot{L}(x) \geq \epsilon/2$ whenever $x \in U \equiv \{x : \|x - z\| \leq r\}$. Define

$$h = \max_{x \in U} \sqrt{\sum_{j \in N} \left\{\frac{1}{p_j(x)} \sum_{v \in N} (p_v(x)x_v - p_j(x)x_j)\right\}^2}. \tag{14}$$

By compactness, this maximum exists, so, by (9),

$$\sum_{j \in N} \dot{x}_j^2(t) \leq h^2 \qquad \text{if } x = \phi(t) \in U. \tag{15}$$

We have proved that any solution $x = \phi(t)$ that enters U moves there at a speed at most h, as long as it stays in U.

Let $U' \equiv \{x : \|x - z\| < r/2\}$. Because z is an accumulation point of $x = \phi(t)$, there is an infinite sequence (t_n), $t_n \to \infty$, such that $x(t_n) \in U'$ for all n. By taking, if necessary, a subsequence, we can assume that

$$t_{n+1} \geq t_n + \frac{r}{2h}. \tag{16}$$

Consider now the behavior of the trajectory during the time period $[t_n, t_{n+1}]$. If $\phi(t) \in U$ during this period, then $L(\phi(t))$ has increased at this period at a rate $\epsilon/2$, at least, so

$$L(\phi(t_{n+1})) \geq L(\phi(t_n)) + \frac{\epsilon}{2}(t_{n+1} - t_n) \geq L(\phi(t_n)) + \frac{\epsilon r}{4h}. \tag{17}$$

If $\phi(t)$ is not in U all the time, then there is a last moment t', $t' \in [t_n, t_{n+1}]$ in which $\phi(t)$ enters U, so for $t' \leq t \leq t_{n+1}$, $\phi(t)$ is in U. Now

$$\|\phi(t_{n+1}) - \phi(t')\| \geq \|z - \phi(t')\| - \|z - \phi(t_{n+1})\| > r - \frac{r}{2} = \frac{r}{2}. \tag{18}$$

Because $x = \phi(t)$ moves with speed at most h, while in U, it takes at least $r/2h$ to reach from $\phi(t')$ to $\phi(t_{n+1})$, so

$$t_{n+1} \geq t' + \frac{r}{2h}, \tag{19}$$

and because $\dot{L}(\phi(t)) \geq \epsilon/2$ for $t' \leq t \leq t_{n+1}$, we obtain

$$L(\phi(t_{n+1})) \geq L(\phi(t')) + \frac{\epsilon r}{4h}, \tag{20}$$

and by the monotonicity of $L(\phi(t))$, we obtain (17) again. Thus, (17) always holds, and it follows that

$$L(\phi(t_{n+1})) \geq L(\phi(t_1)) + \frac{n\epsilon r}{4h}, \qquad n = 1, 2, \ldots, \tag{21}$$

which shows that $L(\phi(t))$ is unbounded.

This is impossible, so the contradiction shows that z must be a Nash point.

Corollary 3. If all Nash points are isolated, then each solution converges to a Nash point.

Proof: Let $\phi(t)$ be a solution. Let x^* be one of its accumulation points. By Theorem 2, x^* exists and is a Nash point; and because it is isolated, there exists $r > 0$ such that no other Nash point lies in $\{x : \|x - x^*\| < r\}$. Suppose $\phi(t)$ does not converge to x^*; then it must have some other accumulation point, z, and $\|z - x^*\| \geq r$. Let $W \equiv \{y : r/4 \leq \|y - x^*\| \leq 3r/4\}$. Note that W is compact and contains no Nash point. Because both x^* and z are accumulation points of $\phi(t)$, the trajectory must enter each neighborhood $W' \equiv \{y : \|x^* - y\| < r/4\}$ and $W'' \equiv \{y : \|z - y\| < r/4\}$ an infinite number of times that tend to infinity. A trajectory cannot pass from W' to W'' without entering W; so there exists an infinite sequence (t_n), $t_n \to \infty$, so that $\phi(t_n) \in W$. Thus, W must contain an accumulation point, which, by Theorem 2, is a Nash point. This contradiction shows that $\phi(t)$ converges to x^*, and concludes the proof.

4   Asymptotically stable Nash points

As has been said, each solution that reaches a Nash point at a certain time remains there forever. Is it, however, true that every solution that comes to a small enough vicinity of an isolated Nash point converges to that point? In this section we shall give a negative answer to this question and, moreover, characterize those Nash points that are asymptotically stable with respect to our dynamical system (5).

Theorem 3. Let x^* be an isolated Nash point at which the Nash product $V(x)$ is a local maximum. This Nash point is asymptotically stable with respect to the dynamical system (5).

Proof: Let U be a neighborhood of x^* (relative to ∂S_+). Without loss of generality, we may assume that it is small enough, so $V(X)$ has a unique maximum at x^*, in the closure $\overline{U}$, and that $\overline{U}$ has only one Nash point. Let r be the maximum of $V(x)$ on the boundary ∂U of U. Clearly, $r < V(x^*)$.

Consider the set $U' = \{y \in U : V(y) > (V(x^*) + r)/2\}$. Clearly, it is a neighborhood of x^*. By the proof of Theorem 2, $L(x)$ and, therefore, $V(x)$ increase along solutions $x = \phi(t)$. Thus, a solution that enters U' at a certain time will never leave U. This proves that x^* is stable with respect to (5). Such a solution must have accumulation points, and all are within U. By Theorem 2, these are all Nash points, so they all coincide with x^*. This proves that any solution that enters U' must converge to x^*. We have therefore proved that x^* is, moreover, asymptotically stable.

Theorem 4. Let x^* be an isolated Nash point that is not a local maximum of $V(x)$. In that case x^* is not stable with respect to the dynamic system (5).

Proof: Let U be a neighborhood of x^* such that in an open neighborhood $\hat{U}$ of $\overline{U}$, only x^* is a Nash point. Let V be an arbitrary neighborhood of x^*. Because x^* is not a local maximum, V contains a point x^0 such that $V(x^0) > V(x^*)$. Any solution $x = \phi(t)$ that at some time t_0 passes through x^0 will have $V(\phi(t)) > V(\phi(t_0))$ for $t > t_0$. Therefore, such a solution will not have x^* as an accumulation point. But $\phi(t)$ has accumulation points, and they are all outside $\hat{U}$; therefore, $\phi(t)$ must leave U at some time. This shows that x^* is not stable with respect to the dynamic system (5).

A Nash point that is not isolated cannot be asymptotically stable (although sometimes it is stable), so, in view of the theorems, *the asymptotically stable critical points of the system* (5) *are precisely those isolated Nash points at which V(x) has a local maximum.*

NOTES

1 For precise definitions the reader is referred to Lensberg's paper.
2 Which, as we assume in this paper, always exist.
3 In Shapley's paper the characteristic function happened to consist of convex sets; however, his definition *per se* makes sense in more general contexts.
4 We use S to denote both the game and its feasibility set.
5 Some of the terms may be negative; namely, when player i has to do the transferring.
6 We regard $L(x)$ and $\dot{L}(x)$ as functions of position, defined by (11) and (12). $\dot{L}(x)$ becomes a true derivative only along solutions passing through x.

REFERENCES

Harsanyi, J. C., [1956], *Approaches to the bargaining problem before and after the theory of games: A critical discussion of Zeuthen's, Hick's and Nash's theories*, Econometrica, **24**, 144–157.

[1959], *A bargaining model for the cooperative n-person game*, in: A. W. Tucker and R. D. Luce, eds., Contributions to the theory of games IV, Annals of Mathematics Studies **40**, Princeton University Press, Princeton, pp. 325–355.

[1977], Rational Behavior and Bargaining Equilibrium in Games and Social Situations, Cambridge University Press, Cambridge.

Lensberg, T., [1981], *The stability of the Nash solution*, RM, Norwegian School of Economics and Business Administration, Bergen.

[1985], *Bargaining and Fair Allocation,* in: H.P. Young, ed., Cost Allocations: Methods, Principles, Applications, North-Holland, pp. 101–16.

Nash, J. F., [1950], *The bargaining problem,* Econometrica, **18**, 155–62.

Shapley, L. S., [1969], *Utility comparison and the theory of games* in: La Décision: Agrégation et Dynamique des Ordres de Preférénce, Paris, Edition du CNRS, pp. 251–63. (reprinted as Chapter 19 this volume)